I've known Mark Venit for over 30 years and have always admired his take-no-prisoners style of writing, teaching seminars and consulting. He's known for giving you lots of meat to chew on – with wit, style, humor, and fun. His latest book won't disappoint. It's vintage Mark Venit, taking his lifetime career of working, consulting, teaching and writing in the decorated apparel industry and assembling it into a book that is a MUST READ for decorated apparel professionals. Each chapter offers the reader those Mark Venit gems where you ask yourself "Why didn't I think of that?"

Reading Mark's book will head you in the right direction on everything from how to name – or re-name -- your company, to how to price your work, how to position your company for solid growth, and lots more.

If you're new to this industry, Mark's book will save you a fortune by cutting ten years from your learning curve. But whether you're an old veteran of the craft or a newcomer, I highly recommend this book to everyone who owns a decorated apparel company as well as to your company's key employees.

Scott Fresener, Director
T-Biz Network International, ▪ ***LLC Scottsdale, Arizona***
Co-Author, How To Print T-Shirts For Fun and Profit
A member of the Academy of Screen Printing Technology

Having been in the textile screen printing industry almost since its inception and having watched Mark in action for well over 30 years, I can tell you with confidence that when it comes to marketing in our industry, he's the guru! His strong emphasis in taking care of his clients is through being an innovator as well as helping them determine the most lucrative directions for their companies. Mark provides them with the results they're looking for and I know -- because some of his clients are mine as well and I see the results. Those who'll read his new book will gain insights and new approaches about how to move their companies forward in gaining and maintaining market share in ways they never imagined possible -- or actually affordable!

Charlie Taublieb, President
Taublieb Consulting* ▪ *Greenwood Village, Colorado
Member: Academy of Screen Printing Technology

My first encounter with Mark Venit was more than 30 years ago when I and two other members of our staff traveled to Florida from Vail, Colorado, to attend an Imprinted Sportswear Show. After a very charmed 13 years in the retail side of the decorated apparel business, I was still open to suggestions that would improve our business. Our first seminar with Mark enabled us to return to Colorado with so much knowledge that our sales doubled less than two months! His advice was, and still is, simple to understand, straightforward, easy to implement, and stands the test of time. I'm still using many of his ideas, many of which are in his new book.

This book is truly a gift to the industry. To have all of Mark's knowledge and techniques at our fingertips is a blessing. His tips and quips make it an even better read. (His sense of humor is as strong as ever). For those starting out in this business or thinking of getting into it, this book is a "Must Read," one that'll put you on the right footing and prevent lots of heartbreak along the way. For those who've been in the trenches of this industry for many years and are still looking for the light at the end of the tunnel, Mark's book IS the light! For those who might feel they've learned just about all there is to know in this industry, this book is guaranteed to be an eye-opener, loaded with specifics and real-world examples. Don't let Chapter 38 -- true stories about companies that failed or will soon -- scare you, because the rest of the book tells you how to do it right and not repeat the mistakes of the failed companies he reveals.

For me, an artist, I hope to collect once again more ideas to make my business all it can, and should be.

Lee Caroselli Barnes, President
Balboa Threadworks, Inc.* ▪ *Palm Desert, California
Honoree, 2002 Embroidery Hall of Fame

This book is for the entrepreneur who wants his or her business to be the best it can be. All aspects and questions about marketing your business are covered and easy to understand. Mark's management philosophies focus on the apparel graphics industry, but they apply to almost all types of business. You'll outperform most of your competition if you apply only 10% of the information within these pages. And if being solidly profitable is your ultimate goal, this book is an absolute must!

Ron Lykens, CEO
Xtreme Wear* ▪ *Dubois, Pennsylvania

A t-shirt business is 1/3 production, 1/3 graphics, and 1/3 business savvy. Mark Venit's new book will shorten your learning curve on the last third, making sure you can add pretty dollars to your pretty designs. Distilling a lifetime of practical know-how in these pages, Mark dishes out nuts-and-bolts specifics and winning strategies that will help boost both novices and veterans to their next levels of success. He zeroes in on what works to grow your business -- and what doesn't -- and scores direct hits everywhere. While you can easily put lots of colors onto shirts these days, Mark's insider techniques will help you keep your apparel decorating business ledger running in the black, not in red.

Mike Neer, Publisher
CorelDRAWHelp Magazine ▪ *Fresno, California*
Executive Director of the Association of CorelDRAW Professionals

---

As an editor for Impressions Magazine for 20 years (1981-2001), I became very familiar with Mark's extreme knowledge, experience, and unique expertise in an industry that not many other marketing and business consultants paid any attention to. It's safe to say that he's the number one authority or any marketing or business topic pertaining to the decorated apparel industry.

If you're involved in any aspect of decorating apparel from creation to production to wholesale and retail sales, this is a must-read book. It will dramatically shorten your learning curve, increase your sales, and is the most time-efficient way to set up your business to make money. Through his 30 plus years of consulting with all size and types of apparel decorating businesses across the United States and the world, he knows what works for decorated apparel businesses.

Now you can have the benefit of his counsel at your fingertips!

Deborah Sexton, President
Saracen Communications ▪ *Richardson, Texas*
Former Editor of Impressions Magazine

I met Mark Venit in 1983, early on in my adventure in the apparel decorating industry. At the time, we were operating six retail stores and a small screen printing operation, selling mostly to the US military in Germany. Mark came to Deutschland and kicked our tires hard (3 of which were already flat). His tools and guidance were a major factor in the rebirth and transformation of our business, which I'm proud to say was sold last year as the leading wholesaler of promotional textiles throughout Europe -- with warehouses and sales offices in every major country on the continent. Mark's insight saved me from paying the steep tuition at the "University of Hard Knocks." I can honestly say I used many of his lessons as well as his wisdom and counsel over and over again in building our company into the winning success it became and remains. And he's sharing all that knowledge with the readers of this book. I just wish I had a copy of it to work from at the very start of our company. Take my advice: buy his book and apply its guidance to your own game plan!

Stephen G. Ross, Founder and Retired Chairman
Falk & Ross Group Europe ▪ *Sembach, Germany*

Both W. Edward Demming and Peter F. Drucker, noted business developers and consultants, have stated that in any business enterprise "innovation and marketing produce results... everything else is just cost." Mark L. Venit is the master of innovation and marketing in the decorated apparel industry. He has an uncanny ability to draw upon his years of experience and his own unique talents to help a business owner see his company's strengths, weaknesses, opportunities, and threats. His insight typically leads to the development of a unique market position for the client's company which, combined with Venit's astute and to-the-point guidelines about marketing, operations, and management, puts his client miles ahead of their competitors.

I have worked with Mark since 1998 with several companies I have owned and can state with absolute confidence: follow the advice in Mark's book and you'll greatly increase the likelihood of your company's success; ignore it at your own peril.

Tom Stewart, President
Level 10 Sportswear ▪ *Birmingham, Alabama*

Having known Mark Venit for nearly 20 years and having been an embroidery consultant to several of his client companies, I can attest to how well those enterprises perform their marketing agendas, giving them strong advantages over their competition. In his latest book Mark's strategic and tactical advice will compel you to think -- or re-think -- how your company can achieve its true potential -- even if your company's resources are limited.

I tell my clients that there are two ways to learn: 1), investing in top quality education, or 2), paying the costs of damaged garments, lost production, and lost customers. The first learning path creates opportunities and profits, the second mandates continuous damage control. This book is definitely a smart investment in your future and will save you years of mistakes and guesswork. And you'll learn how to make more money. I'm recommending it as "required reading" for all my own clients and their senior management personnel.

Frank Gawronski, President
Embroidery Educational Services International ■ ***Powell, Ohio***

THE BUSINESS OF T-SHIRTS:

A Textbook for Success in Marketing and Selling Decorated Apparel

By Mark L. Venit

ISBN-978-0-615-45099-5

Printed in the United States of America

First Printing – March 2011

Second Printing – April 2011

This is a work of non-fiction. However, some of the names, characters, places, and incidents may be the product of the author's imagination and used fictitiously to illustrate points made in the content; any resemblance to persons living or dead, businesses, companies, events, or locales is entirely coincidental. While the author has made every effort to provide accurate Internet addresses and telephone numbers at the time of publication, neither the publisher nor the author assumes any responsibility for errors, or for changes that occur after publication. Further, neither the publisher nor the author has any control over nor assumes any responsibility for author or third-party websites or their content. For information on bulk purchases of this book, contact the author at 410.641.7300.

Manuscript edited by Marcia Derryberry

Cover design by Dane Clement

Book design by Adriano Aldini

TABLE OF CONTENTS

DEDICATION

To Judy, Kyle, Hannah, Daniel, Gabriel, Francine, Suzy, Kenn, and Mom and Dad

To industry friends, close associates, and key colleagues Ted Stahl, Tom Stewart, Judge George Coleburn, Marshall Siegel, Verne Packer, Drew Farnese, Lee Caroselli Barnes, Karin Bellinghausen, Pete Bolsoni, Alice and Roger Campbell, Bob Carpenter, Dane Clement, David Dickson, Bob Dundas, Howie Emeson, Beverly Endebrock, Scott Fresener, Frank Gawronski, Alan Gentry, Frank Gizatullin, Jeff Glenn, Jerry Goldberg, Richard Greaves, The Higgins Family, Rich Hoffman, Deborah Jones, Lloyd and Gail Lewis, Gary Littlefield, Ron Lykens, Mark and Terry Mackaman, Jay Malanga, Jake Mandel, Jerry and Marie Mayotte, Sharad Mehta, Jeff Melcher, Jim Mickelson, Robert Mims, Isadore Mitzner, Tony Mucilli, Al Novin, Walt and Gwen Palmer, Marc Polish, Peter Potter, Steve Ross, Steve Rosengarten, Steve Silva, Jan Starr, Charlie Sulzberger, Charlie Taublieb, Bruce Tharp, Larie and Dick Thomas, Bob Werneke, and Tony Williams.

To industry editors Deborah Sexton, Mike Neer, Adriano Aldini, Marcia Derryberry, and the late Carl Piazza

To special friends now departed Buffalo Bob Smith, Art Rhodes, Mike Lemberg, Richard Labove and Keith Caroselli

To my now departed mentors Sid Friedman, Jack Goldenthal, and Harry A. Bailey, Jr.

i

ABOUT THE AUTHOR

Mark L. Venit, MBA, is President of Apparel Graphics Institute LLC, which provides management and marketing consulting and proprietary research to apparel graphics companies throughout the Americas and Europe. Author of several books and nearly 500 articles on management and marketing published in trade magazines and professional journals, Venit has been recognized by *Impressions Magazine* as one of the Top 25 Innovators in Industry History. His columns and articles are featured in the online Impressions Newsletter and in *Imprint Canada*.

He's also chairman of the board of ShopWorks Software, the apparel graphics trade's leading provider of industry-specific business software. Headquartered in West Palm Beach, Florida, ShopWorks serves over 500 apparel decorating companies in the United States, Canada, the United Kingdom, and the Caribbean. The ShopWorks software program is used every day by more than 3,000 professionals working in the decorated apparel business as well in the recognition, promotional products, and garment manufacturing industries.

Venit is engaged extensively as an expert witness, qualified in all US and Canadian jurisdictions in the areas of trademark and copyright applications and business practices in the apparel graphics industry.

His career has included being CEO of USAdvertising Corporation (Philadelphia, PA); President/CEO of Empire Specialty Printing Corporation (Philadelphia, PA); Executive Vice President of Plymouth Mills International (New York, NY). Venit also helped manage the business affairs of Buffalo Bob Smith and Howdy Doody as well as being closely involved in apparel marketing promotions for Bruce Springsteen & the E Street Band, Southside Johnny & The Asbury Jukes, Meatloaf, and The Kingsmen.

A former professor of advertising and marketing, Venit earned his bachelors (Magna Cum Laude 1970) and Masters degrees (Summa Cum Laude 1973) at Temple University in Philadelphia, Pennsylvania. He has presented over 1,100 workshop and seminar courses at more than 250 trade events throughout North America and Europe as well as conducting thousands more management and marketing programs for more than 600 clients and at colleges and universities.

An accomplished pianist, avid boater and whitewater rafting enthusiast, he also enjoys woodworking, fishing, and target shooting. His self-confessed passions are exploring Medieval castles, including researching the histories long-hidden within their walls, and building sandcastles. Venit is a 3-time world champion sand sculptor.

To see some of his work: http://www.maryland.com/ImageGallery/?catid=24 and his online video at www.monkeysee.com/play/2120).

Based in Ocean Pines, Maryland, he can be reached at markvenit@cs.com.

FORWARD

Quench Your Thirst For Knowledge

There's a drought going on when it comes to useful, up-to-date and comprehensive information on the actual business of marketing and selling decorated apparel. Mark L. Venit's book is the life-saving water for which so many have been waiting sp long — an in-depth textbook that's also a practical guide to starting and growing a garment decoration business. It definitively answers the age old questions on how to price apparel, how to find customers, how to keep customers and more, including answers to lots of questions you didn't realize need to be asked! I've known Mark for several decades and it's always an education to speak with him.

No one walks away from one of his seminars or workshops without ideas or plans to improve something about the way they do business. I am thrilled that he's finally transformed his industry experience and hands-on know-how into this content-rich and energizing book. For all you "knowledge thirsty" business owners and start-ups, I encourage you all to drink up.

Cheers!

Ted Stahl
Executive Chairman
GroupeSTAHL

CHAPTER

INTRODUCTION
WHO AM I AND WHY DID I WRITE THIS BOOK?

As a high school student in the 1960s, I somehow took to drawing with Magic Markers™ to "jazz up" my T-shirts and sweatshirts. My mother wasn't thrilled with the idea of "ruining" my knockaround clothes, but since they were inexpensive and worn after school, on weekends, and playing sports in the neighborhood, she didn't make a big deal about my newfound hobby. My interest in decorating shirts faded after high school and remained dormant for a few years.

During graduate school, I moonlighted as a disc jockey doing a late night shift. My first love, though, was playing keyboards and singing lead in my own rock band, Mark's Men. After all, I was trained as a classical pianist -- who learned to love and play jazz, and as a budding opera singer – who learned to love and sing the blues. In 1967 my band was signed to a recording contract by a well-known music industry promoter, Don Kirschner. At the time, he had a popular Saturday night network TV show, "Don Kirschner's Rock Concert," which featured chart-topping rock groups and singers.

Our manager, Hank Hunter, was working for Kirschner's organization, and told us "Don wants you to play country, because he thinks it's gonna' be big." Country? For nice, Jewish city boys? Not in a position to bargain, we recorded our own rock-and-roll tunes, and some country stuff, as instructed, and donned sequined metallic blue-and-silver lamé outfits for promo tour appearances and at college concerts. To little avail, though, as our records bombed everywhere they were radio tested.

While under contract to Kirschner, I got my first look-see at the marketing process, including matters such as why were we told to play country music. It was a coming thing. Why were we costumed as we were? It was to make us look "bigtime." And why were Des Moines, Detroit, and Boston the test markets? Because they had diverse and distinct audiences for testing the popular appeal (or lack of it) of our music. The word "marketing" was never uttered; the word "positioning" hadn't been invented yet.

Nor did I really understand what all that stuff was about – until much later, after the band had returned to the night club-Bar Mitzvah-and-wedding circuit.

Playing private parties and being a disc jockey meant I needed to give out prizes to the winners of dance, trivia, and singing contests. I quickly learned to get freebies from record companies and buy other give-away goodies "wholesale" and mark 'em up to make a few extra bucks for myself. In time I was also "repping" the companies I bought from, selling psychedelic posters, popular T-shirts, and gimmicks and gadgets to metro Philadelphia gift boutiques and head shops. I soon became acquainted with the realm of specialty advertising (as it was called then) as I was buying custom-printed T-shirts, key fobs, pens, and magnets to promote the band. As a musician, a deejay, and sales-man who also was writing radio jingles and creating logos for local businesses, I was earning a nice chunk o' change in addition to earning my teaching fellowship stipend in graduate school.

It got to the point, however, where the chairman of the department I worked in at Temple University asked me what all these "business" calls coming into graduate studies office were about. He made it clear that he wanted an end to these interruptions to the staff. I got Dr. Bailey's message loud and clear and, figuring I had a great opportunity to go into business for myself, I chose to leave the Ph.D. program a year short of getting my degree. At the end of the semester in 1973 I founded my own full-service advertising agency, while still working part-time as a deejay, performing with my band on weekends, and growing my promotional products sales as a service to my agency clientele.

Sales of custom-printed T-shirts trickled in without my really noticing, as they were largely in response to requests from clients, not by anything proactive on my part. At a 15% margin product, (in line with most advertising commissions) the T-shirts were marked up 25 cents a piece, bringing their average selling price up to a whopping two bucks for a finished white shirt printed in one color in one location.

In reviewing the agency's financial performance for 1975, my accountant asked me if I had any idea how many T-shirts I'd sold during that year. I was truly unaware of the sales this item, as it was, or so I thought, a small piece of the pie. He pointed out that I had sold more than 30,000 units – without really trying. When his observation sunk in, I started pushing the product, added a bit more mark-up, and watched my T-shirt sales quintuple through the spring of '76. My supplier, however, couldn't keep up with my orders, causing me to buy my own inventory from a dry goods distributor in downtown Philadelphia: Bodek & Rhodes.

Thanks to a tip from Art Rhodes, I found another supplier, who proved to be constantly late on delivery and even worse on quality than my first supplier. Frustrated with delays and mediocre workmanship, I had had it with contractors. By the end of the year, I took on a partner and started my own screen printing company called Empire Specialty Printing Corporation – or "ESP." I jettisoned most of my ad agency business to focus my time on selling custom T-shirts to businesses, schools, events promoters, and teams. With a competent screen printer stolen from my contractor and a partner who could sell and handle administration while I sold and did the artwork, ESP went into full production in January, 1977. My Dad was supportive of my effort while my mother chided me with a reality check: "T-shirts? Isn't that a fad?" I replied, "Mom, the fad is already 10 years old!"

"Mom, the fad is already 10 years old!" -- 1976

Adding artists, more screen printers, a secretary, production support personnel, and a former ladieswear salesperson over the next few months, I saw the business boom that first year. I expanded into the development and distribution of preprints the following year, and became an ASI-accredited supplier as well. Plugging into my old connections from the music business, my accounts included several major rock bands, including Meat Loaf, Bruce Springsteen & the E Street Band, Southside Johnny & The Asbury Jukes, and Peter Gabriel. The company also became a vendor to Columbia, Decca, and Capital Record companies. ESP was on a roll.

Selling retail lines to department stores was a challenge. During the late '70s, department stores characterized decorated T-shirts as "undignified apparel," the proper retail venue for which (in their opinions) was "tacky T-shirt shops" and low-end resort retailers. Tut, tut, tut, and tsk, tsk, tsk. But when one of my salesmen designed our "Football Widow" line for women whose husbands and boyfriends abandoned them for college football Saturdays and for NFL games all day on Sundays and on Monday nights, major Pennsylvania department store chains such as Gimbels, John Wanamaker's, and Boscov's finally tried our shirts. We had a hit on our hands and the department stores sent us orders and re-orders for thousands of tees and sweats! That success finally earned us attention from Macy's and Alexander's in the New York metro area, which began buying decorated apparel from us as well. For most of those companies, our preprints were their very first foray into printed T-shirts. Who knew I was making history?!

ESP moved to a bigger building in 1980, but two things killed my company two years after the move. First, promotional products distributors had learned about buying blank garments from wholesalers and sending them for contract printing and embroidery, obviously increasing their profits. Since we sold only finished products and 40% of my sales were to the promowares people, our sales dropped dramatically, as long term customers in 10 states found other sources willing to sell just the decorating aspect of custom sportswear.

The recession that began early in President Reagan's first term and drove the prime interest rate to more than 20% in 1982 was the final blow for me. I closed the company late that year. But, with the addition of a partner in my advertising agency, USAdvertising, business there was still good and getting better.

ESP liquidated and paid nearly 100 cents on the dollar to all of our creditors, including the $240,000 we owed Hanes and 40 grand to Bodek & Rhodes.

I was back in my creative groove, but a fashion merchandiser in New York came a-head-hunting – for me! After receiving the proverbial offer I couldn't refuse, I relocated to New York City as Executive Vice President of Plymouth Mills, Inc. The company operated a 200,000-square foot Staten Island manufacturing facility and had its showroom in a suite of offices on the 51st floor of the Empire State Building in Manhattan. At age 35, I had the proverbial and literal "key to the executive washroom!" Dubbed "Philly" by the CEO who recruited me, Alan

Ellinson, it was an acknowledgement that I was a hick from a small metro area --- of only 5 million people. I became immersed in learning the ways of The Big Apple, apparel manufacturing, monster runs of tens of thousands of shirts, and dealing with buyers from Macy's, Bloomingdales, Chess King, Merry-Go-Round, Fashion Bug, and other department store and mall retailing conglomerates.

I loved working in Manhattan, though much less so on Staten Island. Regrettably I spent most of my time putting out fires arising from angry customers and fighting – and eventually defeating – a labor-organizing assault on the company by the International Ladies Garment Workers Union. Though I got a good education about garment manufacturing, importing and exporting, and dealing with the daily challenges of having some 300 employees, my biggest education came in the field of opposing a powerful union and working with lots of lawyers. After a year of battles on many fronts and rather exhausted and unsettled from it all,

I removed myself to Florida for a few years before ever setting foot back in NYC.

I also vowed never again to have a boss, partners, employees, or inventory, vows that have been broken in the latter three categories on several occasions.

In 1979 there was a revolution of sorts in the Textile Division of the Screen Printing Association International. In the previous five years the membership grew exponentially with the influx of textile screen printers from all over the country. By and large, the division's officers were from the manufacturing side of things, in an incestuous system whereby the outgoing board nominated the next group of leaders – usually from the existing board -- and they all ran unopposed. And won. There was never a contested election until 1979, when we young-Turk T-shirts guys ran our own candidates and swept all the offices. We were all 30ish and the "slate" candidate was really old – 40! For our end of the organization, we envisioned programs that helped us improve our craftsmanship, our businesses, and our futures.

The following year, Mark Coudray from San Luis Obispo, Calif. (who's still quite active in the field as a successful business owner and well-regarded genius in screen technology) became the new division president. I was his vice-president and served with Mark for two terms, implementing two-day pre-convention training workshops, among other innovations for "us T-shirt guys." We had arrived and the election of "these T-shirt people" wasn't well-received by the Old Guard at SPAI. But as proof positive of the emergence of textile screen printing as the force in that technology, the association has twice changed its name to reflect changes in print technology -- especially digital printing -- first to the Screen Print and Graphic Imaging Association and later to the Specialty Graphics and Imaging Association (SGIA). The last major bastion for screen printing today is on garments, as other formerly strong areas of the field have been transitioning to digital printing as the primary technology.

In the early '80s, having been awarded SGIA's highest honor, the Magnus Award for leadership in the industry, I was invited to be a speaker at Imprinted Sportswear Shows (ISS) around the country. I accepted – and have been serving the ISS cause ever since. I also began writing articles and columns for Impressions Magazine, which contributed conveniently for beginning my nearly 30-year career as a management and marketing consultant. Working with ISS and Impressions, I developed a close, personal relationship with the CEO at the firm's Dallas headquarters. Marshall Siegel, who also became a mentor to me, gets the credit – or blame – for encouraging me to move into my next career: consulting. Based on his years of being a Colonel in the U.S. Army and his subsequent career as a publishing executive, his advice for me was to simply "do my thing" helping companies grow and prosper. He said that if an opportunity presented itself for me to go back into business or accept a great job somewhere, I'd be able to make another move with ease and, as a consultant, I would be wired in the trade and have a privileged ear for hearing opportunities as might come my way.

In 1983 I founded the Apparel Graphics Institute to provide consulting services to the trade and become a research resource for industry manufacturers in search of data on the industry and its participants, marketing intelligence, trends, and other information that was available nowhere else. I've been at it ever since, helping businesses on a fee basis, helping preprint merchandisers on a percentage basis, providing proprietary research on a project fee basis, and writing my observations in trade journals and magazines for very modest fee about what I see and learn in the field.

Despite flattering offers over the years to relocate and run companies and accepting two one-year assignments for just that purpose to reconfigure them for growth and profitability, my full-time activity since 1983 has been as a consultant to more than 600 industry companies – screen printing, embroidery, retailing, apparel merchandising, and promotional products firms, as well as manufacturers and distributors of garments and equipment and related supply enterprises. My endeavors have ranged from nine years' involvement in a variety of marketing assignments with Fruit of the Loom and helping create (and name) One-Stop Distributors to being engaged for a broad range of other consulting assignments. These firms included Cutter & Buck, NEBS, DuPont, Brother, Disney, Latitudes, Flip-Fold, Balboa Threadworks, T-Formation, ScreenWorks USA, and Falk & Ross GmbH, Europe's largest wholesaler with warehouses throughout the continent and catalogs in nine languages. These are among many other well-respected industry firms on both sides of the Atlantic with whom I've worked professionally.

Accepting start-up businesses as clients over the years has given and continues to afford me unique insights into the dynamics and evolution of the trade, as seen through the eyes and aspirations of more than 50 such companies since 1982. Among these firms of which I'm most proud are Latitudes in Portland, Oregon, which has grown to become one of the largest apparel decorators in the West and one of the top five most sophisticated and innovative decorators in the industry; Red Brick Clothing Company in Pelham, New Hampshire; and One Stop Distributors (Grand Rapids, Michigan). And each year until God calls me home, I'll look forward to continuing to accept two start-ups annually to help their owners launch successful businesses -- and preclude me from becoming jaded and ivory-towered.

As a result of some pro bono industry-related assignments (and occasionally via grants), I've had the joy of working with several Native American (in the U.S.) and First Nations (in Canada) tribal enterprises from the Rio Grande to the Arctic Circle, from British Columbia to Quebec. I've become an honorary member of some of the tribes (Sioux, Mohawk, Haida, and Pueblo), having danced to the North, the East, the West, and the South with them, and have seen their enterprises blossom.

I've been blessed with my share of long-term consulting relationships: for eight years with RBS Activewear in Argyle, Wisconsin; for nine years with Falk & Ross, with Sportop Marketing in Thunder Bay, Ontario, and with Fruit of the Loom in Bowling Green, Kentucky; 10

years with Habitat Software in Montrose,. Colorado; 12 years with J-M Enterprises in Seattle, Washington; 16 years with Northwest Embroidery in Milton, Washington; 22 years with Promark Industries in Evansville, Indiana and with Latitudes; 27 years with Idaho Impressions in Lewiston, Idaho; 28 years with Impressions Magazine and the Imprinted Sportswear Shows; and 28 years-and-counting working directly with Ted Stahl at GroupeSTAHL, the sponsor of this book.

If you're wondering just how much I travel as a consultant and speaker, it's still between 100,000 and 150,000 miles in the air each year and some more on the ground. In 2010, I had the good fortune to work with clients in New Hampshire, Rhode Island, Massachusetts, New York, Pennsylvania, New Jersey, Maryland, Virginia, South Carolina, Georgia, Florida, Alabama, Tennessee, Louisiana, Illinois, Wisconsin, California, Oregon, Washington, Alberta, and Ontario. And this was a very typical year for me, in which I also taught seminars and workshops at eight industry shows in, exhibited at eight with the software company I co-founded, and went to a few others as an attendee for my own edification and enrichment. I also traveled to Italy and France for some R & R and to see emerging trend in color palettes and leisure fashions.

During my career I've taught nearly 1,000 seminars and workshops at trade shows, conventions, and corporate training events reaching tens of thousands of industry participants. I've written three books and more than 400 articles and columns published in Impressions, Digital Impressions, Screen Printing Magazine, GraphicPRO Journal (now CorelDrawPRO), Imprint Canada, and Stitches Magazine. And did I mention that I worked directly with Buffalo Bob and Howdy Doody for two years as the TV legends' marketing manager, licensing agent, and business manager?

In 1997 I entered another phase of my industry career. A client whom I had worked with for three years, Jay Malanga, had put many of my management and marketing ideas into a software program to run his company, JAM Grafix, near Washington D.C. He asked me if there'd be an opportunity to take the program to the industry. Shortly after I saw what Jay had created, we began our partnership in ShopWorks Software, the oldest industry-specific business software developer in the apparel decorating field anywhere on the planet.

Since the founding of ShopWorks, the system has been dramatically expanded and is the only industry-specific business software for the recognition industry (as in awards and engraving), and serves the promotional products industry with the most sophisticated software in that field. The programs we sell today also have extensive custom capability for sign shops, digital printing firms, and virtually every other business in the graphic arts industry. More than 500 ShopWorks systems are operating throughout the U.S., Canada, the UK, and a few other outposts around the globe, including China.

There's one other aspect of my instrumentality in the decorated apparel industry, and that is as an expert witness involved in major litigation on trademarks, copyrights, and trade practices. I've worked on one side or the other in nearly 50 lawsuits, some of which resulted in landmark rulings in many state and federal jurisdictions. I'll admit it's quite nice to be on the receiving end from lawyers for a change instead of being on the other side of the fence.

My career in the apparel decorating industry has been from the beginning a labor of love, which has also provided me a comfortable livelihood. It has enabled me to work throughout America (49 states), and Canada (seven provinces and in the Northwest Territories), and Mexico (six states), other parts of Latin America and South America, and spending more than two years of my life living and working (and playing) in Germany, France, Austria, Spain, Italy, Belgium, Luxembourg, and the United Kingdom.

God has been good to me, even though She sometimes has a weird sense of humor. I thank my lucky stars with a little prayer every morning when I look out across the marshlands and waterway and see my neighbors – mainly mallards, Canada geese, and (for eight months of the year) great egrets, blue heron, and more than 50 other species of feathered friends. My prayer states simply, "Thank You, God, for the great ride I've had along the way and for one more day!"

This book is to a large extent my way of giving back to the industry in return for a career that I still enjoy – nay, relish -- every day. I still love doing the work I do, seeing the places I see, and working with the people I work with. Having flown more than four million air miles, I whine about only one thing -- and that's getting where I have to go. Though getting back home is always a lot easier.

An academic by training, the most challenging aspect of my industry involvement has been teaching, writing, and working on research projects from a wide range of firms in and outside the industry. This includes assignments for several Wall Street firms that track our industry for their investment customers. Sharing what I've seen and learned over the nearly 40 years I've spent in the apparel graphics world through a comprehensive textbook is a goal I've been putting off for the past 15 years. Though I've no plans whatsoever to retire – ever, I figure I'd best write this book now, before it's, uh, too late.

The objective of this effort is straightforward: to share as much information as I can to help thousands of industry entrepreneurs and executives as well as their salespeople and middle management personnel to understand their jobs and opportunities better. This will enable them to be better armed to sell more volume and run better, more successful, more innovative, more profitable businesses.

This book also is being written for the thousands of entrepreneurs who every year explore entering this industry. Until now, there has never been a single work that serves as a comprehensive guide to building a decorated apparel business or a decorated apparel arm of an existing business. How nice it would have been for those of us who joined this industry during the past several decades to have had such a resource to help us learn what we ended up doing anyhow, but without paying the tab for our mistakes and our dumb mistakes, as well as enduring the trials and errors we all experienced.

For companies currently in the awards businesses, sign shops, printing shops, digital printing businesses, and other companies with account bases that would like to buy decorated apparel from your company if they could, my intention is to enable you to better decide how to make a successful transition into selling decorated apparel if you decide to go this route – but without having to invest years of learning our ways, paying for mistakes that could have been avoided, and being crushed under the weight of the learning curve.

What's in it for You?

You're about to read theories, strategies, techniques, and tons of nuts-and-bolts specifics. You likely already know some of this and you certainly have the luxury, of course, of skipping over chapters that you could have written yourself. But I suspect many experienced apparel decorating people will read it for reasons ranging from getting a refresher course to reinforcing what they already know, perusing the book for insights they might have missed along the way, for helping their employees get up to speed more quickly and more intelligently, and moving forward in directions that don't require you to reinvent the wheel.

Along the way you'll read about real businesses that have succeeded in this industry, why they succeeded, and why they continue to be able to provide very generous incomes for their owners and salespeople and respectable livelihoods for the rest of their employees. You'll learn what they did right and sometimes what they didn't do so right. Hopefully you'll apply some of the lessons to your own enterprise and get to the right answer sooner and without paying additional tuition attending the School of Hard Knocks.

Among the many questions this book addresses are: Do I have to learn the technology to be successful in selling decorated apparel? How much technology do I really need to know? How much does equipment cost for a start-up company? Who are the primary buyers of decorated apparel? What are the biggest buying audiences of decorated apparel? Does my pricing have to be the lowest pricing around to makeit in this business? Can you help me find the right name – or the right new name – for an apparel decorating company? Are there ways to save money on buying garments that only insiders know about? What are the biggest mistakes newcomers make? What are the biggest mistakes industry veterans make?

You'll get the answers to these and dozens of other questions. And you can count on getting scores of ideas from this book that'll make you more money faster – without having to pay the high cost of the usual learning curve and continued mistakes. I promise you'll also have fewer arguments with your spouse, your partner, and your employees. I promise you'll pull out much less hair. I promise your return on investment in this book will pay substantial dividends for years to come. And I promise you'll get the truth, without sugarcoating or spin.

Just a few warnings and suggestions:

▶ **Check preconceived notions at the door.** This advice especially is for veterans, because you're going to learn how conventional industry wisdom is dangerous to your economic health. The companies I work with wouldn't have become as successful as they are were they wedded to doing simply what everyone else did – or does.

► **Keep a notepad handy when you're reading this book or tuck a sheet of paper inside the cover.** I am absolutely CERTAIN you'll think of ideas that will directly impact you and your company as you're reading – ideas that if not jotted down right when they occur may very well be lost when you try to remember them a few minutes later. (Writing in the margins, putting ideas on Post-It® Notes and sticking them to the relevant pages using a highlighter are OK, too).

► **Consider requiring your key management personnel, salespeople, customer service people and other important staff to read this book.** Each person who reads it will learn some different things, sees things others might have missed, and will think of new ideas. Your company will earn more dividends as a result. Gee, you might even buy a few extra copies for special people and keep one or two on hand for future employees and for future reference.

► **This book is designed to be a teaching tool.** It is for management, for staff, and for students enrolled in printing management courses at colleges and universities, but it's also for classroom consumption and instruction in your own company. It'll prove to be a valuable tool in developing your employees to think about ways for your company to sell more products and services, to improve its profitability, and to enjoy the special benefits that accrue from seeing your competitors appear further and further away from you in your rearview mirror! So, consider scheduling a few classes in your business, assign chapters to your own "students" from week to week, and then discuss what everyone learned, the ideas they have to offer, and how your company can incorporate and implement them.

Thanks for buying the book! And Best Wishes for Your Success!

Faithfully,

Mark L. Venit

CHAPTER

2

THE MAKING OF THE APPAREL GRAPHICS INDUSTRY

The industry that creates and sells decorated apparel is an American phenomenon that emerged over time as a result of changing lifestyles, technological advances, social and political movements, and evolving consumer preferences. The terminology for this industry today includes "decorated apparel," "apparel graphics," "embellished clothing," or "the T-shirt industry." But whatever you choose to call it, the field encompasses a wide realm of components – from those who design, manufacture and distribute leisure apparel to those who transform "blank" apparel into everything from utilitarian everyday garb to graphic masterpieces and trendy fashion attire.

A brief look into the industry's history will help anyone thinking of participating in the world of decorated apparel understand its roots, its cultural derivatives, and its continuing appeal.

The genesis event that started the T-shirt on its way to mass appeal occurred in 1913 when the basic white T-shirt was made part of the standard uniform of the U.S. Navy. By the 1930s the T-shirt was being marketed as a men's underwear product, referred to as a "gob shirt" or "gob-style" shirt, owing to its association with sailors.

During WWII T-shirts, though officially undershirts, became a preferred choice as a comfortable warm weather garment, favored by American sailors serving in the South Pacific theater. After the war, T-shirts rose in acceptance as an underwear staple and in the 1950s, with navy veterans leading the way, moved to center stage as leisure and recreational apparel. Among the factors driving the increase in appeal and mass acceptance was the leading role performance of actor James Dean in the motion picture, *Rebel Without A Cause* in 1955. Hot on his critical success in *East of Eden*, Dean played a T-shirt-clad troubled teen and in so doing quickly attained celebrity as the reigning Hollywood symbol of alienation and volatility of the mid-50s youth culture. His death on September 30, 1955 effected the beginning of a personality cult following and whose adherents saw Dean's T-shirt as an iconic representation of youth culture.

Marlon Brando, who like Dean embraced the naturalist "method acting," wore a white T-shirt under his leather motorcycle jacket in *The Wild One*. That visual permanently reinforced the "coolness" of T-shirts as the de rigueur apparel of the new American youth culture, as thoroughly masculine, and what any self-respecting teen male, rebellious or otherwise, should be wearing, especially when the ladies were around. Elvis Presley, too, merits mention as another pop culture icon who preferred wearing T-shirts when hanging out with his buds.

In the early '50s screen printed T-shirts -- and sweatshirts -- appeared, initially within the custom arena encompassing schools, colleges, clubs, and summer camps. By the mid-60s, printed tees and sweats had earned permanent positions on the racks and shelves of souvenir stands and college bookstores.

Multicolor graphics emerged as an offshoot of the colorful custom art done on hot rods, particularly in California and Florida, as automotive airbrush artists enjoyed the fun and profit of turning their talents and their high-pressure airbrushes from decorating funky cars to creating funky T-shirts, by then the standard uniform of gearheads.

One popular method of multicolor decorating on shirts was to start with direct-screened black line-art or heat-printed graphics and colorize them by airbrushing additional colors onto the designs. Taking their cues from the street rodders, California airbrush artists made decorated T-shirts a fixture at the beach, too, where colorfully-designed T-shirts quickly become the favorite garb of surfers. As The Beach Boys exploded on the music scene and Philadelphia heart-throbs Frankie Avalon, Bobby Rydell, and Fabian moved into their next careers as stars of Hollywood's new genre – beach flicks – with Annette Funicello and other hot starlets, youth culture in the early '60s was being propelled by AM radio and network TV to mirror whatever was happening in California. And tens of millions of Mickey Mouse Club alumni, the first generation to grow up with T-shirts as an integral part of their attire, made T-shirts the virtual uniform of the Baby Boomers.

In the 1960s, young artists took to decorating their T-shirts and sweats with painted images and words. I was one of those early apparel decorators transforming his and friends' shirts into a medium of personal expression, though my favorite medium was a black Magic Marker™. But such frivolity was prohibited at school.

It was the social turmoil and antiwar protests, however, in the late 1960s that elevated the decorated T-shirt into a medium for mass expression as well as for individual expression. Until the Vietnam war, decorated tees and sweats told the world where you had visited as a tourist, what school or college you were attending, and who your favorite team was. With the T-shirt already the after-class garment of choice for college students, young protesters quickly discovered their T-shirts could, with four spray painted strokes, be emblazoned with a single icon to indicate where one stood on the question of continued American military involvement in Southeast Asia.

It was the social turmoil and antiwar protests . . . in the late 1960s that elevated the decorated T-shirt into a medium for mass expression as well as for individual expression.

It was the social turmoil and antiwar protests... in the late 1960s that elevated the decorated T-shirt into a medium for mass expression as well as for individual expression.

That single icon was the peace sign. This medieval Teutonic rune of death re-emerged in 1958 as the symbol of anti-nuclear activists. Also known in history as "the witch's foot," "broken cross," "crow's foot," "Nero's Cross," and a symbol of the "anti-Christ'" (a crucifix with broken arms), this icon appealed to the anti-nuke movement for its graphic likeness to a B-52 bomber.

Like honking your horn at cars identical to yours, wearing a peace sign on their T-shirts enabled left-wing students to identify like-minded friends. Led at first by these left-wing demonstrators, often wearing the anti-nuclear symbol on their shirts, anti-war protests rapidly moved from the left to the center of American politics. Caught up in the evolving political shift, the anti-nuke symbol morphed into the anti-Vietnam war symbol. Associated as it was with the peace movement, it became better known and remains known as simply "the peace sign." Conjure up a vision of what the crowds and the rock bands wore at the storied Woodstock event in 1968 and you'll see thousands of T-shirts emblazoned with the peace sign.

Whatever your politics, or mine, the peace sign merits the distinction of being the icon that synthesized the union of a T-shirt and an opinion prominently printed on it. This singular icon recast decorated T-shirts as a medium of expression that announced something powerful, personal, and did so publicly.

The combination was a natural, as we know today, and the peace sign was easy for just about anyone to spray paint on a T-shirt. You wouldn't "ruin" a good dress shirt with a spray-painted design, but as a T-shirt was viewed as considerably less dear and easily replaced, it was OK to decorate the humble garment with a few gusts of air-propelled pigment.

Another important, but seemingly unrelated, historical event that served to midwife the decorated apparel industry was the Arab oil embargo of 1973. Americans faced gasoline rationing for the first time since WWII and our national psyche -- our way of life -- was threatened by sheiks and sultans on the other side of the world. When the dust settled on that experience, we were able once again to buy all the gas we wanted without having to wait in line for hours, on any day of the week, regardless of whether our license plate number ended with a certain letter or an odd or even number. What had changed forever, though, was the price per gallon -- which was doubled and tripled -- and the kind of gas station where we'd fill up.

With prices hiked way up, major gasoline providers soon moved to become not only the wholesalers and distributors of gasoline, but also its retailers. The traditional American institution of the service station that dispensed gasoline was earmarked for extinction. Big Oil canceled station leases where it could to eliminate competition from independent operators, reduced the volume available to those remaining operators where it couldn't, and within a few years, the corporate-owned gasoline superstation had replaced its two-pump ancestor. Thousands of small neighborhood and highway gas stations were vacated by their owners, who lost both their leases and the ability to procure the gasoline for resale that provided them with their retail profits and their main drawing cards for customers.

Needing tenants for these highly-visible abandoned gas stations, their owners offered low rents to anyone who could cover the landlord's real estate taxes and monthly mortgages. Enter a cadre of Baby-Boomer entrepreneurs, now in their 20s and 30s, in search of low-cost locations for certain newly-emerging business categories that flourished in these old stations: plant and flower shops, specialty food and produce stores, and T-shirt shops.

These new retail T-shirt stores offered immediate gratification through the medium of T-shirts decorated with heat transfers and/or custom iron-on lettering, and at very reasonable prices. The generation that grew up in T-shirts and wore their political opinions on them in the '60s now opted to wear messages of their own creation and colorful multicolor plastisol graphics. They could buy a while-u-wait custom gift for under 10 bucks, and had an alternative to sporting goods stores for outfitting the teams they -- or their kids -- played on. Customers soon began asking the retailers if they could provide what we today refer to as "custom orders" for schools, businesses, events, and organizations.

These new retail T-shirt stores offered immediate gratification through the medium of T-shirts decorated with heat transfers and/or custom iron-on lettering, and at very reasonable prices.

These retailers knew where to source these purchases from another new group of entrepreneurs, the pioneers in the emerging textile screen printing industry. Both the printers and the retailers were oftentimes competing in the marketplace for the same customers. But with demand for custom garments skyrocketing along with the burgeoning number of accessible providers, there was plenty of business for everyone. Buyers flocked in to place orders at both T-shirt retailers and at local screen printing companies, which had the dual advantages of doing the actual screen printing decoration in-house and supporting that endeavor by having on-site art capabilities.

Custom apparel decorators were selling tens of millions of T-shirts, a fact that didn't escape the attention of the knitwear manufacturers that produced them. Fruit of the Loom®, Hanes®, Russell Athletic®, Stedman® and smaller manufacturers were happy to provide the product, but were cautious in their outlook, viewing the phenomenon of printed T-shirts as a fad. As such, the pioneer retailers and screen printers for the most part had little choice but to buy shirts either individually folded or in bagged 3-packs, as these were the prevailing modes of supply.

Those of us whose careers in this industry began in the '60s and '70s remember bringing in our blank stock and having to unbag and unfold our shirts, remove the chipboard inserts, and peel off little pieces of cellophane tape before laying our goods out flat and stacking them in preparing them for delivery to the press.

By the mid-'70s, we were finally able to buy bulk-folded tees from certain mills that recognized our needs and began to accommodate them. Later that decade, they also responded by offering us new colors: light blue, pink, yellow, mint, and beige to augment the available athletic-based palette comprised mainly of red, navy, royal, kelly, black, grey, and gold. You could buy mill-direct or from wholesale distributors. The wholesalers carried limited inventories of T-shirts, but for most of these companies, what we were buying was still an ancillary category, subordinate to their core offerings -- underwear, hosiery and socks, flannel shirts, pajamas, and jeans purchased for resale by "real" businesses.

A few dry goods wholesalers in each major city -- Bodek & Rhodes in Philadelphia, and Eisner Brothers and Eva in New York to name a few -- would eventually jettison all lines outside what this industry was buying to focus on our booming sector. In some places, a few screen printing companies, such as Virginia Tees in Virginia, found more opportunity in selling blanks to other companies around their region than selling decorated apparel in their backyard. In yet other situations, distributors sprung up strictly in response to our industry, as was the case of J-M and SanMar in Seattle, and South Carolina Tees in Columbia, S.C.

Like many screen printing companies that began in a garage or a basement, South Carolina Tees founder Bill Gregg ran his enterprise initially from his house, eventually filling every room except the bedroom and the bathroom with inventory. As Bill recalled, "When I had to put some boxes in the bedroom, my wife made it clear to me either my business would move out of the house or she would!"

Beyond T-shirts and athletic uniforms, our standard product line grew to encompass sweatshirts, caps, golf shirts, and jackets as core categories.

While decorated jackets and outerwear date to biblical times, sweatshirts, like T-shirts, are an early 20th century phenomenon, with fleece originally starting out as an insulating fabric for lining apparel. Baseball caps and the myriad of styles and fabrications that have blossomed in the past four decades date back as far as, well, baseball teams -- to the mid-1800s.

The history of golf shirts is more colorful, beginning with the tennis shirt. Created in 1928 by French tennis professional Jean René Lacoste, he and a partner established *La Société Chemise Lacoste* that in 1933 started to manufacture tennis shirts commercially. Lacoste wore his signature garment when playing. It had a small embroidered likeness of Lacoste's nickname, "the crocodile" – for his aggressive style on the court. These inexpensive, jersey knit garments with their trademark (which is better known as an alligator) became a popular favorite with athletes for providing comfort and more freedom of movement. It morphed into the "golf" shirt when introduced by The Munsingwear Company in the 1950s. Contributing to its rising popularity was the growing casualization of the American wardrobe, particularly in the workplace, and in the 1970s owing in part the proliferation of embroidery companies whose embellishing process weighs heavily in making the garment serve a variety of applications on the court, on the job and off.

Screen printing has its roots in the ancient art of stenciling in ancient Egypt, as early as 2500 B.C., later in ancient Greece, and circa 900 A.D. in China, when ink was first forced through silk fabric to create images. It was then that ancient artisans first stretched silk fabric across a frame and poured hot beeswax into it. Once the paraffin cooled and hardened, artisans using wooden stylus-type instruments etched designs in it, removing the wax from the lines drawn. Pouring ink in the "silk screen" and gliding a wooden squeegee across the design, the process of silk screening spread throughout Asia as an art medium for decorating paper and wooden panels, although rarely done on textiles or garments, where embroidery prevailed. The inks were made from colorful berries, roots, minerals, and other natural dye sources.

Using multiple silk screens with differentiated art patterns, multicolor designs executed by highly skilled artists were done with an impressive degree of sophistication, including tight registration. It wasn't until the 1880s, in Lyon, France, that silk screening became a viable commercial process for decorating fabric. It wasn't until 1907 when Samuel Simon of Manchester England received the first patent awarded for the process of using silk fabric as a printing screen.

The art of silk screening evolved in the 20th century into the versatile commercial graphic process that flourished for printing everything from huge billboard panels, posters, circuit board panels, glass and ceramics, vinyl, pressure sensitive materials, and acrylic sheeting, to, of course, garments. But to distinguish the modern, scientific, technologically advanced process from its ancestor craft, *screen printing* has become the preferred term. Through continued advances in graphic technology, many of screen printing's non-textile applications have been supplanted by digital printing, a field in the past two decades that has mushroomed to such an extent that it has replaced screen printing as the preferred technology in many commercial and industrial product sectors. At the onset of the 21st Century, though, digital printing came into being as another means to print garments.

A hybrid form of screen printing is flocking. In this early 1920s process, cotton lint was electrostatically charged to cause the lint particles to "jump" onto fabric pre-screened with an adhesive-only graphic and/ or lettering, creating a felt design. This messy and cumbersome technology has been replaced with a flocked material that is CAD-CUT® into the desired graphic and then heat-sealed onto the garment.

The heritage of embroidery dates back 5,000 years, but this medium today has as much basis in the application of computer technology as it does in the artistic tradition of needlecraft. One's personal ability to sew by hand or using a sewing machine is no prerequisite to entry in the field, nor very important to gaining proficiency. Masters of modern embroidery are more skilled in computer programming and electromechanics, graphic art, and a range of abilities that have little direct relationship to handling needles and thread. And do remove the term "monogramming" from your vocabulary as a synonym for embroidery, just as you wouldn't refer to the conductor of the London Philharmonic Symphony Orchestra as "a band leader." Monogramming is the proper term today only for sewing letters or stylized font patterns onto garments, towels, and napkins, or engraving these type designs onto jewelry and other personalized products.

Athletic lettering and numbering has been from the industry's inception a fundamental component of its success and a staple source of income for those companies that market teamwear on a regular basis.

The modern roots of athletic uniforms date from team outfits used in mid-1800s baseball. Team names first appeared by way of hand-cut lettering sewn onto the fronts of players' jerseys. (The Baseball Hall of

Fame in Cooperstown, N.Y., has several such garments in its archives and a few on display). Numbering was introduced by the Cleveland Indians in 1916 – on sleeves -- and was rarely seen again in the Majors until 1929, when the NY Yankees took to the field wearing large numbers on their backs. Initially, numbers reflected who batted where in the line-up. Murderer's Row fixtures Babe Ruth and Lou Gehrig wore No. 3 and No. 4 respectively.

By 1932 all Major League teams wore back numbers; the Brooklyn Dodgers introduced front numbers (an idea which never caught on in baseball).in 1952. Collegiate football introduced player numbers in the 1920s. Affixing player names on the backs of jerseys is a phenomenon of the television era, though the first player to wear such a garment was Eddie Gaydosh, the famous dwarf sent in to pinch hit *one time* by White Sox manager and marketing wizard Bill Veeck in during a critical game in 1951. (Not surprisingly Gaydosh drew a walk, resulting in Major League Baseball's subsequent introduction of minimum player height requirements). Gaydosh's number? 3/4!

Twenty years before the appearance of die-cut numbers on athletic uniforms, die-cut letters first appeared shortly after the stock market crash in 1929, on beanies. Arthur Carl "A.C." Stahl, an employee of the Detroit Flag & Banner Company, upon getting permission to keep for his own use some of the leftover felt scraps from the firm's manufacturing operations, turned trash to cash in his after hours, manufacturing the era's popular brimless caps, or "beanies." (Think of The Little Rascals wearing them in the *Our Gang* serial movie features of the period). Beanies made A.C. a few extra dollars, but he soon discovered offering beanies decorated with the buyer's own initials sewn on to be the value-added inducement that made the product irresistible. Sales boomed and enabled the young entrepreneur to start his own business, Commercial Art Products, despite the onset of The Great Depression.

When Stahl's sales prompted him to look for money-saving, time-saving efficiencies to improve productivity and profitability, his idea to die cut his felt letters provided the needed economies. And in so doing made the young man not only the inventor of die-cut lettering but also the first to die cut fabric.

Die-cutting fabric was first done to make custom-shaped backgrounds for Chenille embroidery for teamwear as early as the 1930s for corporate logos on employee uniforms. A.C.'s early enterprise was the forerunner of today's Stahls' ID Direct, which manufactures its numbers and letters on three continents and is the world's largest supplier of these products. Though the descriptive term "die-cut" is still used when describing letters and numbers, it may be more germane to use the term "pre-cut" since today's heat-seal letters and numbers are manufactured primarily using waterjet, laser, and other technologies, as well as by the CAD-CUT® (computer-assisted design) process.

The process of heat-sealing numbers and letters on garments was an outgrowth of fabric-to-fabric heat-sealing. The first adhesive used in the process was shellac, which after it's rollered onto fabric and dries, is rehydrated by heat in combination with pressure. The first heat print-ing "machines" were household irons and, for larger jobs, traditional horizontal dry cleaning clothing presses. The type of commercial heat presses used today for T-shirts were introduced in the late 1960s along with the first screen-printed plastisol-ink transfers.

Plastisol ink, developed in the late 1960s, was another technical inno-vation that brought about the predominance of decorating via direct screen printing and heat printing on garments. These two technologies along with embroidery apply to more than 99% of all garments sold in the industry.

Plastisol ink, a petrochemical-based product combined with resins (for adhering) and pigments (for coloring), is still the primary ink type used on screen printed and heat printed apparel today.

We've now arrived at the intersection where garments, decorating technologies, historic events, social phenomena, capitalism, and the graphic arts meet and see a moving picture of an industry coming togeth-er, driven by unforeseen, unrelated events -- an industry *happening*.

The defining moment of the decorated apparel industry occurred in Texas in 1977, with the creation of *Impressions* Magazine. By anyone's yardstick, *Impressions* is singularly responsible for the genesis of the industry, its leadership at its inception as well as its continuing edito-rial leadership today, and bringing about the industry's organization as a marketing entity, albeit one diverse in its components, audiences, and applications.

Founded by Dallas entrepreneur Bill Windsor, *Impressions* brought all the centripetal forces in the industry -- garment and equipment manu-facturers and distributors along with their customers around the U.S.

-- under one umbrella. Windsor coined the "imprinted sportswear" industry and synthesized his publication by drawing together equipment, garment, heat transfer, and technical supplies manufacturers and their distributors who sought a vehicle to advertise their products to audiences comprised of apparel graphics marketers in the screen printing, embroidery, sporting goods, promotional products, and retailing sectors of the newly-emerging industry. Windsor delivered both necessary ends of the equation – buyers and sellers -- to one another. With readers hungry for editorial content, especially in technical expertise and expanded sourcing, and advertisers hungry to reach their prospects and customers efficiently and affordably, *Impressions* Magazine was an instant success.

Windsor bought lists of names from suppliers, capitalized his magazine, wrote articles about things that had never been written about before, and mailed out his first issue in 1977.

I remember receiving the charter edition of *Impressions* and experiencing what thousands of other recipients were experiencing: "*What?! We have a magazine now?!*" We did indeed, a place to find lots of new vendors, education, training, and a means of communication with one another around the country. It also told us there were lots more folks out there doing this and that there might actually be a future in it!

The birth of *Impressions* was the catalyzing event, The Big Boom, if you will, of our industry today, which, like the universe, will continue to expand indefinitely. But there have been huge developments that have altered the landscape. What has changed over time is the fragmentation of the industry, the simplification of technologies, and the extraordinary expansion and proliferation of computer software applications.

When the industry started, screen printed apparel meant largely T-shirts, though sweatshirts, golf shirts, and outerwear became growing categories. The products were sold mainly by screen printers, and to a lesser extent, the traditional uniform industry. Enter the growth of embroidery and its impact on screen printers and the uniform industries. Early on, the bulk of embroiderers' work was on orders placed with them by screen printers and uniform companies, and in time, promotional products distributors.

Many screen printers – about 15% of them currently -- opted to buy embroidery equipment to recover market share and keep customers from straying elsewhere. Promowares companies changed the dynamics by selling their service as all-inclusive, one-stop shopping, and have inexorably been gaining market share in decorated apparel at the expense of screen printers and embroiderers. Smart embroiderers discovered heat printing and bought heat transfer machines and custom transfers to compete more effectively with screen printers and promotional products distributors.

Meanwhile, the traditional uniform industry lost ever-increasing market share to local screen printers and embroiderers, then to the consolidation of local uniform retailers by national companies, then to Internet marketers, and finally to Wal-Mart. What was once the province of uniform retailers with brick-and-mortar locations became largely the province of smart e-commerce firms and big box stores. Today when nurses need scrub shirts and pants, their most convenient and oftentimes the most convenient source is Wal-Mart, which stocks broad selection, broad size scale including up to 4XL garments, and sells them one at a time, cheap. I know; my wife's a nurse. (She wears a medium). The uniform industry has been decimated.

With declining fortunes, retail printing shops doing letterheads, envelopes, business cards, and brochures were seriously impacted by the advent of millions of people having computers and desktop printers to supplant their need to visit their local print shop. To augment their sales and profitability print shops, sign shops, awards companies, sporting goods retailers, and other businesses became outlets for promotional products and many learned to augment their sales with heat-printed garments done in-house with a heat-transfer machine. Big box stores such as Staples and Office Depot began offering decorated apparel and promotional products.

The dynamic we were experiencing during the industry's evolution from its infancy into its toddler stages was a burgeoning network of roadways all bringing customers to the same destination – our decorated apparel neighborhood. But apparel decorators were constantly expanding their sales as well into other buying sectors and technologies. The crossover selling came and went in several directions, but all were converging on the same buyers who can today buy custom decorated apparel, promotional products, signs, awards, vehicle graphics, and other related product lines from so many different types of companies – or from ONE company for everything. Technologies once limited to one segment of producers became available to almost all of them; and where one vendor chose to expand his available in-house production, others opted to outsource it.

With the exception of manual screen printing, the advancing digital age propelled the evolution of many decorating technologies into becoming output devices for computer graphics programs. Embroidery, laser engraving, digital printing, CAD-CUT®, sublimation printing, and direct-to-garment printing are all done on output devices or other digitally-driven internal programs. The learning curve has, in part, been shifted from learning operating apparatus and performing pre-production tasks to learning as much or more about computer graphics programs and equipment-specific applications.

That's where you'll find the world of custom decorated products today. You'll find it's a world of opportunity for apparel decorators who elect to explore moving into other realms, but also a world of opportunity for those in other technologies who want to explore the opportunities in decorated apparel.

That said, the author's focus in this book will be on marketing decorated apparel, though we'll take some time along the way to look at those places on the map where there's ample justification to take occasional side trips beyond the confines of apparel.

While the apparel decorating industry's history is largely an American phenomenon, its development elsewhere has been exponential as well.

Canada's apparel decorating industry closely followed that of what was happening in the USA, though it took until the early 1990s for garment manufacturers to develop a network of distributors. Prior to that it was largely a system of mill-direct supply, a reality that caused Canadian entrepreneurs to source a chunk of their garments needs in the U.S., incurring in the process duties, broker's fees, customs delays, excessive freight charges, extra paperwork, and other time- and money-consuming hassles.

The United States – Canada Free Trade Agreement, signed by President Ronald Reagan and Prime Minister Brian Mulroney on January 2 ,1988, took effect on January 1, 1989 after enabling legislation was passed by each partner. The pact was designed to reduce and in most cases eliminate barriers to and tariffs on trade in goods, services, and investments between the U.S. and Canada by January 1998. In the decorated apparel industry, the agreement helped Canada's industry to quickly achieve parity with its U.S. counterpart in technology, quality, and customer service.

The agreement was suspended on January 1, 1994 when the North American Free Trade Agreement (NAFTA) went into effect, mandating free trade in areas that had only been principles of agreement in the U.S.-Canada agreement. Within a few years any noticeable differences in the apparel decorating industries of the two nations had been largely eradicated.

Europeans, especially West Europeans, dress better than Americans. The idea of wearing slogans and advertising -- especially on T-shirts -- was a hard sell to Europeans, though over time they've been catching up to their American cousins. The most pervasive use of decorated apparel across the pond is in Germany, where the presence of the U.S. military has been pervasive; our military personnel wear there what they'd wear here. Screen printing was consistently 10 to 15 years behind whatever we were doing on this side of the pond through the late 1990s. Walk into a screen printing or an embroidery shop today in Germany, however, and you'd feel right at home.

In the United Kingdom, the industry stayed well behind the growth we saw here, though the industry in and around London was evolving quickly and achieved parity with the U.S. in many ways by the 1990s. In France, while producers there do credible work, the culture is still 20 years behind the U.S. in decorated apparel. Its primary uses there are for athletics, schools, and events, but to a considerably lesser degree for business application. Where you'd see more T-shirts -- printed and plain -- in France is along the Mediterranean coast, where there are sizeable communities of immigrants from North Africa and the Middle East who routinely wear decorated apparel.

In Africa, especially sub-Saharan Africa, T-shirts are everywhere. After all, it's hot there and T-shirts provide great value – comfortable, launderable, inexpensive, durable, colorful, and, to the joy on the growing cadre of screen printers and micro-retailers there, are printable. The Republic of South Africa has a vibrant industry along with Nigeria and Ghana in the west and Kenya in the east. But T-shirts are evident throughout the continent.

Much the same can be said for our counterparts in the Indian subcontinent and throughout most of Asia. T-shirts are everywhere. Australia and New Zealand also have very strong decorated apparel industries as well.

Latin America is and has been fertile ground for printed T-shirts for decades. In Brazil, a nation approaching 200,000,000 souls, T-shirts have long been "the uniform" for most of the population; and for its growing middle class and corporate marketplace, golf shirts and upscale leisurewear have long been staples.

Note that I titled this chapter "The Evolution of the Apparel Graphics Industry." I thought titling it "The History of the Apparel Graphics Industry" would be a bit presumptuous, since what I've written about it is a combination of what I've learned about it as well as what I recall personally as both an observer and one of thousands of actors on the stage. It is an accounting that's admittedly biased and but one man's perspective. Other writers and future industry historians will write other things, new things, distill the past, and give you their own spin on what is by any standard a work in progress.

In 2002, I was cited by *Impressions* Magazine as one of the Top 25 Leading Industry Innovators, an honor about which my father would be proud and my mother would believe. While it's a nice accolade and I was humbled to be included in such esteemed company, I take myself and my role in this industry's evolution with a grain of salt. (After all, all I was trying to do was make a buck). Were the same list to be compiled by the editors of *Impressions* today, there would likely be some new names inserted to replace older ones. It's a safe bet some of those new names are reading this book.

While the traditional view of history is a summary of events and the people that influenced them, this industry's history reflects the powerful impact of politics, social forces, technology, and a host of phenomena that won't be seen in context until many years from now. But if I can place one factor at the top of the list on what has brought about this industry and fostered its continuing success, it is the magnificent energy that springs from human creativity – in what we design and manufacture, dream about and implement, and synthesize from among seemingly unrelated things. Obviously any industry's past has a bearing on its present, though its future is a matter of conjecture. My view of this industry's future is that whatever forces will shape its course, it will continue to be propelled by creative thinkers who aren't bound by the conventions of the past or the present.

CHAPTER

3

THE MARKETING PROCESS IN THE APPAREL GRAPHICS INDUSTRY

Marketing is far from an exact science, and different authorities on the subject offer different views on what should be included within the context of the marketing process. Those of us whose careers center on marketing – albeit on very diverse levels of expertise, input, training, and insight -- place differing emphases on the various components of marketing by virtue of our own personal and professional experiences. What we'll explore within the scope of this chapter has been developed by this author to reflect his apparel graphics industry-specific bias in addressing the needs and perceptions of his industry-specific audiences. In other words, to all my former colleagues in academia, butt out, this is a family affair!

A general overview of business operations shows three primary areas: production, finance, and marketing. Let's look at the marketing process as much more encompassing, though, since everything we do to build our apparel graphics companies in the custom-decorating sector is impacted by our success -- or lack of it -- in generating new customers and keeping them happy and sufficient to merit their continued patronage while we look for still more and more new customers.

What is a market? Simply put, it's people or an audience with the need for our products and services, the authority to buy them, and the money to pay for them. Need, authority, and money are critically necessary for us to have a chance at selling something to someone. Where one of these fundamentals doesn't exist or is severely compromised, no opportunity or market exists for us to pursue on a practical basis.

The first issue, the need for our product, is one that might not seem apparent at first glance. Where a prospect doesn't perceive or know that he needs what we're selling, we have the challenge of convincing the prospect he can benefit from our products and services.

Where a prospect doesn't perceive or know that he needs what we're selling, we have the challenge of convincing the prospect he can benefit from our products and services.

Creating someone's authority to buy, if he doesn't have it to begin with, is beyond our power. But we do have the ability to learn if the prospect we're talking to has influence on decision-making, to what extent, and how he might be enlisted to help move the decision to buy closer to its ultimate source.

Creating the money for the buyer is at first glance a very tall order. But if we're effective in ascertaining, identifying, creating, and, when possible, demonstrating the prospect's need for our product by explaining its value and its benefits and advantages, a prospect can then decide he'll have -- or will find within his resources -- the money to pay for our products.

Six Main Market Sectors

In the apparel decorating industry, there are six main market sectors of custom-decorated apparel or, as characterized by the industry's own lexicon, "general custom" (or just "custom"). We'll refer to these six market sectors throughout the book. In Chapter Thirteen, we'll look at each sector, outline the subsectors within each category, and catalog the primary applications of decorated apparel in each sector.

▶ **Businesses**
▶ **Schools & Colleges** *(including Universities, Pre-Professional Training, Trade Schools)*
▶ **Organizations, Clubs, Interest Groups**
▶ **Athletic Organizations, Teams, Leagues**
▶ **Governments**
▶ **Events**

Left off the list is a seventh sector, "preprints." This category includes decorated apparel created for sale to retailers -- both the brick-and-mortar variety and online stores -- for resale to consumers or retail sales made directly to consumers by apparel decorators either from their shops and stores or online.

An industry-specific term coined in the 1970s, preprints refers essentially to the broad spectrum of apparel products merchandised to retailing sectors and a broad spectrum of targeted end-user audiences. The buyer's motivation for purchasing these products ranges from use in his or her personal wardrobe to demonstrating a personal affinity for one's favorite endeavors, teams, celebrities, personal causes, or other individual aspirations and lifestyle choices.

Some of these products are sold within the scope of branded apparel (such as Nike, Reebok, Polo, etc.) and licensed apparel (Major League Baseball, NFL, Disney, etc.) regardless of where and how consumers purchase the products.

The marketing of apparel for retail sales differs dramatically from the cultures and methodologies used in the creation and marketing of custom-decorated apparel to the other sectors discussed here and in many subsectors of the events sector. Because the nature of developing and marketing apparel product lines in the retail world entails vastly different cultures, objectives, and functions from the selling of custom-decorated apparel, this book excludes this sector from further examination.

Where sales in this sector function largely as retailing to mass audiences, albeit at specific venues or to specific audiences, the products here would be better characterized as being within the realm of preprints.

CHAPTER

4

THE EIGHT STEP IN THE MARKETING PROCESS OF DECORATED APPAREL

The Eight Steps in the Marketing Process for Decorated Apparel (Figure 1)

Figure 1. = The Eight Steps in the Apparel Graphics Marketing Process

8. Reviewing Your Success (or the Lack of It)

7. Delivering the Product

6. Selling the Product

5. Producing the Product/Service

4. Determining (or Creating) Your Product/Service

3. Researching the Market Potential

2. Analyzing the Needs of the Market (or Segment)

1. Targeting the Market (or Market Segment)

Beginning with the foundation of the eight steps, let's look at the marketing process for decorated apparel with regard to how each phase impacts your decisions in becoming a successful seller and marketer of decorated apparel.

1. Targeting the Market (or Market Segment)

In this first step, our intelligence in choosing a viable target market wisely will go a long way toward solidifying our chances of ever making any money in this business. Pick the wrong, unrealistic or unfeasible market and everything you do from this point will be futile. Marketing begins with identifying and targeting the market or markets in which we think we can succeed.

Imperative in understanding any given market is to further investigate its segments and subsegments. You frequently hear the term "niche marketing" in conjunction with targeting an audience. Is it good to look for smaller niches or go after the broader market? (You'll know the answer to this question in due time, I promise).

Let's say you determine that a potentially desirable market for your company to investigate is schools. First, we'll need to refine that choice to a level where we're more likely to succeed more quickly, with less competition, and at a reasonable return on investment.

Narrowing down this particular market to more manageable proportions means we need to consider geographic boundaries, types of schools, size of schools in terms of the number of students, the character of the community the schools are in, and how sophisticated the students are, among a host of other important issues. Looking at just this one example, we'll need to get smart fast and answer the right questions – that is, once we figure them out. Schools. Hmmm . . . All the schools in America or just those within a half-hour's drive from our business? Public schools, private schools, parochial schools, or *all* schools? Elementary, middle, high schools or all of them? Vocational-technical schools? Colleges and universities, too? Rural, suburban, or urban schools? Schools with students who are city kids who watch MTV or country kids who listen to Rascal Flatts, Taylor, Leann, and Reba? Do the local schools have average enrollments of 2,000 students? Or 200?

The questions here illustrate the process – and perhaps the frustration -- of attempting to narrow down where you're be more likely to see a better return on your investments of time and money. Wrong answers will prove costly, but asking these questions is the first step in the challenge of finding the answers. By focusing on those potential areas where you have more advantages and opportunities, the rest of the process will become more instructive and lead you to better conclusions and, eventually, better choices.

DUMB MISTAKE No. 1:
Thinking your company can be all things to all people.

2. Analyzing the Needs of the Market (or Market Segment)

What characteristics of the market might make your company a more desirable vendor? What can you offer that sets you apart from the competition? Ascertaining qualitative information if you can find it --which you'll indeed find if you look for it -- will help determine those areas in which your company can move to the head of the class. Key findings here will shorten the learning curve and its marketing costs.

Using the school exercise above, we can expect that school buyers' needs are likely to differ from some of the key factors a businessperson would consider paramount. For schools, you'd want to learn how their buying habits and needs can be accommodated by your company to make your advantages theirs. You've got the best art staff in town, but do the schools you're targeting care about that? Do they buy on concepts, quality and great graphics or it is simply all about price? How, when and how much do they buy? Do they need everything yesterday? Do they take precise-to-the-number-of-garments orders from the students before purchasing? And if they do, will they demand guarantees that you'll cheerfully produce after delivery of the initial order nine more shirts with 5-color designs at the same 288-run price they pay when they buy at the 288 level? Do they require personal presentations and samples or is their purchasing done on bids limited to their own specs? Would they favor (and must they favor via local ordinance) buying from firms who pay taxes in their school district even if the price of the local supplier is 10% higher than out-of-state vendors? Were you an out-of-state vendor, would the equation change if the local guy's price is, say, 15-30% higher than yours?

When you can meet the school buyers' needs -- or exceed them -- and develop policies that satisfy needs that the buyer hadn't identified but would appreciate, your chances of success in a given marketplace rise dramatically. But if you don't ask and don't seek, you won't find, and you sure won't compete effectively.

Businesses have their own hot buttons. But the particular practices of a business buyer differ from schools in that a decision can be made much faster than where decisions are impacted by school committees, bureaucracies and paperwork. That means a business caller who needs a price right now needs a price right now. And unlike school buyers' objectives, price to a businessperson is more likely to be viewed with an understanding that quality and service, better art and better workmanship, and the like may have a worthwhile – read: beneficial -- bearing on price.

How often do teachers, coaches, principals, student buyers, and PTO moms demonstrate the same level of understanding? Oh, sure, school buyers might give lip service to such qualitative issues, but their general lack of experience and understanding about value makes their decisions weigh much heavier on price than would be the case in the eyes of a businessperson willing to pay "fair value" for superior quality and service.

The smart business buyer will be generally more concerned with how his recipients -- ranging from customers and prospects to employees and senior staff -- will react to the garments if the graphics and execution are mediocre, if the garments don't hold up through repeated washings, or look "ordinary." School buyers might appreciate these factors, too, but more often do so after the fact, whereas the business buyer needs his expectations met and assurances delivered up front.

A school buyer, oftentimes a volunteer, may need to meet with sales reps in late afternoon, in the evening or on weekends, whereas the business buyer wants you to be open early and answer your phone on the first ring. He can approve artwork five minutes after it's e-mailed, while the school situation may require that two or more people must sign off on an approval -- and that extra step may take an extra day or longer.

Analyzing the needs of the buyers in a given market and accommodating these needs, if you can, means you're still in the game here. If you can't service their needs, it's back to the drawing board to investigate other markets or segments or develop other questions. But if you can not only satisfy the identified needs but gain advantages by addressing them better, you're a big step closer to winning the game.

Because there are so many directions you can take and still make money, targeting the market and analyzing its needs are the toughest to comprehend and often quite confusing among the many challenges you'll address in your search for the right markets. Once you've made your determinations about which markets you'll pursue, the rest of the steps in the marketing process are considerably more finite. But you can expect that the challenges and confusion of choosing the best directions will likely get tougher before they get easier. That's because, as you'll learn throughout the course of this book, there are so many good market options you'll want to explore.

3. Researching the Market Potential

Researching the market potential means ascertaining whether a market is sufficiently large enough to actually give you a chance at making money. Schools, as discussed above as a possible focus of your business, are certainly a large-enough market. And it's probably too large were you to try to attack it in its entirety. But were you to select an audience within that arena that's way too small – say, French teachers and their senior year classes in your own school district in the U.S. -- there's likely not enough business to make it worth your time and effort. Spanish, maybe, but not French.

To reiterate, a market's potential is essentially an evaluation of how much business is being done with a product (or product category) in a given area, how much could be done if the circumstances were right and conducted over a specified term, and whether there's enough sales volume now or down the road to justify your investments of time, effort, and cash. What you're ultimately looking for is finding enough demand in terms of units and dollars to see if there's room for one more competitor -- you!

To illustrate the point, I was contacted in the mid-90s by Sue Horner, a woman whose screen printing company had sold custom shirts for several years to a group of greyhound aficionados for their special events. She told me she thought there was an opportunity to develop a decorated apparel business that focused on the greyhound market. As my only personal familiarity with that market was as an occasional bettor at a local greyhound track when I lived in Florida, I wasn't knowledgeable about whether the greyhound world had sufficient potential for income. My charge to Sue was for her to research the size and scope of the market. She called back after a few weeks of fact-finding to report "There are about 300,000 people who have something to do with greyhounds" – they love greyhounds, own them, race them, frequent greyhound tracks, show them, breed them, adopt them after their racing days are over, are members of greyhound clubs, yadda yadda yadda. 300,000 greyhound enthusiasts to sell to? Score! The potential was more than sufficient to pursue that market, so I became Sue's consultant. Starting out with innovative designs, including rhinestones, for an upscale audience that knew only boring designs, Greytwear (www.greytwear.com) was born and became an instant success. She quickly beat her competition by several lengths. Today, with more than a decade of extraordinary growth and success behind her, she remains well in the lead and truly the Big Dog in greyhound apparel.

Determining how many units of garments and a detail of styles and colors are purchased in various trading markets and for how many total dollars is an exercise in futility vis-à-vis the apparel graphics industry. This level of data is unavailable, unlike the sophisticated and accessible statistical documentation for an industry as large and critical as, say, the automobile industry, where you can learn sales figures, units and models sold, along with hundreds of other finer details to the nth degree.

The good news is that the vitality of decorated apparel in virtually every market in North America means you needn't worry about finding where there is sufficient demand for custom-decorated apparel among the markets or market segments or subsegments you'll explore.

4. Determining Your Products and Services

In general, you know the products the industry offers. Knowledge of the apparel decorating technologies available to you entails, however, considerably greater exploration of your options, especially for beginners. Yes, the most widely used technologies are screen printing, embroidery, and heat printing in terms of production volume. But the cost of the equipment, the space necessary to house the apparatus and put work on it, and the technical learning curves can present barriers to entry.

In its broader sense, the services you'll need to offer, whether you perform them in-house or outsource them, include preparing artwork, personalization (particularly regarding team numbers and names), and a range of other standard customer services, may appear to be more than you can handle. Except in the most highly automated operations of Internet-based businesses, selling decorated apparel and providing customer services means promptly handling inquiries, coaching customers and negotiating with them when necessary, getting approvals on graphic designs, addressing last-minute surprises, and accurate, timely invoicing, among many other functions.

At first glance, the industry's product categories are quite familiar: T-shirts and fashion tops, fleecewear (crewneck sweatshirts, hoodies, sweatpants, etc.), placketed goods (golf/polo shirts), outerwear, athletic garments, caps, poplin and denim shirts, shorts, and infant and juvenile garments. Every category, however, includes in most aspects, dozens of colors, a wide variety of shapes and styles, a variety of fabrics including jersey knit, pique knit,100% cotton, cotton/polyester in various applications, 100% man-made fabrics, moisture wicking fabrics, and different applications of fleece, among key considerations. In golf shirts, a myriad of styles enables buyers to select from hundreds of different color combinations, trims and piping, bottom finishing options, sleeve finishing options, fabrics, pockets, and more.

When it comes to outerwear, the choices expand even further, encompassing an extraordinary range of weather-related applications – from the types of outershells, front closures, pockets, neck styling, linings to internal hoods, zip-out linings and zip-off sleeves.

In addition to the plethora of garments available to apparel decorators, there are yet other categories to learn about, including bags, aprons, beverage insulators, and should you elect at some point to offer them, thousands of items in the realm of promotional products.

Though it takes time to get a firm grasp on what's available, with the supply chains serving the marketplace, current demand, evolving trends, and the breadth of technologies for decorating apparel, new industry entrants and would-be decorated apparel marketers can get a crash course and further information on the industry today by availing themselves of some of the free resources provided by popular industry websites such as www.impressionsmag.com, www.stahls.com, www.imprintcanada.com.

5. Producing the Products and Services

The same resources listed on the above and other websites also provide guidance about choosing which technologies you should consider doing in-house vs. outsourcing them to specialists. But a broader set of considerations about how much of the process an entrepreneur can handle on his or her own becomes necessary to address the actual fulfilling of orders from the time a sales order is secured through to getting paid for the order.

Three frequently asked questions regarding this aspect of the marketing process are discussed below and the answers to each will give you a solid understanding of the issues at hand and, hopefully, an added level of command and confidence in determining your courses of action.

Question 1: Is it imperative that I handle in-house all the functions of executing the orders I sell?

Question 2: How much technical knowledge must I attain to be successful in the world of decorated apparel?

Question 3: If I choose to outsource some or all of my work, how confident can I be that my contractors will provide good quality work? And will contractors keep the business I do with them confidential?

Let's get to the answers.

Question 1: Is it imperative that I handle in-house all the functions of executing the orders I sell?

Answer: No. Many successful sellers of decorated apparel who may a.) lack the personal financial and credit resources to transact business and be able to pay their bills on time or b.) choose to focus primarily on selling the products enter into relationships with full-service apparel decorating firms, promotional products distributors, or other trade agencies that are equipped to handle a variety of critical functions. These range from purchasing, invoicing, credit card processing, and collection to providing the full gamut of production functions, including the preparation of graphics, comprehensive in-house decorating production services, packaging and shipping.

But the single, biggest part of making money in the apparel decorating business is in the mark-up on the goods. Except in some comprehensive athletic orders -- where the price of applying the team graphic along with multicolor numbers and names, and perhaps adding league insignia may well exceed the charge for the garment -- in most decorated apparel orders the single, largest component of profit derives from marking up the cost of the actual garment.

As such, those who can buy and sell the garments, regardless of whether the seller does in-house decorating or outsources it, usually make more money than those who rely on other sources to handle the risks of buying for them. The key risks of buying come down to two main issues: 1. Who pays for garments damaged during the decorating process and replacing them?, and 2. not getting paid (or paid in full) by the customer and having to absorb the cost of the items.

The most prevalent arrangements with another entity handling some or all of the responsibilities in executing orders include:

► Working on an independent contractor basis with a vendor. This means you run your own business and do your thing -- mainly sales -- to earn your money and pay the vendor or vendors for those services you contract for. It also means you pay your own federal, state, and local taxes on what you earn as well as self-employment tax, and any other mandated employment taxes, fees, and permits. Of course, this arrangement means you also have to collect your own receivables and assume all the financial risks of running a business.

► Working as a commissioned independent sales agent. In this arrangement, your job is primarily to sell orders and develop accounts. The company that you elect to sell for processes your orders, procures the goods, handles getting them decorated, and collects the payment due. Most of the time, the commission is paid to the sales representative upon the company's receipt of payment, a system known in the trade as "pay-on-pay."

As with the first arrangement, you are responsible for paying all of your own federal, state, and local taxes on what you earn. If you earn $600 or more per year, the company – or each company -- you sell for is required to send you a statement as to what you received as compensation. In the U.S., that's IRS Form 1099; in Canada it's Revenue Canada's T-5.

► Working as a commissioned employee of a decorated apparel company or a sales organization. In this arrangement, you have a boss -- along with a "home" and the responsibilities of maintaining your position. This means the company has responsibilities to support you, diligently execute the orders you generate, and handle just about every function of the process except for finding customers and earning their patronage.

This arrangement also requires the company to pay its share of employment taxes, and pay its mandated percentages of your earnings for workman's compensation, unemployment compensation, and other requisite taxes. If the employer provides its workforce with healthcare, retirement, and other benefits, you'll receive these advantages as well. The company will withhold taxes as required by law and issue a year-end statement of your earnings as an employee – the W-2 Form in the U.S. and the T-4 slip in Canada.

In this relationship you trade your independence and most of your risk for a more stable income, all the support functions the company performs, more predictable hours, and what may well be a variety of competitive advantages.

Some of these commission arrangements are accomplished with the benefit of a draw-against-commission, a system in which the company provides a consistent minimum or "floor" level of financial support in anticipation that the sales representative will over time earn his keep on a more consistent, predictable basis. A commission-draw levels out seasonal and other cyclic variations in sales performance. As long as the sales rep performs in conformance with the financial basis of the arrangement, both sides can be comfortable with the relationship. Sometimes these arrangements are structured with a base salary plus a performance component for meeting or exceeding goals established for the individual salesperson or all the salespeople.

As for straight-salary arrangements with outside salespeople in the decorated apparel industry, they're few and far between and rarely endure successfully on a permanent basis.

Question 2: **How much technical knowledge must I attain to be successful in selling decorated apparel?**

Answer: It depends on to what extent your company will actually be doing the work or if you'll be contracting all or some of it to service providers. If you'll be executing the decorating in-house, you need to be intimately knowledgeable of the processes you're offering but not necessarily personally skilled enough to do the work yourself. If you're selling and doing screen printing, it means knowing something about getting the art prepared, the basics of screen making, the nuances of screen printing, and be familiar enough to be able to diagnose or anticipate technical challenges or trouble before it happens. Do you need to know how to do the artwork, make screens, set up presses, and select and "pull" squeegees? Absolutely not. It's nice if you can do some of the graphics or prep chores and handle production, yourself, in a pinch. But these functions are the province of people who earn their livelihoods generally at a lower rate of pay than that of the boss, who don't want the risks of owning a business, and prefer to be on the receiving end of instructions about which orders to run and when they're due.

To be sure, though, there are indeed tens of thousands of successful, lucrative small apparel decoration operations whose owners wear several "hats" – from being the primary artist, screen maker/digitizer, machine operator, bookkeeper, salesperson, and/or janitor on a regular basis. Some do quite well financially overall and are smart enough to outsource production jobs that are over their heads in terms of size or sophistication.

For most entrepreneur-owners, though, who'll devote most of their time, money, and effort to sales and marketing, overseeing their operations, and performing the "visioning" function of the enterprise, attaining production-level technical knowledge and skills are not critical determinants of a company's success.

From a practical point of view, the owner's requisite level of understanding of the technical processes would best be characterized as "slightly dangerous." Essentially, a decorated apparel entrepreneur needs to be sufficiently familiar with the technical processes to be able to sell intelligently, buy intelligently, and be able to ask intelligent questions when troubleshooting production snafus and researching equipment and technology purchases.

Question 3: **If I choose to outsource some or all of my work, how confident can I be that my contractors will provide good quality work? And will my contractors keep the business I do with them confidential?**

Answer: While the quality of work depends on the culture and skill of the contractor, those contractors that specialize in the technology you need done are generally quite good at what they do and oftentimes are better than most of their competitors doing the same type of work. That's because contractors have to satisfy their customers on a regular basis if they're to merit repeat business and referrals from their trade accounts; they cannot afford to do bad or mediocre work if they want to stay in business.

Oftentimes contractors are skilled at doing the kind of work many full-service companies are incapable of executing. Many typical screen printing companies cannot run jobs requiring advanced-level specialty inks, such as high-density, suede, discharge, caviar beads and other such elements; many typical embroiderers aren't skilled at sewing 3-D/puff embroidery or sewing jobs calling for appliqués. But most experienced, superior-skilled screen printing and embroidery contractors accept often complex work as routine assignments. Do ask a potential contractor for references to satisfy yourself before sending out your work. But as a general observation, most contractors do excellent work!

The question, "And will contractors keep the business I do with them confidential?" derives from a very legitimate concern, especially for newcomers. The answer here is that professional contractors wouldn't have gotten where there are by stealing business from customers or tipping off more favored accounts about orders they run for you. Again, check references and use common sense.

When visiting a contractor's facility where it's convenient to do so, the contractor will be happy to "show you around the place" the first time you visit. After that, smart contractors keep contract customers – you and your competitors -- out of production areas except when absolutely necessary to allow them "in the back." That's because while the contractor's integrity may be pristine, some of their other customers might be folks who want to snoop around and stealthily observe what other orders are being run to get a look-see at the accompanying paperwork. It's these people you need to be concerned about, not the honorable contractor.

6. Selling the Product

For too many companies in our industry, selling amounts to a religious experience where thousands put their faith on the line: they wait by the phone and pray for it to ring. Selling doesn't happen by itself. Someone has to do something, or more precisely, satisfy three objectives to get the phone to ring, have customers walk in, get customers to mail back a reply card, or generate an online inquiry.

First, you have to *create awareness* of your company. You have to tell people you've "arrived," you're alive, and introduce yourself to them. Achieving awareness takes time and effort. It may also take money.

Second, you have to *inform* folks about what you do, along with why they should buy from you. They need to know your hours, your location, and how to go about doing business with you.

Third, you need to *solicit business*, meaning: you "ask for the order." Soliciting business means going after the account, not waiting for it to come to you.

Creating awareness, informing prospects and customers, and asking for their business are accomplished by a variety of techniques ranging from traditional advertising and sales promotion to one-on-one selling. What works best to get the message out and the inquiries in will vary by situation, resources (read: money and talent and effort), and the characteristics of a market. There's no single guaranteed medium or message nor a one-size-fits-all cure. But we'll look at overall strategies and specific techniques in several upcoming chapters.

Not selling isn't an option. Companies in our industry that don't pro-actively sell find themselves stagnating and blame their lagging per-formance on the economy, unethical competitors, and other perceived – usually imaginary -- bogeymen. They'll find excuses for whatever is ailing them except the real one: their own lack of effort. Companies that do market are the ones that grow bigger and smarter and more profitable every year; they're the ones who thrive at the expense of the dinosaurs.

Not selling isn't an option. Companies in our industry that don't proactively sell find themselves stagnating and blame their lagging performance on the economy, unethical competitors, and other perceived – usually imaginary -- bogeymen.

7. Delivering the Product

Delivering the product or service doesn't just mean getting it to the customer, it means getting it to where it's going on time, in budget, and done right the first time. Lots more on this later in the book!

8. Reviewing Your Success (or Lack of It)

Ed Koch, New York City's colorful and popular mayor during the '80s, became associated with his signature phrase proffered to the voters and the media: "How'm I doin'?" That's the question we need to ask ourselves at least once a year on a more formal, more comprehensive basis. Sure, we do it to some degree every day, but not in the context of really sitting back, taking an overview of the interaction of all our efforts, and analyzing our efforts with an eye to making the system better. What I call "The Five P's" will help focus your self-evaluation process:

PRICE: Are you charging what you *need* to be charging? Do you have an opportunity to increase your prices without jeopardizing sales or market share? Do you have any choice in the matter? Based on what we know from the field, are your prices out of line and in need of rethinking? You'll find more about this in Chapter 12 about the real meaning of price and why you don't have to be at the bottom of the pack.

Dumb Mistake No. 2
Thinking everything you sell has to be sold at the lowest possible price!

PRODUCT: Are you selling the market what it wants to buy? Are you ahead of your customers' needs or behind them? Is the quality of your work where it needs to be or should it be upgraded vis-à-vis the competition? Does your quality command attention and respect? And earn you re-orders?

POSITION: How is your company perceived by your customers? What do prospects and other not-yet-customers think about you? Do you live up to what you say about yourself and your service in your advertising? Have you been correct about where you've focused your marketing efforts? Are you getting your message out effectively, relative to what your strategy is? (We'll talk lots more about the art and science of positioning in Chapter 7).

PROFITABILITY: Well, uhhh, are you making any money? Are you making what you should? What does your profit-and-loss statement tell you about what you should be doing to gain efficiencies that'll lower your expense ratios, or where appropriate, spending more to achieve them? Is your sales volume sufficient for realizing your financial goals?

POTENTIAL: To what degree are you maximizing your efforts, relative to your resources? Are you really performing qualitatively and quantitatively on the level you're capable of? Do you have ample room to grow? *Lots* of room? What do you have to do to be all that you can be? (With apologies to the U.S. Army.)

For too many companies in our industry, selling amounts to a religious experience where thousands put their faith on the line: they wait by the phone and pray for it to ring.

Hopefully you'll see the marketing process not so much as a continuum of effort, but an interactive system that's constantly adapting and evolving, able to refine, define, and redefine your goals and opportunities as necessary to produce more revenue and realize a greater profit.

Historically, business developed around production. Until the mid-20th Century, the common proposition for a company selling products, as opposed to selling services, was that the enterprise produced its wares and then searched for customers to buy them. But in the post-WWII era, businesses worked to provide products and services for audiences that were receptive to these products because the products were designed and marketed to satisfy their tastes, their needs, and their desires. This approach led to an explosion of innovation, niche marketing as well as mass merchandising, and more customer-friendly ways of doing business. The high tech age we're in now is a wonderful example of how marketing thinking is supposed to work.

Some apparel graphics entrepreneurs sincerely believe that doing good work and selling it at a reasonable price is the foundation of good marketing. But a true understanding of the fundamental role of marketing recognizes the company as a vehicle that *looks to the marketplace -- the buyers! – for further direction and inspiration* and responds through a well-integrated system that produces desirable products, and more importantly, respectable profits.

Responding to the marketplace doesn't necessarily mean following what everyone seems to want, but rather delivering what an audience demands and expects. It also means creating new solutions wherever possible and identifying unfulfilled needs and satisfying them better and faster than someone else does. And hopefully you'll accomplish all of this before the other guy figures out what you're doing, so you can witness his former customers switching alliances and becoming *your* customers.

In Section 4 (Positioning Your Company in the Apparel Graphics Marketplace), we'll use our understandings of the marketing process as a guide to examining current marketing realities in the decorated apparel industry, how they impact apparel graphics companies, and how we can develop strategies for moving our own company forward and positioning it for sustained, long-term growth and profitability. Before we get there, let's look at the various technologies used to decorate apparel -- the technologies you're already using, those you'll be considering when starting a business, or those you'll be looking into soon or down the road as you entertain ways to expand your enterprise.

CHAPTER

THE TECHNOLOGIES FOR DECORATING APPAREL IN THE 21ST CENTURY

On a visit to the Caves of Lascaux in Southwestern France in 2010, I marveled at breathtakingly beautiful images of animals painted on the upper half of cave walls, images created by Cro-Magnon artists 14,000 to 20,000 years ago. Recent discoveries by archaeologists working in other parts of the world show that this level of talent, creativity, and technology is today thought to have been achieved as much as tens of thousands of years *earlier*! I'll venture that if early man could figure out how to go deep into a cave, build scaffolding to stand on or lay down on, provide enough lighting in the cave to enable him to see his stone "canvas" to paint on it, and make pigmented materials to express his thoughts graphically, I think it a safe bet that he also occasionally decorated his leatherskin vestments with the name and logo of his favorite team or magical spirit, local pub, hunt club, or vacation destination. Suffice it to say, folks have been decorating garments for eons.

From silk screening's artistic roots in 1st Millennium China and the advent of commercial textile screen printing in 19th century France, the process didn't change much for another 80 years when plastisol ink was invented in the 1960's, propelling the field of textile screen printing from an art into a science. Embroidery goes back to Biblical Times. Electro-mechanical embroidery machines and "punched" tapes came about in the early 20th Century and didn't change much until computerized embroidery arrived in the early 1970's. The first computerized embroidery equipment sent digitally crafted instructions to the machine as to where to position itself and what its needles should sew.

...folks have been decorating garments for eons!

Today screen printing (including screen printed heat transfers) and embroidery are the two processes that command the overwhelming bulk of production of decorated garments. There are, however, other newly developed technologies that accomplish the same ends. Let's look at a quick rundown of how garments and textile fabrics are decorated and with reference points for the minimum capital requirements. The dollar figures given are for new equipment and requisite supplies and accessories. The figures do not include training costs, the working capital required for sustaining a new business during its umbilical period, or the inventory to be decorated.

Screen Printing

Modern screen printing involves making a "screen" for each color of imprint in a design. A screen is a device whereby mesh fabric is stretched across a frame and secured to it. The screen is coated with a light-sensitive emulsion and a graphic image or design is then placed on the screen either with a transparent medium with opaque graphics on the film (or a milky white substrate called Vellum™) or imaged onto the screen via a digital process that directly applies ink onto the screen's emulsion surface. The imaging process will eventually permit only the design elements to be washed out of the screen. After the screen is dried and sometimes touched up to eliminate imperfections, it is positioned onto another device -- a screen printing press -- to hold it in place during the printing process. In this technology, ink is forced with a squeegee through the screen's mesh onto whatever's underneath it – a T-shirt, a jacket, a sign or banner, pressure-sensitive label stock, etc.

Setting up a textile screen printing shop with new equipment will run between $10,000 and $20,000 at minimum for basic manual equipment (a press, an infrared dryer, an exposure unit for imaging screens), start-up supplies and hardware.   Used equipment is also available. A new automatic press will run anywhere from $16,000 to $80,000.

The learning curve of textile screen printing will take but a few days of training, practice, and hands-on experience to gain a basic ability to screen print on a manual press, one without motors, robotic arms, or any high-efficiency add-ons. Learning how to operate an automatic press will take a few additional days to learn. But achieving a *command* of the subtleties, nuances, and a myriad of variables that ensue with mastering the process will take months. And as some highly-skilled screen printing technicians will attest, it can take perhaps years when it comes to being able to see a highly complex job and quickly evaluate it as "a piece of cake!" Training, instruction (including some great video training), and technical experts throughout the nation are widely available. And affordable.

My colleague, friend, industry pioneer, and the craft's premier technical educator, Scott Fresener, published the first edition of his "*How to Print T-Shirts for Fun and Profit*" in 1978. Though updated over the years, the book's basic instructions are still operative today. This landmark work, which has sold tens of thousands of copies since its first release, was the catalyst for launching thousands of screen printing businesses, whose owners had little technical training beyond what was printed in that book. The point here is that learning how to screen print isn't all that difficult; learning to print *well*, however, is!

Embroidery

The modern process is seemingly simple, accomplished using a sophisticated sewing machine that sews designs onto fabric. The image or design to be embroidered is "digitized," creating a digital file by which a computerized embroidery machine "reads" the programming instructions that tells the needles where to sew stitches to create a visual design with thread. Machines range in capacity from a single embroidery "head" that can embroider only one garment at a time to multi-head equipment that can sew from two to 12 garments at a time. Machines are equipped to sew several colors in a production run at finished sizes that range from a few square inches to a few square feet. The bigger the machine, the greater the number of heads, the greater the thread capacity, and the faster an order will be completed -- and the more a machine will cost in initial outlay.

The embroidery process can be seeming easy, though it does have its own learning curve. The basics of operating the machinery are learned with a few days of instruction and practice. But understanding the realm where graphic design, machinery, computer programming, and thread and needles come together entails learning that comes best from "the doing." According to Frank Gawronski, the embroidery industry's top industrial engineering and production management consultant, "Think of it as learning to play the piano. You learn the basics from your teacher and you can play a few rudimentary tunes in a few days. But appearing at Carnegie Hall isn't in the cards for beginners." The finer points and nuances of executing professional quality embroidery need to be experienced in a way that formal instruction won't accomplish. And as Gawronski notes, "Some people can become astute embroiderers in a few months, while some folks who've been doing embroidery for years still produce rather mediocre workmanship."

As with screen printing, on-site training and video training programs in embroidery are widely available throughout North America and are affordable.

Start-up costs for a single-head embroidery operation will run between $10,000 and $20,000 for basic commercial machinery, start-up supplies and hardware, and three days of training. Add $10,000 to $15,000 for a two-head machine and considerably more (another $20,000 to $50,000) for high-output equipment with six to twelve heads. 24-head machines area available by special order, but have small design fields.

Heat Printing

The most prevalent type of heat transfer product in the decorated apparel industry consists of an image imprinted onto a substrate (various types of paper) by means of screen printing, inkjet, or lithography. The heat transfer is then placed on a garment or textile surface and through the application of heat and pressure, the image, itself, is transferred to the textile surface.

A heat-transfer press is a device that has top and bottom metal platens, the top of which is electrically heated, and is engineered to hold the platens firmly in place together above and below the fabric for a prescribed number of seconds, the time for which is determined by the type of ink employed and the type of garment being imaged. Rhinestone transfers work a little differently, but the principles of how rhinestone or nailhead graphics are transferred onto a garment are essentially the same as with heat transfers with inked graphics.

By using *professionally manufactured* heat transfers and transferring images onto a garment using a *superior quality* heat-transfer press, a decorated apparel creation done with heat printing technology is absolutely indistinguishable from one decorated on a screen printing press.

Heat transfers also can be made through sublimation printing, a process involving special inks on specially manufactured paper, that can be made by inkjet or laser printers and on specially designed photocopiers.

The resulting heat transfer can then be applied to a textile surface using a heat press. Sublimation printing can also be transferred onto ceramics, glassware, wood, and metal. Cylindrical objects, such as coffee mugs, can be decorated on a specially-engineered cylindrical heat press that wraps around the surface to be decorated and uses a combination of heat and pressure to cause the image to transfer on to a specially coated mug. It's the coating on the mug that is actually heat printed.

Heat printing is the most affordable technology for start-up apparel decorating entrepreneurs, where an investment of between $1,000 and $3,000 for a commercial-quality heat transfer press, start-up supplies, and accessories, are all that's needed to get into business as an apparel decorator.

By using professionally manufactured heat transfers and transferring images onto a garment using a superior quality heat-transfer press, a decorated apparel creation done with heat printing technology is absolutely indistinguishable from one decorated on a screen printing press.

Many heat printing apparel decorating businesses choose to do their graphics in-house, which can be accomplished with a graphic software program and a few days of training or prior experience. Some of these companies also will elect to produce their heat transfers in-house with the purchase of one or more types of machines – from inkjet printers to screen printing presses. Most heat printing apparel decorating businesses, especially in their infancy though often for the life of the company, will opt to order ready-to-go heat transfers from companies such as Transfer Express that specialize in providing the actual finished heat transfers.

These vendors can work from the customer's prepared graphic art files, but also are fully equipped to execute both the graphics necessary for the designs as well as the production of the heat transfers. Some of these vendors offer extensive art libraries for use by their customers at nominal fees – or free. Also available from these companies are heat-transfer (or "iron-on") letters and numbers in a broad variety of fonts, sizes, colors and applications and are available as single-item supplies – one number or one letter -- to boxed alphabet and number kits.

The situations where heat printing is a smart option include:

▶ **Starting an apparel decorating business with minimal capital:** Heat printing is the most affordable way to enter the industry. Period.

▶ **Hedging on quantities:** When customers tell you potential purchase volume -- especially those designs with multicolor graphics -- but don't want to tie up large amounts of money because they're not confident they will use or sell as much as they think, heat transfers present you and the customer with a way to test their confidence with considerably lower risk. For example, the customer suggests she thinks she'll sell 200 T-shirts with multicolor designs on front and a one-color design on back.

Ordering finished tees up front will cost upwards of $1,000. But she could order 50 or 100 transfers for $4 each or $2.50 each, respectively, which is an outlay of between $200 and $250 plus the cost of blank shirts and application charges. In this scenario, she'd be able to buy blank garments in lots of ranging from a few pieces to a few dozen. If the total volume never reaches the hoped-for 200-unit level, the only downside is, say, $100 in unused transfers instead of several hundred dollars of unsold finished inventory. Meanwhile, orders can be placed by the customer and produced on an as-needed basis, ensuring minimal risk of waste and eliminating the need for and cost of repeated set-up charges. If the customer needs shirts for an event but isn't sure how they'll go at the shirt table or kiosk, heat printed garments also offer the advantage of being produced in minutes, on demand, even while the event is happening.

▶ **Handling names and numbers on teamwear:** Heat-printed letters and numbers "to go" means no screens, no number screens and no numbering machines, no screens for printing names, and faster turnaround. It also means replacement garments or add-on units can be done while the customer waits!

The team design can be ordered as heat transfers with the customer buying a few extra pieces to accommodate the inevitable changes and additions to the team's initial line-up as well without facing additional set-up charges and production delays. CAD-CUT® materials and a computerized cutter (see section below) provide a fast, economical way to produce even one garment quickly, and with minimal risk. All the seller needs to do is cut the design and/or names and numbers, and then heat press them as directed onto the garments as needed.

Those interested in learning more about getting into business using heat printing technology can get extensive technical and sales information and start-up guidance from Stahls' ID Direct, the firm that invented the technology for the apparel decorating industry. The company [www. stahls.com] also is the world's largest manufacturer of heat printing machines, heat-transfer supplies, and, via its Transfer Express division, ready-to-go finished heat-transfer products, which usually ship within 24 hours of receipt of your order.

Direct-to-Garment Digital Printing

Though inkjet printing has been done on textiles since the 1970's (primarily in Japan on fabric rolls), digital printing on *finished garments* is a very new addition to the apparel graphics industry. Arriving at the beginning of the new millennium, direct-to-garment printing is a technology by which garments are printed by inkjet with four-color process inks, though many designs incorporate fewer colors in the graphics. Initially this technology was available for printing only on white or light-color garments, but a decade into its existence, the process has since progressed to now handle work on dark-color garments as well.

With a wide variety of manufacturers selling "D2G" machines, this technology now gives excellent quality, and garments decorated by this method can be machine washed and dried with confidence that the ink won't fade or degrade. It's a great solution for executing small orders requiring on-demand delivery or multicolor printing without the burdens of making and setting up screens or installing and housing cumbersome screen printing equipment.

That said, the technology has limits on its seemingly attractive advantages. For small orders of one unit up to a few dozen, decorated garments produced on D2G machines are competitive price-wise with multicolor screen printed garments. On larger runs, though, from three dozen garments and up, D2G-printed shirts become more expensive than similar jobs done with traditional screen printing. As the order quantity escalates, the price and speed advantages of screen printing over D2G accelerate. That's because the per-unit cost of the special ink for D2G – from $.50 to $2 per imprint -- is way more expensive than plastisol ink and the time necessary to print orders is vastly slower than screen printing. Compared to high-volume orders produced on automatic screen printing presses, direct-to-garment printing is downright expensive and wholly uncompetitive at higher levels of production.

Moreover, the cost-of entry into direct-to-garment printing starts at $20,000 for a single-head machine and nearly twice as much or more for dual-head equipment. D2G should be considered primarily for doing short runs, for retail stores and kiosks, and for orders needed "right now" or "yesterday," where its technological advantages shine. For larger firms and companies specializing in selling to retail markets, D2G does offer major advantages and opportunities to "test" designs used in the solicitation of orders. It's also useful for printing actual samples for getting fast approval from customers of how an order's design specs will actually appear.

As with gaining a command of any apparel decorating technology, there is a learning curve that comes with the territory in direct-to-garment printing. But anyone thinking of starting a D2G business needs to acquire a strong command of graphic software applications along with learning how to run a D2G printer. Learning the graphics programs is an endeavor that will likely entail considerably more time and effort than learning the D2G process itself or entail hiring someone with previous graphics training and experience.

CAD-CUT® Technology

CAD-CUT®, the acronym CAD is for "computer assisted design," is a technology whereby a substrate – vinyl, paper, or fabric, among other materials – is cut by tiny "knives" into shapes, letters or other images cut only deep enough so you can separate the design and text on the substrate. These substrates are available with adhesive backing for applying and transferring the graphics onto another substrate, such as a T-shirt.

The learning curve in CAD-CUT® technology used to entail having a broad command of computer graphics. That learning curve has been shortened considerably with the advent of CAD-CUT® Designer. Developed by GroupeSTAHL in 2008 to enable users to create cuttable artwork more easily and faster. CAD-CUT® Designer is an online design service that takes the hassle out of creating artwork for garment decorators, (Currently – in 2011-- there are 6-month free trial memberships offered online for both CAD-CUT® Designer and CAD-PRINT® Designer, a module for creating full-color artwork for output to printer-cutters. Go to CadworxLive.com to learn about these and other tools for apparel decorators).

Entry cost to the realm of CAD-CUT® technology begins with the heat press you presumably already own plus $1.000 to $5,000 for a computerized cutter, start-up inventory, and accessories.

Dumb Mistake No. 3
Limiting your apparel decorating capabilities to only
ONE technology.

For example, you can peel away (or "weed," as it's referred to in the trade) a design on adhesive-backed vinyl from a carrier sheet, apply it to a garment, transfer it using a heat transfer machine, as discussed earlier, and end up with a perfectly decorated garment. You also can complete it with personalized player names and numbers. Or, by using another type of pressure-sensitive vinyl that is backed with an adhesive that requires no heat sealing, you can place a CAD-CUT® image on a magnetic sheet and create an easy-on/easy-off vehicle sign (yeah, like what real estate salespeople put on their cars). Or you can place it on a variety of paper, cardboard, fabric, metal or plastic sheeting products and create a sign, a flag, or a banner. CAD-CUT® materials also can be used to directly letter trucks, heavy machinery, boats, PWCs, snowmobiles, submarines, time machines, spacecraft, and wooden boxes, among a host of other things moveable or stationary. The technology opens up tremendous opportunities for selling custom CAD-CUT® decorated products well beyond apparel and teamwear.

The learning curve is relatively easy with CAD-CUT® equipment, though learning computer graphics also is essential.

Acquiring CAD-CUT® technology runs between $3,000 to $5,000 for entry-level equipment, supplies, software, and start-up inventory. Another level of CAD-related decorating technology is available in combination with digital printing equipment (see below).

Digital Printing

A technology that has revolutionized the gamut of printing methodologies, digital printing has expanded the means and alternative pathways to decorate apparel as well. The use of the word "digital" in garment decoration is commonly associated with full-color graphics that are produced using an inkjet or laser printer. At the entry-level end of investment you can use either a desktop inkjet or laser printer with a paper or substrate appropriate to your job application to create your own digital heat transfers, which are then transferred using a heat press. An undesirable limitation of most commercially available papers is, however, that they leave on the image a "ghosting" background within and/

or around the image applied. Fortunately manufacturers of these papers keep improving their products and the introduction of ExactPrint™ by Stahls' ID Direct eliminates the need for decorators to trim the ghosting from digital transfers made via laser printers.   Today, having a heat press and a laser printer provides the most affordable means to enter the world of digital garment printing.

On a more sophisticated level, digital printing involves the use of a wide-format inkjet printer, used primarily for producing signage, posters, and banners.   These printers range in output capacity from 30" to 54" across (and larger) and print continuously on rolled media (substrates wrapped on rolls in pre-cut widths and lengths).   For decorating apparel with solvent-based inks or eco-solvent (read: environmentally green) inks, a variety of transfer media are available.   For entry into the higher end of digital printing, your initial capital investment will range from $20,0000 to $100,000 or more.

Cut-and-Print Technology

The cut-and-print process is a hybrid technology which combines digital printing with cutting. This methodology, despite its sophistication, carries a surprisingly user-friendly learning curve. Essentially, a digital printing machine does the graphics and/or text and is equipped with a sharp-edged component that is a built-in cutter. A quick way to make a variety of multicolor heat transfers and custom-cut twill for doing appliqué designs for embroidery, the technology enables apparel decorators to do short multicolor runs on garments competitively, cut their own multicolor letters and numbers, and beef up profit-making embroidery capabilities by cutting custom-shaped appliqués. All this, and you also possess the operational abilities to add signage, vehicle markings, banners, and other products when and if desired to expand into additional products lines and conquer new markets

To move into entry-level cut-and-print technology you can expect start-up costs to be in the $20,000 to $30,000 range, including machinery, supplies, and software. Used equipment is available, but the technical advances in this process mitigate against buying anything other than recent-model equipment.

Industry veterans are well-aware of most of the technologies outlined in this chapter. For successful apparel graphics companies, though, considerations of the various apparel decorating technologies beyond screen printing, embroidery, and heat transfers, should be seen with regard to the relative ease in entering, accommodating, exploiting, and mastering the new apparel decorating media.

That's because if you've been in the business for a while, there's a strong likelihood you already own some of the critical resources that'll enable your enterprise to leapfrog its way into these new avenues of opportunity. Many of the key aspects of screen printing, embroidery, and heat transfer printing resources that you already possess are prerequisites for the other, newer technologies. Seen from an operational vantage point, direct-to-garment printing, CAD-CUT®, and digital printing (as well as laser engraving and other graphic decorating technologies) are all output devices for a computer graphics program. Ergo, you're already at the starting gate, should you decide to enter your horse in any of these derbies.

Your other existing resources and advantages include:

► **Available Manpower:** Are all of your employees busy every hour of every day? In a word: NO.

Given the seasonal cycles in our industry and the economic challenges of the current economy, keeping your best employees working -- and paid -- can be challenging. But acquiring any of the newer apparel decorating technologies entails virtually no additional personnel cost beyond the arc of the learning curve, which will certainly add some investment in training your personnel.

► **Existing Customer Bases:** You already have an account base. In-house production of alternative technologies gives you a huge advantage over your competitors, especially sales agencies, whose turnaround is days or weeks behind yours.

Your ability to deliver more products more quickly to trade accounts means you'll also have a potentially strong, new level of wholesale or contract business if you already sell through independent intermediaries in additional to or in lieu of doing your own direct selling. And the cost for marketing your new capabilities to your existing account base is next to nothing.

► **Little or No Additional Overhead:** Most of the new output devices require very little space or electrical upgrades. Most entry-level and mid-size equipment for CAD-cutting, sublimation printing, direct-to-garment printing, and digital printing (as well as laser engraving and cylindrical ceramic decoration) fits comfortably on a standard-size desk or in a similar size footprint for the equipment and work areas.

New Profit Centers, Crossover Selling Opportunities

Owning the means to produce more than one decorating technology means opportunities for more prospects, more solutions for decorating, a better use of staff, more long-term security, enhanced profitability, improved account loyalty, increased transaction frequency, and amplified marketing horsepower. It also means more wearables business from new accounts you land through other product decorating portals. The potential crossover selling opportunities for apparel graphics companies that move their enterprises beyond apparel into limited production of signage, awards, mugs, giftware, and a host of other products are out there, should you elect at some point to add additional technologies. Many of the non-wearable products you might someday be decorating aren't as constrained by seasonal selling cycles, so they provide their masters with year-round work and income -- even in first quarter!

For more information on the new technologies, I'll suggest once again, contacting Stahls' ID Direct, a pioneer in the development and distribution of textile decorating technologies beyond screen printing, embroidery, and heat transfer printing and a world leader in advancing non-textile technologies.

And, hey, hold on a minute!

The author's intention here in outlining the lay of the land in apparel decorating technologies is to provide a general awareness of what's available, how the technologies are similar and how they differ, entry capital requirements, and other opportunities the various apparel graphics methodologies present in the way of developing additional product lines beyond apparel. For production companies in the industry, most apparel decorators focus on one technology, while some 15% do two or more processes in-house. Most screen printers (85%) sell embroidered apparel, though most contract their decorating to other producers. Nearly half (47%) of all embroiderers sell screen printed apparel, and/ or provide heat-transfer decorating. As you might expect, the longer a production company has been in the apparel graphics business, the greater the likelihood it has expanded its capacities to produce additional product lines with additional technologies. [Source: Apparel Graphics Institute – Trends Survey 2005].

For new entrants, however, a major issue is deciding whether they should or shouldn't do more than one technology in-house and with what outcome.

Here are some recommendations about this issue:

► **Start-up embroiderers** also should purchase – at some point, and sooner rather than later – a heat transfer machine. They'll quickly learn how to supplement their embroidery sales by decorating T-shirts -- the single, largest category of garments sold in the trade in terms of units -- as well by doing them in-house (except for large-volume orders, where using the services of a contractor might offer economies and faster turnaround).

► **Start-up screen printers** should learn how to sell embroidery immediately. In doing so, they'll be able to offer the higher-ticket products and significantly add to their profitability, boost their competitiveness in the marketplace, and protect themselves from losing important business to other sellers and producers. Start-up screen printers should buy a heat transfer machine upon entry to avail themselves of the opportunity to offer teamwear, sell upscale rhinestone designs, apply heat-sealed patches to caps and garments, and be able to handle orders for small quantities of multicolor designs faster and more competitively.

► **Start-up heat transfer enterprises** should quickly establish relationships with contract screen printing and embroidery firms. For orders calling for larger quantities and more sophisticated decorating, doing jobs solely with heat transfers alone will restrict competitiveness and opportunities to sell larger quantity orders.

► **Start-up direct-to-garment businesses** should quickly establish relationships with contract screen printing and embroidery firms as well as purchase a heat transfer machine for all the reasons cited above. The idea that D2G technology gives a company the ability to do and sell *everything* a screen printer can is folly and, moreover, virtually guarantees the firm will be utterly unable to compete for larger orders, teamwear sales, and jobs calling for specialty inks. The equipment simply is not able to provide competitive advantages on larger orders and more sophisticated work compared to the efficiencies and attributes of screen printing.

▸ **Start-ups focusing on CAD-CUT®, digital printing, print-and- cut technologies** for doing their apparel decorating should, from the outset, offer products lines beyond apparel. Some of the technologies here have inherent limits in producing large orders of decorated apparel, printing specialty inks, and decorating higher-ticket apparel products. As such, these businesses should establish relationships with contract screen printing and embroidery firms. Then again, sometimes heat printing can be the only viable solution in certain mass-production situations.

Offering signage, vehicle markings, banners, and pressure-sensitive products present huge opportunities to sell high-margin orders to virtually any type of business, government entity, event, and organization. Within days of getting started you can be selling vehicle markings and window banners to radio stations and to companies with fleets of cars or trucks. And for booster clubs, churches and organizations in need of new ideas and new items for fundraising, your company can be a wonderful resource.

CHAPTER 6

PRODUCTS, PRODUCT SOURCING, PRODUCT SELECTION

The core products of the decorated apparel industry encompass a broad range of categories. Most of the list below shows product categories you're quite familiar with, but it also shows categories with products you might not have at first considered. It's possible that these other categories may be where you find opportunities you might otherwise have missed.

▸ **T-Shirts** – The largest category, which covers more than two-thirds of all the units decorated in the industry, includes traditional adult and youth sizes in some three dozen colors, which vary somewhat from year to year as manufacturers replace weaker-selling colors with new ones. Long-sleeve and pocket tees capture a small percentage of the total for most companies. White is by far the largest selling color, accounting for some 40%-plus of all T-shirts, followed by black and grey (or variations on the color, such as ash and grey heather). These three colors account for some two-thirds of all units of standard T-shirts manufactured for the North American market.

But the fastest growing segment of T-shirts includes specific styles for women and girls. More fashionable vis-à-vis current trends, cut to better reflect the female anatomy, and the fact that females are demonstrably more concerned (than males in general) about being more fashionable in their apparel tastes, feminine garments feature new styling silhouettes and subtle though noticeable detail changes from year to year.

T-shirts are made from jersey-knit fabric in a variety of weights from 100% cotton, blended cotton-polyester in varying percentages of fiber mix, and 100% polyester. A niche category growing in popularity in recent years is moisture-wicking fabric, an all-polyester knit that "breathes" to allow the more rapid evaporation of sweat. Its application is mainly for use in activewear, worn in warmer climes and for recreation and athletics. This fabric is referred to in the trade also as "moisture management" and "performance" fabric.

► **Fleecewear** – This is the industry term for what civilians call sweat-shirts. Available in different weights for different seasons and different applications, fleece is a three-layer knitted fabric that is known for its comfort, warmth, durability, and soft feel against your body. Hooded sweatshirts, dubbed "hoodies" several years ago, and traditional crew-neck sweatshirts are the two primary products in the category, followed by sweatpants. Styling elements include zippers, drawcord hoods, ribknit fabric cuffs and collars, and self-collars. Manufactured since the early 20th century for the collegiate and industrial markets, fleece garments today are a staple category in the North American market.

► **Golf Shirts** – Also called "polo shirts," this knitted garment features a collar, two- and three-button closures just below the neckline, and hemmed or trimmed sleeve ends. Manufacturers call the category "placketed" goods (a placket is the section of the garment with the buttons and buttonholes on the "column" of the garment.) This garment has been the No. 1 category in unit production for embroiderers since the industry's inception as an industry in the 1970s, as the vast majority of golf shirts are decorated with embroidery. Lower-ticket, jersey-knit styles items, however, are occasionally screen printed or decorated with heat transfers.

Placketed shirts are offered in a variety of cotton, cotton-poly blends, and moisture-wicked fabrications in jersey knits, pique knits, and inter-lock knits. There's a myriad of styling variations from solid colors, which account for the overwhelming majority, to models with sleeve and collar trims, piping, color-blocked bodies, stripes, notched sides, and "backtails," among the most prevalent enhancements. Far removed from its golf and tennis origins, golf shirts are a staple in North American and European wardrobes – male, female, young and old -- and in every nook and cranny and climate on the demographic map.

► **Poplin and Denim** – Made of woven fabric, often twill, these shirts are usually styled with button-down collars, front buttons, buttoned cuffs, and pockets. Styling variations range from solid colors (in the overwhelming majority of the category) to pinstripes, contrasting collars and cuffs, and other detail enhancements. Nearly all denim and poplin garments are decorated with embroidery. When first introduced into the industry in the 1970s, denim shirts were called "prison shirts!"

► **Shorts** – Made in fabrics from jersey knit, fleece, and nylon to moisture-wicking and polyester mesh,   shorts come in a huge variety of colors and styles for applications ranging from pure leisurewear to athletics use and everything in-between.

► **Bags** – If you can imagine it, it's been made – and it's probably a stock item. Roll bags (also called barrel bags and gym bags), tote bags with and without gussets (the bottom flair that adds capacity), garment bags, fanny packs, backpacks, "manbags," diaper bags, and scores of other more esoteric varieties are easily screen printed, heat printed, and embroidered. Each style presents tremendous opportunities for added profits. Colors of every imaginable hue and combination, sizes from a few inches to superlarge equipment bags, and a wide variety of trims are the hallmarks of the category. From $1 items to high-ticket specialty gear, bags also can be custom manufactured for clients who demand specially designed pockets, special closures, and other specified features for surprisingly affordable prices.

► **Teamwear** – From jerseys to full uniforms for every sport under the sun, teamwear has been a core staple of the industry from its inception. Decorated via many technologies, teamwear commands good margins as well as the added profit gained through providing player names and numbers, decorating accessories, and equipment bags and covers.

►**Outerwear** – Jackets are the highest price echelon of the industry and are available in styles and weights to accommodate whatever climates you target – from the tropics to the Arctic Circle. Basic styles wholesale for $10, while well-known national branded selections eclipse the $100-mark. The lower-end items often are screen printed or heat printed, but the bulk of the items in this category usually are embroidered. Outerwear also includes wind shirts, insulated jumpsuits, skiing gear, and just about everything else worn over indoor clothing. Hundreds of stock items are offered by the industry's leading suppliers for virtually every imaginable application – except maybe space suits for astronauts.

▶ **Caps** – The ultimate category for styling diversity – in thousands of styles – caps are relatively inexpensive to buy and command higher selling margins. Ball caps are, for sure, the biggest category, followed by visors. But add to these all kinds of special application caps, jeff caps, straw hats, bucket hats, painter's caps, and, well, you get the idea on the variety of available inventory. There's big money to be made here.

▶ **Other noteworthy categories** – There are yet further product categories. Some are huge, some are small. Among the bigger ones are children's apparel -- from infants and toddlers to pre-school garb -- and workwear. While children's clothing is a business unto itself -- complete with its own distribution channels and trade events -- our industry certainly provides its share of custom-decorated kidswear.

And while workwear can be thought of as its own industry, apparel decorators are claiming an ever-increasing percentage of market share, so much so that our industry today is vastly bigger than the uniform industry. And there are yet other product categories, albeit smaller, such as petwear, towels, fan hands and stadium cushions, beverage insulators, pillowcases, placemats, doormats, scrubwear (for both the medical industry and as beachwear), executive accessories (printable and embroiderable portfolios and computer accessories), and banners, among other product lines decorated by our industry.

Sourcing Goods

Apparel decorators are blessed with a wealth of reliable vendors with well-stocked shelves. Our distribution chain is a basic dichotomy of manufacturers and distributors. For the gamut of basic and mid-range T-shirts, fleecewear, and golf shirts, the prime manufacturers include well-known national and international firms such as Fruit of the Loom™, Hanes™, Gildan™, and Jerzees™, among several other large, reputable firms. Sourcing directly from these larger firms, due to their minimum order and capital requirements, is essentially limited to buyers with huge warehouses and multimillion-dollar financial resources.

Obtaining these branded garments is therefore accomplished through a network of wholesale distributors; major national players such as Bodek & Rhodes and San Mar and larger regional firms such as Imprints Wholesale in the West and New England Sportswear in the Northeast, among others. In addition to carrying the better-known consumer brands, these firms also offer their own branded apparel lines along with wide selections of outerwear. Most distributors also stock limited selections of caps, bags, and aprons, among other specialty textile product categories.

Standard pricing for most apparel categories among and between the wholesalers is relatively similar, though there's considerable latitude when it comes to their proprietary offerings. From time to time, all distributors conduct special sales to trim unsold inventory on selected items or categories for periods ranging from a few days to a few weeks, especially toward year-end and late summer. For creditworthy buyers, all provide reasonable credit terms. However, if you're new in the decorated apparel business, you'll likely be required to pre-pay via check or credit card or pay C.O.D. with cash or a certified check.

Most wholesalers offer free-shipping deals from the warehouse to your door when you buy a certain annual volume or meet thresholds of a specified dollar amount (usually a few hundred dollars) on a single order.

Who can buy from wholesalers? Most suppliers will only sell to firms with track records in the trade (as documented by an internal industry-specific organization that monitors the activities and credit of trade buyers) and/or proof of holding licenses to collect sales tax. As a basic rule, the general public cannot buy from our wholesalers, who are all careful not to make their wholesale-to-the-trade pricing available to end-users online or otherwise. Obtaining access to this information requires a buyer to have a password. Published pricing for use in your selling to end-user accounts is displayed at twice the standard trade price, meaning trade buyers receive a 50% discount on the prices shown to end-user buyers.

Some apparel decorators merit built-in discounts below the standard trade price, usually in the form of "case pricing," or having the ability to buy units at the case price but without being required to buy full cases. Additional discounts and concessions accrue to more loyal, bigger buyers – those who satisfy stated purchase-volume or per-shipment-volume thresholds. The lowest pricing tiers include perks such as an added 2% discount below case pricing, free freight on all orders, advertising allowances or rebates, and for the very largest volume buyers in the trade, additional support in the form of yet further discounts, extended credit terms, and promotional and display allowances.

Most wholesalers offer free-shipping deals from the warehouse to your door when you buy a certain annual volume or meet thresholds of a specified dollar amount (usually a few hundred dollars) on a single order.

Just about all wholesalers offer limited quantities of free catalogs and price lists to their customers for use with their accounts. More worthy buyers are awarded larger quantities of promotional catalogs with their own customized cover imprints.

Whom you buy from is, of course, up to you. *But knowledgeable buyers learn in time that it pays to place as much overall general purchases – T-shirts, fleecewear, golf shirts, etc. – with ONE wholesaler and develop an alternative, smaller-volume relationship with a second vendor.* That's because gaining any type of advantageous pricing or other special leverage with any one wholesaler means demonstrating a consistent pattern of loyalty and predictable purchasing volume.

A common mistake of newcomers, as well as veterans who get into a perpetual bad habit, is to shop the wholesalers every week, every day, or, for some, on every order to save a few pennies on every garment. It's quite do-able to achieve those per-unit savings, but making this procedure the rule in your buying practices rather than the exception means spreading your purchasing among too many vendors and not becoming a regular, valued – and noticeable! -- buyer to any of them. Measured over time, this practice usually doesn't save money. It *costs* money -- and effects the unintended consequence of truly being penny-wise and pound-foolish.

Buying in the industry is done for the most part over the telephone, a declining preference, or online, as more and more companies do for most of their buying. More than 99% of all wholesalers' orders are shipped to the decorator or contractor. Certain key customers, however, in major metropolitan areas avail themselves of direct deliveries where offered once or twice a week by some wholesalers, while some folks pick up their goods in person at the warehouses.

A word to the wise: Endeavor to deal with a wholesalers whose distribution center is within one day's UPS delivery if possible. It saves time, but more importantly, saves on shipping.

Newcomers can be assured they'll have ample opportunity locating sources for all of their garment and accessory needs. And once a business has registered on various websites and has had its e-mail address captured on search engines, it's only a day or so before industry vendors will begin to solicit the new enterprise's patronage. While veterans have good reason to limit vendors' e-mail access to those they really care about, newbies are advised to communicate with all trade solicitors during their umbilical period.

Offering Your Garment Selections

Now, allow me to give veterans and newcomers alike some wisdom about selling garments and what you *should* be offering your customers.

There are three philosophies on offering various styles and brands to customers:

One philosophy says that you should open your favorite wholesaler's catalog or link it to your website and simply let your customer choose exactly what he wants without regard to brands or other limitations. Assuming the vendor stocks everything well, it sounds fair enough. Right? If the customer is a knowledgeable, experienced buyer, the system works. But only to a point, a matter that we'll look at shortly.

A second philosophy says that you should open *several* of your favorite wholesalers' catalogs or link all of them to your website, giving the customer maximum selection flexibility and without limitations. This way a customer gets the best of all possible worlds – as some might think. Sounds OK, assuming all the vendors carry deep inventories of everything they show. Right? If indeed the customer is a very knowledgeable, experienced buyer, this system works to everyone's advantage, or at least some would argue.

A third path – namely, mine – is that the customer should be able to select only from those brands and styles the seller designates. There are several reasons why I advocate this system and not the others. First, with the exception of only the very most astute customers, most buyers haven't a clue as to which brand is really better, how wide or deep your preferred wholesaler stocks everything offered, or how the garments print or embroider; nor do they care. The typical customer doesn't understand the differences and nuances between similar-looking terms, such as "heavyweight," "Beefy™," or "megaweight," much less more specialized terms such as "ringspun," "open-end," or "moisture management." Most customers basically know just colors and fabric content (100% cotton or a cotton-polyester blend).

While some customers may have insisted on receiving Hanes, Fruit of the Loom, or Russell brand products years ago, the fact is that today they buy what you tell them to and they don't challenge your choice.

What YOU know (or will learn sooner rather than later) is which wholesalers stock which brands better than others and in what depth. You also know which brands (in your opinion) print or embroiderer better and/or run more efficiently on your equipment, which wholesaler offers you deals (free freight, extended terms, etc.), and which brands carry a wider latitude in sizes. The system I advocate you follow means that by taking control of the brands you sell in the various categories, you gain significant benefits by limiting your purchases wherever possible to those brands YOU want to buy and decorate. Here are more reasons as to why I preach about limiting choices.

▶ You speed up the selling process. Your customers are shown only those items you want them to see, particularly when it comes to brand. They won't have to spend time – wasting it really – to see the same items from another manufacturer and another and another, dwelling on esoteric perceived differences in color.

▶ Being "invested" in a brand means if you need to buy additional goods to accommodate possible overruns on a particular order (especially on larger orders) and replacements for errors, you can make your purchases in a brand that helps you build some on-hand inventory if you use little or none of the add-on units you brought in for a particular job.

▶ When you calculate that ordering some additional stock when buying for orders on hand will help you meet a threshold level that gets you free freight from your supplier, you don't risk ending up with lots of odd-ball leftover items of diverse brands. Such garments will likely sit and accumulate on your shelves for a long time, tying up space and money. One thing newcomers probably don't know when they go into this business is that customers don't like to receive shirts of the same style and color that are delivered to them in assorted brands.

▶ Because sourcing just a few garments in extra-big sizes (2XL – 5XL) of goods in your preferred brand likely means you pay extra for freight. You can save money and time by keeping some on hand and avoid delays occasioned when these items are out of stock at your supplier's warehouse. And ordering only the few XX+ pieces only when you need usually means you might well have to delay production on the order until these needed items arrive.

▶ Accumulating inventory on selected items in your preferred brands means from time to time drawing down those holdings for routine orders or drawing down for a panic rush order where the customer will buy whatever you say you have on hand. On these orders, your stock has been purchased at the lowest possible price and without immediate freight costs, which is the dividend for intelligent buying and planning.

▶ For companies that do retail sales of "one-sies" and "two-sies" to individual customers, the extra stock for retail customers purchased in the preferred brand always is available in a pinch for custom orders as well, bought right, and without paying freight.

Each of these advantages gives you a few pennies of pure profit every time you draw from them. In the normal course of business over the year, it can add up to savings of hundreds of dollars in outlay and hundreds more in labor savings and/or freight charges.

Dumb Mistake No. 4
Letting customers make all the decisions about
what you should sell them.

What some argue is a downside is, to my way of thinking, just the opposite. "What?! I shouldn't take out the wholesaler's pretty catalog, not put it in my customers hands, and not let his fingers do the walking?," they say. That's *exactly* what I mean. Instead, show instead YOUR OWN mini-catalog for the key volume items. It's easily constructed from your vendors' websites and printed out on your computer, on heavy stock, or put in clear plastic sleeves in a 3-ring binder.

Taking the time to organize these key items as such means virtually every time you show only the limited selection to a walk-in customer or one you're calling on means that order is done more quickly and you maintain better control of the price, the quality, and the outcome. The time you save then can be put to better use in upselling imprint colors or additional locations for printing or embroidery, upselling graphics or specialty inks, showing complementary items, or educating your customer about additional products and services you offer. Everybody wins -- especially *YOU*!

The same limited selections on key items can be done on your website in conjunction with your vendor's entire gamut of offerings. You simply present your own recommended selections in the key categories via an "express section" for quick ordering. In time, your customers will understand why it's easier for them to source from this section instead of wasting their own time looking at a plethora of redundant choices. By the way, the subtleties of colors printed on paper, which are difficult enough to discern, are even more indistinct to customers seeing your products online. In Chapter 16 I'll help you construct your own express catalog.

Many of the clients I work with no longer even show the vendors' catalogs or links to their websites – except when, once again, the customer is an experienced pro. In this case, the nice, pretty catalogs are made available and the full-line website version is controlled by a password given to the customer. The result? As most of these clients report, "Our customers, even the big players, generally don't want to waste their time either and are quite happy with how we've made it easier and more convenient for them." *Quod erat demonstratum!*

The big lesson you should understand about of this chapter is that showing garment selections to your customers and prospects should be part of a process that includes a whole lot more than simply letting someone choose what he wants – or thinks he wants. The selections he's offered should be determined in conjunction with a buying strategy that enables the seller to sell efficiently AND to buy intelligently.

To illustrate the principle here seen through the eyes of a promotional products distributor, the firm's sales rep offers a prospect a low-end ballpoint pen solution -- say, one selling for $.25 to $1.00 each. She could furnish her customer with 10 or 20 catalogs with very similar selections in each. But how many buyers really want to look through a stack of catalogs for every possible nuance among the essentially redundant item groups -- or have the time to do so? The sales rep does herself and her customer a favor by limiting the choices to one catalog, and in so doing gains her company more leverage with that manufacturer over time by building up sales volume. Read: loyalty and credentials to earn end-quantity pricing and/or other benefits and advantages. You get the idea, now. Right? Good.

Before you begin reading the next five chapters, let me tell you this is what I consider the single, most important section of the book. It's also the one that was the most fun to write, recollect, and research! You'll learn why along the way.

CHAPTER

"Positioning" is the term coined by marketing gurus Al Ries and Jack Trout in their 1980 landmark book *Positioning: The Battle for Your Mind*, which explains the critical concept of getting your business into the minds of customers and prospects in a manner that accurately reflects the company's attributes, advantages, and missions. As a former professor of marketing, I consider this book the very best marketing book ever written; and it offers more insight and understanding better than any Marketing 101 course ever offered. I assure you it'll change the way you think about marketing your company and I'm confident you'll agree that reading it will prove to be a catalyst in your business planning for years to come. (Be sure to buy the most recent edition of the book).

That said, you need to gain a working command of what positioning is and why it's critical to any discussion of marketing your business.

In their groundbreaking treatise, Ries and Trout gave marketing professionals a new handle on how to determine where a product or company belongs vis-à-vis the association a person will assign in his mind to a given product or company. The crucial words here are "association" -- the relationship or connection between concepts -- and "in the mind." Association is the process; in the mind is where it happens. Grasp these two elements and you're able to see that how you shape your company's identity by intelligently *defining* it, is the shortest route to getting people to view your company as you want them to see it and be able to associate who you are with what you do.

If YOU don't define your company, people will define it for themselves, drawing their own conclusions and perceptions that may differ considerably from what you'd like them to think.

When entrepreneurs go into business for themselves, they have a good idea of what they want to do. But most are too busy and too excited when starting their businesses to take the time to articulate how they want to be seen. So, most fail to define themselves until they've been around for a while. What usually gets them thinking about doing it is learning over time that they're unhappy with how folks think about them. Or worse: people don't think much about them at all or think they only do such and such when they're really offering so much more. What's even more painful is that people might very well think of them, what they do, and their products as simply "commodities," where, in their minds, what they sell and do is pretty much what every other company in the field sells and does.

If YOU don't define your company, people will define it for themselves, drawing their own conclusions and perceptions that may differ considerably from what you'd like them to think.

To overcome these perceptions and to hopefully make them right from the get-go, you're obliged in the positioning process to make your company stand for something distinct. It should be differentiated in the minds of your customers and prospects from your competitors by your name, your message, your performance, and your other attributes and advantages.

Positioning -- or Re-Positioning -- for the Long Haul

If you're to measure where you've been, where you are, and where you're going, you'll need a marketing map that shows you the routes and your options. Positioning is that map.

Dumb Mistake No. 5
Skipping Section Four of this book!

You had a vision for your enterprise when you started it. For too many, the vision proves to be little more than wishful thinking, a dream lost in the minutiae of getting the company up and running and keeping it moving. But for the entrepreneur who'll succeed in building his dream into reality, his vision is well defined, well planned, well watered – and kept in his sights. It'll be groomed, trimmed, fed nutrients, and placed in a location where it can get maximum sunshine and year 'round visibility.

In new companies, defining who and what you want to be is the first major marketing challenge and it's the critical prerequisite for creating the message you'll engineer into the process of generating leads. (Addressed in Chapter 28: Lead Generation and Lead Processing Strategy).

CHAPTER

WHAT'S IN A NAME?

In initially defining your company, you're stating your vision and staking out your position -- or at least your claim to it -- of where you think you should be located on the marketing map in your customer's mind.

Choosing your company name will be a key focus in properly positioning it for success. Finding the right name will entails lots of the considerations you're about to explore. But finding an effective name will address and answer several questions: Does it tell who you are and what you do? Does it tell your story well? The whole story? Is it memorable or catchy? Is it dated or does it limit you?

Let's look at "Downtown T-Shirt Company," now 12 years old. It started as a textile screen printing company, branched into embroidery in its fourth year, and today does 38% of its sales volume in (and earns 43% of its profits from) embroidery. The firm added a tag line to its name two years ago in an attempt to better describe itself as "Your One-Stop Source for Custom Screen Printed and Embroidered Apparel." It certainly helped to tell a more complete story, but it's kind of long, isn't it? And a T-shirt company? Hey, it's a lot bigger than that today. Would someone quickly associate this aspect of the name with being the best or first place to go to buy top-of-the-line embroidered Cutter & Buck® golf shirts for an upcoming golf tournament that an investment firm is sponsoring?

Downtown? They firm moved to an industrial park, uptown, 18 months ago. The "downtown" derivation of its name was for the major urban center in which the company was first located, an area that had become blighted and seedy and no longer had a positive connotation. Screen Printing & Embroidery? Well, that's what it does, but is this the most effective way to position a company that offers so much more? After all, it's got the biggest and best showroom around, a user-friendly catalog and price list, the coolest website, not to mention the best customer service and sales people in the state. It has a massive warehouse right on site that's jammed with inventory. More importantly its salespeople are skilled at creating entire promotional apparel campaigns and the art department is downright world class and blows away anything else the other guys can come up with. Does the name "Downtown T-Shirt Company" tell that story?

How 'bout just calling it DTS? It's easy, it's fast, and it does have an "ear" to it. Sure, let's destroy the company's identity and position altogether and go with dumb letters that will forever relegate the company to being another alphabet-soup corporate non-entity. Over my dead body we will! "DTS" is a poor solution, albeit one we see all too often when companies can't figure out what to call themselves after evolving beyond their original visions and roots.

Maybe it's time to re-think the company's name. Duh. And while the owners are on the subject, maybe it's also time to re-think and revitalize their entire marketing agenda, and go in for a facelift in their advertising, which is sure showing its age these days. Little about it has changed in years, though the list of products and services they offer has been greatly expanded. Considering that the company has been contemplating launching a new lead-generating advertising campaign, could this also be the perfect opportunity to re-merchandise itself in new, better, more effective ways and incorporate the name change into the campaign? Yes. It is the right time, because the longer the company delays changing its name, the more it will cost and the harder it will be to execute.

Let's say *you* are the owner and founder of Downtown T-Shirt Company. You agree the firm is long overdue for a better, more accurate or more advantageous name, one that tells what the company really is today and that'll cover the enterprise's development over the next decade or beyond. The ball's in your court; got any ideas for a new name? Go ahead, take a stab or two. Uhhhhhhhhh... Well... Crank up your imagination. Seriously, stop for a few minutes and really try to suggest a few new names for a successful company that has grown well beyond the founders' wildest dreams; moved to a beautiful new plant; has plenty of business; plans to open satellite sales offices in nearby cities in the near future; has successfully expanded into promotional products; is looking at bringing in digital printing as a separate division – including devoting a part of that beautiful new building for doing vehicle graphics, etc, etc. This is, to be sure, a company on the move and confident of its future.

Choosing your company name will be a key focus in properly positioning it for success.

Thinking of a few new names for Downtown T-Shirt Company will give you some practice in assessing -- and exploring -- many of the considerations that go into such decisions. Now, put the book down for five minutes, or for an hour. Have a cup of coffee. Or a cold beer. Think of some names. Let your mind go fishing. And then come back and continue reading. In due course, I'll reveal the result of the sought-after solution to Downtown T-Shirt Company's quest for a new name. Seriously, get lost for a few minutes!

Welcome back to class.

The issue of a good name isn't hypothetical or discussed here just for illustration. In fact, it's an important part of what I and other marketing consultants and ad agencies do every day, which is essentially to position or re-position companies for growth. Here's some food for thought: Of the 600+ companies I've worked with in this industry, I've advised almost half of them that to continue marketing under their existing name would be counter-productive in the long run, entailing the investment of more time and money into an entity that would be locked even further into a name that had already outlived its usefulness. As an matter of personal ethics -- being unwilling to waste my time and a client's money -- in many cases, I've made my continued service to a client contingent on effecting a company name change.

Some clients strongly resist a name change and have understandable misgivings and jitters. Oftentimes I have to counter conventional wisdom. But as I work from a position of advocacy, I continue to force the issue and in almost all cases my clients eventually "come around" and eventually become energized, themselves, in the process. Hey, just doin' my job.

Here are stories about eight real companies that have developed highly effected names or executed effective name changes.

▶ **1988: A start-up screen printing company in Portland, Oregon.** A woman with a fashion merchandising background decided to go into business and purchased a small company, Sport Screens, a local screen printing company specializing in teamwear. I accept two start-up companies each year and found this candidate to be a natural for our industry, so I agreed to help Larie Thomas reposition her fledgling company and provide necessary industry-specific counsel. The new owner's vision was to create something much broader and much bigger. After brainstorming for a few hours and grasping her vision and understanding the types of lines she wanted to develop, I blurted out, "Latitudes!" She immediately said, "That's It!" Period. Done. As luck would have it, the owner's initials, L.A.T., coincided with the proposed name.

Latitudes today is one of the largest apparel design and decorating firms in the Northwest and among the top 100 companies on the planet in technical sophistication in both screen printing and embroidery. The firm provides year-round employment to more than a hundred dedicated staffers and its clientele includes some of the world's most recognizable apparel merchandisers. Owners Larie and Dick Thomas remain at the helm of the little company launched in 1988 that now operates from a 70,000-square-foot plant in Portland. [www.latitudespdx.com]

▶ **1988: A growing apparel decorating and specialty label printing company in Evansville, Indiana.** A sporting goods retailer whose company had branched into screen printing and started to provide products to some top corporate accounts in its region invited me to help move the firm into a better position for further growth. When I landed in Evansville, the company was trading as Campbell's Printing, a family firm operating under the corporate name "KARM Corporation."

KARM was an acronym for daughter **Kena**, Mom **Alice**, Dad **Roger**, and son **Mike**. The clients agreed the Campbell's Printing name had limiting factors: a) it sounded like a paper printing company; b) when folks heard the family name, they thought of soup; c) and the traditional nomenclature sounded "mom-n-pop."

CEO Roger Campbell felt the company's name didn't tell the whole story of his firm's expansion into highly-sophisticated label printing and packaging for major regional and national manufacturing and pharmaceutical companies. He sought a name that was succinct, better represented the high level of professional competence in the very complex world of security labeling, and a name that could provide an umbrella to encompass future directions. Reconfiguring KARM into MARK and putting PRO in front of it, the new company was reborn as ***ProMark***, and has prospered and grown exponentially ever since. Today, Roger and Alice are semi-retired and Kena and Mike are at the helm of management and sales. [www.promarkin.com]

▶**1994: A start-up wholesaler in Grand Rapids, Michigan.** Apparel decorators in mid-America know this upscale garment distributor. What you might not know is that the company's initial positioning was as an alternative to two major industry wholesaling powerhouses, Broder Brothers in Detroit and A & G in Chicago. About midway between these two giants, the company was an outgrowth of a retailing company with stores throughout western Michigan, The Depot. I convinced founder Bob Palmatter to also offer plastisol ink and other essential screen printing supplies as a means to attract more customers, defray the cost of the customers' shipping, and increase transaction frequency. I developed ***One-Stop Distributors*** as an easily remembered name for covering the two categories of products.

The firm further positioned itself as one that provided exemplary customer service based on the founder's extensive background and success in training retail personnel in his very successful retailing business. You know the company, you know the (newer) name, and the history of this popular megamillion-dollar distributor with fiercely loyal customers speaks for itself. The company tweaked its original name several years ago to ***One Stop Imprintable Fashions*** to further refine, redefine, and differentiate itself from the pack.

▶ **1999: An apparel decorating company on life-support in Columbia, Missouri.** A successful retailer from Hawaii wanted to return his family to its hometown roots in Missouri and bought a 20-year old firm called Burrito's. The name for this screen printing and embroidery was a dog from the company's inception, but a second owner kept it anyhow. Most people who drove by the shop and saw the name thought the company had something to do with catering Mexican food. With the company in serious straights, I was brought in to help the new owners get out their bind and immediately indicated a name change would be critical to long-term goals for growth and repositioning as well as a vital mechanism to separate the company's future from its past. Looking for a moniker that engendered thoughts of the area's heritage, sounded historic and charming, I developed the new name, *Missouri Cotton Exchange*. I also suggested a logo that presented an image of a mid-19th Century agricultural institution.

Launched through a direct mail campaign to existing and former accounts and supported by radio advertising to inform the community, the new name took hold and the owner revitalized his sales efforts – landing some huge orders through exceptionally creative graphic design and hard work. A successful turnaround was underway. Within six months, the company had returned to profitability, sported a new look and feel, generated massive increases in sales volume and has never looked back. CEO Jeff Glenn today runs a technically advanced enterprise, serving hundreds of active accounts throughout the Midwest with a broad range of custom products, licensed apparel, and specialty retail lines. "MoCotton" moved into its brand new 11,000-square-foot facility in 2008. [www.mocoton.com]

▶ **2001: A start-up embroidery company in Pelham, New Hampshire.** The fledgling one embroidery head business was a good candidate for success in this market as the owner had a strong business background and was an exceptionally astute networker. Accepting Marie Mayotte as a client was an easy decision and working with her and husband Jerry in Maryland for our first meetings was pure reinforcement for my confidence in the company's future. One stumbling block: the company name, Breakthrough Embroidery. When that subject came up, the happy camper asked my opinion. Having obtained her permission for complete candor, I told her it sounded to me like a woman's joy having finally fulfilled her dream to go into business for herself. I felt that a name change was in order pronto forthe firm, before investing in a broad campaign to accelerate the expansion of its account base.

The new name drew from New England's manufacturing heritage and the ubiquitous 19th Century brick factories built throughout the region. I proposed a new name, which sounded a little awkward at first, but then grew on Marie and Jerry. The name was "warm" in tone, struck a chord with the natives, and was a perfect fit for what I characterize as a "dream name:" That's a name that can work as a company name, a product line trademark, a label, a retail store name, a catalog name, a domain name, or a name that could be extended to brand other businesses and product lines.

Drum roll, please…welcome to **Red Brick Clothing Co**. Jerry sold his other business shortly thereafter, joined Marie at Red Brick, and the company has flourished ever since. Adding more embroidery heads year after year, adding a full-service screen printing department, and promotional products, the company now handles, among large accounts, the retail uniform program for several area archdiocesan school systems. What started out in the Mayotte home now boasts a 9,000-square-foot facility in Hudson, New Hampshire, with a staff of 20, including son Keith. [www.redbrickclothing.com]

►**2003: A start-up embroidery company in High Point, North Carolina**. Don and Hilda Allen had deep, long, and successful careers in the textile industry. Both held masters degrees in textile sciences. Hilda was a fabric designer for a major textile manufacturer in Greensboro, North Carolina, and Don was a senior sales executive for Mitsubishi Chemical, calling on major textile manufacturers in the South. Seeing the handwriting on the wall, they left corporate America to start an embroidery business. Upon accepting them as clients, I had confidence they'd succeed. Their biggest shortcoming, I observed, was their company name, AdVentures in Embroidery.

I found the name perhaps a bit too cute to accurately capture the professionalism of the owners. I also found the name somewhat distant from their core product and service and felt the term "adventures" could be perceived adversely by prospective customers, as in, "Oh, yeah, just what I need – an adventure in embroidery!" Customers don't want an adventure, I maintained, and noted that it as the antithesis of what customers do want -- which is a pleasant, trouble-free endeavor. I counseled that before we embark on investing in a marketing campaign, we should first re-think the name. So it was back to the drawing board for a new name. After a few weeks of e-mailing back-and-forth and fine tuning, the new name emerged as *Alpine Graphic Apparel*.

The derivation of the name was the wonderful memories Don and Hilda had of living in Switzerland for three years and constantly looking back on that magical period early in their marriage – especially with a beautiful photograph Don took of the Matterhorn that they see every day in the lobby of their plant to remind them. "Alpine" was, in the lexicon of marketing strategy, an "aspirational" name, evoking a positive force, the splendor of high peaks, of being "on top of the world." It translated well when transformed into the company's new logo, which has elements of peaks, a touch of green marketing, and typography that's refreshing, airy, modern and stately. The new name fits well, the Allens love it, and they're motivated by it. And the name was well received by their customers. The rest is history. Today, the Allens have a strong, thriving business that includes providing company stores for national corporate clients and major universities in addition to their local custom accounts. [www.alpinegraphicapparel.com].

▶ **2007: A start-up embroidery in Bell Haven, Virginia**. Rosemary Bosworth left a secure job as a corporate CEO to start her own business in a building behind her home. Beyond the regular agenda I conduct with start-ups, the business name here was a key first objective. And it came quickly.

Rosemary and her husband, Dr. Bruce Bosworth, live in a quiet waterfront area of Virginia's idyllic Eastern Shore. It is an area with a colorful history and a culture laden with lore and feel of the crabbing and oystering trade in the Chesapeake Bay trade that goes back to early colonial times. A highly specialized boat for oyster dredging, a skipjack has a V-shaped wooden hull with a square stem. Its mast is hewn from a single log and supports two sails. Only a few of these boats still ply their trade on the bays and just a few dozen remain in existence, most being 50 to 100 years old. When I proposed *Skipjack* (to which Rosie selected the rest of the name) *Custom Apparel*, she lit up with a big smile. The name, a keeper from the get-go, quickly helped position her company as an integral part of the Eastern Shore Virginia business landscape from the time she opened for business.

▶ **2008: A struggling start-up screen printing company in Clarksville, Tenn**. Jim Hosey was a former U.S. Army AH-6 Little Bird helicopter pilot who served in Operation Desert Shield and Operation Desert Storm. His storied unit in Iraq is rumored to have played a key role in capturing and guarding deposed dictator Saddam Hussein. Jim's a real-life military hero, a combat veteran who was awarded 10 Air Medals, the Bronze Star for Heroism in Action, and the Distinguished Flying Cross.

Entering the apparel decorating industry after retiring from active service in 2006, he formed TDC Screen Printing. Having experimented unsuccessfully with a preprint line geared to what active military personnel wore off the base, Hosey saw his enterprise fall on hard times as a small local custom and contract printer. Seeking a more forward position and a brighter outlook for his line -- which I summed up as "too traditional, too square, and too ordinary" to attract much attention from twenty-somethings -- Hosey came to Maryland to work with me at my home base.

During our sessions, we repositioned his line to have a more spirited, hipper look and Jim dubbed it Zero6™, a term to describe the key decision-maker in the command structure of the elite forces. Geared to military personnel, focused on major armed forces divisions, and especially positioned for the elite groups such as Marine Recons, Army Rangers, and Navy Seals, the line quickly proved itself on the shelves of stores located near military installations catering to base personnel and their dependents.

To reposition the company away from production and into preprint sales, a new company name was in order. Given Hosey's background as a Chief Warrant Officer and his marketing focus on things military, we scored a direct hit with the name ***Wingman Apparel Company***, which just happens to be headquartered close to the U.S. Army base at Fort Campbell, Kentucky. Attracting a growing following among enlisted men and women and commanding strong re-orders, the Zero6 line has already earned its wings so to speak on the shelves of Wal-Mart, army-navy stores, and outdoor retail outlets throughout the nation.

There's a little more to Hosey's story. Jim looks the part of a combat pilot, too, and publicity about him caught the attention of Hollywood. Selected for a role in the movie, "*Black Hawk Down*," Jim hit the silver screen playing the role of a pilot flying his chopper and dodging surface-to-air missiles in the battle scenes about the 1993 military action in Somalia. [www.wingman06.com/about.html]

Now, as for a new name for Downtown T-Shirt Company...

The company became **Great American ShirtWorks**. It eventually morphed into a retail chain, flourished for several years and grew to five locations in suburban malls. Upon the tragic accidental death of its 40-year old majority shareholder, the company imploded in a legal bloodbath among the surviving partners and amid demands from IRS. Sadly, the company exhaled forever, as the partners had never completed their Stock Redemption Agreement and never got around to purchasing cross-insurance policies on its principals. And with due deference for the late radio personality Paul Harvey, "And now you know the r-r-r-r-est of the story!"

Dumb Mistake No. 6
Selecting a company name without testing it for applicability to the company's position, its mission in the marketplace or its shelf life.

So, what's in a name? Latitudes, ProMark, One-Stop Fashion Imprintables, Missouri Cotton Exchange, Red Brick Clothing Company, Alpine Graphic Apparel, Skipjack Custom Apparel, and Wingman Apparel Company should all give you some insight into how a company's name underscores its positioning goals. Names such as these also become a valuable long-term asset – a saleable asset at that! – to a business looking to reach its desired customer bases and achieving its full potential. (More on this below).

Here are some guidelines I use and offer for your consideration in weighing whether a company should change its name. Ask yourself these questions:

▶ **If the existing name is still adequate for now, can it be expected to serve as well in the future?** Included in this question are concerns about whether a company name has some deficiencies that limit or inhibit the company's growth and improved positioning.

▶ **How much is the name really worth in terms of good will? Will changing the name cost it any customers? Or will it serve to help attract many more?** Do note that rarely, if ever, does a name change of a good company result in any loss of customers.

▸ **Is the name -- or has the name become -- tired, trite, dated, or has simply lost or outgrown its groove?**

▸ **Are there special attributes in the name that are absolutely indispensable?** Some major issues here include names that have been in use for decades and have earned status as virtual community "institutions" or have become thought of as "brands."

▸ **Would the owners of the company really like to change the name, but don't know quite how to go about it, haven't yet calculated potential downsides or risks, or aren't yet totally convinced of the substantial benefits?** Oftentimes, though, a catalytic comment -- from a consultant, an astute customer or vendor, a key employee or salesperson or words in a book – is what spurs management to take a closer look at a name change and ultimately take the plunge. Once a name has been selected, though, after what can be a frustrating exercise in a squishy medium that's more art than science, management and staff usually become energized in the process and get to work on implementing the new name immediately.

Below are 10 categories of variables and tips to help you open your search for your company name or to ponder when contemplating a name change. Keep the list handy in your brainstorming sessions.

1. Local factors. The geography, culture, history, landmarks, flora and fauna, and climate of the primary trading area or targeted market or market niches. Names derived from such attributes tend to endure and usually are far stronger than the names or initials of the owner or owners. *Missouri Cotton Exchange* (even though such an entity never existed!), *Red Brick Clothing* and *Skipjack Custom Apparel* are perfect examples.

2. Personal factors. Your interests, special talents, family background or ethnicity, personal achievements, favorite pets, some important event in your life or a special period or experience, and your passions. *Alpine Graphic Apparel* and *Wingman Apparel* fit this concept well.

3. Matters of convenience and other customer-friendly and professional attributes. Speed, quality, service, status, and performance. Names like *ProMark* and *One-Stop Fashion Imprintables*, *FastSigns*, and *Jiffy Lube* illustrate the concept.

4. Market-oriented factors. Related to business, schools, organizations, government, events, athletics, leisure and recreation industries. Names such as *Team Spirit Promotions*, *Military Outfitters*, and *Mark's Workwear* (a franchise company in Canada), are good examples.

5. Positive, uplifting, aspirational, inspirational, innovative, exciting attributes. Superior, premier, peak, reputation, first, excellence, winning/winner, victory, triumph, forward, advance, professional, challenge, and power are words that stimulate further thinking and lead to other routes in lots of different directions. Sometimes a turn off the main road, as you know, can result in wonderful surprises! *Higher Ground Designs*, *New Age Fashions*, and *High Peak Sportswear* are illustrative here.

6. Fun stuff. Magic, enchantment, wizardry, animals, literary characters, movies, goofy names, and the like will get you headed in the right direction here. Two favorites of mine are the names of a retail client in Arlington, Virginia – *Ballyhoo*! -- and a powerhouse apparel decorating client in Columbia, South Carolina -- *Eat More Tees*. [ballyhoo@ ballyhoostore.com], [www.eatmoretees.com]

7. Application-related. Corporate identification, advertising, uniforms, awards and incentives, promotion-oriented, giftware, fundraising, recruitment, spirit and pride. *AdWear Promotions*, *Winning Ways Awards & Engraving*, and *Executive Gifts On Demand* tell the story here.

8. Garment specialization. Infants and juveniles, children, seniors, plus sizes, maternity, outdoor, uniforms *Planet Baby Clothing and Accessories*, *North Face Apparel*, and *Mom-to-Be Fashionwear*, for example.

9. Invented, Crafted, Hybrid, and High-Tech Sounding Names. If you can develop a good one, it works, though finding and creating such names is a whole lot easier said than done to get one that works. Such names include crafted nomenclature such as *MicroSoft, Verizon, HoopMaster, America Online, ShopWorks, Frigidaire* (for "frigid air," invented a million years ago!), *Mediacom, Accuweather, Xerox, iPod, Zazzle, eHarmony, Adidas* (a contraction of the founder's name, Adolph "Adi" Dassler), *USAirways, MasterCard, Cisco* (from San Francisco) *Systems* and *X-Box,* among hundreds of others you've heard of.

10. One-word names already in the language. These are words or terms that have been around for years or forever, but are claimed by a business or product to brand or title something altogether different from the original meaning. Some might connote something good or positive in its new incarnation. Think of how one came about, intuitive or otherwise, and try to understand it.

And if you don't understand the associative properties or its derivatives, it really doesn't matter because these names just plain sound cool or fun or perfect in some way. But do realize that the name, itself, helps the entity to become important, successful, and earn its own meaning, a name that can oftentimes become massively more powerful than the original meaning. Genius world-class example, you ask? One word: *Google*! Google is a brand, of course, but today has in its decade or so of existence earned the status of a verb in the English language. Other good examples include *Amazon, Bing, Apple, and Blackberry.*

Speaking of Google, a tip from a knowledgeable friend suggests doing a Google search of your ideas and seeing what comes up, possibly stimulating further ideas from seeing similar terminology, attributes, or other applications of the word or words.

In the course of playing the name game, you will inevitably try to find a great name and one that's available as a domain name. However, the odds are high that the great name is not also available as a domain name. Of course, you can continue to check for names followed by .net, .biz, .us, and other dot-whatevers. But with a little creativity, brainstorming, and a willingness to be reasonable about the quest, you'll likely find a solution that's close to or sufficient for your desired company name. Research some of the tricks of the domain name game, but for starters, try a few of the remedies below.

Example: Your sought after domain name is BlueSkyPromowear. com, but you find it's not in the cards as is online and other dot-whatevers aren't available either. (Capital letters are used below to make it easy to see)

• Try numerical prefixes and suffixes:
>123BlueSkyPromowear.com   > BlueSkyPromowear123.com

• Add your town or metro area, address, zip code, or region
>BlueSkyPromowearDallas.com > BlueSkyPromowearAmerica.com
>BlueSkyPromoDowntown.com   > BlueSkyPromowear54321.com
>BlueSkyPromowearTriState.com > BlueSkyPromowearNewEngland.com

> BlueSkyPromowearNYC.com   > BlueSkyPromowearDallas.com

• **Add the local airport code or a well-known abbreviation**

> BlueSkyPromowearDFW.com   > BlueSkyPromowearPDQ.com

> BlueSkyPromowear2Go.com   > BlueSkyPromowearUSA.com

> BlueSkyPromowear007.com

• **Abbreviate parts of your company's name or use phonetic spelling**

> BlueSkyPromo.com   > BluSkyPromowearDallas.com

> BlooSkyPromo.com

The list above could have yet more sections, from Latin and Greek root words, modern foreign languages, mythology, Bible stories or characters, nursery rhymes, legends, and on and on and on. I trust you get the idea. A name can be about you, your life, your neighborhood or your world, your dreams, your vision, what you do for fun, something that *used to* mean something but now means something else, is silly, contrived, or means nothing at all – yet! Remember, the goal of the list is just to help you get the naming process started. An old adage comes to mind about the process when you begin it: You might not know what you're looking for, but you'll know it when you see it – and hear it.

Allow me to share a few pointers about two other types of names that have inherent limitations, evince little creativity, or are weak in developing a distinctive, differentiated business name.

1. Overused and Trite Names. Avoid company names that are overused. Even though you probably don't see industry databases too often, I can tell you two particular forms of company names guarantee your vendors and industry peers will yawn when they see them: Anything with the words "creative" or "unique' in the title. Using these terms usually denotes companies that aren't very creative or unique. Yes, while names might seem attractive to you at first, my admonition here may seem counterintuitive.   But trust me on this.

2. Obvious Nicknames. If your business is in Chicago, New York, Detroit, Seattle, Dallas, Denver, Minneapolis/St. Paul, Nashville, or San Antonio, do you want to join thousands of other enterprises using Windy City, Big Apple, Motor City, Emerald, Big D, Mile High, Twin Cities, Music City, or Alamo in their names? If you take these easy cop-out solutions, you can count on getting lost in the shuffle, becoming another gallon of water going over Niagara Falls.

3. Letters, Initials, and Personal Names. Wherever humanly possible, avoid resorting to using personal names (first and/or last), your initials, or contractions of earlier names. It creates no buzz and serves in most cases to devalue a company when an owner decides to sell the business. Just because Al and his brother Frank go into business does not mandate the company be named A & K or A-K. Woo-Wooooo. . . zzzzzzzzzzzzzz. It also guarantees a mom-n-pop connotation, deserved or not, which becomes an inhibiting factor when trying to sell to Corporate America. Two Brothers Screen Printing isn't much better. Get my drift?

Oftentimes, letters are the easy shortcut to trimming existing company names because the name is too long, no longer describes what the company does, or has developed negative connotations as perhaps after a scandal, a bankruptcy, or a crisis stemming from a discrimination lawsuit, pollution violations, and the like. Sometimes abbreviations or letters are chosen in conjunction with a company going public or to conceal ownership, but it's still unlikely to become a winning marketing asset.

In research done on company names, the findings on names formed with abbreviations, initials, or contracted words have shown a range of inherent weaknesses, the biggest of which include the loss of identity and loss of association with the company's core product or service. There is, however, a huge exception to this general admonition, which is that the use of initials to brand a company works best for companies whose earlier and much longer names had broad commercial awareness, positive connotations and economic success. That's why using letters proves to be successful for re-branding firms such as Atlantic Telephone & Telegraph (AT&T), International Business Machines (IBM), American Broadcasting Company (ABC) and its rivals Columbia Broadcasting System (CBS) and the National Broadcasting Company (NBC), and the National Biscuit Company (Nabisco).

And then there are Dream Names.

Though an elusive undertaking, try if you can to achieve a "Dream Name." That's my term for a name that provides the ultimate flexibility in marketing; a name that can work as a company name, a product line trademark, a label, a retail store name, a catalog name, a domain name, or a name that could be extended to brand other businesses and product lines. Finding a dream name isn't an absolute necessity, as I'd rather discover a great name that gives the company and product strength, staying power, and other wonderful benefits than a dream name that's already taken and cannot be trademarked nor is available as a domain name. But don't give up. Then, again, what's getting more difficult every day is finding great names and dream names that are able to merit trademark approval as well as a domain name that doesn't cost you as much to secure as a powerful politician.

Allow me to get personal here and tell you the names I chose for my own business. My hobbies and interests range from fishing, gardening, woodworking, painting, travel, French (I speak it), and history to politics, cats, genealogy, whitewater rafting, cooking, playing piano (I was trained as a classical pianist), singing (opera!), restoring antiques (well, OK, junk!), target shooting and hunting, boating (aboard *The Guilt Trip*), and diving, among other pursuits. But my *passions* are even more telling. My house is modeled on the interiors of European castles, complete with thrones, tapestries, heraldry, huge animal mounts on the wall in the great hall upstairs, dark wood furniture, and lots of items and fabrics with fleur de lis designs. The license plate on my UK-made car reads "CASTLES." My cats are Emperor Charlemagne ("Charlie") and Louis XIV ("Louie-Louie").

So, what did I draw from in my own existence to name my management consulting company? Clues: knights, castles, things medieval, King Arthur, Merlin, and Camelot. My *passions* are anything about medieval days and the Renaissance, castles (I've explored over 300!), and building . . . *sandcastles*! (You can see some of my work at www.oceancity.com/ImageGallery/index.php?catid=24 and at www.monkeysee.com/play/2120-how-to-build-a-sandcastle). My management company is called . . .ta daaaaa . . . ***Round Table Management Systems LLC***. It's about what I love, connotes working as a team to build something strong and permanent and good, in a Camelot goal-oriented type of environment, yadda yadda yadda. What are *YOUR* passions and how might you develop a business name that relates to YOU, that you'll love forever, and pleases your clientele as well?

Round Table Management is the company that encompasses my professinal activities outside the apparel decorating world. But the company I represent when working inside the apparel decorating industry is the Apparel Graphics Institute LLC. The name focuses on what revolves around consulting, educational and research services and has an academic ring to it. I'm also in a partner in ***ShopWorks Software***. While our company focuses on the decorated apparel industry, it also develops and sells proprietary software programs in other fields (from small carpet installation businesses to large waste management companies). An apparel graphics industry-specific name would be quite limiting and confusing in marketing to businesses beyond apparel decorating.

Does that mean the name solution is sometimes a second name? Or more? Indeed! Read on, in Chapter Nine.

I'll venture that reading this chapter has been slow going for you, due to the several pauses you made in the course of being stuffed with ideas because an idea might have hit home or stimulated more ideas and variations of names you've already had in mind. Hopefully you've gotten some more food for thought.

And should you happen to come up with a name that's so good and so strong that you'd like to protect your use of it for a long time and throughout North America, consider trademarking the name for your own protection and peace of mind. You'll need to do some homework here, but to research names and marks that might already belong to someone else, especially if an existing mark could present potential conflict in the apparel category, look at the resources available through the Trademark Electronic Search System (TESS) from the United States Patent and Trademark Office. [www.uspto.gov].

CHAPTER 9

SECOND NAMES, TAGLINES, DESCRIPTORS, AND DIFFERENTIATING YOUR COMPANY FROM THE PACK

Additional Company Names

In cases where changing an existing name is highly problematic, oftentimes a second and/or third name becomes a smart, practical option. This alternative is particularly useful when you're looking to strengthen your position in one or more specialty or niche markets. For example, your business, *Northern Lights Custom Apparel*, chooses to further your penetration into volunteer fire companies in search of fundraising campaigns. This is an area where your firm has had some success and has developed its own such programs. A second company name that might attract more interest could be *Hook & Ladder Apparel* or *Firehouse Fundraising*. Or for marketing to fishing clubs, your second name might be something like *Fish On Shirts, Deep Sea Designs,* or *Freshwater Fashions*. For a chess clubs, it might be *Checkmate Sportswear*. For amateur astronomy clubs, *Sportswear for Starry, Starry Nights*.

Handling phone calls to the new second company can be done with a dedicated phone line (an additional line) or simply answering your phone with both names (e.g., "Good morning! Great American ShirtWorks and Freshwater Fashions. This is Mary Lou, how may I help you?"). The second company name is easily implemented as well with a separate web address. As you develop yet additional special markets and product lines, you might need to add additional names and/or resources to properly segregate the divisions.

In cases where changing an existing name is highly problematic, oftentimes a second and/or third name becomes a smart, practical options.

Taglines

Sometimes, in addition to second names or in lieu of going that route, you use a "tagline" to better define who you are and what you do. A tagline is a word, a catchword, a phrase, or a short sentence that helps get your message across as to who you are, what you do, who you serve, where your company offers advantages, or other particulars. Properly promoted, displayed, and reinforced over time, a tagline becomes part of the identity of or associated with a product, company, person, group, event or place. With famous folks, certain such phrases become a signature element in their personas. When a Major League team wins a championship, you're bound to hear the phrase, "I'm going to Disneyworld!"

Let's play 20 Questions. See if you can correctly identify the catch phrase associated with:

a. DiGiorno Pizza®

b. Nickname of hockey legend Wayne Gretzky

c. Comedian Henny Youngman

d. Comedian Rodney Dangerfield

e. M & M's®

f. Crowd cheer of New Orleans Saints fans

g. TV commentator Bill O'Reilly

h. President Obama's campaign slogan

i. Morton Salt®

j. Fox News®

k. Burger King®

l. McDonald's®

m. Bounty® towels

n. December 7, 1941

o. Milk

p. Pork

q. Moses

r. GEICO®

s. Fed Ex®

t. Wheaties®

[The correct answers appear at the end of this chapter].

Getting the answers for all 20 questions is nearly impossible because of your age or personal interests.

If you're under 40, you probably never heard of Henny Youngman, a famous mid-20th Century comedian. You also probably can't associate the famous phrase about Japan's attack on Pearl Harbor spoken by President Franklin D. Roosevelt, the spark that triggered America's entry into Word War II. And if you've never followed ice hockey, you never heard of Wayne Gretzky, one of the sport's all-time greatest players.

Anyhow, how'd you do? Congratulations to all the winners! Because if you got one right, you understand taglines and positioning statements and the associative relationship of a company, product, person, event, or other entity with a certain phrase.

Obviously some taglines are better than others; some are unknown to older or younger readers. Some are easier to remember than others. Some are known only to people who use the product or service. But each phrase came to be associated with something else -- by happenstance, through long-term advertising investments, personal involvement or memory, or whatever. Shorter is usually better, though a longer phrase can be successfully effected with gazillions of ad dollars behind it. That was the case of a year-and-a-half McDonald's national ad campaign in which millions of people learned that a Big Mac® consists of "Two all-beef patties, special sauce, lettuce, cheese, pickles, onions on a sesame seed bun." It was first run in 1976, but remains in the minds of millions of people several decades later.

The correct answer for question L (about McDonald's) might be "*I'm Lovin' It*," but if you answered "*McDonald's is your kind of place*" (run in 1967-1971) or "*You deserve a break today*" (run in 1971-1975 and revived twice -- 1980-1983 and 1989-1990), score it as a correct answer. This illustrates the point that campaigns and taglines change over time to what suits the company's evolving objectives for itself and vis-à-vis its competition. (If you'd like to see a few dozen other McDonald's slogans, go to "http://en.wikipedia.org/wiki/McDonald's_advertising."

A classic tagline developed by industry pioneer Dan Gray, better known as "Daffy Dan," starting in the 1970s, focused on the famous Cleveland entrepreneur's innovative concept of imprinting his "DD" icon on sleeves of the shirts his company decorated. Say Daffy Dan's to someone from Cleveland and he's likely to think or say out loud in response, "*If your T-shirt doesn't have a DD on the sleeve, it's just underwear.*" Dan is still a well-recognized celebrity in Cleveland, known for his signature handlebar mustache. But even more so for his company's catchy, memorable, and powerful tagline that has been hard at work helping position the firm ever since its debut. Despite its age, it's still proudly proclaimed in the firm's advertising and marketing materials. And the company's shirts still get the double-D icon treatment. [www.daffydan.com]

In a campaign I designed several years back for a client in a midsize

Midwestern city, I developed the tagline, "*Instant Answers, Fast Quotes, and Guaranteed 3-Day Delivery.*" Radio was the primary medium used to get the word out; the airtime budget was $16,000, run over eight weeks on three stations -- soft rock, country, and the Rush Limbaugh Show on a news-talk station. The tagline addressed the frustration prospects had with the competition, which consistently proved slow on response and evasive or impossible on giving quotes to callers seeking information and pricing. Typical competitors' phone responses included, "We don't quote over the phone;" "We have to see your art before we give a price;" "You have to speak with the owner and he's out until about four;" and "We'll beat any price."

The campaign struck a nerve and it scored more than 40 new accounts, whose purchasing volume over 12 months (measured from the onset of the radio spots) totaled $141,000. And that was in addition to the additional business stimulated from former customers and existing accounts. Given that some 80% of these accounts will continue to buy from the company for many years, the value of this campaign could easily chalk up a half-million dollars in five years as well as generate more volume through referrals.

Here are some taglines I've used successfully for decades that are still popular with my clients. Borrow what you'd like from the four below, a small gift from me to you for buying this book.

▶ Targeting business customers? "*We make good companies look great!*"
▶ Targeting teams and leagues? "*The best-dressed teams in town come to* [your company name]"
▶ Positioning against slower competitors? "*Guaranteed 3-Day Turn around*"
▶ Positioning against low-balling competitors? "*Get the good stuff*" And...

The most popular tagline among my clients for the past 30 years? "*We sell attention!*" Sometimes this one takes the form of, "*We sell attention! You get results!*"

By the way, all the ideas contained in this book are yours to use as you see fit, except the one tagline above: "We sell attention!" Please note that it's protected via copyright and its use is restricted only to companies that have secured legal authorization. (For details on obtaining a license, please contact the author).

Differentiating Your Company from the Pack

The tagline or taglines you'll develop on your own help differentiate your company. Why is this effort necessary?

For example, let's look behind the tagline, "*We sell attention!*," to determine its goal or goals.

The offer, claim, and positioning strategy addresses specific aspects of prospects' perceptions about what they're buying. Or, rather, what they *think* they're buying.

"*We sell attention!*" is designed to jog would-be buyers minds' to expand their thinking past the notion that all sellers and producers of decorated apparel do the same thing, on the same products, with the same results. The typical unknowledgeable buyer believes all he needs to know to differentiate one vendor from another is the prices they're charging. He believes you, what you sell, and what you do are commodities. The thinking here goes that if he's buying flour, sugar, eggs, milk, gasoline, salt, tissue paper, or toilet bowl cleaner, it's all pretty much the same, so why pay more for any of these commodities? That's essentially the same thinking he has about apparel decorators and apparel decorating – we are simply, in his mind, a commodity. .

When pressed to think that there could be differences among any of the commodities suggested above, folks might adjust their thinking, though not by much.   Demonstrating why your company is a better choice is what you need to do to combat the commoditization factor to successfully differentiate your company from the others. Your failure to change this perception leaves prospects committed to one main standard of differentiating you from the next guy: price.

Dumb Mistake No. 7
Allowing a prospect to believe the only difference between you and you competitor is the price you're both charging for similar items – and not doing anything about changing that perception.

Differentiation is a critical function of positioning; think of it simply as explaining why you're different, or better, or friendlier, or easier to do business with, or smarter, or whatever else sets you apart from the pack. You need to say it, you need to show it, and you need to prove it, if you are to make your case successfully. You'll see lots more specifics throughout this book to help you accomplish all that.

Descriptors

A descriptor is a significant word, phrase, or specific terminology used to help your customers and prospects get a quick handle on just what it is that you do, or sell, or offer in the way of other benefits and services. It's easiest to explain it by presenting it in conjunction with a company name.

True North Custom Apparel and Promotions sells and does lots of different things. To get people who see its ads, web sites, signage or other materials zoned in quickly, True North has added a few words that get right to the point.

True North Custom Apparel & Promotions
SCREEN PRINTING· EMBROIDERY · GRAPHIC DESIGN · PROMOWARES
We make good companies look great!

Kinda says it all, doesn't it? The company name, its descriptors, and its tagline. Now, take your ball and run with it!

Answers to 20 Questions:

a) It's not delivery. It's DiGiorno! b) The Great One   c) Take my wife… please! d) I don't get no respect e) Melts in Your Mouth, Not In Your Hand f) Who Dat?! g) Caution. You're about to enter the No Spin Zone h) Change you can be believe in i) When it rains, it pours   j) We report. You decide k) Have It Your Way l) I'm Lovin' It m) The Quicker Picker-Upper n) A day that will live in infamy o) Got milk? p) The other white meat q) Let my people go! r) So easy a caveman can do it s) When it absolutely, positively, has to be there overnight. t) Breakfast of Champions

CHAPTER

10

WHAT'S IN A LOGO?

A logo is the visual component of your company's identity, a graphic signature, or an iconographic shortcut to your identity. Just as we've established the critical importance of a good, effective name—and perhaps augmenting it with a tag line and descriptors -- your company needs a distinct, attractive, memorable graphic symbol. It should be something that shows you're cool, you're professional, you're friendly, and -- especially in our craft -- you're as good as you claim to be at creating great garment graphics.

In the course of a year I see hundreds of logos of apparel graphics companies – from clients (and often those of their prime competitors when doing research on them), from attendees at the seminar and workshop programs I conduct at trade events, from business cards of visitors to the ShopWorks Software booth at trade shows, and from cruising company websites. Despite the fact that the apparel decorating industry is a proud part of the graphic arts industry, too many apparel graphics companies have logos that say anything but. Most are rather, shall we say, uhhhh, *under*whelming. And I'm being kind and generous in making that observation.

Your company's logo should be distinctive and attractive because, to everyone who sees it, it makes a first impression; and everyone who sees it makes a judgment about your company. When your enterprise shows itself through its chosen symbol, it speaks volumes about your creativity, your taste, and your own graphic prowess – or lack of it. Were you to pose for a family portrait, certainly you'd want to look your best for generations. Likewise for a logo, though its useful life may be considerably shorter, as businesses routinely freshen their logos from time to time to reflect evolving changes in the marketplace.

When you reach the epitome of logo design, your logo should be in the realm of *unforgettable*. Ergo, it's something that shouldn't be taken lightly and is the antithesis of a hastily prepared afterthought. A good logo may prove to be a clincher as to whether you get a prospect's call or his order – or if he places his call and the order elsewhere.

Despite the fact that the apparel decorating industry is a proud part of the graphic arts industry, too many apparel graphics companies have logos that say anything but.

Use your logo on every visual image your customers and prospects will see, because it's one of the most cost-effective ways to increase your advertising reach, frequency, and continuity.

While the importance of a company logo cannot be minimized or understated, your *first* logo needn't cost a fortune, nor does it have to be original. Oftentimes a stock icon selected from a commercial collection of logo templates will suffice. Do make certain that you have the legal right to use one before you run with the ball. Once you've got a few months or years in this business under your belt, your logo will need to be revisited and retooled. By then you'll have a much better handle on what you'll want it to say about your enterprise. And consulting with and investing in a designer's creativity will pay long-term dividends in upgrading your company's identity and imprimatur.

In selecting or designing your company's logo, there are certain properties about the logo to weigh before committing yourself to a final choice – "final" at least for *the present*. Here are some cogent additional logo considerations:

▶**Flexibility:** Your logo will see lots of duty across the full gamut of business communications – on   business cards and stationery, in advertising and web materials, on signs, on vehicles, on promotional products, on catalogs, invoices, purchase orders, and on checks, among other applications. A complex, highly detailed logo won't work on a pen or on other small-format placement areas. So whatever you choose, it has to reproduce cleanly and completely on everything from a business card to a banner to a billboard. To determine if your logo is, in fact, flexible in applications, first make sure it looks good in black and white *as well as* when printed in white *on* black.

If you'll be creating your logo from scratch, work first *only* in black and white, which will enable you to focus on your concept, the shape, and overall impression. The vast applications of your logo will be done in only one color, usually black, so don't get sidetracked by letting the emotional effect of color influence your direction. Yet.

►**Simplicity:** King KISS (as in, "Keep it simple, stupid") rules the Realm of Logoland. A confusing or complicated logo that tries to convey too much information won't get your point across and it'll look a mess. Look at the great logos you see everyday – on your car, your computer, your home appliances, on tools, on your cell phone, and scads of consumer products – and you'll see what simple means. Don't confuse a logo with what you see on official city, state, and provincial seals; most of them were created before the word "graphics" was even part of the language of communications. Take a quick cruise online or leaf through a favorite magazine to get some inspiration.

Many global companies use only letters. For IBM and Sony, their logos say it all. For apparel graphics companies or any graphics arts producer, I strongly advise that your own iconographic image serves to reinforce your prospects and customers with the fact that you are a graphic arts provider.

Your logo doesn't have to be a representation of your product, though that's certainly an option. A silhouette of a T-shirt says a thousand words. But Nike's swoosh tells a story, too, even though it says little about clothing, fitness, style, or comfort. But Nike's worldwide recognition, with billions of dollars invested over time in its advertising and marketing, nonetheless makes the value of its seemingly unrelated trademark worth even greater billions of dollars as an asset called "good will."

►**Continuity:** Once your logo is essentially what you want, don't tweak it every time you run it.Consistency brings about faster recognition for your company.

►**Typography:** Different fonts give you the ability to convey different attributes. Fonts communicate ***STRENGTH*** or ***discretion***, can be ***feminine*** or ***masculine***, express ***tradition*** or ***modernity***, *excitement* or ***composure***, ***whimsy*** or ***sensibility***, ***superiority*** or ***deference***, ***simplicity*** or ***sophistication***. Or just about anything else you want to portray. So, whether you opt for creativity or elect a conservative cast, think about how different fonts can effect different outcomes for a distinctive look and feel.

►**Color:** Once you like what you see in black and white, consider what color you'd like your company to wear when color is a suitable option. Two-color logos can be lovely, but not necessarily twice as good as a monocolor logo. Using three or more colors isn't three or four times as nice, nor will it properly show in many smaller applications. But there are logos and names that scream for color (i.e., Celebration   Sportswear, Rainbow Fashions, etc.) Use two, three, or even four colors to create impact, but always be sure to design your logo in such a way that it maintains its integrity in all monocolor applications. The final word on color: there's no one-size-fits-all answer as the issue of color or colors is one that comes down to chocolate or vanilla. Both taste good.

Dumb Mistake No. 8
Designing a logo that doesn't work well in one color.

When you think you're done, you're not. You won't have a finalized logo until you've shown people whose opinions you value have had a chance to weigh in. When it comes to logos, you're not looking for "cute," you're looking for smart, you're looking for effective, and you're looking for impact. But your ultimate decision shouldn't be "democratic." Not unless those weighing in have as much money at risk as you have. Yes, do get input, but this decision is one conserved only to the owner or owners of the business.

Before you embark on your logo mission, reflect on some selected recent statistical conclusions compiled in a review of the logos of the firms listed in Business Week's top 100 global brands. The study was done by an enterprising 20-something blogger, graphic designer Jacob Cass.

► 94% - The brand name does not describe the product sold. In most cases, a logo is used to identify a company, not its product or service.

► 90% - The tagline is not included in the logo.

► 84% - The font style is clean and clear.

► 74% - The logo design uses only one color (if at all) other than black and white.

► 66% - The logo design is rectangular in shape.

► 48% - Logo designs including the trademark symbol placed the ™ at the top-right (54% of all brands display the ™).

▶ 52% - The name is six letters or less.

▶ 52% - The background is filled and solid.

▶ 44% - The brand uses upper & lower case letters (excluding acronyms).

Source: http://logodesignerblog.com/100-best-global-brands-of-2009/

Second Marks

As a little boy I met a real, live celebrity who worked near Grampop's house in Atlantic City outside of the Planter's Peanut Store on the Boardwalk. Mr. Peanut™ has been hard at work on Planter's® product labels since 1918. I still have my Mr. Peanut drinking cups proudly displayed in my kitchen.

The Morton Salt® girl has been holding her umbrella on packaging since 1916 (the current version had her most recent makeover in 1968). Leo the Lion has been roaring in the Metro-Goldwyn-Mayer logo since 1927. Rice Krispies' Snap, Crackle and Pop® got their working papers in 1933. These characters could, however, be the Michelin Man's grandchildren, since he hit the street in 1898. His grandchild could be Tony the Tiger, who has been working for Kellogg's Frosted Flakes® since 1952.

People have been poking Poppin' Fresh's belly since 1965 and he's been giggling on Pillsbury's payroll since then. And Keebler's elves have been baking cookies since 1968.

Perhaps your kids – or YOU -- own M & M toys, likenesses of "Red" and "Yellow," who debuted as "spokescandies" in 1954 and have gone on to becoming a best-selling toy brand. The Energizer Bunny®, now a 20-something, has grown beyond merely being a battery company's CBO (chief bunny officer) to boasting his own line of toys as well. Maybe your kids have a close personal relationship with Ronald McDonald®, who first appeared in 1963, portrayed by Willard Scott who went on to become NBC's legendary weatherman. (Scott also played Bozo the clown on Washington D.C.'s WRC in the late 1950s).

The Roaming Gnome™ is instantaneously recognized as working for Travelocity™, though his travel shtick is the result of his proclivity for being kidnapped. Met Life™ is represented by one smart dog, but Snoopy® is old school compared another insurance company's representative reptilian. He does have a name, Martin, but most of us know him simply as the GEICO® Gecko. Note though that some see Martin as a "scab," however, since he got hired in 1999 when the Screen Actors Guild went on strike. We also know GEICO employs cavemen from time to time as well.

Oh, yeah, and Budweiser has Clydesdale horses.

Who knew that long-standing recognition could come from "second marks?"

A "second mark" is a device that serves in a supporting role to your logo when the logo might be insufficient in certain applications. This second mark could be a mascot, an anthropomorphic character or some other representation of your company. It can serve as a spokesperson for your company in newsletters, advertising, product and package labels. It also can enhance a mountain of applications where your logo and identity need reinforcement or a convenient ready-to-go helper to make your visual image go that much further when the situation warrants.

Who knows? Someday your own second mark might holding a sign in your print ads, heard in radio spots or seen in cable TV commercials, skipping across the screen on your web site, be seen dashing across a football field at halftime, or marching in your town's July Fourth parade. Those are among the many advertising roles second marks have played in helping my own clients reach new customers.

You'll find this second mark a convenient way to build your identity when a logo doesn't do the whole job.

Second marks also can be part of your branding strategies, especially when used as sleeve or collar icons on the garments you decorate. Just as Daffy Dan's double-D has amplified his company's total marketing persona and increased the value of his brand, your own second marks not only can reinforce loyalty from the people who'll wear them, but they'll also generate millions of advertising impressions to everyone who sees them.

Hmmmm, what's that sound I hear? Ahhhh, it must be the creative wheels in your head spinning!

CHAPTER

IMAGE VS. IDENTITY

While you hear the term "image," frequently with regard to a company's marketing persona and its approach to its audiences, you rarely hear the term "identity" used in the same context. Identity is, however, what you really want to achieve. Let's see why.

Your image is what you say you want to look like in the minds of your audiences as well as being an ideal you strive -- or at least profess -- to live up to. Image is, however, better characterized as how you look with your make-up on. After all, when you go a-courtin' your prospects, you want to look your very best in hopes of attracting some attention. Image is cosmetic. Identity, however, begins with being seen with that same make-up on, but extends much deeper. Identity encompasses your personality, your style, your values, your heritage, your history, your reputation, your workmanship, your technologies, and everything your company represents and professes to believe in. Image is only skin deep; identity goes all the way down.

Your image might suggest you're youthful and hip in your look, but an identity adds the "feel" and backs up your image. If there's integrity to your identity, your youthful, hip image would be reinforced by your use of high-tech communications and cutting-edge decorating technologies. It also would include your shop using up-to-date equipment, being on the ball with your service, demonstrating fresh approaches to graphics, offering more in the way of fashion-forward colors and styles, and having energetic salespeople on the front lines.

Image is only skin deep; identity goes all the way down.

Perhaps a company wants to present itself with a more corporate image, complete with a Wall Street-genre logotype and high-brow graphics in its catalog. But what would corporate buyers think if they visited that company and saw the employees dressed down in beat-up tees and jeans, saw a disheveled showroom, walked through a production area that looked like The Terminator just wasted 10 bad guys, saw misprinted old garments strewn about, and last week's used coffee cups and soda cans sitting on top of the dryer or on your hooping table? "Corporate" might be the look on paper, but the on-site identity says "unkempt, untidy and unprofessional." Perception would be made worse if the company had no current price list, and incoming callers were serviced only by whomever was available, handled poorly by people who sound unknowledgeable and as if the call is interrupting them.

Allow me one more example to explain identity. An old neighborhood that's undergoing gentrification has a landmark Victorian home that stands in disrepair, but has just been sold to well-known local restaurateurs. They've announced they're pouring a few hundred grand into the place and will open it this spring as an elegant restaurant called, "The Victorian."

Look at two scenarios that could evolve from here:

Scenario 1: An up-and-coming young architect and builder are teamed up to re-do the place. They go to work meticulously restoring the exterior to its grandeur of the 1880s. Inside, the old mansion has been gutted and reconfigured with vaulted ceilings, skylights, and wild, contemporary wall treatments. Art reproductions include imitations of a Renoir here, a Diego Rivera there, along with some Dutch masters, a Leroy Neiman and a Zippy the Chimp original. The place is eclectic to say the least, but nonetheless impressive. According to the press release announcing the gala grand opening, "our menu will feature Nouvelle Americain and Thai cuisine," while the bar staff and servers will be outfitted in 22nd Century attire. Additionally, Nine Inch Nails will be playing in the lounge and, for the older crowd, an Elvis impersonator will work the banquet hall.

Scenario 2: An up-and-coming young architect with several historic restoration projects under his belt is teamed up with a contractor who, himself, has been restoring old buildings for more than 25 years. They go to work meticulously restoring the exterior *and the interior* to its grandeur of the 1880s, complete with elaborate crown mouldings and stained glass windows rescued from a recently demolished mansion. The menu will feature traditional American and mid-19th Century English fare. The bar staff will be "in tails and top hats," while the servers will be outfitted as butlers and maidservants. The grand opening will feature a vocal ensemble doing Gilbert & Sullivan favorites.

Identity? The second scenario is thoroughly Victorian. The first one is anything but.

Dumb Mistake No. 9
Finding out you're the only one who believes your company's image is a good one. Or worse, not finding out you're the only one who believes it!

What story does your company's identity tell? Has it been carefully crafted as part of a marketing strategy, or is it simply something that has evolved over time to whatever people define as your company today? Does your identity energize prospects to want to be associated with your company? How you answer these questions will reveal how much you've done to proactively build an identity or how little attention you've given toward achieving a better one.

CHAPTER 12

FOUR KEY CUSTOMER CONCERNS: CONVENIENCE, SPEED, QUALITY, AND PRICE

The primary marketing sectors that purchase apparel graphics products are: Businesses, Schools & Colleges, Organizations & Clubs, Athletic Teams & Leagues, Government, and a hybrid market, Events.

Common to nearly all these sectors are issues of convenience, speed, quality, and price (or "value"), though these issues will vary in importance between and within these market sectors.

Convenience

Convenience to some buyers means a company has a local showroom and extended hours in the evening and Saturdays. Convenience to schools that are distant from providers' showrooms might mean you loan out jacket samples for a week in five different sizes for "try-on" days to help you get orders from the students.

Convenience to many buyers might simply mean having access to a great catalog and an easy-to-read price list – in hard copy and/or online -- and fast telephone or e-mail responses to inquiries. For some, it's being able to call on a toll-free line and pay with a credit card.

Making it difficult for customers and prospects to get the information they're looking for means more than just inconvenience. It frequently means your company is leaving itself wide open to the advances of a more astute competitor, one who makes it easier to do business with his company.

Speed

Speed is a relative term. To some, speed, or more precisely "turnaround time," means on-demand, instant gratification, or one-day delivery time. To others, it means three- or five-day turnaround. Folks not in a big hurry are fine with two-week turnaround. But when a company defines its production turnaround time as "taking our own sweet time to complete an order" based on overall production volume, staff resources, and seasonal factors, it invites a competitive assault by a smart, well-managed company that guarantees turnaround time in 72 hours. This firm is one that is certain to consistently gain market share against a slower, complacent competitor.

Quality

The quality of garments is generally a function of price, though even our industry's most basic garments are made well and provide good value for whatever money the buyer is willing to spend.

For the most part, the bar for buyers' expectations on what constitutes acceptable garment quality is set rather low, due to the overall quality offered at virtually all levels of garments available from reputable industry manufacturers. Some end-users, however, think nationally recognized brands are at the higher levels of quality because, at retail, these brands (e.g., Polo®, Nike®, Bill Blass®) sell for prices considerably higher than Hanes, Fruit of the Loom, Gildan, or other well-known industry staples. The fact of the matter is that the quality of our standard brands – stitch for stitch, detail for detail, and fabric specs – is every bit as good as the better-known, logoed goods, price differences notwithstanding. The logoed goods may, however, have *additional* detailing or features that justify being priced accordingly. Brands such as Cutter & Buck® do indeed set a significantly higher standard and command much higher prices for those whose budgets allow for purchasing this luxury level of garment.

The quality of the graphic treatments, the quality of the decorating, and the sophistication of the producers, however, evince very discernible differences between one apparel decorator and another.

But here, too, the bar for buyers' expectations on what constitutes acceptable decorating quality is set rather low, due to the fact that most sellers of decorated apparel do a respectable job of delivering good-quality workmanship.

But there is a noticeable distinction between *average* quality graphics and superior quality graphics. While most designs look fine as presented, others rate an immediate "WOW!" upon presentation. What transforms "It's fine" and "It's nice" into "That looks smashing!" are matters of talent, experience, and extra effort on the part of the artist or digitizer, even if the design itself is comprised of only a logo or rudimentary illustration and text. Whether the design is enhanced with shadowing or beefed up with thickened embroidered outlines or other textural elements, the graphics look sharper, better, and more alive.

When it comes to illustration, of course, superior talent helps move graphics from being merely a component of the decorating process to becoming a distinguishing difference between competitors – a position that wins attention, demonstrates visibly better outcomes, and word-of-mouth advertising, among other benefits.

Price

At the beginning of Chapter Seven (What is Positoning?), I briefly mentioned that in the minds of most prospects, "people might very well think of us, what we do, and our products as simply 'commodities.'" After all, "in their minds, what we sell and do is pretty much what every other company in our field sells and does."

For apparel graphics companies, the critical component for being thought of as something beyond being producers of a commodity is positioning. And if you were wondering why I've devoted an entire section of this book to the topic of positioning, it is as the antidote to being summarily commoditized. Without differentiating your company in the minds of your prospects and positioning your enterprise to be viewed as something better than the rest, your price is relegated to being set in the commodity market.

By virtue of the fact that I have a bread machine at home and occasionally use it to make very passable fresh bread in a variety of palatable offerings, once or twice a month I can lay claim to the title of "baker." A key ingredient in most of the recipes I follow is "bread flour." Except for what I've learned on the Internet (that bread flour has a slightly higher gluten content than all purpose flour), I'm clueless as to the differences between the bread flour packaged under Gold Medal®, Pillsbury®, or the store brand. To me, bread flour is a commodity. Of course, when the difference between the most and least costly is $.25 a sack, whichever brand I drop in the shopping cart isn't a big deal. But when the price quoted by two competing screen printers for 144 T-shirts is $.25 per shirt – or $36, why should someone buy from the vendor selling at a higher price?

Likewise, when two embroiderers vying for a 36-piece golf shirt order on identical goods with similar designs are a dollar per shirt apart from one another, how could the one charging the higher price ever hope to win the order?

Left with little or no real understanding of the differences from one vendor and another, the buyer makes his decision as to who gets the order on the only basis he knows: price.

Unless a company has crafted its position and its identity on a range of factors – its reputation, guarantees, better graphics, better workmanship, user-friendly customer service, more reliable and faster delivery, among other attributes -- price remains the primary determinant on who wins patronage.

Educating prospects and customers and demonstrating that the company is in fact all it claims to be are easier said than done. But making conscious, strategic decisions to develop and promote an enhanced position are ultimately what separates who makes money in this business from those who at best make a living. Who would you rather be? And will you make the necessary investments in marketing, advertising, better technology, and better training of employees?

I've taught pricing seminars at industry trade shows for 30 years. Attendees come to class thinking pricing is mathematics. Ninety minutes later, they leave understanding it's marketing. And positioning.

Isn't pricing based on costs? To some extent it is, and I'll acknowledge that costs certainly present a basis for calculating the break-even amount that has to be covered. But pricing, when properly determined and intelligently stated, must represent something much more important: value.

Value derives from a combination of customer perceptions and satisfactorily addressing customer needs and wants. For the buyer whose sole consideration nonetheless is price, the low bid wins – almost regardless of quality and service. Those are factors unhappy buyers learn about after the order has been delivered.

The issue of price begs the question, "Is the sale simply one of garments and graphics?" I'll state unequivocally, NO! It's *value*. It's promising and proving a better return on the money spent. Oftentimes demonstrating value encompasses satisfying the customer's basic expectations, but also providing lots of "little extras" – from individually folded garments, better packaging, better paperwork, better graphics, faster turnaround, prompt responses to inquiries, and saying "thank you" and "please," among so many other simple procedures and courtesies. (For lots of specifics on how to build value and about the "little extras," see Section Five: Merchandising Your Products and Your Company – 24 Way to Get Customers to Love You).

For those who insist that pricing *must* be cost-based, consider Nike T-shirts. Having been in the plants where Nike shirts are manufactured and the plants where Nike shirts are decorated, I can tell you that the production cost of the average Nike T-shirt is essentially equivalent to similar garments produced by Hanes, Fruit of the Loom and Gildan. It costs no more to print Nike T-shirts than other T-shirts. At retail, though, consumers will pay double or triple for Nike compared to T-shirts with similar graphics but not branded Nike. Lower-end Nike tees sell for $18 – $22; higher-end tees go for $28 (2010 figures). Including the garment and screen printed decoration, Nike shirts cost between $2 and $4 in labor and materials. Without discussing wholesale pricing for reasons of confidentiality, I can tell you that the cost of producing Nike garments has very little relationship to what consumers -- quite willingly – pay to own and wear a Nike product. But Nike buyers, to be sure, aren't buying shirts. They're buying identification with the brand, perceived value, and, in their own minds, coolness.

While retail value is admittedly a whole 'nother subject, the price issue of custom decorated apparel takes different shape in different markets throughout the distribution chain.

For example, the nature of decision-making in privately owned local businesses is quite different from those of big national corporations and local school districts. Local businesses can usually make decisions faster and oftentimes one person has complete control of the process. Dealing with any bureaucracy in a governmental agency or school district (though sometimes in business as well) means fast turnaround capabilities usually won't be of paramount concern to such buyers. Positioning a company with "guaranteed five-day turnaround," however, will appeal to local businesses in a way that event organizers, government buyers, and school buyers wouldn't appreciate to the same degree of interest or need.

Dumb Mistake No. 10
Thinking you can win an order by giving a ridiculously low price
***and* thinking you can make it up on subsequent**
orders or over time.

While price is an issue that concerns all buyers, for business buyers the concerns of pricing may only mean that a price needs to be somewhere in the ballpark of perceived value, not an absolute rock-bottom number. Business buyers are far more likely to acknowledge that service, quality, speed, convenience and other qualitative matters all go into the "value equation." A municipal agency that buys strictly via low-bid contracts and teachers who make their decisions on price alone fall into profiles where the decision-makers' product knowledge, awareness of graphic style, and ability to assess decorating competence would be on the low end of the scale.

But by positioning your company to be perceived as "progressive," with user-friendly catalogs and explanatory literature in its efforts to educate buyers (if they're educable to begin with), you might elicit a little more respect from such decision-makers, who traditionally view your products as commodities. And if you demonstrate through an astute sampling program your extraordinary mastery of graphics, printing and embroidering, you might generate interest from buyers who wouldn't otherwise respond to your lead-generating campaigns. You might be able to convince these low-awareness buyers that getting shirts from you that are so much better looking than what they've ever had in the past could yield big dividends. Meaning: if higher sales accrue because your stuff is so much more attractive, more colorful, classier, and hipper that the school or organization would make more money than ever before -- even if your price isn't the absolute lowest -- they learn doing business with you is better for them in terms of earning more revenue, even though they could have found a "cheaper" price.

Through teaching seminars at trade events and in sessions with clients, I have developed a simple pledge for everyone involved in the decorated apparel industry that sums up the ultimate lesson in pricing your products.

That pledge is: "I am allowed to make money!"

Repeat after me, class: "I am allowed to make money!"

"I am allowed to make money!"

Price also can be a marketing device that helps a company position itself in the pack, or below it, or above it. Allow me to share with you the counsel I give to virtually every apparel graphics company I work with as to the ideal position for its custom-decorated apparel. How my clients should be thought of by their customers and prospects comes down to this: "Well, they're a little high, but they're worth it!"

CHAPTER

NARROWING YOUR FOCUS:
LOCAL ECONOMIC FACTORS, GEOGRAPHY, AND
AGE-SPECIFIC AUDIENCES

Trying to be all things to all people generally doesn't work in the decorated apparel business. There are many other matters to weigh about who's most likely to buy from you and what you might do to make your company appear more attractive to them. In Chapter Four (The Eight Steps in the Marketing Process of Decorated Apparel), we looked at some of the function involved in developing your marketing. Of particular relevance in the chapter now at hand are the steps involving targeting the market or market segment, analyzing the needs of the market or segment, and researching the market potential.

In narrowing your focus, allow me to present some more food for thought about some specific considerations that'll help you determine where you can make inroads against existing competitors, tailor your product offerings and services to specific audiences, and perhaps consider specializing in certain segments that existing competitors either don't address or do so only to a generalized degree.

Local economic factors

What is the primary economic engine (or engines) of your local area? Regardless of how well the economy is doing, certainly some areas of economic concentration matter more than others. Can your business compete better at some things or offer advantages that competitors don't or don't focus on?

Say the local economy has its emphasis in the tourism industry. On what part or parts should your marketing be positioned? The hospitality industry (mainly hotels and, restaurants)? Attractions? Retailers? The tourists, themselves? Certainly all of these sectors buy decorated apparel -- for applications ranging from uniforms to souvenirs.

But if there are already plenty of existing companies currently addressing their needs well, entering the market as simply one more competitor doesn't bode well for your success. So you look further. Perhaps you want to focus on those who provide products and services to the hospitality industry, the attractions, and the tourists and/or locals. These potential customers could include plumbers, carpenters, electricians, landscapers, insurance and real estate agencies, automotive and marine repair firms, institutional catering firms, trucking and transportation companies, or local governments. It would be easier to penetrate those types of accounts faster than to commit the bulk of your time and money to targeting the larger local players who likely have good relationships with the existing decorated apparel providers. The latter option can wait until you're in a better condition to attack.

You also might consider going after those sectors that have little at all to do with tourism, including the year 'round buyers -- local manufacturers whose markets are well beyond just the locality or region. Potential accounts are schools, colleges, local governments, state and provincial agencies, radio stations, and healthcare providers. Yes, you'll run into existing competitors, but you have a far better chance to get orders from the sectors that are less dependent on the primary local industry.

In the long run, you always want to become a stakeholder in the primary local economy, but working around the edges will yield better initial results and generate critical cash flow and experience. When you've secured a sufficient base of accounts to keep your company running and growing, that's the better time to initiate your forays into the primary economy. It's also likely you'll have developed a few of the "plum" accounts along the way through referrals and your own networking efforts.

Geography

Urban, suburban, small town, and rural areas all present challenges and opportunities for apparel decorators. The advantages of being located in a large metropolitan area are mitigated by the amount of competition in it. Whatever your geography, the opportunities for successfully generating business lay in carefully defining the territory you can reach and intelligently determining how to reach it.

Case in point: Argyle, Wisconsin. Located in the southern central part of the state, at ground zero for the cheese producing industry and an hour and a half southwest of the major population center of Madison, *RBS Activewear* grew by developing team and school business throughout the Upper Midwest and well beyond the region, too. Its core markets were and are well serviced with a strong customer service effort, direct mail, Internet marketing, and fast – three days on some 97% of orders – turnaround. Selling to the local environs was not a concern or an identified target; whatever local business the company did beyond team and schools was accomplished on a haphazard basis.

But in calculating the population of the territory in a 60-mile radius from Argyle, I advised the company's owners that there was sufficient "critical mass" for developing a separate company to serve an extended local trading area. Despite there being several times more cows than people, the area nonetheless is home to thousands of dairy farms and small businesses, lots of smaller public schools, a few local colleges, and, of course, lots of dairy-related enterprises. In researching RBS's competitors, my findings were that there were a handful of small local shops that sold accounts within a fairly narrow radius from each tiny town.

Using radio to reach the rural communities supplemented by advertising in small local newspapers and targeted direct mail, the brand new division, Thunder Bridge Trading Company, reached mid-six figure sales within three short years. The geography, which at first glance appeared to have inherent limitations, proved to be ripe for an ongoing, organized effort. The keys to success were defining a wider trading area (but one with similar culture throughout), ascertaining what cost-effective media to use to reach the distant and diverse audiences, and hiring a full-time, boots-on-the-ground salesperson to service accounts and develop relationships.

Dumb Mistake No. 11
Defining an expansive territory for marketing without having commensurate resources to reach the target audience(s).

In a large metro area, broadcast media and big-city newspapers are prohibitively expensive. But the number of potential accounts means there's usually plenty of business to go around, even for newcomers. Focusing on either smaller parcels of territory in the city and/or specializing in handling certain size orders or certain types of accounts (e.g., local businesses, professional offices, nearby clubs and organizations, elementary or private schools, and church groups) and/or particular aspects (e.g., fundraising, neighborhood events, festivals) will yield better outcomes than trying to compete in the general marketplace with the already established players at all levels of endeavor.

Age-Specific Audiences

Buyers for audiences in specific age groups present opportunities for specialization. The products high school audiences seek differ from what pre-school and elementary school audiences need. The former buys the gamut of apparel for a variety of applications (athletics, fundraising, spirit wear, etc.), while the latter groups' needs are narrower (e.g., drawstring bags and basic kids-sized shirts).

Becoming an expert on and marketing greater selections of custom-decorated clothing for infants and toddlers will enable you to reach buyers who don't see what they're interested in from companies that address more general audiences and with more traditional product lines.

Specializing in selling to seniors in nursing homes and assisted living centers and to those who attend to the populations living in them presents a market with millions of residents and hundreds of thousands of employees. Few decorated apparel companies and promotional products distributors call on these locations, creating an invitation to a potentially large and lucrative niche with little competition.

Women of child-bearing age include millions of prospects. What groups or businesses cater to them? Children's furniture companies, organizers of Lamaze classes, diaper services, and, of course, hospitals.

Maternity is big business – and a major profit center -- for hospitals that devote big bucks to attract would-be mothers for utilizing the institution's staff and medical resources, including becoming paying customers in their maternity departments when it's time for the big event. And after the new mothers go home with their newborns, there are yet more businesses catering to their needs and aspirations, firms with healthy appetites for decorated apparel and custom-printed promowares.

One demographic group in North America continues to grow larger each year: senior adults. Millions of seniors participate in sports and recreation programs and a plethora of clubs and organizations attract their loyalty and enthusiasm. Given that people are living longer and more people than ever are collecting retirement benefits, it's a wonder so few companies in our industry are addressing the needs and aspirations of this humongous audience. Maybe you'll be among those few who elect to mine this audience's riches?

Narrowing Your Target Audiences

As mentioned earlier, the primary marketing sectors that purchase apparel graphics products are: Businesses, Schools & Colleges, Organizations & Clubs, Athletic Teams & Leagues, Government, and a hybrid market, Events.

One demographic group in North America continues to grow larger each year: senior adults.

But on closer inspection, each of these groupings has its own subsectors and internal audiences.

Below is a list that should help you see how to further narrow the focus on your targeted audiences. Each category also contains a quick summary of the applications of decorated apparel within the category. It's provided as a reference tool to get you thinking about just how much you want to bite off. Narrowing your focus means you'll also be able to market to and test various subsectors at much lower cost, with less risk, and with a greater likelihood of success.

▶ **Businesses:** Small, medium, and large. Urban, suburban, and rural. Local, regional, national, international. Professional, semi-professional, technical, manufacturing/industrial, and commercial.

Primary Uses and Applications of Apparel Graphics Products include: corporate identification, advertising, special occasions, uniforms/required dress, employee incentives, customer incentives, promotions/premiums/gifts.

▶ **Schools & Colleges, Universities, Pre-Professional Training Institutes, Trade Schools:** Small, medium, and large. Urban, suburban, small town, and rural. Kindergartens, elementary schools middle schools, and high schools. General education, academic/college preparatory, vocational-technical. Local, state/provincial, regional. Public, semi-public, private, and religious. Alumni, faculty, staff, fraternities, sororities, and campus organizations.

Primary Uses and Applications of Apparel Graphics include: School spirit/pride, student identification, promotion, special events, fundraising, uniforms/required dress, recruitment, bragging rights, revenue generation.

► **Organizations, Clubs, Interest Groups:** Small, medium, and large. Urban, suburban, small town, and rural. Local, state, regional, national. Governmental, public, private, religious, political, athletic, labor, social, civic, unions, ethnic, etc.

Primary Uses and Applications of Apparel Graphics Products include: Spirit/pride, member identification, promotion, special events, uniforms/required dress, fundraising, recruitment, bragging rights, revenue generation.

► **Athletic Organizations, Teams, Leagues:** Small, medium, and large. Urban, suburban, small town, and rural. Local, state, regional, national. School related, governmental or public sponsored, private, alumni, boosters, etc.

Primary Uses and Applications of Apparel Graphics Products include: Spirit/pride, member identification, promotion, special events, uniforms/required dress, fundraising, recruitment, bragging rights, revenue generation.

► **Governments:** Local/county, state/provincial, federal, Native American/First Nations, military, public corporations,

Primary Uses and Applications of Apparel Graphics Products include: Spirit/pride, member identification, promotion, special events, uniforms/required dress, fundraising, recruitment, bragging rights, revenue generation.

► **Events:** Local, urban, small town, rural, state/provincial, regional, national, international. Holiday related, athletic related, business related/business sponsored, school related/school-sponsored, organization related/organization sponsored, conventions, competitions, consumer shows, trade shows, promotions, fairs/festivals, and concerts.

Primary Uses and Applications of Apparel Graphics Products include: spirit/pride, advertising, participant/fan identification, staff uniforms/required dress, fundraising, recruitment, bragging rights, revenue generation, promotions/premiums/gifts.

CHAPTER

THE PRIMARY APPLICATIONS OF APPAREL GRAPHICS PRODUCTS

There is a broad variety of applications of apparel graphics products. Here's a quick rundown of the most important uses of our products.

Employee Identification

Whether for businesses, schools, or government, identifying employees is big business. From uses for security to customer service, the applications vary from building pride, making it easy for customers or constituent groups to spot staff members or service employees, and celebrating events to being welcome incentives and/or recognition for employees (for achievements in safety, sales, length of service) and as employee gifts. Among the largest drivers for decorated apparel products is for employee use in conjunction with policies requiring employees to be identified at all times when on the job.

Advertising & Promotion

Who gives away shirts? Just about any business or non-business entity that wants to promote its goals, activities, services, products, brands, or special programs gives away shirts. Or, in many cases, sells them to target audience members who want to identify with whatever the cause is.

Included in this application is the use of decorated apparel as incentives. Test drive a new Ford 150 and receive a cap emblazoned with the embroidered logo of the area's favorite team. Anyone who drops 25 pounds in a Weight Watchers® program merits a well-deserved "Big Loser" T-shirt. Take the stage at Murphy's Irish Pub's Wednesday night karaoke event and earn a cap; command the biggest applause and win an American Idol-like embroidered jacket; get the loudest boos and earn a "Biggest Fool" T-shirt! Show up at a local supermarket's grand opening and receive a free oversized canvas bag. You get the idea. And chances are good you've gotten a few freebies yourself over the years.

People get free stuff and then promote the donor company to hundreds or thousands of people over the life of the garment or accessory.

By the way, I'm often asked if there's any data as to the advertising reach – and cost-effectiveness – of decorated apparel as an advertising medium?

In a study I was commissioned to undertake for a major apparel manufacturer as to the number of advertising impressions generated by custom-decorated T-shirts, the results were astounding. Worn while outside the home during a full day of typical routine activity – excluding attending sports events, concerts, and gatherings at other big venues or crowd centers -- a T-shirt with a full-front imprint is seen by some 200 people. Worn once a week, that's more than 10,000 advertising impressions in one year. And if worn to class, a mall, or a public event, the 200 impressions a day can escalate to thousands of advertising impressions within a few hours!

Let's say at a selling price of $7 per custom shirt, $1 invested in a T-shirt with a full-front design does in fact generate those 200 advertising impressions per day. After wearing the garment ten times, the body it's on has produced 2,000 advertising impressions. That's about $.0035, point-three five, or just over one-third of a penny per advertising impression. In some major markets, that same figure would be competitive with mass communications media such as a news-hour commercial on television or a billboard on a major artery!

On an attractively decorated shirt that the user enjoys wearing regularly, the impact on customer loyalty and awareness -- every time the user sees the design when she washes the garment, takes it from the dryer, folds it, puts it in a drawer, takes it out later, and sees herself in the mirror wearing it -- is empirically inestimable in dollars and cents. But I'll bet the qualitative impact on the user is downright huge.

Membership and Participation

People who are proud of the group or activity they participate in want to brag about it. It's easy to do that bragging by wearing decorated apparel to broadcast their affinities. In some cases, shirts or caps or bags are given to members as part of their membership package, registration fee, or as a reward for participating in an event or program.

Revenue Generation

For some buyers of decorated apparel, selling their garments is a way to make additional – sometimes substantial -- money. If they're successful at it, that success is derived largely from the fact that their customers love the place, product, or service, want to identify with it or remember it, and find the selling price represents good value for the item.

Fundraising

Organizations of all types need money to serve their members and fulfill their missions. Selling decorated apparel provides them an opportunity to build revenues wile providing products their members and supporters want to buy and wear or give as gifts. Of course, it would help a great deal if the items are made attractive and relevant.

There are yet other applications, and I have every confidence you'll discover – and hopefully be successful at establishing -- even more!

But there's another "category" of sorts that shouldn't be overlooked: hybrids of those cited above – such as combining advertising with membership, or revenue generation that provides additional incentives. Such hybrids occur when selling shirts or caps at a profit or distributing them without charge; and when the garment is worn to the advertiser's location, the wearer receives a dividend or benefit. For example, when worn on Friday to a local eatery, the shirt or cap earns the customer receives a free soft drink with lunch, or when worn to a popular bar, earns the wearer free admission by getting the establishment's cover charge waived.

Your acuity in identifying those areas, factors, and applications where you're more likely to succeed and harnessing these factors to your creativity in combining two or more elements to create new and unique market positions gives you tremendous near- and long-term opportunities to grow and prosper.

Limited capital shouldn't be a constraint on your thinking here and may, in fact, be of value in forcing you to narrow your focus.

Hopefully what you've gained in Section Four is an understanding that making a proactive effort at properly and more intelligently positioning your company gives you far better strategic firepower than leaving such weighty matters to happenstance.

CHAPTER

LEAPFROGGING YOUR WAY PAST THE COMPETITION

"Leapfrog marketing" is a term I coined in the 1970s with clients of my advertising agency. I developed it to describe the process of doing all that you can to make it as difficult as possible for a rival to duplicate your performance. It also can make it virtually impossible for any future challenger to ever be in a position to catch or pass you. If yours is a start-up company, you've got some catching up to do. But, as you'll see in this chapter, there are lots of things you can do to hit the ground running and things you can do that your competition – including those who have been on the scene for many years – doesn't do.

Leapfrog marketing isn't just going the extra mile; it's going the extra *two* miles. It's polishing your marketing vehicle to look its very best, pouring in high-octane additives to make your marketing engine run smoother and more powerfully, and installing a few luxury accessories that make the journey all the more pleasurable. The ultimate goals of leapfrogging are two-fold: 1) to preclude your ability to settle for "good enough," and 2) to demolish and, over time, *demoralize* the competition.

To understand leapfrog marketing, imagine you and a competitor are on the starting line, ready to run a race.

Your rival has been in business for 20 years, has all kinds of technology going for him, a showroom that displays his main offerings, and lots of accounts. But on closer review, I'd characterize his company as being in business one year, 20 times. He has no catalog, nor a price list. His web site is rudimentary, doesn't give pricing, and doesn't do much in the way of telling a prospect why buying from his company would be a better choice. His showroom, though adequate, looks tired, has several dated samples, and the whole place could stand a good cleaning and a new coat of paint. His promotional products displays aren't particularly well-organized and they haven't been dusted in months. His employees are nice people, casually dressed (and without the company's logo on their apparel), and most of the time staff members do business standing behind a counter.

You're the newer kid on the block, in business just a year an a half. It might still take a while to catch up with the other's guy's technology, but you have a sufficient command of it now and you're proactive about learning and doing more. So, what can you do from the current starting line to put some dents in the other's guy's image and customer service culture?

Lots! You have all the same catalogs as the other guy, but *you'll* have a printed "express catalog" that showcases your selected key garment and accessory offerings. Equally important, you'll have a price list that goes with it to give your prospects. Right there, you've moved way ahead of the competitor. Customers are sure to appreciate being able to compare things for themselves and, if they want to study further, can take the catalog home. And unlike your rival, *you* respect the customer's time and intelligence by providing a real price list in hard copy and online. Your catalog and website tells lots about your company, explains who you are and what you've accomplished in life, and shows your picture, among other friendly gestures.

To differentiate your company from the other, you have a counter for quick transactions, but your showroom also has a convenient table and attractive, comfortable chairs. The table enables you to lay out catalogs and samples and gives you room to work. The chairs enable your buyers to get comfortable and not have to stand on their feet the whole time. Your showroom is well organized and each item in it is tagged with pricing information that helps customers tell which items cost what, relative to other similar-*looking* garments on your racks.

Your customers can figure out all by themselves which price range they can afford or choose to look at in determining what they'll buy – even if you're on the phone finishing up a call while the buyers are browsing unassisted. *Your* showroom has attractive graphics and clean displays. You show examples of your work (or facsimiles if you're brand new and haven't yet developed your own collection of prints and embroidery you've done, yourself). You have refreshments at the ready (coffee, juice, water, soda) and some munchies, candy or other goodies – and napkins. The showroom windows and carpet are clean, the room is well illuminated, and everything is orderly.

Leapfrog marketing isn't just going the extra mile, it's going the extra two miles.

With what your showroom and website tell about you and how your company looks and feels to a visitor, you've already mitigated some of the advantages of your competitor. You appear to be a whole lot friendlier and more professional. You and your staff wear embroidered golf or poplin shirts and wear engraved name badges. Your staff has been trained in the basics of good customer service – because you invested some time and effort in your people.

Overall, your company makes a much better first impression. Let's say at this point in the race, you've caught up to your opponent. But now you take a few leaps' lead by following up your phone and e-mail requests with written price quotations, and sending the appropriate catalog and price list via snail mail or via easy-to-access-and-understand web links. If it's an inquiry from a local customer, you invite her to your showroom or offer to visit her yourself or send a sales representative. You send out or e-mail a "propaganda" sheet (more on this later in this chapter) that details the advantages of buying from your company, explaining lots of important details without the customer having to ask (e.g., which credit cards you take, your regular business hours, your guarantees, standard production turnaround time, etc.), and you do further follow-up with a friendly phone call. You're now putting some distance between you and the other guy.

When the prospect visits, you suggest some great ways to improve the design at little or no additional cost. Additionally, you show ways to further customize and personalize the items being reviewed. And when she leaves to do a little more pondering, you send her off impressed with your professionalism, better informed about what you sell and how you sell, and with about $5 (your cost) in materials to help her remember your company and her positive experience working with you. You know better than to give away a cheap plastic pen or lame key tag. Your five bucks includes a nice quality pen, a clever calendar magnet, an attractive memo cube, a handy keyhole flashlight, or a rain bonnet, all with your company's imprint – plus she left with your catalog, price list, propaganda sheet, and written quotations.

Leapfrogging forward, word is getting out about you and your company. You see the former rival dropping further away in your rearview mirror.

Unlike the competitor, you've been marketing all along – in the mail to local businesses, networking in the community, and making some good ol' fashion prospecting calls over the phone. And as a result of your efforts, *you're getting leads* (some of which are from the other's guys existing accounts) and are converting them into customers.

Meanwhile, the competitor quite predictably, hasn't done a thing to change the way he does business. He still has no price list; the website still is boring and without pricing information or personality; the showroom still needs cleaning, brightening and organizing. Because he's clueless about what you're doing to gain market share and doesn't bother keeping tabs on his competition, you continue to win some of his accounts one by one by one. And you keep at it inexorably every week.

Dumb Mistake No. 12
Learning about a competitor who's beating you with better marketing and better customer service and thinking you can fight back by lowering your prices.

That's leapfrog marketing. By the time the other guy starts to feel the impact of your leapfrogging efforts, your lead has lengthened and your positioned has strengthened. Given what you've being doing, how many things does the weakened rival have to do to identify as to what you've been doing to even attempt to counteract your results? How will he learn how to go about it all, and how deep is his commitment to revitalize his marketing? He won't and whatever he might actually do, it'll be short lived at best.

What's eminently predictable is that he'll lower his pricing, he can badmouth you as the new guy, and he can try to advertise his enterprise. But by dropping his price, he won't win back much and will weaken his own company. Badmouthing you leaves people cold, especially people who've already started buying from you and like what they saw and love what you delivered! And as for the other guy attempting to advertise more, it's extremely unlikely he'll do it right or continue it for long. That's because it isn't working for him, because it was bought on price or trade, or was done hastily and without much in the way of positioning his company. Thoroughly leapfrogged, he comes to accept his declining fortunes as long as he can eek out a living doing lowball jobs. It's heads you win, and tails he loses. He's now relegated to the world of leapfrog losers. You have been a good leapfrogger and he is the retreating leapfroggee.

Lots more leapfrogging ideas await you in the next nine chapters. Keep a pen and paper handy.

CHAPTER

24 WAYS TO GET YOUR CUSTOMERS TO LOVE YOU

▪ Identity-Builder W2GC2♥U No. 1:
Your Company Catalog

> **mer·chan·dis·ing** | mur-chuhn-dahy-zing | – ***noun***, the planning
> and promotion of sales by presenting a product to the right market at
> the proper time, by carrying out organized, skillful advertising, using
> attractive displays, etc.
> *Source: THE RANDOM HOUSE DICTIONARY OF THE ENGLISH LANGUAGE*
> *– The Unabridged Edition (1971)*

The well-worn 20-lb. dictionary that occupies a position of honor on
my desk was a gift from my parents when I finished my first graduate
degree. They figured I'd keep it around. They were right and I think
of them every time I reach for it. When I checked dictionary.com for
the same word 39 years later, the copy was 100% identical. Yes, the
definition of merchandising is still valid, but I wish Mr. Random had
expanded on that word, "product." A product also can be an idea, a
belief, and any other "ism." It also can be your business.

This section, Section Five – Merchandising and Selling Decorated
Apparel – 24 Ways to Get Customers to Love You, began with an
explanation of Leapfrog Marketing. Now I'll shift the concept into gear
and head out on the highway of opportunity, which I'll call Highway
24. I'll be driving a convertible – with the top down -- so you can get
lots of sunshine and fresh air. Sure, put some tunes on and crank up
the volume. I'll be making 24 stopovers, each of which will help give
you the horsepower that'll enable you to start to see your competition
in the rearview mirror -- and dropping further back in the pack. The
24 Ways to Get Customers to Love You **(W2GC2♥U)** are organized
into nine Identity-Builders, three Customer Relations Vehicles, five

Goodwill Tools and Loyalty Incentives, three Customer Satisfaction Extras, three Quality Control Mechanisms, and The Ultimate Leapfrog Signature (a very unique guarantee you'll learn about in Chapter 24).

Identity-Builders
(Chapter 16) W2GC2♥U No. 1 -- *Your Company Catalog*
(Chapter 17) W2GC2♥U No. 2 -- *Your Price List*
(Chapter 18) W2GC2♥U No. 3 -- *Your Showroom*
(Chapter 18) W2GC2♥U No. 4 -- *Your Website*
(Chapter 19) W2GC2♥U No. 5 -- *Your Company Stationery*
(Chapter 19) W2GC2♥U No. 6 -- *Business Cards*
(Chapter 19) W2GC2♥U No. 7 -- *Self-Promotion Brochure*
(Chapter 19) W2GC2♥U No. 8 -- *I.D. Garment Labels*
(Chapter 19) W2GC2♥U No. 9 -- *Your Packaging*

Customer Relations Vehicles
(Chapter 20) W2GC2♥U No. 10 -- *Customer Surveys*
(Chapter 20) W2GC2♥U No. 11 -- *Newsletters*
(Chapter 20) W2GC2♥U No. 12 -- *Customer Advisory Board*

Goodwill Tools and Loyalty Incentives
(Chapter 21) W2GC2♥U No. 13 -- *Open House Events*
(Chapter 21) W2GC2♥U No. 14 -- *Christmas Gifts*
(Chapter 21) W2GC2♥U No. 15 -- *Valentine Cards and Other Special Occasion Cards*
(Chapter 21) W2GC2♥U No. 16 -- *Premium Offers and Frequent Buyer Clubs*
(Chapter 21) W2GC2♥U No. 17 -- *Crackerjack Marketing*

Customer Satisfaction Extras
(Chapter 22) W2GC2♥U No. 18 -- *Individually Folded Garments*
(Chapter 22) W2GC2♥U No. 19 -- *Accepting Credit Cards*
(Chapter 22) W2GC2♥U No. 20 -- *Shipping Notification and Pick-Up Notification*

Quality Control Mechanisms
(Chapter 23) W2GC2♥U No. 21 -- *Quality Control Calls*
(Chapter 23) W2GC2♥U No. 22 -- *Quality Control and Re-Order Reminder Card*
(Chapter 23) W2GC2♥U No. 23 -- *Packer's Personal Assurance*
And . . .
(Chapter 24) W2GC2♥U No. 24 – *The Ultimate Leapfrog Signature*

Several of these ideas fall into more than one category, but each is listed only once. Select one or more items from each heading to leapfrog past the competition. Each of the 24 ideas presents a specific leapfrog technique. The more leapfrog techniques you can execute well, and on a regular basis, the greater your chances of achieving a near-100% level of account retention.

The great news about your competitors is that most of them have never seen most of the leapfrog items along "Route 24" on any roadmap and never heard of most of the towns on your route. Of the small percentage of industry owners and managers who have heard of some of the little towns on Highway 24, most nonetheless are driving on the Route 24 Bypass, opting to ignore the slower Business Route 24.

Gentlemen and Ladies, start your engines…We're headed first to the realm of Identity-Builders (Items 1 through 9), all of which are designed to help establish who you are and what you sell as well as position your company as customer-friendly and professional.

In the section on "Offering Your Garment Selections" (Chapter 6: Products, Product Sourcing, Product Selection), I laid out the case for limiting your key offerings for a variety of money-saving, time-saving and practical reasons.

Allow me now to help you construct a four- to six-page "express line" catalog, limited to the items that really matter to most buyers of our products.

Identity-Builder W2GC2♥U No. 1 : Your Company Catalog

Start with an 11" x 17" sheet of paper (stock details to follow), which gives you, when folded in half, four 8½" x 11" pages. I recommend the front cover be used as a front *cover*! – nice graphics, your company name, tagline, and descriptors (see Chapter 9) along with your address, phone numbers, and website information.

Or consider a sheet that's 25½" X 11," which folded into thirds gives you six 8½" x 11" pages. Rarely will an "express catalog" format require more than six pages (including the cover). By shortening the extreme right-hand interior page, you can develop a format that will create a finished product that has a tab-like fold on the right and looks like a file folder. This format is called a "gatefold" in the world of printing. For the record, virtually all of my clients prefer the space and flexibility of the six-page format to tell their stories.

I've personally designed more than 50 such catalogs and my clients have produced hundreds more.

Recommended stock is at least an 80-lb. or a 100-lb. cover stock. By comparison, typical copy paper is 20-22-lb. stock. Your favorite printer can show you samples of these as well as various styles and colors of textured stock. (I like linen stock, budget permitting, because it looks like fabric!). Heavier stock cost virtually no more to mail and is many times more likely to be kept by the recipient. Lightweight stock just doesn't command the same level of respect and importance.

The front cover of your custom catalog is a *statement* about your company and needs to make you look astute about your graphic prowess and your (high) level of professionalism. First impressions count! The interior pages contain the "meat" of the catalog. It's the items you sell.

▶ **Brands are *never* mentioned.** Why? Because most buyers accept what you tell them. Yes, a few brand loyalists might insist on what they've grown accustomed to or insist on; we'll attend to their requests to the extent necessary. But even these customers will usually buy the brand you recommend – the one you prefer and for whatever reasons you please (availability, price, printability, transferability, embroiderability, "hand," finishing, etc.).

▶ **Style numbers are never mentioned.** Why inform your competitors about what brand and styles you're promoting, especially when dealing with buyers who are shopping prices? You'll know what items you selected. If you need to insert style numbers for clarity, for customers' purchase orders, or for your sales staff to use when writing orders, create your own alphanumeric codes, but do so in such a way as to conceal the official manufacturer's style codes.

▶ **Iconography or photos?** Use an icon to indicate each section of garment category or style. An icon of a T-shirt is self-explanatory, especially when the word to the right of it says, "T-Shirts." An icon can be a simple outline of the product or a solid silhouette. It makes referencing an item in your catalog easy to locate. In the text for the item, show sizes and colors available and, if desired, brief descriptive copy (e.g., 100% cotton, 50% cotton/50% polyester.) For more varied categories such as golf shirts, the copy might indicate 100% piqué cotton, hemmed bottom (or drop-tail back), woodtone (or matching color) buttons, etc.

Photos obviously show your products well. You can use items as shown on your wholesalers' or the manufacturers' websites. Most sources are happy for you to "borrow" their photos, though, technically speaking, you should get permission to use them.

Yes, photos are great, but will the use of photos instead of line-art icons significantly increase your sales? No. I say this from long experience. In some cases, though, printing photographs can significantly increase your printing costs. But if your catalogs will be produced in small quantities (say, 50 to 100 at a time) from digital files printed out on your own computer printer or on a commercial printing company's equipment, the additional printing costs can be quite moderate.

Do you need the shirts to be shown on models? Not really. People know what a T-shirt and a hoodie look like. Professional models can cost several hundred dollars (and up) per day for photo-shoots. But if you do want to show people, your staff, family, children, grandchildren, and friends will suffice as models for most express catalogs. If you insist on doing a color catalog with people wearing your garments, should the people all be beautiful and young? That's your call, but I'd consider using a variety of folks – young, middle aged, seniors, men, women, kids, the whole shebang. And since not all women are "a size five" nor are all men possessed of six-pack abs, consider using *real* people.

Whether you opt for line-art icons, photos, or a clever combination of both (i.e., photos for categories and icons for the specific styles in each section), the goals of your company's custom express generic catalog will be met: faster shopping for your buyers, better control of your sourcing, and reduced expenses for mailing.

▶ **Key Apparel Offerings.** Below is a list that includes the overwhelming bulk of the items sold in the industry, excluding items specific to athletics.

▶ **T-Shirts** – As noted in Chapter 6, T-shirts is the largest category in the business in terms of total units sold. And they certainly are the No. 1 staple of screen printers and heat press companies. Show icons (or photos) for both adult and youth styles. List the colors available, but be careful to avoid using exact manufacturers' names for the specialty colors, as it'll give away the brand. If you see colors termed canary yellow or spring green, you can call them "daffodil" and "meadow green." Rarely do express catalogs include the stacked color displays you see printed in the wholesalers' catalog. Use descriptive words instead for the colors offered. The fact of the matter is that catalogs printed on glossy paper don't show precise duplications of how the colors appear in fabric. And colors look different under incandescent light, fluorescent light, and sunlight. So, since there's no need to show color scales and the reproduction colors on glossy paper aren't accurate, don't trouble yourself. Remember, this is an express catalog, designed to get buyers zoned in on what they really want and what you really want to sell them.

On basic tees, most express catalogs do detail offerings in both 100% cotton, 50% polyester/50% cotton, and in recent years moisture-wicking fabrics.

Whether you decide to include long-sleeve tees, pocket tees, and tank tops in your express catalog is a matter of what part of the country your company sells in. (Tank tops have a real short season in Maine and North Dakota). If any or all of these items are important in your mix, give them separate treatment. Otherwise, you can group them in a collage-type set of icons and refer buyers to call your sales office or consult your price list.

Yet another emerging category is a growing array of T-shirts and other activewear styles tees created from moisture-wicking fabric. If performance garments are happening in your market, treat this category as it deserves. Or you can include it in the catch-all graphic group with tank tops, long-sleeve tees and pocket tees.

▶ **Ladies' Tops/Fashion Tops** – Some folks like to include various ladies' tops in their T-shirt section, while others prefer creating a separate heading for these items. Ascending in popularity and the fastest-growing segment of the general T-shirt category, ladies' shirts come in a huge array of styles. Pick two or three for your express catalog and show the corresponding icons for each. To attract the customer looking for something she doesn't readily see, mention in your text: "To see our complete collection of ladies' fashion tops, visit our showroom or call our sales office."

▶ **Fleecewear** – The best sellers here are hoodies, crewneck sweatshirts, and pants. Show icons for each item with descriptive copy. Which weight in these items you'll include in your mix varies by latitude; the farther north your market is the more likely you'll be touting 11 oz. goods. The farther south, it's the 7 oz. goods. You can always mention which weight fleece you sell, though don't devote too much space in the catalog beyond what's absolutely necessary, instead referring the buyer to your price list. In some areas, you might want to include in this category one or two Polar fleece selections (e.g., a vest, pullover, zip front, or quarter-zip front).

▶ **Golf Shirts** – Also called "polo shirts" and "coach's shirts" in some markets and diverse regions, the key items here are:

a) 100% cotton jersey knit golf shirt: It's inexpensive, sells well, and with screen printed or heat printed graphics, it's a very affordable alternative to traditional T-shirts and a low-priced alternative to the more upscale offerings in this category that usually are embellished with embroidery.

b.) 100% cotton piqué golf shirt: Moderately priced, it's the top item for most embroiderers.

c.) 100% cotton piqué golf shirt with a back tail: It's priced somewhat higher than the standard piqué golf shirts, it sells well. The back tail extends below the front hemline and usually has short (1"- 2") vented or V-notched sides. You'll also see this feature termed by different vendors as "extended back length with vents" and " drop-tail back with side vents."

Golf shirts beyond the three cited above are available in a myriad of styles, some with long sleeves or with pockets, and in a huge variety of collar trims, sleeve trims, and diverse fabrics featuring jacquard and herringbone patterns, stripes, color blocking, a variety of buttons and button colors (woodtone, pearlized with colors that match the fabric color, etc.), and other detailing. Fabrics range from jersey knit to piqué to interlock and other finer materials. Golf shirts also come in nationally branded styles (Nike, Bill Blass, etc.). Because of the dizzying array of offerings in this category, my suggestion is to keep the express catalog limited to the three general styles above, but with text that reads (and modify it as you like):

IF YOU DON'T SEE IT HERE...

To see additional golf shirt selections in herringbone, jacquard, or pigment-dye treatments, to golf shirts in other fabrics such as silk, inter-lock, moisture management, breathable mesh or with specialty options in custom styling or unique finishing, please visit our website [INSERT HERE] *or call your friendly local* [INSERT COMPANY] *sales representative. Or visit our showroom, open Monday through Friday 8am - 6pm and until noon on Saturday.*

▶ **Poplin and Denim** – These items have proven popular for decades, particularly in long-sleeve styles and those with a chest pocket (or two). Select one denim and one poplin and advise in the text that other selections are available on your website or by calling your sales office.

▶ **Shorts** – Frequently thought of in conjunction with athletic offerings, the shorts category is a sleeper. What has been demonstrated year after year by companies that offer shorts in their express catalogs is that they sell reasonably well, usually as an add-on sale and at very favorable margins. Offer three styles that make sense for your market. If you'd like to increase your sales by a percent or two, include shorts in your catalog and watch what happens!

▶ **Bags** – A perennial favorite, bags are something everyone can use. A bag is a great one-size-fits-all   solution – literally -- for giving or selling to event participants, club members, employees, tourists, and students. Bags are easy add-on sales and present you with better-than-average profit margins.

Two styles that matter most:

a.) Tote bags: From items that cost you a dollar or less to more durable styles, the two main variables here are size and whether or not the bag has a gusset. Show one icon (or a small collage) and list three or four sizes and available colors or color combinations.

b.) Roll bags: Also called gym bags and barrel bags, these Tootsie Roll-shaped bags will earn you extra business with schools, businesses, events merchandisers, and teams. Show one icon (or a small collage) and list three or four sizes and available colors or color combinations.

▶**Outerwear** – We're talking jackets here for the most part in a gazillion styles, weights, colors, color combinations, linings, and applications. Select four to six jackets that are appropriate for your customers and your climate. Base part of your offerings on cost (and selling price) to give your customers flexibility in their budgets. While most jackets in the industry are embroidered, one in particular lends itself to screen printing, particularly on the back. This style is the least expensive in the category, and it's commonly referred to as a coach's jacket. Features include a snap-button front, drawstring bottom, two front slash pockets, and elastic cuffs. It is available unlined, with a flannel lining or, for buyers in colder climates, with a heavier linings.

An important matter here is to call your jackets not by their style numbers or style names, but by terms that both help merchandise them and make it difficult for competitors to tell exactly which suppliers' jackets you're offering and quoting on. To position the jackets, use applicable terms such as "Mountaineer," "Mariner," "Whaler," "Tundra," or by towns, landmarks, and other features of your area.. If your company is located in New England, you might merchandise its outerwear selections dubbed "Green Mountain," "Bradley" or "Logan" (airports), "Winnipesauke (a lake)," "Newport," "Killington" (a ski resort), "Cape," "Yachtsman," "Clipper," "Berkshire," "Pilgrim," Patriot," "Yankee," "Town Square," "Paul Revere," "Nor'easter," or….well, you get the idea.

Note that express catalogs won't satisfy a certain percentage of buyers and you'll likely be showing these more astute buyers additional styles in your showroom and online. Also, an item that's sometimes hard to categorize is windshirts, which can be included with outerwear.

▶ **Caps** – Here's another category that could fill volumes of catalog pages, given the available styles, colors, graphic treatments, different types of construction, and other detail variables. For the express catalog, pick three styles: a low-profile cap, a visor, and a high-profile cap (or what I affectionately call a "geezer cap"). List colors and color combinations as you see fit for your market. And for the most demanding customers, once again refer them to your website, showroom, or to call your sales office.

▶ **Other Noteworthy Categories** – There are yet further product categories. Some are huge, some are small. And there are categories that go beyond decorated apparel, which are either too large to do justice to them for inclusion in an express catalog or are too small to merit space in your catalog, I've developed a simple way to handle such matters in the express catalog format. Essentially, do not even attempt to address them in any specific detail.

Instead, cite them in a section of the catalog to let the buyer know there's more to your story than just the key categories shown and that you welcome the opportunity to help buyers in search of these products.

It usually takes one-third to a half page to cover them. Your decisions are to determine which you choose to include and which to ignore. Below is a rundown on these categories and some text you might want to use to get your message across. You'll need to select which sections apply to your company and modify the text to suit your particular capabilities. I sometimes label this section "…and more!" I recommend you put the headers in reverse bars and add some simple iconography that illustrates the header. (I've suggested an icon or two for each category for your consideration.)

…and more!

Beyond our ability to provide you with superior-quality decorated wearables, [INSERT COMPANY] *is the* [area/town]*'s most comprehensive producer and supplier of custom graphics products. Below are some other things we can help you get right here in your own backyard!*

• *TEAMWEAR, LETTERING, AND NUMBERING* [*Suggested iconography:* baseball, football, hockey stick, basketball, soccer ball, darts, etc.]
   From head to toe, we've got you covered! Come to the official supplier of the [area/town]'s best-dressed teams for team uniforms along with multicolor team graphics and lettering along with multicolor player numbers. And get it all on one call!

• *KIDSTUFF* [*Suggested iconography:* Teddy bear, tricycle, bucket and shovel, etc.]
   Little folks get our attention, too. (As if they don't get enough already!) Tees, sweats, jackets, bibs, onesies, rompers, playsuits, and dresses. Infant wear from 6 months and toddler togs from Size 2 in a bunch of fun colors.

• *APRONS, TOWELS, BANDANAS, PILLOWCASES, LINENS, PLACEMATS, BATHING SUITS, SCRUBS, FAN HANDS, BEVERAGE INSULATORS, GOLF BALLS, STADIUM CUSHIONS, EXECUTIVE PORTFOLIOS, MOUSEPADS* [*Suggested iconography:* an asterisk]
   As one of the most experienced/most innovative textile decorators in [the area], we're fully equipped to meet your needs, specifications,

and deadlines. If it's made from fabric or foam, you can be certain we can decorate or personalize it!

• ***WORKWEAR*** [*Suggested iconography:* tractor, oil rig, CSR with phone]

You've come to the right place to outfit your employees, whether they work in casual wear, scrubs, shorts or heavy-duty winter gear. You'll find attractive, affordable solutions for them for working indoors, outdoors, and on the road. You also can have us design an online company store to make it easy for you and your staff to order directly from us or from you.

• ***SWEATERS*** [*Suggested iconography:* pullover vest, button-down sweater, collegiate cardigan]

From pullover vests to deluxe cardigans, you'll find sweaters in a wide array of styles and colors. And, of course, with embroidery, a sweater looks even sweeter!

• ***CRITTERWEAR*** [*Suggested iconography:* horse wearing a blanket, doggie cape]

For customized blankets for horses, customized pet carriers, doggie blankets, bird cage covers and just about any animal-related wearables or covers, you can count on us to work our magic!

• ***SIGNS & BANNERS*** [*Suggested iconography*: pennant, real estate sign, vehicle door sign]

We sell visibility for businesses, schools, churches, offices, and special events. Enjoy one-stop sourcing and in-house production of custom digitally printed, screen printed, and CAD-cut vinyl signs and banners.

• ***VEHICLE GRAPHICS*** [*Suggested iconography*: van with markings, race car, PWC (personal watercraft), trailer]

Vehicle advertising doesn't cost money. It *makes* money! We're your factory-direct, in-house production specialist for weather-resistant exterior markings for cars, trucks, vans, trailers, snowmobiles, space ships, tractors, boats, submarines, horse trailers, and off-road vehicles. We sell visibility for businesses, schools, churches, offices, and special events. And we install everything we sell!

• ***CERAMICS & GLASSWARE*** [*Suggested iconography:* coffee mug, beer stein, travel mug]

Looking for a local source for decorated mugs, tiles, ceramic plates, glassware, and bottles? Need it fast, too? Need just one mug or a thousand beer steins? Our in-house production gets you great quality, prompt turnaround, and affordable pricing.

• *PROMOTIONAL PRODUCTS* [*Suggested iconography:* calendar, desk set, balloons]

If you've seen it or need it invented, we can source it! We're PPAI/ASI-accredited direct distributors for custom imprinted pens, pins, calendars, key tags, executive gifts, balloons, emblematic jewelry, and thousands of items to fit every budget and every promotional application.

• *PROFESSIONAL GRAPHIC SERVICES* [*Suggested iconography:* artist's palette and brushes]

Our full-service art department creates graphics for all of our product lines. From concept to completion, [INSERT COMPANY] is your one-stop source for everything involved in delivering your order accurately, faithfully, on time, and in budget. To see some of our graphics, visit our showroom or visit our website.

• *TROPHIES, AWARDS, AND ENGRAVING* [*Suggested iconography:* trophy, blue ribbon]

Recognition of your players, members, top producers, and honorees of all types is what we provide for you to present your recipients. Our laser engraving capabilities enable us to work wonders on stone, acrylic, metal, and wood on a myriad of artistic, contemporary, and traditional awards media. And we can design it all in our art department to save you time and money.

• *COMPANY STORES* [*Suggested iconography:* computer monitor with an arrow pointing to an order form]

Our art department and I.T. professionals are ready to help you set up online stores for your business, school, organization, or special event to reach your members, participants, and fans. It's surprisingly affordable and will make your job easier!

• *BAGGING, TAGGING, CUSTOM PACKAGING, FULFILLMENT, WORLDWIDE SHIPPING* [*Suggested iconography*: Gift box with big bow, bagged T-shirt, shirt with tag]

If it's "presentation" you need such as bagging, tagging, gift boxing, or other finishing services, contact our sale office to discuss enhancing the packaging and delivery of your orders. Put our crew to work for you!

Select the applicable merchandising sections, twist 'em, turn 'em, and add sections as you need to tell the rest of your story. As for touting those decorating technologies you provide in-house, if they're not part of your company name or descriptors, you can add a brief paragraph in the "….and more!" section or with the use of simple bullet copy on the front cover, as shown below:

- *SCREEN PRINTING*
- *EMBROIDERY*
- *HEAT PRINTING*
- *CAD-CUTTING*
- *DIGITAL PRINTING*
- *SUBLIMATION PRINTING*
- *PAD PRINTING*
- *ENGRAVING/LASER ENGRAVING*
- *HOT STAMPING*
- *SANDBLASTING*
- *RHINESTONING*

Once you've assembled the elements of your own custom express catalog, you've done most of the work for adding an express section to your website.

2. Catalogs from Wholesalers and Manufacturers

The industry's leading manufacturers and distributors of apparel "blanks" (undecorated shirts, as they're commonly referred to in the trade) develop their catalogs and websites for use by both their customers and their customers' customers. These beautiful, full-color catalogs are quite comprehensive in their treatments of the available offerings as to styles, sizes, and colors. They're also excellent tools for researching products, product specifications, colors as accurately as possible for printing on paper, and, in my humble opinion, are ideal for use with certain types of customers. The operative words here are "certain types." Said certain type customers include those who are inanely fussy and who think they know what they're looking at; and those who are knowledgeable, more sophisticated purchasers of decorated apparel. This latter group possesses solid experience, a modicum of expertise, and usually has the authority to buy large quantities -- at least hundreds of units or hundreds or thousands of units.

Do you need the shirts to be shown on models? Not really. People know what a T-shirt and a hoodie look like. Professional models can cost several hundred dollars (and up) per day for photo-shoots. But if you do want to show people, your staff, family, children, grandchildren, and friends will suffice as models for most express catalogs.

Offered to trade buyers with the front imprinted with the buyer's company name, address, phone number, and website, the professionally produced distributors' catalogs with lovely models and generally perfect people are provided (in most cases) free of charge. (Additional quantities can be purchased at reasonable fares). The quantity of free catalogs is commensurate with the volume of annual purchases, the vendor's judgment as to the potential volume that can be developed and other subjective issues. While these catalogs promote the various brands of apparel offered, there is no disclosure of the distributor, so sellers can be confident their customers will not see where the goods are being sourced by the decorator.

Dumb Mistake No. 12
Attempting to offer every conceivable garment and accessory to all customers without placing reasonable and intelligent limits on their choices.

Now for the downsides and deficiencies of the beautiful catalogs....

• Rarely, if ever, do the garments shown appear with decoration – that's the reason why people buy from *you*!

• They are expensive to mail -- $4 to $6 each depending upon the carrier.

• Since they're available to virtually every trade seller, many companies in the same areas and markets all show the same vendor catalogs to their customers. The only discernable difference a customer sees is the seller's imprint. Using these catalogs is the antithesis of good positioning strategy, clear differentiation of your company, and efficient selling.

• The catalogs are premised on the conventional wisdom that says in effect, "Just hand the customer the catalog or show it online and let the customer buy whatever he or she chooses" – without regard to selecting brands that you, the decorator and/or re-seller, prefer to promote and decorate.

• The offerings oftentimes confuse buyers as to what they think they should buy, causing you to spend additional time explaining details and, in most cases, getting the customer to buy what you wanted him to buy anyhow!

My strong bias against using the distributors' catalogs is derived from the reasons above and decades of observations that, for most buyers, the garments they buy are essentially what industry professionals recommend to them. My experience, and counsel, here is to use these resources mainly for their primary intended purpose – to inform you about the products you need to buy. For those buyers who know what they're doing and understand what they're looking at, yes, giving them the distributors' catalogs is a worthy effort. But you'll find even most of these buyers usually will end up agreeing with your recommendations. The fact that our distributors provide the bulk of these catalogs to apparel decorators with the seller's imprint without charge, however, means you can accept the largesse of your vendors for use with special customers and save your own money for producing literature that serves your own purposes, not your vendors'.

When we look at developing your website (in Chapter 18), my opinion about availing yourself of using the distributors' website programs will be quite different and to the extent that I endorse most of the vendor website programs as affordable, worthwhile resources.

One final comment: Of the 24 ways to get your customers to love you, do note that I chose to make developing your own catalog the first discussion of these merchandising mechanisms. That's because I view this effort to be the most important of all, but only so when combined with developing your own price list to go with it.

And a piece of great news: once you've completed assembling the elements of your express catalog, you've also completed taking care of one of the most critical responsibilities of building your website insofar as showing your key offerings. In the next chapter, I'll be addressing the next most important function: your price list.

CHAPTER 17

24 WAYS TO GET YOUR CUSTOMERS TO LOVE YOU

▪ Identity-Builder W2GC2♥U No. 2: Your Price List

The Art and Science of Pricing

The apparel graphics industry executive entered the Secret Chamber of Truth and bowed reverently to the serene figure sitting cross-legged before him. After a moment of meditation, the Shaolin Priest, spoke: "Welcome, Grasshopper! What wisdom do you seek today?"

"Master, I come to you in search of the One True Path regarding the mysteries of pricing custom screen printed and custom embroidered apparel."

The century-old sage listened patiently as the entrepreneur recounted his frustrations in pricing decorated apparel. After reflecting on the petitioner's woes, the priest turned to his T-shirt clad student and warbled in a low but audible tone, "Ahhhh, pricing! Yes, it is indeed the elusive muse of your noble apparel graphics craft. It is true that an understanding of its ways can be achieved, but one must first prepare spiritually for a journey into such multiple enigmas. Snatch these pebbles from my hand, Grasshopper, and look deep into them for the answer. As you gaze, free your mind of the conventional wisdom that teaches "pricing is simply a matter of numbers in which you a.) in put your costs, b.) mix in some hopefulness and good luck, c.) add a dash of intuition, and then d.) tack on what you think would represent a fair return on your investment of time and effort."

"Then, is there actually One True Path concerning pricing, Master? And how will I know when I have come upon it?"

"You will encounter Many Paths. Which one is true for your company, Grasshopper, will manifest itself to you soon enough. Now, go in search of the wisdom you seek on pricing."

So much for the Kung Fu Theory of Pricing, except that the truth about divining the key elements of pricing indeed entails a great deal of introspection and investigation. More importantly, you'll come to a realization that apparel graphics pricing is more art than science.

For some apparel decorators, pricing seems like a watching a TV game show where the host scurries out from behind the curtain and announces: "OK, contestants, let's go to the Magic Pricing Wheel. Darts ready? . . . Fire!" Still others profess that their own process of pricing simply comes down to finding out what price they have to beat and beating it.

I'll first address some Big Myths in our industry about how prices are or should be determined.

BIG MYTH No. 1: You need to know what it costs to run your shop per hour (YN2K). Once you know this, you'll know what to charge to break even. Oh, yeah, and then you need to add a profit.

This You-Need-To-Know myth --"YN2K" for short -- has been around since the industry's infancy. It's the "system" you've been fed by technical consultants and others with no backgrounds whatsoever in finance or accounting, nor who've ever actually done what they advocate. I say this because it's a practical impossibility in addition to being a methodological farce.

YN2K is bad science and intellectual chicanery. My affectionate term for it is MythMath! Here's what its proponents say you should do to calculate your prices:

1.) You determine all your business expenses over the course of a year even though some expenses are fixed and some are variable. But, hey, you have to start somewhere.

2.) Decide how many weeks you plan to work per year and then divide your yearly costs by the number of weeks you plan to work. While it might seem logical to divide the weekly overhead by 40 (hours), you need to identify how many hours per week your machine really runs.

3.) Then compute your cost by impressions or stitch count, determining how many impressions your equipment can print or how many stitches your machine can sew per hour. Of course, you also need to know how many minutes per hour your equipment is actually printing or sewing, so you can adjust your formula accordingly. (Still with me?)

4.) When you're done calculating all these figures, you can the figure your costs per printing impression or per-thousand-stitches. From there you add profit and -- voila! -- you've done your pricing!

This is pure baloney. My advice on YN2K is that a.) you should actually try to determine all these figures ONCE, b.) write 'em down on a piece of loose leaf paper, c.) fold it into a paper airplane and d.) launch it from the top of the Empire State Building on a windy day and see how far it flies. For better results, write your numbers on sturdier stock.

Readers of this book who are industry veterans have heard this Myth-Math many times before, but I don't know a single successful entrepreneur in this business who actually uses it to determine pricing. Not *one*!

BIG MYTH No. 2: Pricing must be based on cost.

Knowing your costs is certainly important. But the perceived value of your products has considerably more bearing on what you charge -- or should charge -- than your costs. I'll explore the mechanics of cost-based pricing in depth shortly, along with discussing how marketplace realities impact the math.

BIG MYTH No. 3: For most customers, price is the most important factor in their decision on sourcing decorated apparel.

If you firmly believe this myth -- that pricing is the most important factor for buyers, your career in this industry is probably doomed to failure or at best earning only a marginal living someday.

Pricing has to be seen in its proper perspective. Too many -- perhaps most -- screen printers and embroiderers believe the idea that all customers are hung up on price. But you already know that those buyers who make price their first -- and only -- concern aren't likely to let you make much money, if any, on the deal to begin with. You also know these people are usually the most troublesome to work with and often prove to be among the most difficult to collect money from, too.

Why not just leave the ridiculously cheap work to your low-ball competitors in their never-ending struggle for viability and profitability? If someone else in your chosen marketplace consistently wins orders at prices you find unfathomable, let him! Your counter strategy should be 1.) to concede such orders to these competitors, who will in time be eliminated by the laws of economics; and 2.) to rethink and reposition your marketing and selling efforts to reach better-quality accounts.

But there's at least one good reason to enjoy having a couple low ballers in your neighborhood: eventually you can pick up their equipment at bargain basement prices when their businesses fail.

For most legitimate buyers, price is only ONE factor in their decision. Far outweighing a customer's decision to buy on price alone are the collective matters about service, quality, rapport, and trust. After you've survived the math assignment that looms ahead, you'll learn how to educate your customer about the non-financial aspects of pricing. These include the strategic issues and tactical mechanisms that'll help you sell your goods at prices sufficient to enable you to make money, build equity in your company, and sidestep bottom-dwelling competitors. I promise!

Allow me to digress for a moment. I have been teaching seminars on pricing at the Imprinted Sportswear Shows and at Imprint Canada Shows since 1982. I've also created literally hundreds of price lists for clients in different ends of the industry and throughout the Americas and Europe. What I've learned and can share with readers from my forty years' experience is that using the conventional wisdom methodologies encompassed in the various pricing myths cited above provide no solution to creating effective price lists nor for engendering profitability. Read the rest of this chapter with a very open mind.

Incorporate its concepts into your thinking. And when you create your next – or your first – price list, know you'll be making adjustments along the way, modifications that reflect competitive pressures as well as opportunities to expand your margins as your craftsmanship, marketing position, and reputation grow.

Putting the three Big Myths irrevocably behind you, how then is pricing properly accomplished? Is there a simple formula that does the job? What are the most important factors in determining what to charge?

First, you need to realize the real purpose of your company is to make money, not to subsidize your customers or competitors by unrealistically underpricing your wares.

OK, let's do some algebra. Algebra!? You know, that course in you took in high school that you were certain would be worthless for the rest of your life?

Just as there are thousands of companies in our industry, there are seemingly thousands of pricing systems. Whatever formula you've been using in your business may have worked until now, but the math expressed in the equation below will help you better understand the key components of pricing as well as enable you to refine your own pricing system to make it work to your advantage.

I'll also look at other prevalent pricing methodologies later in this chapter.

Figure 1: COST -BASED PRICING FOR DECORATED GARMENTS

$$\left(\left[\cfrac{\left(\cfrac{[(G \times 1.W) + D]}{R \text{ of } m}\right)}{R \text{ of } P}\right]\middle/ R \text{ of } C\right) + F$$

= The Selling Price of
a Decorated Garment

G = Garment
W = Waste
D = Decorating Cost
R = Reciprocal
m = Overhead & Administration
P = Profit Margin
C = Commission
F = Inbound Freight

I'll define the variables in this formula, track the algebra, and arrive at a correct answer. I'll be inserting component prices in the equation along the way, so you can follow the math using real numbers.

1. G = Garment

G represents the garment you're pricing -- undecorated, the way it comes into your warehouse or staging area from your vendor. In this formula, G is expressed as a single unit (as opposed to a dozen).

2. W = Waste & Spoilage

W represents the factor used to account for waste and spoilage, whatever its cause or source. Screw-ups come with the territory. And on rare occasion, you receive a shirt with a manufacturing defect that makes it unsalable as first-quality merchandise. Who pays for these garments? You? The mill or the distributor you buy from? The customer? All of your customers?

Regardless of how you answer, it has to be paid for, unless, of course, you diligently return defective merchandise to its source for credit or replacement.

The **W** figure is expressed in hundredths. That means, if you determine that in your shop 3% of what you buy is lost to workmanship errors and/or manufacturing defects, the W factor is .03 and must be added to your garment cost. The way to capture it in the formula is by multiplying the garment cost, **G**, by 1.03.

So, for a garment that costs you $3.00 (excluding freight in) in a company with a 3% shop error rate, you'll calculate your garment cost with a 3% upcharge. How you compute this is: $3.00 x 1.03, giving you a more realistic and more accurate garment cost of $3.09, as shown in Figure 2.

Figure 2: $[(G \times 1.W) = \$3.00 \times 1.03 = \$3.09]$

In case you're wondering what the average waste and spoilage percentage is for the industry as a whole, it's about 1½ %. (Source: Apparel Graphics Institute surveys since 1982). This doesn't necessarily mean that you ruin 1½ garments per 100 shirts in production. More likely, your orders run well and there's normally little or no waste or spoilage. What generally causes headaches, however, is when you screw up an entire order. (3% waste and spoilage would be a very high and unacceptable rate to be sure).

Think of the inclusion of a waste and spoilage component in your formula as insuring yourself against the likelihood of screw-ups, giving you a built-in revenue source for covering misprints, rejects, samples that disappear, walkaways, and covering irksome customers who refuse to pay you, even when you've scrupulously followed their instructions and get their approvals every step of the way. Waste and spoilage is one of many areas totally unaddressed by the YN2K myths.

3. D = Decorating Cost

D is the cost-per-unit you incur in screen printing or embroidering a garment or the price you pay for a heat transfer and applying it. **D** also covers any other decorating process such as embossing and foiling as well as the aggregated cost for any combination of apparel decorating processes. Decorating costs will vary from shop to shop, by complexity of the job, and the length of a production run. (Computing this figure in your shop is a major topic in itself, one not covered in this book due to its complexity and the realistic limits of space). For now, **D** means whatever decorating cost you assign for doing the job you're setting out do. This element includes both the labor and the materials consumed in the process (ink, solvent, spray adhesive, thread, backing, etc.).

The formula's top bracketed component -- [(G x 1.W) + D] -- now captures what you've paid for the garment (G), accommodates errors (W), and recovers what you spend on decorating (D).

Using an assigned decorating cost of 50 cents, say, for a one-color print, and inserting it into the equation in Figure 1, you'll arrive at $3.59.

Figure 3: $[(G \times 1.W) + D] = \$3.00 \times 1.03 \ (= \$3.09) + .50 = \$3.59$

4. *m* = Overhead & Administration

m is the pricing component you need to include to cover your overhead and administration costs -- all of the *other* costs in running your business. It'll be expressed in hundredths.

The optimum method for determining your company's *m* factor begins with maintaining timely and accurate accounting in your monthly Profit & Loss statement. With careful tracking, you simply add up all of your fixed and variable costs excluding, however, a.) garments and inbound freight; b.) production labor (including what your company pays in mandated employment taxes and benefits); c.) consumable materials; and d.) sales commissions. In figuring your overhead expenses, do include salaries and wages and employment taxes and benefits paid to owners, officers, administrative personnel, and non-commissioned sales and customer service personnel. (For learning how to properly organize these items in your accounting, read my article, "Industry Operating Ratios: The Measure of Success" on pages 30-62 in the February 2001 issue of *Impressions Magazine* and review the Apparel Graphics Institute's "Recommended Chart of Accounts for Apparel Graphics Companies" found on page 63 of that same issue).

Once you arrive at your total costs for overhead and administration, divide this figure by your total revenues. The resulting ratio is the figure you input for *m* in your pricing.

Before I return to *m* and where it goes in the equation, I need to discuss reciprocals. With apologies to mathematicians to eschew a discussion about the mathematical theorems behind reciprocals, all you need to know for your purposes here is that "a *reciprocal*" is simply one of two numbers that add up to the number 1. Simply put, the reciprocal of .6 is .4, the reciprocal of .3 is .7, and the reciprocal of .21 is .79. What is the reciprocal of .56?   If you answered ".44," you understand what you need to know about reciprocals to work the whole formula.

I'll input the **_Reciprocal of m_** into the formula to arrive at a figure that tells you your break-even point in pricing. After that, you'll calculate for profit as well as accommodate whatever percentage you pay for sales commissions, if any.

I'll assign a figure of 17% to cover overhead and administration. The reciprocal of .17 is .83. You can now add your overhead and administration by dividing the total of [(G x 1.W) + D] by .83 (to cover the 17% you're spending to keep the doors open).

Figure 4:

$$\frac{[\ \underline{(G \times 1.W) + D}\ ]}{R\ of\ m} = \frac{[\ (\$3.00 \times 1.03)\ +\ .50\ ]}{.83}\ {\scriptstyle(=\$3.59)}\ \begin{matrix}= \$4.33\\ {\scriptstyle (\$3.59\ div.\ by\ the\ reciprocal\ of\ .17)}\end{matrix}$$

You're dividing the $3.59 total of the garment-plus-waste-plus-decorating cost (from the figure above) by .83. This new subtotal is $4.33, the amount you've paid for garments, labor, and your general overhead. Excluding preparation charges (for which most companies invoice separately) and the corresponding preparation expenses for them, you've now arrived at the "break-even" price.

At this juncture, neither your company nor your salesperson has made any money. But at break even, you can at least keep the doors open while you -- the owner -- of course, still work for free. Now let's get to rewarding your company and then compensating a salesperson.

5. P = Profit

P is the pricing component you elect to earn on the sales you generate. The **P-factor** also is the primary reason you went into this business. Think of it as oxygen, without which, you suffocate. The amount of profit you're building here is purposely engineered to be calculated *prior to* allowing for the payment of commissions to salespeople, which I'll address momentarily.

What's a fair profit level? Is there a "correct" level of profit in our industry?

"Fair profit" is a subjective term that varies from entrepreneur to entrepreneur. And, no, there is no one-size-fits-all "correct" profit level for the industry, occasioned by the same subjectivity issue. Sure, we'd all like to maximize our return-on-investment, but the marketplace, the economy, and your competitors all have some say on what you can charge and within what price latitudes.

I'll save my discussion on "pricing as marketing" until later; but for our purposes here and now, I can safely say a profit figure for insertion will typically be in the latitude of 20-40% for custom orders (not retail orders of one or a few garments, nor contract work run on someone else's garments). Remember, this window does not include what you'd pay in commissions or keep as additional profit if no one's receiving any commissions.

From my experience working inside more than 600 apparel graphics companies for the past three decades, I can tell you that a realistic overall figure for building profit into your formula is in the 25-30% range *at this juncture in the formula*. The figure will likely be much higher for small orders and somewhat lower for larger orders.

To insert a profit (or more precisely, a "margin" as used here), divide the total of everything you've done so far by the reciprocal of whatever level of profit you think you can achieve. For this example, I'll assign a profit level of 25% into the equation, the reciprocal of which is .75. In Figure 5 below, you can see it applied in the equation.

Figure 5:

$$\frac{[\ (\mathbf{G \times 1.W}) + \mathbf{D}\ ]}{R\ of\ P} = \frac{[\ (\$3.00 \times 1.03)\ +\ .50\ ]}{.75} \; (= \$4.33)$$

$$\frac{R\ of\ m}{R\ of\ P} = \frac{.83}{.75} = \$5.77$$

Earlier, I calculated that the break-even point on this garment was $4.33. Now, building in a realistic 25% margin into the equation, the company earns (on paper, anyhow) $1.44 on this one unit ($5.77 - $4.33 = $1.44).

To this point, you've paid for all your garments, charged your customer a small "insurance premium" (the **W** factor) to cover possible mistakes, paid everyone in production and in the office, and paid for your supplies to net your company $1.44 on this garment. The only key component yet unapplied in your formula is what you'll pay a salesperson.

6. C = Commissions

C is the percentage paid as a commission to a salesperson. Whether this individual works full-time or part time, inside or outside, is classified as an employee or an independent contractor are not issues in this discussion. What we're providing for right now is simply a mechanism for compensating a salesperson.

Continuing with the formula, I'll assign a commission level of 10% (a typical ratio in small to medium orders), the reciprocal of which is .90. In Figure 6, divide the $5.77 price by .90 and arrive at $6.41.

Figure 6:

$$[\underline{(G \times 1.W)+D}]=[\underline{(\$3.00 \times 1.03) + .50}] \; (= \$4.33)$$

$$\frac{R \; of \; m}{} \;=\; \frac{.83}{}$$

$$\frac{R \; of \; P}{R \; of \; C} \;=\; \frac{.75}{.90} \quad (= \$5.77)$$

$$R \; of \; C \;=\; .90 \qquad = \mathbf{\$6.41}$$

I've now calculated everything and everybody except one specific cost: Inbound freight.

7. F = Freight (or "Landing Cost")

F is the actual amount you pay for getting the garment from its source to your door. Why has it been included as the *last step* of the equation instead of being included at the beginning of the process lumped in with garment cost, as most companies do?

Had I added the freight-in cost to the garment cost and went through all the math here, a 10¢ freight cost would become about 21¢ cents in the final price. Though we're talking pennies, it would have just added slightly more than 11¢ additional to the price -- 11¢ that you don't have to add. What's the big deal? Answer: The reality is that a dime too high here and there can kill a sale. Since your main goal is to sell an order and make money on what you sell and do, I, for one, don't believe you need to mark-up freight, rather merely recover it as a pass-through charge.

This same principle of not marking up what you don't have to can be argued for the W factor. The nine additional cents added for "error insurance" in Figure 2, calculated through the formula, ends up in the final price at just over 20¢. Had I added the 9¢ at the back end of the equation – as a pass-through item – I'd get a selling price that's about a dime lower.

I've shown in the equation one possible pass-through item (W) at the front end of the formula and another pass-through item (F) at the finish line. So, which is correct? Should you calculate freight-in and waste at the beginning of the equation, or add either or both at the back end? Well, how you elect to handle this and whichever answer you give is the correct answer. The arguments for including such things as freight and waste factors at the front end and working the costs through the formula's subsequent phases come down to a.) "I don't think the slightly higher price (20¢ total in this example) makes much of a difference;" b.) "I can get away with it;" and c.) "I know I'll have some built-in room to maneuver when I need to shave some coins off my price."

The argument favoring back-end pass-through is that it helps keep the price a few percentage points lower, and hence, slightly more competitive. Each justification on both sides of the fence here is valid.   Pick the rationale that works for you.

To complete the final phase then, I'll assign 10¢/unit for freight-in and add it to the $6.41 figure you arrived at after you built in a 10% commission. You're now at $6.51 ($6.41 + .10 = $6.51), which I'll round off to $6.50.

Now, I'll use the formula to price an embroidered golf shirt that includes 7,000 stitches. The garment cost is $8.25 with a 3% waste allowance and I'll assign a decorating cost of $2.45 per unit. As in the first example, *m* will be 17%, the profit margin at 25%, the commission level at 10%, and I'll recover 30¢ per unit for freight-in. (I'll round all figures as I go through the paces).

Figure 7:

$$\frac{[\ (G \times 1.W)+D\ ]}{\begin{array}{c} R\ of\ m \\ R\ of\ P \\ R\ of\ C \\ +\ F \end{array}} = \frac{[\ (\$8.25 \times 1.03)\ +\ 2.45\ ]}{\begin{array}{c} .83 \\ .75 \\ .90 \\ 30\cent \end{array}}$$

(= $10.95)
(= $13.19)
(= $17.59)
(= $19.54)
(= $19.84)

Call it $20.00, $19.95, or $19.75 when you're ready to apply it to quantity breaks and the size of the order in units, which to this point I haven't addressed. What do you do with these $6.50 and $19.95 prices vis-à-vis the quantity breaks you're offering? I'll look at applying these figures shortly, but I'll have several options for distributing the pricing, some better than others, and all subject to your own preferences and thinking.

Pencils ready? Here's your final exam to see if you've learned the formula....

Price an embroidered golf shirt. G = $7.50 with a 2% W factor. The assigned decorating cost for this is $2.00/unit for 6,000 stitches in one location. *m* is 13%, the profit margin is 30%, the commission level is 10%, and you'll recover .25 cents for inbound freight.

OK, you do the math on this and then review the calculations below to see if you scored a bullseye.

- •
- •
- •
- •
- •

The correct answer is **$17.85.**

The math is:
$ 7.50 (G) x 1.02 (W)   = $ 7.65
$ 7.65 + 2.00 (D)   = $ 9.65
$ 9.65 (÷) .87 (the R of .13 *m*)   = $11.09
$11.09 (÷) .70 (the R of .30 P)   = $15.84
$15.84 (÷) .90 (the R of .10 C)   = $17.60
$17.60 + 25¢ (F)   = $17.85

Congratulations if you got it right. (Still having trouble? E-mail me at markvenit@cs.com for help).

Having addressed some of the underlying assumptions, sales tools, and marketing objectives in determining your pricing, you can now proceed onto the next phase of the process.

The expanded context for how you're about to make decisions on pricing and quantity breaks allows you to now to sprinkle in marketing components that help you get higher prices, add more (perceived) value for your products and services, increase sales, and propel you toward improved profitability.

You'll be putting that $6.50 price you arrived at a few pages back in play momentarily as I begin the discussion of quantity breaks. $6.50 isn't the final price or the only price for the $3.00 garment you started with in the first example. I call this $6.50 price "a marker price," one that will be ratcheted higher and lower to meet both marketing and reasonable profitability goals as well as customer expectations.

Quantity breaks in our industry are traditionally expressed in dozens, but there's no standard for these breaks. Some companies create their own levels based on competitors' breaks, guesswork, or the "It's what we've always used" theory. I'll recommend, however, a set of quantity breaks that creates price *incentives* and *disincentives* for buyers.

Specifically, I generally favor breaks in the range of one, two, four, six, 12, 24, and 48 dozen intervals. (For smaller companies selling custom embroidered apparel, I usually recommend one-half dozen pieces as a minimum). Many industry companies, though, have additional or fewer breaks and at differing intervals.

Typically, quantity price breaks are priced in units (not dozens) and appear on price lists in either of the two formats shown in Figure 8

Figure 8: **Traditional Formats for Quantity Breaks**

a.	12	24	48	72	144	288	576 + Up
b.	12 - 23	24 - 47	48 -71	72 - 143	144 - 287	288 - 575	576 + Up

Line a. shows it simpler and cleaner, expressed in numbers divisible by 12. Line b. is the common form used by companies whose owners feel they need to talk in more precise terms. Either form works, but a lesson I learned from my accountant in the mid-1970s forever changed my thinking.

We were reviewing a proposed price list when he turned to me and declared, "Hey, you and the egg people are the only folks on the planet who think in dozens! *Normal* folks think in tens, twenty-fives, and hundreds." I explained how our goods are packaged and sold to us in dozens and pieces by our vendors, blah, blah, blah. Given that many other industries think in dozens – such as for toys and baked goods to name a few -- his argument was a bit of an exaggeration. But he made his point and sure got my attention when he asked, "Would you mind if I showed you a way to make things easier for your customers AND net you a 4% increase in sales for the *rest of your life -- without spending a penny extra*?"

I perked up, took the bait and said, "Show me!"

"Stop thinking like an egg man! Think like a *normal* person!"

"*Goo goo ka choob!*," was my reply. (Note to younger readers: the term "*Goo goo ka choob!*" is from the Beatles song, "I Am the Walrus.")

So where was my extra 4%?

He continued that "Someone who's placing an order for 144 shirts doesn't exactly take orders for exactly 144 shirts, right? They're looking at next-quantity prices to see if buying that next quantity makes better sense price-wise." Other than the one dozen minimum that I held was the minimum I wanted to offer, egg man or no egg man, he suggested we increase our 24-unit bracket to 25, 48 to 50, 144 to 150, 288 to 300, and 576 to 600. It all made perfect sense. And from that day on, all the price lists I've engineered for clients have reflected his idea, which has paid my clients back many times over for my professional fees.

Figure 9 below shows how virtually all of my clients arrange their prices for custom decorated apparel, in my "4%-Bonus Price List" format.

The additional units you'll sell are yours for the taking. Think about

Figure 9: **"The 4%-Bonus Price List"**

▶ Traditional	12	24	48	72	144	288	576 + Up
▶ +4% System	12	25	50	75	150	300	600 + Up

how many more thousands of dollars this device will be worth to you during your company's lifetime!

Now, let's see where the $6.50 T-shirt price fits best.

Two facts about orders provide insight here. Both are derived from surveys conducted by the Apparel Graphics Institute measuring average orders. Fact 1: The *statistical average* order for custom screen printed garments is 6 to 10 dozen. Fact 2: The *statistical average* order for custom embroidered garments is 3 to 6 dozen. Sure, there are lots of small orders of lesser amounts and some giant orders of a thousand units or more, but the average orders are in fact in the stated ranges. This means that you have to be reasonably competitive in these ranges while also keeping a price that's high enough to make some money. Hence, the $6.50 T-shirt price you calculated earlier should be inserted where you need it most -- at the 75-unit break (or 72, if you don't "get it" yet).

What should the rest of the price distribution be?

Figure 10: **Inserting the Marker Price**

At this point, your arrangement is:

Quantity (in units)	12	25	50	**75**	150	300	600 + Up
Price				**$6.50**			

Since you know smaller orders cost you more to administer and produce on a per-unit basis, the 50-unit price logically should be somewhat higher than the 75-unit price, high enough to give you some additional margin and higher enough to make the 75-unit price look more attractive if the customer can commit to this higher quantity. My call here is to put another 50¢ per unit in the cash register for you, translating to a 50-unit price of $7.00.

You need to plug in even higher prices for the 25- and 12-unit quantities. I'll add a dollar to the 25-unit level and another buck at the 12-piece minimum. I know from experience most firms in our industry can get these prices. Moreover, if I don't add these dollars to the shorter quantities, you probably won't make any money, a reality I trust industry veterans agree with and understand well. See Figure 11 for lower quantity prices.

The same logic applies to higher quantities, except now you're

Figure 11: **Price Distribution** (*based on the $3.00 unit price of the first equation studied*)

Quantity (in units)	12	25	50	75	150	300	600 + Up
Price	$9.00	$8.00	$7.00	$6.50			

acknowledging the customer's expectation that more goods should cost less per unit. In effect, you need to satisfy this expectation as well as provide incentives to entice the buyer, if possible, to buy more, as shown in Figure 12 below.

You, of course, can set your own prices at higher and lower levels to

Figure 12: **Price Distribution**

Quantity (in units)	12	25	50	75	150	300	600 + Up
Price		$9.00	$8.00	$7.00	$6.50	$6.00	$5.75 $5.50

reflect what you believe will provide appropriate pricing incentives and disincentive for your customers, in *your* area, and with at least some deference to the "going rate" of your competitors.

And for those readers who want to take a slightly more "sales-y" approach, you might elect to massage your numbers as most retailers would, as seen in Figure 13.

For a second example of price distribution, I'll apply the same prin-

Figure 13: **"Sales-y" Price Distribution** (*compared to the pricing in Figure 12*)

Quantity (in units)	12	25	50	75	150	300	600 + Up
Price		$8.95	$7.95	$6.95	$6.49	$5.95	$5.75 $5.49

ciples to the embroidered $8.25 golf shirt I priced earlier at $19.84. You'll recall that the statistical average order for custom embroidered garments is between three and six dozen, as cited earlier. See Figure 14 for an approximation of the price points.

My own preference is for the prices in Figure 13, but this is a choco-

Figure 14: **Price Distribution**

Quantity (in units)	12	25	50	75	150	300	600+Up
Price		$24.95	$21.95	$19.95	$18.50	$17.95	$16.50 $15.25

late-or-vanilla matter -- either answer is correct and essentially depends on your own perspective.

To get started on your price list, use the formula to set your marker price for five to 10 key items: a 100% cotton heavyweight T-shirt, a cap, a mid-range golf shirt, a 50/50 sweatshirt, a promotional tote bag, a denim shirt, etc. Then, distribute the prices using good judgment and your own experience. You'll get the hang of it quickly enough and realize that there's ample room for opinion and interpretation on how the numbers play out and interact.

Once you've priced your company's basic T-shirt offering in white, move on to pricing light, dark, and premium color garments. Calculate the costs of the corresponding youth sizes. You'll find that a color T-shirt that costs 50¢ to $1 more than white can be inserted into the equation by adding somewhere between 90¢ cents and $2 in the key bracket ranges -- a little more for lower quantities, and a bit lower in the higher quantities. Other garments can be shown with a relatively constant add-on price, as in showing prices for XXL through XXXXL, pocketed tees, and long-sleeve tees.

The first comprehensive price list you make -- a total of 30 to 60 items -- will cover (based on Apparel Graphics Institute survey data 97% of what you sell. This exercise will be stimulating, challenging, frustrating, and it'll take a tedious day or two. But after doing your first real price, the process will become easier and faster the second time. By the third time you do a price list, you can zip through the assignment in a few hours. The payoff is not only a smart marketing communications document, but a resource that'll eliminate many redundant tasks when you're quoting, selling, and processing orders.

By now you should see pricing as a merchandising tool to discourage unprofitable orders and *en*courage profitable production runs. Your price list and your brand of salesmanship should be designed to provide incentives for buyers to go for more ink colors, higher stitch counts, additional areas for decoration and move up to the next higher-quantity price breaks in more productive runs wherever appropriate.

I need to add a word here about pricing large orders, say, 50 to 100 dozen garments and up. When you're quoting on this volume range or publishing major-quantity pricing on your price lists, high volume numbers need to be kept on the conservative side. Why? Because collective experience says that customers buying these quantities don't ask you for pricing, they often *tell* you the numbers they want to hear. They're also in a position to demand considerably lower fares.

Smaller apparel graphics companies must be careful not to fall into the dangerous price pit when quoting on or listing pricing for large orders that require production capacity or resources greater than what your firm has in house. Many owners of small companies peremptorily rule out sending their work to contract printers and embroiderers, insisting on doing everything in their own shops.

But for small companies handling big orders, pricing high quantities based on screen printing them in house with manual equipment or embroidering them on one- or two-head machines is folly. Even if it's produced in house, the job would have to be priced as being done on an automatic press or a 15-head machine if it's a price that will "fly." That's how the big guys are pricing it, and either you set prices in the prevailing ranges or you forfeit ever being in contention for large orders.

It's also recommended here that such orders won by small companies are better farmed out to contract printers and embroiderers. Contrary to the assertion by small-company entrepreneurs that no one else can equal their level of craftsmanship or run even nearly as conscientiously as they do, the fact of the matter is that a professional contract house can do at least as well as you can, and very probably better. It *has* to, or it's out of business!

Dumb Mistake No. 13
Having any type of catalog, but not making a price list available to your customers and prospects.

Being concerned about what your competitors are charging for the same type of products, services, and quantities is always going to be an issue -- a big issue for many and a small issue for others. A little low-level industrial espionage to ascertain pricing on key categories, however, does have its place and can go a long way in helping a company keep a pulse on the marketplace and establish some reference points for maintaining its pricing within the context of a company's market position. (It doesn't take a lot of imagination to figure out how to go about getting prices, catalogs, and price lists from competitors and learning more about what they do right -- and hopefully what *you* can do better).

Being asked to meet competitors' prices if they're significantly lower than yours is a perpetual challenge. But if your prices are in the general ballpark of your area or special market, the quality of your marketing efforts as discussed earlier is where your pricing becomes less of an issue for a buyer who really wants to do business with you for all the right reasons. If anyone reading this book still thinks price is everything, ask yourself: "How come most of the biggest and the most successful custom apparel decorating companies in America are consistently at the top of the price spectrum?"

More than 30 years ago, I learned a lesson about how to make money in this business -- or any business – from my own business mentor, a Hartford, Connecticut restaurant furniture manufacturer named Jack Goldenthal, who was a client of my ad agency. Jack, 40 years my senior and a seasoned executive, taught me things my ivy-towered professors didn't cover in class. My relationship with Jack was in some ways like father and son. In other ways, Jack was the Shaolin priest to me playing the role as Grasshopper. One day he explained to me that, as a manufacturer, he made and sold the same type of furniture as did his many competitors all over the country, but "we've all got to be somewhere in the same ballpark price-wise. You can be at the upper end of it, in the middle, or toward the lower end. But if you're charging less than the ballpark price, you won't survive. If you're selling above the ballpark, you can't grow and you might die from a lack of customers." The conversation ambled to Jack's explanation of why his company was so profitable, even though his pricing structure put him in the very top price echelon in his industry's ball park.

"We all pay about the same for our materials and our manufacturing costs are pretty much the same. But if I can buy a just a little bit better, operate just a little bit smarter, and make our goods just a little more efficiently than the next guy -- and keep our good employees well paid -- I can make money forever!"

When I asked him how he could maintain his success for so many years against the cutthroat low-ball competitors in his industry, just as we have in ours, he acknowledged, "Sure, the competition has its effect your prices, but don't worry about what your competition's doing, Mark. Keep your focus on doing what you do better than what the other guy does well. Make the other guy worry about what you're doing and you'll never have to follow his lead! In time, he'll have to follow yours!"

Jack's paramount teaching on pricing was "Base it on what it's worth to your customer. Concentrate on value, not price."

Value is the yardstick by which astute buyers make their judgment on who'll get the business. With a price that's somewhere in the ballpark, buyers also expect reliable service, quality merchandise and good workmanship. While lots of companies can provide all three, where the industry's most successful companies leave their competitors in the lurch is their ability to generate leads and referrals (the byproduct of nurturing strong relationships with customers), and gaining over time the trust, confidence, and loyalty from everyone who does business with them. Historically, low-ball operators in our industry don't market, don't have a culture for nurturing clients, and lose as many customers as they bring in. The principles of what Jack's lessons translate to in our business come down to 1.) better buying, 2.) efficient operation, and 3.) improved productivity. For us, earning an extra nickel or dime or more in each area will make us a respectable fortune over time.

Here are some specifics on how to extract these nickels and dimes in each objective.

1. Better Buying: The single, biggest cost in custom work (as well as preprints) is for garments. It follows that buying intelligently and strategically is critical to profitability. If you can learn to buy effectively, more efficiently and on a more organized basis, you can effect savings of 10-20¢ per unit on T-shirts and a quarter or more on golf shirts. It comes through working with your top one or two wholesalers to find solutions to limit what you pay for shipping, learn what you can do to get a little extra consideration on pricing, and select more carefully what you're going to offer to most customers. Developing good relations and a good track record on payment with your preferred wholesalers is, of course, a given prerequisite.

I *know* that you can buy better! Look at all the internal redundancies most companies in our business commit every time they buy. Typically, they buy several times a day, frequently buy the same things they bought just hours ago or a day before, and schedule in too many shipments, which arrive in too many inefficient, overpriced, smaller, lighter cartons. (Those who routinely pay hefty COD fees and per-box surcharges lose another dime or more on every garment they buy). Each call to the wholesaler takes time, and each additional purchase order's processing takes time. Each level of redundant paperwork and order processing amplifies the time and money expended. All this clerical time becomes more costly than it should be, whether you're doing it, yourself, or paying someone else to do it. Moreover, you lose the additional time you *could be* spending on selling, marketing, planning, organizing, and running your business, not to mention losing the option to leave the office early and take whole weekends off (!) to pursue other interests, see your family, and have a life. Remember? Like it was before you went into business?

Developing your own brand preferences and limiting most customers to seeing only those goods you've chosen to show and sell engender further economies in garment purchasing. The trade's conventional wisdom of buying only what you need when you need it might work in the short run, but do note that nearly every major player in the trade keeps some or all of their key inventory items in stock in house. Building a working inventory over time doesn't mean you have to own a warehouse bulging with goods. But keeping a few dozen garments in your frequently ordered styles, sizes, and colors saves a small fortune in redundant phone calls, paperwork, and unnecessarily overpriced shipping charges. And having at-once access to key items saves money on production costs, especially when there's been an administrative error, miscommunication with a customer, or decorating flubs.

As long as you continue buying the way everyone else does, you can't gain those extra nickels and dimes on each garment -- and insert those coins in the slot above your bottom line.

2. Efficient Operation: Is there anything you can do to improve your company's internal systems and workflow in order processing and pre-production endeavors? Significant cost savings -- and faster turnaround to boot -- can be accomplished by investing in upgraded business software, newer generation graphic and digitizing programs, and new communications equipment. Sure, you'll incur some capital costs, but we all know it takes money to make money. Then again, there are probably some old geezers out there using dial telephones and asserting, "At least they're paid for!"

As long as a business continues running "the way we've always done it" and the way most other companies do it, a company loses the additional nickels and dimes on each garment that would be gained from operating smarter.

3. Improved Productivity: What can be done in your shop to decorate faster and qualitatively better?   Moving up to retensionable screens? Bringing digitizing in house? – or contracting it out? Buying new equipment? Using heat transfers to handle small-quantity orders calling for multicolor prints? Most likely you've already got a "wish list" of things you've thought about getting, but either haven't gotten around to it or feel you can't afford it. Investing in better productivity pays for itself. Perhaps the question here should be expressed as "Can I afford not to make these improvements?" Gaining yet another nickel or dime or more per item in labor savings goes right to the bottom line.

For most custom apparel decorating shops, labor is the second largest component of cost. As such, the upgrading and streamlining of your production operation isn't just a nice goal to achieve someday, it's a necessity. And doing it sooner costs less than doing it later.

Buying, operating, and producing more efficiently can quickly propel a company with little profitability into the black. Add a serious commitment to regularized marketing and a once-weak enterprise becomes a money machine. Doing what it takes to collect all those new nickels and dimes we've been talking about means effecting measurably lower costs. Lower costs means either you have the option of selling for less and becoming more competitive or being able to stick to your price gun and put those extra coins in your personal piggy bank. (I favor the latter outcome).

Pricing nuances come with the territory and help us gain command and control of the process. Getting a handle on the tricks of the trade, overcoming mistakes (often the hard way), and finding where your pricing intersects with demand will require conscious efforts on your part to master both the art and the science of pricing.

Other Ways to Price Decorated Apparel

Beyond my counsel and opinions, there are to be sure other pricing methodologies. Let's look at two of them.

1. Spreadsheet Programs

Using a spreadsheet software program such as Excel, you can develop an extensive price list quickly.   Essentially the software does its magic by executing the formula above (in one form or another). But at what quantity breaks? And should you add decorating into the front end or charge for it as an *a la carte* item (just as most firms do with prep charges)? Hmmm . . . Suddenly, spreadsheet pricing gets a lot trickier.

As chairman of the board of ShopWorks Software, the largest provider of industry-specific business software in the apparel graphics business worldwide, I can tell you our program sells an interactive system that includes a price-calculator spreadsheet program. ShopWorks includes our price calculator as a part of the software configuration in response to our customers' demand for it, not necessarily because I personally believe spreadsheet technology is necessarily the best way to go about pricing.

The two major benefits of using a spreadsheet price calculator are speed and convenience. The downsides are that you'll do a lot of guess-work in assigning margins for each price-break category; you end up with hard-to-read numbers that end in lots of different digits (although you can instruct your software to round up the last pricing digit to the next .00, .05, or .10). Also, there are no factors in the resulting figures that take into account the impact of the marketplace, your competition, or the psychology of buying.

Proponents of spreadsheet pricing nonetheless maintain the advantages far outweigh the disadvantages. They argue -- quite correctly -- that computing the hundreds of styles and thousands of sku's required to create a price list from wholesalers' CDs and downloads is made radically faster and easier. Indeed it is.

I maintain, however, that the downsides of spreadsheet applications for pricing run contrary to what I aver are the marketing advantages and more real-world aspects gained from using more traditional (and admittedly time-consuming) pricing methodology. Pick which side you're on in this debate. Or do both – use spreadsheet calculators for the overall gazillions of sku's from wholesalers' pricing data, but use the lessons here for calculating the pricing on your top categories or top 30-or-so express catalog items (e.g., T-shirts, fleece, shorts, golf shirts, caps, bags, jackets, etc.).

2. Using 100% Mark-ups of Wholesaler Pricing and Adding Decorating Charges

Distributor pricing usually is shown at net prices (what you pay for the garments). Some, however, also provide price lists published at a retail mark-up of 100% over cost. Whether you choose to increase the price by 100% over what you're paying for goods (or perhaps less than a 100% mark-up) or elect to show the wholesaler's retail pricing and then add decorating charges (not costs), you can determine what you'll charge customers for your finished products. How you handle inbound freight charges, waste and spoilage, sales commissions, overhead, or other variables are up to you. If you follow the 100% mark-up policy typically incorporated in this particular pricing methodology, you will, however, end up with prices that generally won't fly once you get beyond prices for a few dozen units when there's serious competition.

The user-friendly pricing, the system I recommend that uses the algebraic formula discussed earlier in this chapter, is based on several assumptions, having the recommended sales tools, and having well-defined marketing objectives, the major points of which have been discussed in the previous chapter and other earlier chapters.

Whatever system you utilize to develop your pricing, I can assure you all your prospects and customers want easy-to-read price lists. Since most of what they buy is predictable, a shorter price list showing your key offerings -- to cover the items in your express catalog -- helps customers make decisions faster and with fewer complications for themselves and you. "Easy-to-read" also means prices that end in "0" and "5" (e.g., $4.95, $4.60, $4.25 instead of $4.97, $4.62, and $4.23, figures generated by spreadsheet programs). Whether it's screen printing and/or embroidery or heat printing, and whatever model you use for your pricing (e.g., everything à la carte, incorporating the decoration into the garment price, or a hybrid method), these simplified price lists average between two and four 8 1/2" x 11" pages and provide you with ample space for helpful customer-friendly information about your policies, procedures, and particulars.

Do make sure you print an effective date and a termination date on your price list. I suggest the date be two to three months earlier than the actual release date. Doing this means you have the option with your better customers of honoring the old price "this time" or charging new customers the new rates.

Whatever your pricing system, you'll have a strong desire to streamline your procedures for selling, order processing, purchasing, and production scheduling wherever possible. Accomplishing these things saves you time and money, and reduces the possibilities for costly surprises and mistakes. Offering fewer items to the vast majority of your customers means faster selling, easier data entry, simpler ordering, more predictable production scheduling, and better overall performance in the critical area of customer service as well as on your bottom line.

More than three-quarters of apparel graphics companies have no reliable, operative price list of any kind. Most of the rest work from some sort of price list used only internally. A handful use a price list from a spreadsheet or an industry-specific program using downloaded wholesaler pricing of thousands of sku's; very few actually print out the document, which might cause some serious deforesting of America

The overwhelming majority of industry firms are forced to reinvent the wheel every day every time somebody asks for a price, which I call the price-du-jour method. It wastes time, makes a company look unprofessional, and significantly increases the cost of customer service while reducing the likelihood of actually making a sale.

A common pathology I observe in our industry is the conscious decision by nine out of 10 firms to withhold making any kind of price list available to customers and prospects whatsoever. What are the objections to having a price list and making available to prospects and customers?

Let's look at the three most common explanations -- or rather, excuses -- people use to avoid publishing a price list. The rationalizations – or more precisely, excuses -- for not publishing a price list come down to four arguments.

a.) "My competitors will find out what I charge." Who's fooling whom? They know your prices and you know theirs. You hear about their prices and deals regularly in the course of having your hands and ears on the pulse of the marketplace. (Of course, I shouldn't presume to think that people who read my books and columns would ever stoop to pose as a customer to call a competitor to get his price on a certain order. Yeah, right).

b.) "My customers will use my price list only as a 'starting point' to chisel me from there." If your prices are reasonable and fair and reflect the pricing "ballpark" of your area, why should you feel obligated to make concessions to chiselers? Sure, you negotiate when you have to, based on the size of the order, how badly you want or need it, the terms, or the value of the order in the context of starting or continuing a relationship with a customer who's worthy of receiving special pricing or discounts. But using this argument about price lists as "starting points" for chiselers doesn't warrant forfeiting the powerful marketing advantages a published price list gives a company.

c.) "It takes too much time and it's a real pain to do." Let's say it takes just four minutes to check some vendor price lists to get the information to then make up a quote on the spot. Next, you call the prospect or customer back to tell him how much you want to charge. Add two more minutes to do this, for a total of a six minutes to communicate a price. If you get two calls a day for price quotes and multiply this six minutes by the 10 times it happens a week and multiply that by 52 weeks a year, you can now see that you spend 52 hours a year reinventing the wheel every time you're asked for a price. And this is a very conservative figure that, in reality, could easily be 100-200 hours a year. Add in the interruption factor a few hundred times, the caller's/visitor's perception of getting lousy service, and the negative impact of all this on what could be an otherwise decent marketing agenda, and it adds up to thousands of dollars in wasted payroll, lost sales, and lost opportunities. Any issue about whether you can afford to dedicate the time to create a price list is better framed by estimating how much it's costing a company to NOT publish a price list.

d.) "Sure, I guess I could do a price list after all, but how do I cover my butt when vendors increase prices on me?" You issue a revised price list or, until you can get around to doing one, simply print an addendum stating which items have been re-priced! Hey, it happens, it's no big deal, and life goes on.

The prevailing methodology in our industry is in fact "the price du jour pricing system." It's based on the price a company can buy goods for today, not tied to what it quoted someone else yesterday, and often reflects the mood of the person quoting, the perceived urgency of the buyer, and how much work is in the shop at any given time. If this "system" sounds familiar to you, you're in trouble insofar as marketing goes.

The Smart Price List

My definition of a Smart Price List is a document that's printed on real paper, can be seen, understood, held, and owned by the recipient for his personal use and when it's convenient for him to use it. In my view, a price list that doesn't satisfy these considerations doesn't count as a *smart* price list.

A price list is a selling tool, a silent salesperson who works with a customer long after normal business hours and particularly when the customer needs a "ballpark" price. A pricelist is a powerful merchandising advantage, not a handicap! When perusing a catalog and a pricelist, most customers simply want a general idea of what things will cost them. They use these tools for ascertaining what and whether they can afford to buy and get a general estimate on the total price to see if it's affordable before they actually sit down to construct a purchase order and send it to you or call in an order.

Oftentimes this effort is done after hours and frequently the customer doesn't want to contact the vendor until he has a general, personal command of the variables. Most of the time, an exact precise-to-the-penny price isn't even an issue until the time of ordering or where a firm price is needed -- for drafting an actual purchase order, getting prior approval for budget purposes, or relative to pre-sales to end-users who are placing individual orders (as in the case of many a school or organizational order). And what a buyer doesn't understand, he'll be sure to ask you about.

Dumb Mistake No. 14
Forcing customers to call every time they need to get a price.

Regardless of their excuses, vendors without price lists often are perceived as having something to hide and are probably quite "negotiable." The epitome of this impression occurs when an inquiring caller is told "We don't quote over the phone." Oh, I see…so, getting a price on shirts must be a matter of national security?

Think about your own reaction when shopping online or receiving an interesting advertisement in the mail and not being able to see what things sell for. What do *you* do? You go on to the next listing on Google or toss out what came in the mail.

The company that furnishes its customers with an easy-to-read price list doesn't lose orders, it *gains* orders! For those still unconvinced or still reticent to issue a price list, when you consider that the largest and most successful companies in our industry all distribute price lists and catalogs (in hard copy and/or online) and spend big bucks to get the information into the hands of buyers, the arguments against publishing price lists fade. All the major players in the decorated apparel world consider having a price list not a luxury, but an absolute necessity.

This chapter is about pricing. But learning about the math and accounting aspects of calculating pricing, as shown earlier, provide only an entry-level understanding of the task at hand. Hopefully, you've gained some appreciation of the fact that pricing also is marketing and that focusing on one without the other won't make you any more money. My strong opinion about learning how and what to charge for your products is that the marketing component of pricing is far more important than the numbers and formulas. We'll discuss the marketing aspects of pricing and attending to price quotations in greater detail in subsequent chapters.

Pricing Preparation Costs

Though this chapter doesn't specifically cover the mechanics of pricing preproduction services, we can, however, address certain pricing principles that impact your decisions as to what and how to charge.

My view of these matters is that creating art and digitizing, making screens, and setting up presses and embroidery machinery are really marketing support functions. As a practical reality, you're obliged to provide these services for your customers, even if you contract these services from outside sources. That's because if you didn't take care of these things for your customers, you can bet they'll find someone else who can. A big philosophical divide between me -- seeing this industry through my marketing and management eyes -- and my friends and colleagues on the technical side is whether prep charges should be seen as profit centers.

Notwithstanding the fact that most technical consultants preach that prep work should be a profit center, it's my very strong counsel that preproduction services don't have to be profit centers and they rarely are. Indeed you should do everything possible to recoup all your costs for preparation, including a realistic amount for overhead and administration, and -- most definitely -- building in a commission for the salespeople who have to sell these services. But it's my experience that few companies in the course of a year *ever* make any money on set-up charges.

We all know some customers are charged set-ups in sharpened-pencil situations and customer-relations efforts, while other customers often get these charges "thrown in." My judgment and advice to clients is that the goal for charging prep fees is simply to recover as much of these costs as possible. Most companies to be sure would love to be able to operate their art, digitizing, and screen prep departments in the vicinity of break-even, but few do. But with an eye to the real world, I'm satisfied that a goal of achieving self-sufficiency in revenues for preproduction or somewhere within a few percentage points of doing so is all that's necessary. Do make preproduction charges seem logical and fair and do commission your salespeople on these items, even if your company earns virtually no mark-up on them beyond covering your costs and paying commissions. *All* of my clients follow these basic rules and, as a result (because prep charges are commissionable), their salespeople rarely waive prep fees except on very large orders or for huge accounts.

Another thorny issue in preproduction prep pricing that can be corrected with the additional of a single word comes in whatever you do charge customers for art, screens, and digitizing. Whatever your price, add the word "preparation" to the description when inserting the charges on your order form. The better and safer terminology becomes "Art *Preparation* Charge" instead of "Art Charge." Restate "Screen Charge" as "Screen *Preparation* Charge," and "Digitizing Charge" as "Digitizing *Preparation* Charge."

In a practical sense, using the term "preparation" means that what you've done for your customer, given the relatively modest fees billed in our industry for these efforts, doesn't belong to the customer except when orders involving these things are executed by your company. Spell it out clearly on your price list with the following language: *"Unless otherwise arranged prior to production, all artwork, screens, digitizing and programming materials prepared by (your company) remain our property and will be maintained on our premises for our exclusive usage in performing your orders."* [Source: Apparel Graphics Institute]

REALITIES

I've dealt with a litany of pricing considerations. But when you really get down to it, how much say do you really have in setting your own prices? The truth of the matter is: you don't set your prices. The *marketplace* does! You can be in the infield or the outfield, but you *gotta'* be somewhere in the ball park.

Any idea that you can just run through a formula and post your numbers without regard to the going rates in the markets you target is nonsense.

So, be confident in pricing your products and focus on selling them to accounts who place equal or greater value on purchasing from a company that sells quality workmanship and quality merchandise, delivers on time, and services its customers on a friendly but businesslike, professional basis. Making money and boosting sales isn't a function of any particular pricing formula, including mine or anyone else's. More profits and higher sales volume happen only when you proactively market your wares and do so within the context of a well-organized strategic platform that includes constant attention to purchasing, operations, and productivity.

The truth of the matter is: <u>you</u> don't set your prices. The *marketplace* does!

The way I lay it out for my clients is this: "We're going to organize your company in ways that make you more attractive to your customers, a good place for your employees to work, and a profitable venture for your owners and investors." And I don't care much about what it costs to run per hour, because the marketing strategy I advance is simply, "to generate so much sales volume that your in-house production capacity won't be able to handle it all!"

Be less concerned about scientifically pricing your goods, and more concerned with selling more and better goods to more and better accounts. The ultimate goal is to put positioning and pricing in their proper perspectives. If you're doing a good job in sales and marketing, the issues of pricing and profitability will for the most part take care of themselves!

CHAPTER 18

24 WAYS TO GET YOUR CUSTOMERS TO LOVE YOU
▪ Identity-Builder W2GC2♥U No. 3: Your Showroom

Let's turn to the subject of creating a winning showroom – the physical kind of showroom that real people walk into to see real samples that they can touch with their real hands. Not all decorated apparel companies will have showrooms, of course, especially if their marketing model is limited to selling online, via direct mail or other communications paths that don't involve being in a physical one-on-one environment.

But for all the businesses that operate in the real (as opposed to the virtual) world, the purpose of this chapter isn't to tell you what a showroom is, but to tell you what it should be.

First and foremost, your decorated apparel showroom, which will display mostly undecorated apparel, should appear to the first-time visitor as an immediate confirmation of your company's marketing position, its identity, and everything else good that you want people to know about your company. Indeed first impressions are lasting ones.

Secondly, your showroom should inspire the visitor to have confidence in your professionalism. How so?

Say you're planning on doing some remodeling at home and a new kitchen is your first priority. You can research a custom kitchen or your dream kitchen at different types of places in the real world, in catalogs, and at online showrooms.

You can visit a nearby plumbing supply house and look at various components and fixtures, but you might not see total kitchen environments – leaving such matters for more full-service vendors. You also can visit a kitchen remodeling workshop and see samples of more components. But if you want to see and "feel" different styles of kitchens in terms of size, style, décor, convenience, and get a handle on what's available to you at varying budget ranges, it might be best to go to a kitchen showroom. You know, the kind of place that shows lots of kitchens as you'd see at a kitchen retailer or Lowe's or Home Depot. You can see a broad collection, speak with a salesperson, get literature and some planning aids, and then go home and mull it all over. Perhaps you'll take out a pencil, graph paper and a tape measure, roughly configure what you'd like to see, and then go back to the store when you're closer to making a purchase.

Your showroom should say to someone the same thing a well-organized, neat, clean, attractive kitchen showroom says to a prospective buyer. Simply put: You're in the right place, you'll find helpful, knowledgeable people to help you, and you'll be able to get everything you need right here! You'll also get competitive prices, ample selection, and when you're finished with the project, you'll love the results!

Does your showroom tell your story accurately, attractively, and present your company as neat, clean, efficient, friendly, up-to-date, and accommodating? Does your showroom inspire confidence in your professionalism? I'll leave the answers to you.

As for neat and clean, you might wonder why that even needs to be mentioned here. While many companies take great pride and devote great effort to keeping their showrooms attractive and up-to-date, the majority of showrooms in our industry leave much to be desired, especially when it comes to neatness and cleanliness. The way showrooms atrophy and become dirty is a result of being taken for granted by owners and staff who get used to how the place looks and don't take the initiative to freshen or clean it. If reading this comment causes you to think about the current condition of your showroom, you obviously need to pay some attention to this vital element of your company's persona. It ain't rocket science to get it up to speed and up to snuff, is it? Of course, you could also invite some of your good friends, employees, and customers to tell you what you need to hear in terms of observations, suggestions, and ideas. And the sooner the better.

Just as I've advocated crafting an express catalog to limit your offerings for the reasons proffered, I advocate that your showroom should mirror your express catalog overall. But there's ample room and reason to display certain categories of garments and accessories in greater depth and selection – though limited to what's realistically speaking going to sell your products or what's needed to better position your offerings and your standard pricing (even if some of the items probably *won't* sell!)

If there's an ultimate goal I can recommend to you in developing your existing or new showroom, it's to make it as self-service as possible. Provide as much fundamental information as you can to the extent possible for a showroom visitor to be able to see what you've got, see his options, and get a good grip on comparative pricing.

Does your showroom tell your story accurately, attractively, and present your company as neat, clean, efficient, friendly, up-to-date, and accommodating? Does your showroom inspire confidence in your professionalism?

To that end, each item presented in the showroom should be tagged with the sizes available, fabric content, and pricing. The tag itself can do its job on an area no larger than a standard business card. Available colors can be shown on a swatch card attached to the garment where it can be quickly seen and referenced. Whether your pricing system includes the first color imprint in one location, includes up to x-number stitches, or displays only the undecorated garment pricing to be used in a completely à la carte pricing model, the clearly marked dollars-and-cents enable any shopper to see the price ranges within a category of garments. The effect on buyers is predictable and quite advantageous to you: oftentimes buyers see for themselves that spending a little extra to get a higher-grade garment may be well worth the difference. When showing higher-ticket items, such as jackets, you'll see that customers frequently buy "up" to get extra detailing such as a concealed hood in the collar, an extra interior pocket, or other options.

The selections for golf shirts, poplin and denim sportshirts, and outerwear sections of your showroom all should offer more choices than what's shown in your express catalog. But limit what you show to items you can source with confidence and in brands you know provide solid value. Just because you can source virtually anything under the sun in garments doesn't mean you want to *show* everything under the sun – and you'd need the area a small department store to accomplish all that.

Good, solid, presentable showroom fixtures are a must. Look at what's available to you before designing your showroom. To get started, Google the term "store fixtures." Look at competitors' showrooms (if you can find a good one) and stores in a nearby mall to get your brain into showroom design mode. For merchandising apparel you've got lots of latitude as to what'll work for your environment -- slatwall displays with waterfall arms, rounder racks, standard racks, grid walls, outrigging displays, and more.

Don't forget about including literature racks, signage and banners, proper lighting, and the type of flooring that will work best for your purposes. Keep the look of your showroom consistent; mixing chrome racks, wood racks, and painted racks can look cheap and unsightly (though I've seen some notable exceptions to the rule). Also, take care of the seemingly little details, such as what type hangers you'll be using.

Got room for mannequins? Apparel displayed on mannequin forms attracts attention more than "rags on racks." We're all hard-wired to be drawn to human faces and to human forms. With some mannequins on your payroll, you have the opportunity to tell a story – about teamwear, business attire, kids clothing, and school spiritwear (using the apparel, bags, caps, and accessories in the display area). You also can consider using "torso forms" and other specialized head, hand, foot, and leg displays.

Mannequins are available in a variety of "people" and positions -- male, female, and child forms, standing, sitting, with full-face make-up or weird, spacey looks. Using mannequins, you'll find creative solutions to energize your showroom – and your sales. Mannequins and sharp display fixtures increase perceived value as well, oftentimes mitigating extreme concerns about the price of your offerings.

Explore what's available in used store display fixtures, too, which often look like new – but sell at bargain prices. Local store fixture retailers usually are happy to help you with layout and design at no additional charge. And, of course, budget permitting, you can hire a local visual merchandising professional to do her or his magic; the investment will be well worth it and you can be confident of recovering your investment for years to come.

I'm frequently asked if samples should be decorated. My answer is, YES, *some* of your samples should be shown decorated. If you use waterfall displays, the garment in front of the pack should appear decorated; the others behind it on that arm needn't show decorated items, but there's no law against it. Items on hangers on horizontal racks needn't be decorated. The main samples that should be decorated are the ones that are immediately visible. The items without visible fronts or backs can remain blank.

The object here is that when someone comes to your showroom, it should create the immediate impression -- and reinforce the idea -- that *decorated* apparel is what you sell. A variety of printed and embroidered garments also will tell your story that you sell the gamut of technology and graphics.

The wall space above your displays is a good place to show full-front screen printed or heat printed designs; these displays can be on textile (or Pellon™-type) squares, preferably framed. Also, show designs on a variety of different color backgrounds. The effect is that of a graphics gallery, a feature that your customers are certain to peruse to get some ideas to see which type graphics and colors they might like to see on their own garments. By the way, old (used) wooden screen printing frames make great frames for mounting prints!

For displaying embroidered designs, many companies do so by continuously adding designs to cloth banners and putting them into display books in the showroom. Though you don't see them often, wing panel display units work particularly well, conserve space, let the customers' fingers do the walking. They also are more readily able to be changed, expanded, and updated.

Counters, table and chairs, or both? Most companies in the industry that have commercial facilities have 42"- to 48" -high counters, over which they conduct business while buyer and seller both stand. Counters do speed up the process a bit. But whether you have a sales counter or not, I always recommend having a table (about the size of a dining room table) and four to six chairs around it in your showroom for those occasions when you'll be showing a lot of samples or catalogs. It also is ideal for accommodating two or more people from the same group to create a comfortable environment for more comprehensive selling. You'll find selling in the table-and-chairs setting keeps buyers with you longer, a situation that almost always boosts your sales. While you're busy at the table, your customers do see all the items on display around the showroom and are very likely to ask about other products.

Making folks feel at home also warrants having refreshments available – water, soft drinks, coffee and tea, and maybe some munchies in your showroom.

Some other ideas that help make your showroom look professional and well-thought out include:

► Bilingual signage

► Small 3" x 5" mini-signs interspersed in your displays that remind customers about other things or advantages your shop offers, such as:
   - "Personalize your garment with names or initials – only $4.00"
   - "Two-color numbers – only $1.75 additional"
   - "Total Quantity Pricing for all items on the same production run"
   - "Guaranteed three-day service on this item"
   - "We accept Visa, MasterCard, American Express, and Discover"

Even though your customers know exactly where they are when they're visiting your business, it's a good idea to have your company name and logo and tag line on display in the showroom to reinforce your identity.

By the way, in case you're wondering which of the hundreds of showrooms I've visited personally wins my endorsement as the best in the industry, it's at the home of Alaska Serigraphics in Anchorage, Alaska. (Stop by when your in the neighborhood!)

Whatever your efforts will entail in designing your first showroom or upgrading your existing showroom, you can expect it'll be a labor of love. And exercising a healthy degree of creativity and some fashion flair will reinforce your company's position as a good choice for buyers to go to when purchasing decorated apparel.

Trade show displays aren't quite the same thing as a walk-in showroom, but allow me a few comments here about creating a booth for use at business-to-business events and at end-user or consumer events.

Trade show booths are a *form* of showroom, though the elements you'll include in any such endeavor will vary with the type of show, the kind of buyers you'll encounter, and whether the function of your exhibit is to generate qualified leads or for direct on-site sales to attendees. While the subject of portable showrooms is better addressed in doing your homework when you're contemplating investing in these venues and creating your own display booth, many of the ideas discussed in this chapter also play well in designing a trade show display booth. These ideas can apply to merchandising the key apparel items in your lines and demonstrating the latitude of your technical and graphic prowess as well as establishing your company's ability to be clever, creative, and up to speed on current trends in colors and styles.

The major differences beyond the size of your portable showroom are that display booths need to be able to be set up and taken down quickly and efficiently, and shipped when necessary at economical rates.

Also, in those cases where you'll be exhibiting in venues when trade unions control many aspects of booth construction (e.g., electrical, carpentry, transporting the display to your floor location, etc.), your booth needs to be able to be erected without the use of hand or power tools. God bless wing nuts, Velcro®, and other devices than enable you to do your own thing.

Perhaps the best education you can get about trade show (and consumer) booths is visiting one. You've undoubtedly attended your share of trade and consumer events, but for the first time peruse the show with a new frame of reference: look at the activities and displays from the point of view of an exhibitor. Should you have any friends or business associates exhibiting somewhere, ask if you can "work" the show with them for a few hours to understand the booth activities, the traffic, and the scope of the responsibilities you'll have being on that side of the aisle.

▪ Identity-Builder W2GC2♥U No. 4: Your Website

We'll talk about web marketing in Chapter 29 (Advertising Mechanics and Strategies), but we'll explore your website here in terms of what it needs to be to get customers to love you. Note that I've grouped the topics of showrooms and websites together in the same chapter because, while the variables evince significant differences in technology, culture, costs, and upkeep, how your site looks and feels will go a long way to reinforcing your intended position – or invalidating it -- and whether or not the visitor to your website will feel like he's in the right place.

My thinking in grouping your showroom and your website in the same chapter is that in many ways your website serves as an online showroom. The effect of both the physical and the web presences needs to be perceived as helpful and organized to enable customers and prospects to have as easy an experience as possible in finding the items they're interested in (and perhaps things they weren't looking for when they arrived). It also should help them get a handle on pricing and their options for spending more or spending less, and making a judgment about whether to do business with your company.

Your website also presents an ideal opportunity to show your technologies and your facilities. In doing so, make sure your camera captures the people doing the work, not just the machines running. And where possible, let your staff do the talking about their roles, be it on the technical side, administration, sales, and post production operations. Even for those technologies that you don't perform in-house, endeavor to show the various processes in operation and make appropriate comments about your instrumentality in preparing the orders or in representing the companies that perform it on your behalf.

Let the story capture your building, inside and out, your showroom, your software at work, and other things that demonstrate your assets beyond the brick and mortar and technology – particularly the people who make your enterprise what it is. In your own way, bring the viewer into the decision-makers' offices. Of course, everything you capture in the audio should be scripted, but with a little rehearsal, people will sound more natural and more confident of their explanations.

You don't need to do anything fancy, and most of the "home-grown" videos I've seen do the job quite effectively. You'll find this weapon helps in long-distance presentations and as a sidearm for salespeople in the field, on the phone, and behind the "counter" at an online company store.

If you think you can get by without a website, you're correct in the short run. In the long run, though, you'll soon find that owning a website, and perhaps several, is absolutely imperative. Here are four good reasons why I say that.

1. Creating a Website Imposes Organization, Discipline, and Focus

The process of building your website imposes reasons to rethink, revisit, and redefine your company's marketing and merchandising appeal, its identity, its unique selling propositions, and its raison d'etre. Given that we've discussed organizing and publishing your own express catalog and price list, you've already done a lot of the heavy lifting in organizing your website. (Conversely, if you start the process with the development of your website, you've got the essence of your own express catalog and price list in hand).

2. It Ain't Rocket Science

If you lack the skills for creating your own website, there are many good providers that'll be happy to execute one for you. Yes, how much you budget for your website will vary by who does it, how extensive it is, and how easy it is to navigate, but even basic websites are affordable today to design and maintain. Your options range from working with leading industry distributors, several of whom have turnkey software and hosting deals available, to creating yours from the ground up. Additional solutions incorporate both aspects to a degree to portray the best of both worlds – a website that provides ample information about your products, services, and pricing as well as telling and showing your company's story. That story includes the company's owners, key people, your production or representation capabilities, noteworthy attributes, and other reasons buyers should favor you with their patronage and loyalty.

Getting your website up and running should be done sooner rather than later. Waiting until everything is perfect and just the way you want it can be a costly mistake, and as too many entrepreneurs can attest, major website development or reorganization is seemingly never completed when promised. Also, decent, effective, user-friendly websites are never inexpensive, though budgets can be established that you can live within. Then again, seen over the long haul, economizing on a confidence-inspiring website may well prove counterproductive and penny wise and pound foolish.

3. It Shortens the Buying Process

Established accounts who peruse your company and its offerings online get real-time, 24/7 answers to their basic questions along with some understandings about their more complex concerns. The issues that aren't addressed for pressing specific situations are the ones you really want to deal with at the time they come up. Your website, properly executed, saves your customers and prospects time and your company time and money. Trying to answer every conceivable aspect of every order and every detail isn't critical and the effort to do so is probably somewhere between folly, unnecessary, and overkill. But those owners who insist that handling routine information and price quotes over the phone gives them a better chance at closing a sale just don't "get it." They don't realize how poorly they look when compared to other companies that show a modicum of respect for the buyer's time and intelligence.

The bottom line: When prospects and customers are ready to call you to ascertain final figures and details -- and maybe to place their orders if they'd prefer not to do so online or need a bit more information -- they've gotten many of their questions out of the way. All this translates to a better prepared, more knowledgeable buyer who spends less time on the phone and issues faster purchase orders. And as your website becomes more sophisticated and more interactive, you'll get one step closer to having customers place new orders online or at least place re-orders online.

4. A Website Enhances Your Credentials

Every company that is a "player" -- or wants to be -- will have a website. It'll be a prerequisite for being thought of as a leader in your market or your backyard.

Marshall McLuhan, the Canadian theorist, educator, and authority on communications, gained fame in the 1960s with his observation that electronic media, especially television, were creating a global village in which "the medium is the message." In basic English, his assertion was that the means of the communication will have more influence on people that the specific information, itself. In other words, if your local TV station runs a news story, it must be important. If you advertise on radio or TV, you're likely to be thought of as a bigger company than your competitors that don't advertise on radio. And if you have a website, there's a whole world of companies who feel more comfortable doing business with you. Perhaps more importantly, there's a world of companies who figure if you don't have a website, your company isn't worthy of their further consideration.

Though the Internet and e-commerce wouldn't come for a generation after McLuhan made his case (he died in 1980), his observation about the relationship of a given medium vs. the information it provides is as cogent today about websites as it was about television.

A century ago, having a telephone was considered to be a luxury only for the rich. Can you remember the time -- only a few decades ago -- when having a toll-free number was perceived to be the province of only big, national companies? Remember when not having a fax made you look small time and less than serious as a business? Not having a website today carries the same stigma.

CHAPTER

24 WAYS TO GET YOUR CUSTOMERS TO LOVE YOU - Business Necessities

Per the materials in Section Four (Positioning Your Company in the Apparel Graphics Marketplace) particularly with regard to choosing a company name, taglines, positioning statements, and descriptors, your use of these assets will be seen well beyond those impressions your advertising and marketing efforts will generate. This chapter is a quick rundown on some of the everyday vehicles that will carry your company's identity. While some new entrepreneurs may consider stationery, business cards, self-promotion literature, labels, and custom-printed cartons to be "old school" or too traditional for their tastes, each still holds an important place is telling your story.

▪ Identity-Builder W2GC2♥U No. 5: Your Company Stationary

Chances are you don't or won't write a good ol' fashioned letter all that often -- anymore. But when you do, your basic business stationery will tell the recipients a lot about your company and its owner or who-ever's signing the document. The times and places for hard copy via snail mail are getting fewer and farther between as Internet communications continue to be the norm. The exception, however, will most likely be for things you consider of great importance – higher level communications to vendors, accompanying large quotes and bids, for special thank-you's and commendations, regarding serious complaints to vendors, and comments and requests to government agencies, among other occasions. Your letterhead and the envelope it's mailed in are your first chance to make a positive impression. So, do make this vital, albeit declining, medium one you'll be proud of and one that demonstrates all the good things about your identity. An attractive, professional letter-head and coordinated envelope won't win you an order or an approval, but it could cost you one. Of course, most letters and the graphics on them are printed directly from your computer these days. To that end, use nicer paper than what your use for photocopies.

Of course, budget permitting, letters with an embossed detail, a touch of foil, or other enhancements do get you extra attention. If you want to spend a little more to get noticed, it's worth the extra outlay.

▪ Identity-Builder W2GC2♥U No. 6: Business Cards

For many professionals, a business card is in many ways your company's signature. Cheap cards, cutesy cards, or cards that lack graphic taste or imagination don't help your cause. The elements of a good business card are axiomatic, but I'll give you two large admonitions here:

a) Do not use oversize cards (dimensions exceeding the standard 2½" x 3"). People who do, think they're getting attention. What they don't realize is that such cards are a nuisance, don't fit neatly in standard business card files or caddies, and suggest to the recipient the giver isn't very experienced in business etiquette. Go oversize at your own risk.

b) Use a horizontal format. Vertical formats can be very attractive and distinctive, but don't do much in the way of making the cards easy to file, store, or reference. Businesspeople overwhelmingly prefer to see horizontal formats. If you want to demonstrate your creativity, make the standard horizontal format and standard size cards stand out graphically – to make other cards look "ordinary."

Specialty stock and special effects usually are worth the added outlay, be it attractively finished card stock, one with a photograph, on magnetic vinyl or other attention-getting medium, such as wood (great for laser engravers, among other smart uses), a holographic imprint, embroidered highlight, embossing, and such.

▪ Identity-Builder W2GC2♥U No. 7: Self-Promotion Brochure

You should put a few goods words in about yourself in your company catalog, but when prospecting for major corporate accounts, grooming advertising agencies for referrals, and bidding large orders, enhancing a buyer's comfort level with more qualitative information about your company may be the difference between being the winner or the runner-up. You can accomplish this in a brochure that tells once again about your management and key people (and show their faces), their technical expertise, background, and training. In a brochure you can show your production facilities, list some of your company's prestige accounts, awards, distinctions, community involvement, and other achievements. List the many advantages and benefits of doing business with your company. If this sounds redundant to your website and parts of your catalog, it is -- and by design.

A business card is in many ways your company's signature. Cheap cards, cutesy cards, or cards that lack graphic taste or imagination don't help your cause.

A quick C-fold brochure will do the trick; make sure it is one that fits in a standard business envelope, catalog, or trimmed to fit neatly inside your folded catalog. This brochure is intended for distribution at trade and consumer events, to walk-in customers, to prospective accounts being seen by sales representatives, and for inclusion with a variety of company communications. Full-color printing and photographs are the order of the day in this endeavor, whether you order in larger quantities from a commercial printing supplier or generate small quantities from your computer's printer on an as-needed basis.

▪ Identity-Builder W2GC2♥U No. 8: I.D. Garment Labels

Your choices in custom labels that identify your company as the producer (or seller) of decorated apparel range from pressure-sensitive I.D. labels affixed to garments (for one-time use) and via heat printing and sewn-in cloth or Tyvek® labels for permanent use.

The third option is mainly for those companies financially strong enough to undertake private-label programs, which are purchases made primarily by companies that maintain large inventory holdings in key categories. A similar approach, though more costly on a per-unit basis but without the onus of making large inventory commitments, is to use custom sewn-in labels in conjunction with the relabeling of garments.

This process entails ordering supplies of labels (available within the trade) with or without size designations on the label (S, M, L, XL, XXL, XXXL and possibly even larger sizes). There's also the option of ordering labels without size designations and using a second label (referred to in the trade as a "neutral" label or "joker tag") that shows sizes.

The U.S. Federal Trade Commission mandates four criteria that must be affixed to the garment: 1, the fabric content; 2, care instructions; 3, identification of the manufacturer and/or seller – via a trademark, a Federal Registry (or "RN") Number assigned by the Federal Trade Commission, or other easily traceable source disclaimer; and 4, the country of origin – specifically, where the goods were manufactured.

Several major wholesale distributors offer private-label programs and/or relabeling services. Expect to pay 15-25¢ per garment per label change, depending on the quantity involved, plus the cost of the label itself, which runs a few pennies each for Tyvek labels and a dime or so for woven cloth labels. The industry's major garment manufacturers also offer private-label programs, but in most cases, the minimum quantity purchase is in the 1,000-dozen range and up. Some smaller manufacturers have much lower minimums.

What's the value to the seller of decorated private-label apparel? Using custom labels conceals the source of the goods, making it more difficult for competitors to steal your customer. More importantly, it increases the *perceived* value of the garment, especially when the custom label is of the woven variety. Some industry firms provide custom garments with the logo and identification of their *customer* in the garment's label, a practice limited mainly to major buyers and major quantities of goods.

Several of the larger companies I work with are routinely involved in private-label programs, while a few others sell to enough accounts to warrant bringing label changing operations in-house by buying a few sewing machines and hiring skilled sewing operators. The operators also sew custom collars on a variety of garments, sew on lettering and patches, and often do double duty in the embroidery department.

If you have a very special customer who buys "tonnage," consider suggesting to the account to incorporate its own custom labels into the products you provide to him. Would your competitors think to offer this? Of course not, and imagine the other guy (chuckle) trying to steal this account after you get the system rolling!

> **Dumb Mistake No. 15**
> **Failing to seize the opportunity to tell everyone holding a**
> **decorated shirt that your company sold that your company**
> **is the source of that beautiful garment!**

The pressure-sensitive I.D. labels I mentioned earlier serve a very specific purpose. To understand it, consider an order of 100 shirts going to a business or an organization or wherever. How many people in the buyer's group receiving or purchasing the garments actually know who provided the wonderfully decorated garments? The answer is: The person or two that placed the order, perhaps the person who picked them up or received them from the UPS driver, and the individual who issued the payment. The other 90-some people who'll wear the garments are clueless as to the source. That's where the I.D. labels -- that cost a penny or two each plus the labor to stick 'em on the garments – come in, to inform everyone else. The label will be seen for a moment or two and removed before donning the garment.

With your own I.D. sticker, every time you sell an order more people will also learn your company name, address, telephone number, and web address. Meanwhile, you got your name out to everyone who got the shirts, including those recipients that own a business or whose spouse does, or play on a team, or are members of other groups, or are on event committees. For a nominal investment, you make a qualitative advertising impression on the recipients. Down the road, when the time comes for some of the recipients to order shirts for other applications or groups, your company might get the call or at least a shot at the order.

If your garment is accompanied by a guarantee for quality, durability, or is available for personalization, your label adds a small degree of value to the product itself and, if nothing else, tells the recipients just a little bit more about your company's identity. (See Chapter 24: The Ultimate Leapfrog Signature.)

Beyond promoting your company's identification, the copy on the label might start out with something like: "Congratulations! You're now the owner a fine quality garment that has been professionally screen printed/embroidered by the quality-conscious technicians/artisans at the production facilities/studios of (company) in (town)." Then go into your guarantees, special instructions, etc.

▪ Identity-Builder W2GC2♥U No. 9: Packaging

Be it previously used cartons, brand new cartons, bags, boxes, or whatever your garments are shipped or picked up in, we know statistically that nearly 90% of the buyers keep what you sold in the packaging you supplied. [Source: Apparel Graphics Institute surveys]

While not every order or every customer may warrant delivery in brand new cartons, for most customers and most orders, garments that arrive in crisp new boxes get more respect, as does the company that packed and shipped them. Printing the cartons with your logo on it and having some fun with the graphics only helps enhance your identity. And as long as the carton stays around, you've got billboard advertising on the box that's seen wherever it goes and by anyone who reaches into it for a garment. Cartons that arrive in good condition from your wholesalers also can be used if they're cosmetically clean. Otherwise, recycle the cartons properly.

As for cartons with a manufacturer's imprint, one way to grab your own attention is to affix decorative labels promoting your company and your offerings. Yes, the specs of the shipping labels that carry the shipping address are mandated by the various carriers, but there's no law against using the boxes for your own advertising. You're in the graphics arts business, aren't you? So get yourself maximized attention for just a few extra pennies per label to use one that's beefed up with your message and dressed up with colorful graphics.

CHAPTER

24 WAYS TO GET YOUR CUSTOMERS TO LOVE YOU

▪ Customer Relations Vehicle W2GC2♥U No. 10: Customer Surveys

What is a customer survey you might ask? For good companies, the answer is: An easy way to have your customers give you compliments – in writing.

An occasional survey sent to your customers – once or twice a year -- is a passive, inexpensive way to remind people to send you some business. That's what you can expect most of the time. Yes, the survey is a real survey, but its impact often is as good as a direct solicitation.

What the survey ostensibly is designed to measure is your customers' opinions about doing business with your company and their perceptions about your firm's level of performance in meeting their expectations and delivering what was promised.

Key considerations in developing a good survey, one that'll merit a reasonable level of response, are that the questions are simple and unambiguous, the responses should be multiple choice with an option for the recipient to write a comment, and the recipient can complete it in a minute or two.

If done entirely online, the survey should be simple to navigate through and send the responses. If done in the mail, the survey should include a postage-paid reply envelope or give the recipient the option to take the survey online. Surveys can be done over the telephone, of course, but some folks won't welcome the interruption, though friendly customers are usually quite happy to help if it's not an inconvenience to them at the moment. And many of the companies I work with include a reply-card survey in every order they ship.

Beyond the usual results that show most *responding* customers are highly satisfied, there inevitably will be some "issues" that arise from unhappy campers. This is a good thing, as most owners and managers understand. That's because negative comments usually emanate from a customer who likely is a lost cause, until someone from your company calls her to discuss her comments and does so with the intent to keep the customer's business rather than have to look for a replacing the account. Essentially an unhappy customer -- if she can be wooed back, will generally be satisfied with some concessions from the company, an explanation and, if appropriate, an apology for any inconvenience caused -- and the account can be retained. (Customers who are bound and determined to leave, however, will rarely be salvaged).

Yes, surveys are a great way to command a little respect from customers and earn you some professionalism points. But the real reason I recommend surveys is what I stated at the opening of this chapter – they earn you compliments. And customers who give you compliments are much less likely to "shop," remain loyal even when price might become an issue (and you come up with a workable solution), and, with the customers' permission, you build a collection of short testimonials for subsequent marketing and advertising.

Here are some quick questions for your use to help you develop your own surveys:

Your opinion matters to us. Please tell us about our service during the past year and, if necessary, how we can improve our service and quality. – (signed by owner, rep, etc.)

1. Was/Were your order(s) completed to your satisfaction?

__ **Very much so**   __ **Overall, yes**

__ **We're sometimes disappointed**   __ **We're not happy at all**

Comment: _____

2. Have our products and imprints/embroidery met your expectations?

__ **Very much so**   __ **Overall, yes**

__ **We're sometimes disappointed**   __ **We're not happy at all**

Comment: _____

3. In your opinion, have you received good value for your money?

__ Very much so   __ Overall, yes

__ Usually   __ We're sometimes disappointed

__ We're not happy at all

Comment: _____

4. Will you be likely to favor us with future orders?

__ Absolutely, count on it!   __ Probably

__ Maybe   __ Probably Not

__ Never again

Comment: _____

Be as businesslike or as engaging or as playful or as personal as you like in formulating your questions. You know your customers and there's no one-size-fits-all style or system for all companies. But whatever you do, make your survey a positive reflection of your identity, your company culture, and your sincerity.

▪ Customer Relations Vehicle W2GC2♥U No. 11: Newsletters

The most common question I get about newsletters is "Do people really read them?" My answer is a resounding YES. Provided, of course, they're properly targeted, particularly to the audience that is most likely to read them to begin with – your customers and key prospects with whom you've begun to establish a relationship, even if it hasn't yet resulted in orders.

Many companies *talk* about doing a newsletter, but few actually execute. And most who do get *one* done rarely get around to doing a second. Producing your first newsletter can be a chore, but it's also a labor of love. And once you get through the first one, if you're committed to following through for the longer haul, the next and subsequent ones become almost mechanical, especially if you produce a regular "format" for this valuable communicator. Your format might include the boss writing a column, as might the art director, sales manager, production manager, etc. Do a feature on a key employee. Include a "Spotlight on

..." section and showcase two or three customers, mindful to tell your readers how these customers use their decorated garments. Put in a few real ads, and an incentive offer or two, especially if you can get a supplier to co-op some or all of the cost.

If you're sending your newsletter in the mail, endeavor to include something three-dimensional – a magnet, a 6" ruler, or other flat, inexpensive attention getter that'll be retained. Ask your wholesalers to help, too, with money, samples, mailing capabilities, or whatever resources they're willing to share. You'll be quite happy to know most are willing to help you get your message across. After all, if you do well, they'll do well, too.

A quarterly edition would be nice, but a two or three times a year will go a long way over time to inform your customers of what you want them to learn about what you can do for them. To that end, whoever is writing in your publication should focus on how you help your customers achieve their own goals -- be it for great looking teamwear, colorful attention-getting graphics, or affordable enhancements that improve the value of their purchases.

People actually like to read about what you're doing and how you're building your business. You build their respect for your efforts, you build loyalty, and you build account activity in the process. A four-page self-mailer will suffice. Newsletters, like any good advertising, don't cost money. They *make* money.

There is, of course, the option of distributing your newsletter via the Internet. Snail mail and e-commerce *both* work. E-newsletters give you the advantage of providing immediate links to key items, although snail mail, based on my experience, is more likely to actually be read and read in its entirety – be it at a desk, in the lunchroom, or in the "loo."

Dumb Mistake No. 16
Not making customer relations an important part of
the company's culture.

How many newsletter copies you mail obviously has a bearing on cost. Quantities of 100 or less can be done on your own office printers. When you'll be mailing 300 or more copies twice a year or more frequently, investigate obtaining a bulk mail permit from the United States Postal Service; the more you use it, the more you save.

▪ Customer Relations Vehicle W2GC2♥U No. 12: Customer Advisory Board

A Customer Advisory Board (CAB) is exactly what the name implies -- a group of customers who'll give you input on how to run your business better in the eyes of customers and prospects. To get started, schedule a meeting, say on a Wednesday at 5:30 p.m. or Saturday morning at 10:00 a.m. for a hour or two at your office. Next, invite a few good customers to join you, enlisting from a cross-section of your account base -- a teacher, a businessperson, an insurance agent, a computer expert, a coach, an elected official. Sit 'em around a table two or three times a year and welcome them to shoot holes in your business, your business model, your service capabilities, and customer service culture. Let them tell you what you need to hear in a conducive environment. The pay? Two shiny pennies reimbursing them for their "two cents" of input, accompanied by a gift certificate to a local merchant, dinner for two, tickets to the movies or a sports event (and with a coupon for popcorn), or a coupon for the local carwash. Whatever you give, try to do it through using the products or services of one of your customers, and, if possible, on a trade-out basis to minimize your cash outlay.

You'll get not only good information from your CAB, but its members will invariably tell other people about their experience as being one of your business advisors. These meetings don't cost you money, they save you money and they make you money. And can you imagine your advisors ever buying from another apparel decorator ever again? Refresh the CAB by inviting different customers from time to time to serve on the board to replace those who can't attend and to get more input and increase your reach into your customer base. Essentially the members of your Customer Advisory Board will quickly become missionaries for your company in your community and beyond.

Though a Board of Directors (BOD) usually is associated with a corporation, your CAB functions in many ways as a BOD albeit without the voting and governance powers. And for those readers whose businesses are incorporated, a working BOD will prove to be a valuable resource for gaining leadership skills, solid advice, and, as with a CAB, a cadre of missionaries in your community.

Essentially the members of your Customer Advisory Board will quickly become missionaries for your company in your community and beyond.

CHAPTER

24 WAYS TO GET YOUR CUSTOMERS TO LOVE YOU
▪ Goodwill Tools and Loyalty Incentives
W2GC2♥U No. 13: Open House Events

Wanna add some octane to your 2nd and 4th quarter sales? Host an open house!

You remember the first time you saw an embroidery machines cranking out the stitches onto fabric?

Or when you saw a series of screens produce a multicolor masterpiece or even watched computer graphics happening for the first time? Well, your customers are just as amazed! And veterans and rookies alike all know the delight of watching their customers marvel at your firm's technical resources in operation. An open house event opens eyes and doors to those who've never seen the equipment running. The event also opens wallets. Open house events at your shop also produce the same effect when your goods are on full display. You'll enjoy hearing customers' observations and the predictable compliments on your capabilities and offerings. All that and an ego trip to boot!

But when you liberally infuse the atmosphere with munchies (simple or fancy), familiar liquid refreshment, a little music, scrumptious desserts, lots of people having a lovely time and chatting with one another, and the miraculous appearance of "free goodies" (tees, promowares, etc.), the occasion truly becomes an event. Just as the festive environment of casinos turns people on – and gets them to loosen their wallets -- a party at your shop is a friendly device to help your customers, prospects, and friends to talk to each other, talk about your business, and – *ta da!* – shell out some money.

If you'd like to host a party and cash in on giving your customers the opportunity to buy some stuff for their customers, employees, fans, co-workers, fellow members and aficionados, the holiday season presents an ideal window for your business. As does the onset of spring. Once a year, though, suffices, but if you find the time and energy for semi-annual showcases, go for it.

Some quick tips . . .

1. The invitation – Be creative! Demonstrate your graphic sophistication and technical prowess. Print "the invite" for example on a Fomecore™ T-shirt, a cap, an infant shirt, or a T-shirt-shaped key fob. Add event details and a map on a separate item or card. The object is to attract attendees, so spend a little more to get attention and a good response. Be sure to invite your staff's spouses, perhaps their parents, significant others, and other family members (inviting children is your call) to your party. That way you get a whole bunch more people meeting your guests and bragging about your company's work to the other attendees.

2. Strutting Your Stuff – Update your showroom samples. Endeavor to get your favorite wholesalers' reps and promotional products manufacturers' reps to set up their own displays for you. Be sure to have catalogs and price lists available and custom-imprinted plastic bags, shopping bags, or inexpensive tote bags on hand for folks to collect their literature and goodies.

3. Free Stuff – Buy what you have to, but do ask your vendors for free stuff for distribution to your guests. You'll be pleasantly surprised how cooperative and generous many will be. Show the stuff you're giving away being decorated while your guests are in attendance, demonstrating what you do in-house on unchallengeable direct terms.

4. Food and Drink – Demonstrate more creativity here. Consider offering T-shirt- and cap-shaped cookies and hors d-oeuvres, a T-shirt cake, custom-printed candies, and other beyond-the-ordinary treats. Booze? Keep it to beer and wine to be on the safe side, limiting both cost and your liability for trouble. And soft drinks, punch/juice, and coffee are much more interesting served in custom cups, which, of course, you just happen to note on a small tent card on the serving tables are available with the attendees' own imprints for quick delivery.

5. Music – Hire a DJ or a band if you've got room for dancing at an evening event or just want to move the open house into party mood and mode. But any music is good, whether it's a classical string quartet or guitarist, a local band, a barbershop quartet, or whatever's reasonable on cost and appropriate for your audience.

6. Other entertainment ideas – Have a magician working the crowd with close-up tricks, celebrity look-alikes, a mime, a juggler, an artist doing caricatures of your guests, and/or anything that helps elevate the occasion to event status. These special treats serve to generate buzz afterward – especially if you take digital photos and e-mail them out to attendees the next day or send out in inexpensive, perhaps custom printed, frames.

7. VIPs – Inviting local politicians, local newspaper reporters, coaches, and community leaders guarantees lively conversation, and oftentimes, photo ops and hopefully media coverage.

8. Dress – For success! Your staff should wear what you sell. Your wholesalers can help provide garments at a deep discount or free. Outfit your crew in a variety of tees, hoodies, poplin sportshirts, polos, caps, vests, scrubs, and lightweight outerwear to exhibit your product lines. Make sure, of course, everything's decorated with your logo, but be clever and cool – adding pride-worthy terms somewhere on the garment (sleeve, right chest, and/or back) to explain who's wearing what -- terms such as "Embroidery Wizard," "Senior Screen Printing Technician," "Solution Provider" (for salespeople), "Paperwork Expediter," "Inventory Miracle Man," "Creative Genius" (for art staff), and "Master Digitizer." The boss can have lots of fun telling about himself or herself -- "Jack of All Trades," "El Presidente," "Janitor," "Master Juggler," "Advertiser's Best Friend," etc.

9. Follow-Up – Thank your guests with something tangible after the event and be sure to ask for an order. And thank your vendors, too. Do follow up your event with a press release and some good photos to your local newspapers, your chamber of commerce, trade publications, and anywhere else you can amplify the occasion's beneficial impact on your reputation, your enterprise's good will, and your customers' good sense!

10. Training Your Staff in Good Manners, Common Courtesies, and How to Accept a Compliment – Don't assume everyone understands that first impressions are lasting ones. Be sure to explain to your staff that it's easy to say "thank you for your business," "nice to meet you," and "we're glad you came to help us celebrate."

And . . . if you want to know one other IMMENSE benefit of hosting an open house – one perhaps equal to the effort at increasing sales -- it's creating a fixed-deadline opportunity to thoroughly clean and organize your shop, offices, production areas, showroom, and exterior. You know how your house gets a thorough going-over when "A-List" company – like your mother! – is coming to visit? Now, you've got a great excuse for getting around to doing what you've been putting off for way too long.

▪ Goodwill Tools and Loyalty Incentives
W2GC2♥U No. 14: Christmas Gifts

What do most apparel decorators send their customers at Christmas? Well, more than half send nothing at all. Not even a card. Sure, seemingly everyone talks about sending out something, but it's one of those things in the height of fall business that's gets put off until it gets too late to do anything. And the same phenomenon occurs year after year. So, if you plan to send something, put it on your marketing calendar. But will customers miss not getting something from a vendor? Not really, unless, however, another vendor who sells the same things sends them something. At which point, it might appear that you don't love them anymore or care about them only when they buy something.

Dumb Mistake No. 17
Not taking advantage of easy opportunities to demonstrate your talent and creativity.

For those who send something to their customers, what do they send? Most send a Christmas card signed by the owners, or everyone in the shop, or by the sales rep who calls on the account. Period.

Some companies send a card *and* a gift. The gifts range from promotional products (with calendars topping the list) fruit baskets, and gourmet food assortments to an item produced in-house. Certainly, these gifts show the recipient that the sender values the relationship and cares enough to want to express it in a special way once a year. And customers do appreciate the thought.

Usually the gifts crafted and/or decorated in-house sport the vendor's logo, though occasionally you'll see an item done with the recipient's initials or an attractive graphic unrelated to the vendor's name and logo.

But if you're going to send out a Christmas whatever, think less about what you'd like to send out and more about what your recipient will think of your offering -- and by extension the impression your company makes on the recipient.

What would *you* rather get? A laser-etched desk set with the vendor's logo or a laser-etched desk set etched with *your* name, *your* initials, or some graphic than means something to *you*? A fly fishing enthusiast would take extra note of something having to do with fly fishing. A Revolutionary War re-enactor is likely to appreciate a patriotic graphic more than your logo. You get the idea.

What a great opportunity to "strut your stuff" to your customers. If they think you mainly do simple one-color work, blow their minds with a spectacular multicolor rendering on fabric, wood, glass, metal, or whatever. And if it's suitable for framing, frame it! See to it the hardware for mounting is already in place. If what you send is worthy of prominent display in a client's office or kitchen, making it ready-to-hang gets it where you hope it goes a lot faster -- reminding your client who you are, what you do and can do, as well as reminding the recipient of your thoughtfulness. And if you think sending a creative work done in your shop will *cost* you money -- what with materials and postage, think again. As with so many elements of advertising and marketing, gifts like these don't cost you money -- they *make* you money.

By creating and sending out a work of art, you maximize the impact of your craft, gain much more recognition for your artistry, and provide a year 'round reminder of your company. And it's a one-size-fits-all solution that costs but a fraction of the good will and good vibes it generates.

Here are a few suggestions for holiday offerings:

- **A small, detailed work, about the size of a 3"x 5" index card:** Framed (and perhaps matted as well), the finished size will be 5"x 7" or 8"x 10". To keep costs down, always endeavor to design your work to fit in a stock-size frame, available for about $1-3 at Family Dollar, Dollar General, or similar emporia.

- **A larger work for display in an 8"x 10" to 16"x 20"frame:** Using digital transfers or screen printing for the background, execute foreground (and perhaps middle ground) highlights with your own technological magic.

Here are some quick concepts to help you visualize your creation: A subdued background of a forest, a country landscape, or a mountainscape, highlighted with embroidered elk, birds, sunflowers, or geese on the wing ...an undersea background highlighted with embroidered fish, whales, dolphins, sea horses or other marine accents ...a background of Jerusalem, the world, or a pastoral scene highlighted with embroidered symbols of the major world religions . . . a snowscape or Victorian houses with secular Christmas icons such as Santa, wrapped gifts, tree ornaments, etc... a nautical background highlighted with embroidered sailboats, divers, a lighthouse -- and/or the client's name or initials in embroidered nautical flags! If you don't do embroidery or don't want to contract it out, use specialty inks for the highlighted graphic. Suede, high-density, and other texturized inks will do the job quite respectably. How 'bout rhinestones or foil to enhance your art? Whatever you do, don't waste the opportunity by doing something ordinary; do something special to earn your stripes.

To get more ideas, glean through some magazines and Christmas card catalogs for inspiration. Open a few books or surf the 'Net. Browse through your stock design templates. Given the many sources at our disposal -- or snoozing in your art morgue, you're certain to find a wealth of stock art available at very nominal cost or already in hand. For those looking for real wow-factor reaction, consider executing high-end mixed-media designs.

While many creations might look best under glass or mounted on wood or marble bases, some will look better *au naturel*. I'll leave all these decisions to your discretion, based on the particulars of your in-house processes, creative horsepower, and budget.

Should you put your company's name and/or the artist's name somewhere on the item or the graphic? Perhaps, but oftentimes it's more effective to do it discreetly, in small type somewhere in the background. Or consider delicately hand writing the title, year, or other descriptive information on the mat or base.

And perhaps your holiday masterpiece is worthy of serial numbering as would be a fine limited edition run.

Your gift should be accompanied by a personally autographed card and, where appropriate, include a short explanation of the significance of the design along with credits to the artists, technicians, and other staff instrumental in producing the finished work. This information also can be affixed on the back of the item for future reference and identification. Some companies prefer to note the year on the design. This is a particularly good idea if you commit to making this effort an annual ritual. Years down the road, you can expect that your customers will proudly display them all, usually in sequence.

Many of my clients have been doing "holiday masterpieces" in one form or another for many years. I've been doing them myself for more than 30 years and can count on hearing from a few folks I cull from the list, especially those who were saving a place on the wall for the next annual edition -- but hadn't sent me any business in a while (I'll give 'em three years before hitting the delete button). And once they've contacted me and then receive the item, I can count on business from them in the year ahead).

In case you're wondering if every customer who placed an order with you should get your new, annual, limited-edition gift, the answer is generally "yes." Then, again, some very small customers probably don't warrant more than a card, while some giant buyers might rate a considerably more substantial type of thank-you.

If you've got significantly different categories of active customers, consider establishing different tiers for different levels of customers. The tiny ones (under $500 a year in purchases) might rate a calendar and/or a card. Customers who purchase, say, $500-$1,500 annually, get a card, a calendar, and your limited-edition framed artwork, while your major accounts might get the above items plus a food basket, theater tickets, or some other higher-ticket gift -- or a personal creation -- commensurate with the value you place on your relationship with them.

Sending something to customers at holiday time is a time-honored business tradition, but one in which few companies really invest much brainpower.

As part of your effort to build customer relationships, consider sending something that demonstrates all at once your creativity, your impeccable taste, and your technical mastery -- a gift that'll stand out among the other folks' traditional, predictable offerings. Why settle for conventional giftware and conventional results, when you can wow 'em with your own wizardry!?

As for the substrate, depending on the decorating methodology, you can decide from among Pellon™, linen, jersey, silk or satin and do present it already framed.

■ Goodwill Tools and Loyalty Incentives W2GC2♥U No. 15: Valentine Cards and Other Special Occasion Cards

Other celebrated holidays and annual milestones present additional opportunities to remind your customers you value them, look forward to renewing your relationships, and welcome re-orders. Your other good-excuse occasions to make some noise include Valentine's Day (you love your customers, don't you?), the Vernal Equinox (the first day of spring), May Day (pre-schoolers, anyone?), July Fourth (you value your freedom and independence, don't you?), Labor Day (especially if you sell to unions), the Autumnal Equinox, Columbus Day, and for those who miss Christmas or want to arrive outside all the other hoopla, New Year's.

Sending something to customers at holiday time is a time-honored business tradition, but one in which few companies really invest much brainpower

■ Goodwill Tools and Loyalty Incentives W2GC2♥U No. 16: Premium Offers and Frequent Buyer Clubs

Perhaps you're old enough to remember getting a glass tumbler every time you filled up your car with gas or had your choice of a kitchen appliance when you opened a savings account. The things you got were "premiums." The two big differences between promotional products and premiums are that the latter is given in exchange for some type of performance on your part, not simply something given as a goodwill offering, and oftentimes is presented without an advertiser's imprint.

Some of the most successful companies in our industry build purchasing loyalty by adding value to an order in the form of points, credits, or other measurable and collectible incentives – much like credit card companies do with airline points, hotel stays, or other goodies that can be earned over time with cumulative purchases.

In our trade, premium programs include a variety of Frequent Buyer programs, with prizes that range from a free decorated apparel item after a threshold dollar amount has been attained to points that can be redeemed for a small color TV (costing you $50-75 at Wal-Mart), a weekend for two at a nearby bed & breakfast ($200-300), a month of free gasoline (up to, say, $100), or a year of free car washes. Where possible, try to secure a premium with a high perceived value that you can obtain at a bargain price or on trade with the seller. For schools and organizations, your premium may become a door prize that can be raffled off or awarded to a deserving member. With some buyers (teachers and coaches come immediately to mind), the gift will be scarfed up for their personal use (without anyone else knowing about it). Frankly, we really don't care what happens to the prize or where we're instructed to ship it, as long as it keep buyers buying from us!

To initiate a Frequent Buyer Club, you can establish dollar goals or point goals, develop a selection of worthwhile, desirable awards and do what airline companies have been doing for years to build loyalty, market share, and make customers think twice about flying on another airline – even when the fare's a little cheaper. In the point system arrangement, you organize your products by point values (a T-shirt = 1 point, a sweatshirt = 2 points, etc.) or offer points per invoiced amount.

▪ Goodwill Tools and Loyalty Incentives W2GC2♥U No.17: Crackerjack Marketing

The caramel popcorn and peanuts in Crackerjack are yummy, but talk about this product and the first thing people associate with it is the prize. (Talk about establishing a great *position in the mind!*) Crackerjack marketing is an original term I coined in the 1970s for putting a goodie in the carton, which my company did and got a reputation for being a fun company. The prize needn't be at all expensive: a small calendar, Good & Plenty, a memo cube, a box of funky plastic paper clips, a bag of marbles, a pen knife, a bottle of bubbles, or simply, a box of Crackerjack! A visit to your local dollar store will yield all kinds of neat stuff and cheap, too. Just remember to put the goodie at the top of the carton, please.

Here's an example of how my company added goodies to out shipments. In January each year, the Girl Scouts in my home town sell cookies and I'd buy a few hundred boxes every year from a neighbor's daughter, Patty, who became the perennial top cookie seller in her troop. We placed a box of Samoas in every shipment starting immediately after her Dad delivered stacks of cartons of cookies to the plant. Every shipment with the cookies added a little bit of sweetness and delight. During February and March, we earned tons of good will from sending the cookies to our customers and the local newspaper's predictable story touting Patty's annual achievement always included a plug for our company. We also helped Patty's volume even further by including an order form for Girl Scout Cookies in our December and January shipments. Customers loved it and were reminded we were the company that put a prize in every order.

But any cool gadget at 50¢ or a buck is worth a mint in good will, especially when your customers tell their friends about your little trick (or treat) and your company. P.S.: If you're concerned that your intended recipient might not be the one who opens the carton, put it in a bag with the targeted recipient's name written on it). Fun, eh?

CHAPTER 22

24 WAYS TO GET YOUR CUSTOMERS TO LOVE YOU
▪ Customer Satisfaction Extras
W2GC2♥U No. 18: Individually Folded Garments

For most screen printing companies, individual folding is a charged-for option. But in astute operations, the nickel-a-garment cost is absorbed as value-added merchandising. We're talking "presentation" here, just as you would expect to see with dinner or dessert at a fine restaurant. The garments appear neater in the carton, customers appreciate the nice extra "touch" and convenience, and the company gains enhanced status for demonstrating it goes the extra mile in pleasing its customers.

Most embroiderers do individually fold their customers' garments, recognizing that a $14-30 embroidered golf shirt or sweatshirt or a $30-70 embroidered jacket just wouldn't look right arriving in bulk folds. Screen printers can take a lesson here from Rodney Dangerfield: Even T-shirts deserve a little more respect from their decorators.

Many companies that go this route leapfrog this finishing option by inserting each dozen garments in a clear plastic bag and placing on it an easy-to-spot sticker with the size of the garments in the bag. This makes retrieval faster and easier for the customer. The bag costs two cents but the great impression it creates is priceless.

For massive quantities of T-shirts, especially when sold at very close margins, folding each garment might prove too costly. But for standard quantities of a few dozen to a few gross, this extra effort demonstrates a company's commitment to high-quality service and professionalism.

▪ Customer Satisfaction Extras
W2GC2♥U No. 19: Accepting Credit Cards

Most apparel graphics companies take credit cards, but very few make it a practice to *encourage* their customers to use them. Why? The conventional wisdom is that accepting credit cards isn't viewed as a competitive advantage and that the cost of doing so takes an unacceptable percentage of the profits. The logic here ostensibly measures costs against benefits -- but without really weighing and understanding the benefits.

Try this argument on for size: Somebody visits you and tells you: "If you turn over all of your receivables to me, 1.) I'll guarantee to pay all of your invoices within a day or two; 2.) You'll have virtually immediate use of your receivables the moment they occur; 3.) You'll never have to send monthly statements again; and 4.) You won't ever have to chase your money or make collection calls again." The role of this "somebody" is what in essence taking credit cards on all of your orders would do for your business.

Would you take this deal at about 2½ % per invoice to get all these benefits? In addition to better cash flow, you also get a heapin' helping of peace-of-mind.

Here's a look at the mechanics and costs of accepting credit cards.

When you process a credit card electronically through a service provider, you pay a transaction fee – 15-35¢ and rates ranging from under 2% to as much as 3% of the gross sale. Affiliating with trade groups, your local chamber of commerce and local business organizations are fast routes to get lower rates.

The actual percentage you'll pay is determined by several variables: the size and transaction frequency; whether you see the cardholder, handle the actual credit card, and/or get a live signature (vs. taking card payments over the phone); projected annual volume; whether you process the transactions electronically or manually; and whether you're affiliated with a trade group that gets you better rates than you can get on your own.

The hardware for a manual card machine, or "imprinter," costs less than $50 -- and way less on eBay. Swipe systems cost a lot more, but can be leased monthly. (And sell on eBay for peanuts!)

Dumb Mistake No. 18
Thinking the cost of accepting credit cards is higher than the cost of losing a customer to a competitor that does accept credit cards.

Most companies in our industry conduct a high percentage of their business over the phone, especially with repeat customers. But even small orders for a few dozen decorated items can amount to several hundred dollars in sales. Since it costs the credit card service provider just as much to process a $15 Denny's guest check as it does for a $600 embroidery sale, it means that almost any service provider would find your firm to be an attractive card-processing customer -- one deserving lower rates.

Most of the companies I work with not only encourage their customers to pay with credit cards, but request -- and usually get -- or mandate *full prepayment* from customers who pay with credit cards. In most cases, the customer doesn't receive his credit card bill for two weeks or longer and has two to three weeks to pay, oftentimes gaining more time to settle up than the usual net-30 invoicing allows.

For those who accumulate airline points or other card dividends, they're happy to pay with credit cards. And you'll develop a more loyal customer as well!

A clever client taught me a great line about getting prepayment via credit cards. As he explained it to me, "When a buyer asks for terms or credit, our response is "Our Credit Department is YOUR credit card." End of discussion.

In addition to the benefits cited earlier, you also won't have to compromise a C-O-D policy with that customer who remembers to stop in to pick up his order but forgets to bring a check with him. (We all know this guy!) While a dissatisfied credit card customer still has recourse to dispute a charge, it's uncommon and not an issue for companies that deliver good work and when promised.

For the customer with not-so-hot credit, buying your products with a credit card lets him avoid the embarrassment of doing the whole "credit application thing" and precludes your risk of losing a customer.

Beyond all the aforementioned benefits you'll reap, you'll get a customer who's also more likely to spend more and remain more loyal, as documented by years of survey research done by credit card issuers.

As a consultant working inside more than 600 apparel graphics companies during my career, I can state   unequivocally: Show me a company that proactively encourages its customers to pre-pay orders with credit cards, and I'll show you can company that generates higher sales-per-transaction and higher annual sales volume.

If the question about whether your enterprise should accept credit cards wherever possible is one where you've asked yourself, "Can I afford to do this?," I'll suggest the issue is better framed as "Can I afford not to?" With today's technology, payment processing software systems enables companies to handle transactions via a laptop or other wireless devices. This makes life a lot easier for apparel decorators, especially those who work fairs and festivals or just about any off-site venue where they're selling their products. Walt Palmer, general manager of Lewes, Delaware-based Mugs & Stitches, whose business encompasses events merchandising and online retailing as well as custom screen printing, embroidery and promotional products, uses a program called PC Charge, one of several PC-based point-of-sale (POS) payment processing systems . He explains that, "I've eliminated the need for a separate phone line to process credit card purchases." He adds that by using the software, "I don't have to buy or lease any credit card processing hardware except for the swipe unit. And when I'm on the road [doing embroidery on-site] at HAM-radio gigs, boat shows, and community festivals, I can process cards from my [wireless] laptop in a few seconds."

Show me a company that proactively encourages its customers to pre-pay orders with credit cards, and I'll show you can company that generates higher sales-per-transaction and higher annual sales volume

There are lots of similar programs and at very affordable fares. To learn more about what's available to you, I'll suggest you start your investigation by simply Googling "payment software" to get a quick handle on current technology, service options, and pricing: Also investigate the many advantages of collecting payments through PayPal™.

Besides covering your receivables quickly, the greatest advantage of credit cards is simply that it makes it easier for your customer to do business with you. Another method that enables customers to pay conveniently if they so choose is accepting electronic fund transfers from a customer's bank account into yours. Whatever small courtesies you can extend to customers to help get their bills paid quickly should be made, from including convenient reply envelopes with statements and promptly issuing invoices as soon as the order becomes a receivable to happily taking credit and debit payments over the phone.

But what about those good customers who've always promptly paid their bills to you? Can you still give them net 15 or net 30 or whatever terms on which you've been successfully selling them? Of course, you can, and should, since their track records warrant your continuing to do business with them as usual.

■ Customer Satisfaction Extras
W2GC2♥U No. 20: Shipping Notification and Pick-Up Notification

When you order from a reputable, reliable company, you usually receive both an acknowledgement of your order and subsequent notification when the order leaves the warehouse. The shipper also usually issues a tracking number from UPS or USPS as a courtesy, so you can follow the package along its way to your door. Few firms in our industry issue acknowledgments or shipping notification. That's the first reason you should do so. The other reasons are that it's smart business, it demonstrates your company's professionalism, and it's appreciated by your customer. And it doesn't cost you anything other than a few seconds of time.

In most industry companies, when an order for pick-up has been completed, it's placed in a pick-up area in the shop and sits until the customer calls or shows up. For the customer who'll be picking up her order at your location, the simple courtesy of a phone call or an e-mail telling her it's ready is appreciated and helpful, especially if it's accompanied about a reminder of payment due and the amount, directions or a map if appropriate, and your hours of operation. It also saves the customer the nuisance of having to call and ask whether the order is done. A few seconds invested in helping this customer gets you brownie points and generally precludes the situation where someone forgets to bring payment and puts you in an uncomfortable position of deciding whether or not to release it to a C.O.D. customer.

CHAPTER

24 WAYS TO GET YOUR CUSTOMERS TO LOVE YOU
Quality Control Mechanisms

Maintaining quality control usually is thought of as being a concern that's addressed internally. And it should be. But in-house oversight of quality isn't bulletproof, nor is it as comprehensive as most companies would like it to be. That's why it's important to rely on the input of salespeople – who oftentimes catch things that production personnel don't and who communicate more often with customers. Salespeople usually are on top of things that don't go as well as planned and are quick to tell management what's not up to snuff. Customers, though, might not express their concerns and/or dissatisfaction directly to you and, as often as not, simply vote with their feet -- taking their business elsewhere when they're unhappy with your results or your people.

That's where external quality control comes in, and is most easily and directly accommodated by three techniques: quality control calls, in-pack quality control and re-order reply cards, and a packer's personal assurance.

▪ Quality Control Mechanisms
W2GC2♥U No. 21: Quality Control Calls

When was the last time an owner or CEO of a company called you to inquire if you're getting treated well by her staff, if your orders are handled well and on time, and if the product lives up to what was promised at the time of sale? Chances are that it's been a long time or, more likely, never.

In seeking quality control input from customers, the boss, a salesperson, or customer service coordinator calls each customer a day or two after decorated merchandise has been delivered to make sure the customer is satisfied. Most of the time everything is fine and what you'll usually hear is "Thank You" and/or receive a bevy of compliments. Such expressions are great and we like to hear these things. But if for any reason the client isn't happy, you can take action right then to remedy the situation and save an account in the process. The call is appreciated by the customer and the company gains respect and credibility. These are the calls that, if not made, can cost you customers that could have been saved.

My recommendation always is that the boss makes the first quality control call; subsequent calls can be made by other personnel and the boss can do an occasional follow-up just to let the customer know the boss cares about her account and cares enough to call her personally.

▪ Quality Control Mechanisms
W2GC2♥U No. 22: Quality and Re-Order Reminder Card

The Quality Control and Re-Order Reminder Card card is a short form (usually 8 ½ " x 11" , on index or heavier stock) that's inserted with the order, taped inside a carton flap or laid on top of the finished goods so it is seen as soon as the box is opened. Differing from general customer surveys (See Customer Relations Vehicle W2GC2♥U No. 10: *Customer Surveys*), this mechanism focuses on an order that has just been shipped or delivered. The top half of the card is a vehicle for enabling your customer to tell you whether the order was delivered on time and done satisfactorily or what issues, if any, need to be resolved.

The bottom half, separated from the top by a perforation, is a quick recaps of the order.

The device serves two purposes. First, the customer is given three easy ways to get in touch with your company if he wants to do so. It gives him an easy way to communicate with you by a.) putting the reply card in the mail (the reverse side of this half is imprinted with a business reply permit number), b.) contacting your via the e-mail address on the card, or c.) calling you at the telephone number on the card.

It puts all the contact information in one place without the respondent having to look for an invoice, a packing list, or check for the phone number or e-mail address elsewhere. The second function is to give your customer a tool for determining what, how many, and when to re-order.

The quality control card asks four simple questions:

Your opinion matters to us. Please tell us how we did and, if necessary, how we can improve our service and quality. – (name, title)

1. Was this order completed to your satisfaction?

☐ **Very much so**   ☐ **Overall, yes**   ☐ **It was "OK"**

☐ **We're disappointed**   ☐ **We're not happy at all**

Comment: _____

2. Did the items and imprint/embroidery performed on the items meet your expectations?

☐ **Very much so**   ☐ **Overall, yes**   ☐ **It was "OK"**

☐ **We're disappointed**   ☐ **We're not happy at all**

Comment: _____

3. Did you receive good value for the price you paid?

☐ **Very much so**   ☐ **Overall, yes**   ☐ **Not quite**

☐ **We're not happy at all**

Comment: _____

4. Would you be likely to favor us with future orders?

☐ **Absolutely, count on it!**   ☐ **Probably**

☐ **Maybe**   ☐ **Probably Not**   ☐ **Never again**

Comment: _____

Statistically you can expect 10-20% of recipients to respond, and most responses will be quite positive.

[Source: Apparel Graphics Institute surveys]

Dumb Mistake No. 19
Thinking every dissatisfied customer will take the initiative to call you to tell you about it.

On the bottom half of the card – the recap shows: a.) "Your Purchase Order was > No. _____; b.) Your Work Order (or Invoice) is > No. _____;" c) "Your order was shipped on (date) _____ /20XX and included (total count) _____ (shirts, shorts, jackets, etc.)."

The customer now can easily reference how long it took to distribute or sell the items, helping him better plan the quantity for a re-order. He also can easily reference order numbers when calling in or e-mailing a re-order. The re-order reply card includes a friendly note which states, "We'll confirm your re-order with you to update the quantity, sizes, pricing and any other details or necessary changes to your original order prior to our production of your re-order."

Because the bulk of customers store their garments in the carton or bag they were delivered in, advise the customer to leave the card in the carton or bag. As inventory dwindles, if the item remains viable, a re-order is virtually assured without the customer having to look for any other paperwork. Customers like the convenience and thoughtfulness of a re-order card and are impressed by your professionalism and courtesy

▪ Quality Control Mechanisms
W2GC2♥U No. 23: Packer's Personal Assurance

The Packer's Personal Assurance is a 4¼" x 5½" note (for printing them 4-up), a 2" x 3½" label affixed to a carton flap or outside a bag, or printed on the back of a business card that tells the recipient who counted the items in the carton and confirms the count. It's *neatly and legibly* signed neatly by the individual who counted the items. Its function is to inform the recipient that a real human being counted the items in the order before the carton or bag was sealed. It reads "I personally counted the items in this order twice and am responsible for any discrepancies." You'll be pleasantly surprised how quickly the number of customers calling you to tell you there was an undercount will be reduced to near zero; that's because the note is personal and subtly obliges the customer to re-count the number of items before alleging a shortage – and jeopardizing an employee's job. At the bottom of the note is your office telephone number.

Customers like the convenience and thoughtfulness of a re-order card and are impressed by your professionalism and courtesy

For more quality control questions you might consider asking your own clientele, look at a "customer satisfaction" service card (such as those you see at franchise restaurants) and "borrow" whatever ideas you glean from it about what management wants to learn from their patrons.

CHAPTER

24 WAYS TO GET YOUR CUSTOMERS TO LOVE YOU
▪ W2GC2♥U No. 24:
The Ultimate Leapfrog Signature

Consider this scenario: Six days after receiving a delivery, a customer brings back a T-shirt that has a direct screened plastisol-ink imprint that has begun to peel off or fall off toward one side of the design. The cause? As any screen printer worth his salt can tell you, it's his fault and for any of a variety of reasons – damaged heat element, uneven squeegee pressure, not enough ink on a side of the screen, a defective batch of ink, or other technical shortcoming. And how does a pro respond to the disappointed customer? He'll make good on the shirt, by either replacing the garment, issuing a credit or refund, or other means of giving the customer his money back. If at all possible, the printer asks the customer to collect all the garments and return them to him for recurring, either by heat-sealing or re-running the shirts through his infrared dryer. A pro also will replace or credit every garment in that production run for all the right reasons – professionalism, pride, honor, ethics, fairness, and smart business practices. Were the garments returned six weeks or six months later, the pro will make good on the garments, all of them, if necessary.

Plastisol ink, the recipe for which is polyvinyl chloride, resins, and pigments, is amazing stuff, and I got the skinny on its lasting properties in the 1970's from plastisol pioneer Dr. Richard Labov, president and guiding light of Union Ink Co. Armed with a Ph. D. in chemistry, Dick explained that properly cured, plastisol is *permanent* and isn't biodegradable. Imagine that a man is buried in his favorite T-shirt this year and lowered down to his final resting place, in an area of limited geologic activity. Fast forward 10 millennia to a time when the area is sought as a building site, triggering the mandatory archeological site search before construction. The flesh and bones, the coffin, and the deceased's vestments have long since decomposed. But as the archeologists dust a layer of soil away with fine brushes, lo and behold, revealed to them is a plastisol imprint looking back at them, that reads: "Fitzpatrick's Irish Pub – *Where the elite meet and greet*" in an arc over a cartoon leprechaun, under which it still says "Brooklyn, New York."

Per the scenario with the plastisol peeling off, the pro is already guaranteeing his work on a de facto basis for all the right reasons. But since such occurrences are rare or non-existent to begin with, why not make your promise of standing by your work a *de jure* guarantee? That's why most of my clients guarantee the permanence of their screen printing and embroidery *forever*. They know it's true and they proclaim it on their catalogs, their price lists, in their newspaper advertising, on the radio, and in the Terms & Conditions printed on the back of their sales order forms in ***bold italic*** type.

Dumb Mistake No. 20
Letting your competitor be the first company to lay claim to "The Forever Guarantee."

As for a customer returning an embroidered golf shirt six days, or six weeks, or six months after receiving it who is peeved that the thread in the design is unraveling or stitches are coming loose, would that customer merit the same good faith consideration for having the garment replaced or credited at the embroiderer's expense? Again, for all the right reasons, an embroidery pro will make good on it. Whether there was a thread-tension issue or a digitizing glitch, it sure wasn't the customer's fault.

Executed properly, for all intents and purposes, a screen printed design on a T-shirt does in fact last forever. And properly executed with quality thread and correct thread tension during the stitching, embroidery is durable for at least a few centuries. The point here is that good companies stand behind their work. Guaranteeing their work is what good companies do.

So what are the risks and downsides in telling customers the work they buy is guaranteed -- guaranteed *forever*! – when that's what they're already doing? There are no risks or downsides for a pro by guaranteeing the decorating workmanship forever! The marketing advantage here simply is that a proud, honorable company makes its *"forever guarantee"* part of its identity, routinely touts it in its sales pitch, and does so in writing. The way it rolls off the tongue is, "Unlike any of our competitors, we guarantee the permanence of our screen printing and embroidery forever." In writing, it's even more impressive and positions any company that does so as extraordinarily competent and confident in its professional skills.

Executed properly, a screen printed design on a T-shirt does in fact last forever

Remember those I.D. stickers you read about in Chapter 19 (W2GC2♥U No. 8)? It's an ideal place for telling everyone who receives a garment decorated and/or sold by your company about your "Forever Guarantee." Doing so gives you the perfect opportunity to identify your company, its address, telephone number, and website – because *YOU* are in fact the company they'd need to contact were there to ever become a permanence issue.

Below is a facsimile label you might want to clone for wording your own Forever Guarantee. Adapt it as you see fit for application on your other marketing materials.

ABC Apparel Graphics

■ SCREEN PRINTING ■ EMBROIDERY ■ DIGITAL PRINTING
■ CAD-CUT® ■ GRAPHIC DESIGN ■ PROMOWARES

We guarantee the permanence of our screen printing and embroidery forever!

Congratulations! You're holding a first-quality garment, decorated by the caring, quality-conscious, skilled artisans and technicians at our downtown Evansville production facility.

Because ABC Apparel Graphics uses only superior grade materials and executes our screen printing and embroidery processes to the highest technical and professional standards of the apparel graphics industry, we're pleased to guarantee the permanence and clarity of our graphics on the garments you buy from us forever!"

■ **1234 Main Street**   ■ **Your Hometown, XY 56789 USA**
■ **800.555.IDEAS**   ■ **www.ABCtheideascompany.com**

Having been asked the question since I invented The Forever Guarantee (in 1978) as to how risky guaranteeing screen printing and embroidery forever has proven, I've been giving the same response from day one: *Not a single company* ever has had to do anything other than what they would have done anyhow regarding any issues about ink and thread permanence.

Another frequently asked question is whether direct-to-garment printing, sublimation printing, and sign vinyl printing can be guaranteed forever. No, not all. What about heat printing? Heat printing performed using high-quality plastisol transfers on high performance equipment, such as the Hotronix® and Phoenix® presses, is in fact as permanent as screen printing. CAD-CUT® graphics will last for decades, but not forever, so you can add it to your forever guarantee if you wish, since the likelihood of a complaint decades from now is somewhere between negligible and remote. The inks used in direct-to-garment printing and sublimation printing have proven quite stable over repeated washings, though some degradation of vibrancy will occur; but in no way can you safely guarantee such decoration forever.

Lastly, why do I characterize *The Forever Guarantee* as "the ultimate leapfrog signature?" Because I know your competition doesn't have the knowledge or the *cojones* to take such an uncompromising position on their willingness to stand behind their workmanship they way *you* do. Nothing your competition can say even remotely rivals the strength and impressive power of *your* Forever Guarantee!

Remember back in Chapter 16 when we took Business Route 24, headed to 24 stops along the way, while the competition took the Route 24 Bypass? You're about to head back onto the high-speed road, but guess who's now barely visible in your rearview mirror?!

If along your excursion along Highway 24, you came up with some more ways to get customers to love you, please consider passing them along to your colleagues. (www.TheBusinessOfTShirts.com).

CHAPTER

25

THE PEOPLE WHO DO THE SELLING

Some apparel graphics companies have proven that it's possible to close sales without offering or adding human intervention with the buyer. If you're skilled or wealthy enough to garner a search engine position for your company in an online apparel graphics business model – a position that displays your company on the first page or two -- you can skip this chapter, as I'll be talking about real people in the real world, not the virtual world. Moreover, many, if not most, of the successful online sellers of decorated apparel have achieved their success through sales of licensed or other popular merchandise offered at retail prices through niche markets, by virtue of capturing extraordinarily valuable domain names early in the Internet game. They also got there by attaining Internet power through astute expertise in the optimization process, or other unusual resources.

The big difference between the business systems we'll explore in this chapter and well-established online sellers is that the former outnumber the latter by several hundred to one. Also, the online model primarily works in selling to prospects who a.) proactively initiate a purchasing foray online; b.) aren't real price-sensitive – at first, anyhow; c.) might not realize they can get what they want in their own backyard and at lower prices; d.) believe they know more than enough to buy decorated apparel intelligently; e.) initially don't understand the impact of shipping costs and time constraints; f.) don't really care whether the seller and apparel decorator are one in the same; g.) aren't easily accessed through more traditional avenues of selling and advertising; and/or h.) aren't looking for assistance in creative or technical expertise or product guidance.

Until 2000, my opinion was that sales of custom apparel graphics products didn't "close" themselves without assistance from human beings and in fact relied on help and guidance from company personnel.

Advancing technology and farsighted entrepreneurs proved me wrong vis-à-vis companies such as CustomInk.com, CaféPress.com, Zazzle.com, UberPrints.com, DesignAShirt.com, and Spreadshirt.com, among many others.

Using online design software, users can go to any of these sites, create their own graphics, order, and receive their goods in a few days or two weeks later. For most companies in our industry, though, selling to their accounts, especially for the first time, the operative route remains human beings for all but a handful of enterprises.

Which begs the questions: 1.) Do you really need to have salespeople at all? 2.) If so, what type of salespeople? And, 3.) How should you pay them? I'll look at the answers and your options before I get deep into lots of specific concerns, including what constitutes "salespeople."

1.) Do you really need to have salespeople at all? No. The owner or senior staff wears lots of hats and one of them is or can be selling -- that is, if "selling" indicates handling inquiries and helping customers place their orders. You don't have to hire or engage additional *sales* personnel if order quoting and order taking are the primary responsibilities your company requires. If, however, selling becomes a matter of looking for new business, expanding existing accounts, or is deemed critical to developing a better, more loyal, and more service-oriented function of your company, people who'll be dedicated to handling and managing accounts will likely be the solution – regardless of whether you call them "salespeople" or "customer service representatives."

2) If so, what type of salespeople? The choices here are several.
- Full-time or part-time?
- House representatives classified as employees or independent reps?
- Outside salespeople – the ones who work to a large extent in the field? Or,
- Inside salespeople who work the phones, the Internet, and handle other sales-related tasks?
- Customer service representatives, who are essentially on the receiving end of inquiries, as opposed to generating them, and who perform various non-selling tasks (order taking, sourcing, customer mainte-

nance), and contact customers when instructed to do so?

As you can see, the answer is far from simple. (I'll look at these options in greater depth in the next chapter).

3) How should you pay them? Here, again, there are several choices that need to be determined.

- Straight salary (or fixed hourly wages)?
- Straight commission? (And how much?)
- Draw against commission?
- Salary plus incentives (commissions, bonuses, perks)?
- Does the position require a vehicle – owned by the salesperson or by the company?
- What expenses will the company cover (or reimburse)?

Now, I'll look more closely at the questions and answers here to measure your current thinking in your existing apparel graphics company. Also, if you're a new entrant to the trade you'll get a better understanding of your options for that time when you'll determine whether you want to build a sales force and which compensation mode best fits your situation.

There are significant differences between the roles played by customer service representatives, who work almost exclusively "inside" and have fixed hours, and "outside" salespeople.

Outside salespeople work inside and outside, depending on the level of selling, where the customers are, and the particulars of the customer's accessibility and needs. Salespeople are more likely to work — and be willing to work -- in the evening or on Saturdays, when necessary, to meet a customer at his place of business, in your showroom, at the baseball field, or wherever suits the situation.

By definition, salespeople have as their primary or sole responsibility *selling*, as well as attending to those tasks directly or indirectly related to selling. Salespeople earn their livelihoods primarily or solely in direct relation to their sales performance. And while there are many other differences and similarities in the functions of customer service people and salespeople, the major distinctions between the two come down to their levels of personal involvement in *initiating sales, facilitating continued contacts* with prospects and customers over the period necessary to close sales, and *maintaining and building relationships* with customers and clients long after the initial sale. In soliciting prospects, unlike traditional customer service reps, salespeople proactively continue to work at building relationships until such time as they're converted to customers or tossed overboard.

Customer service representatives generally aren't found in younger companies due to the lack of a sufficiently large and active account base that requires extra layers of service. A major, but infrequent, exception to this norm would be a young company that aggressively markets through extensive lead-generation campaigns that effect high lead volume via Internet marketing, telemarketing, social media, direct mail, and broadcast media. But such companies also are likely to have highly skilled personnel whose compensation includes healthy financial incentives (relative to the effort and skills involved) for converting the leads to active accounts.

Where this type of customer service model is successful, the personnel either act as salespeople, themselves, or turn the leads over to more experienced salespeople who have the requisite skill, personalities, and motivation to carry the ball across the goal line. Think of customer service personnel as being better suited to being on "special teams" and adequate for running the ball on first down. But running and passing the ball on the other downs, making more first downs, and scoring are the work of *professional* salespeople.

Customer service reps diligently attend to phone calls and e-mails, send out quotes and literature, take orders, contact customers with details of production, gather approvals, greet walk-in customers, and carry out a host of other administrative duties. But they don't recruit new customers. That's what professional salespeople do as their most important function. In addition, they do their utmost to keep customers happy, satisfied, and coming back for more.

As in any profession, salespeople in our industry have the obligation to maintain their currency in keeping up with product knowledge and trends; product applications; current technology as well as new, advanced technology that enhances the service level, or upgrades the graphics, customer appreciation, and overall value of the product to the buyer. The pro has to keep up with what's happening the marketplace vis-à-vis styling, color palettes, decorating techniques, promotional ideas, and a host of matters that make his counsel that much more valuable to his customers.

And to stay on top of the field, a pro -- and hopefully the company he represents -- is committed to his own continuing education – from reading trade publications, attending trade shows and seminars, and doing what's necessary to keep "plugged in."

An often overlooked part of the professional salesperson's role in selling apparel graphics is serving as the eyes and ears of the company in the field. His input to management about the "real world" -- because he's on its front line -- is an integral part of the company's intelligence-gathering function.

The most productive and efficient outside salespeople today do a great deal of their work inside, working the phones and the Internet to stay in touch with their prospects and customers to curtail unnecessary travel. But if your company sells custom decorated apparel and competitors in your market utilize outside salespeople, some outside sales component will be incumbent on the company.

But the choice here isn't either-or; many companies that opt to engage outside salespeople also employ competent customer service people. These employees oftentimes working in tandem with sales reps in the field to free the reps from as much many non-selling responsibilities as possible.

For salespeople to be successful and productive, smart management assures them they'll be provided with leads, guarantees them defined areas of specialization and/or territorial integrity, supports them with competent back-up when they're out of the office, and furnishes them with catalogs, price lists, samples, and other sales resources. Professional salespeople in good organizations welcome training, be it conducted in-house, by manufacturers' reps, at trade events, vendor clinics, or at professional development seminars and workshops.

To see how the roles of both customer service personnel and professional salespeople serve the company, I'll look inside the workings of a well-developed model company that I'll call *Master Apparel Graphics, Inc.*, or *MAGI*. The model I'm about to examine typifies the sales management system most of my clients have been using for the past 30 years.

Here's a snapshot of this successful business's sales operation and some considerations and explanation about the company's reasoning behind some key policies.

1. A Commitment to Advertising.

MAGI has an ongoing advertising program that generates cost-effective leads. But its owners also know that even when their very proactive advertising may not generate immediately identifiable leads, their total advertising is an effective long-term investment that serves to create awareness and convey information about the company. When outside salespeople are engaged in prospecting activities, there's an increased likelihood they'll find prospects that have some level of familiarity with the firm. The extent of that familiarity ranges from, "Oh, yes, you're the people who 'sell attention,' right?" to those who react only with a general, "I've heard of your company" response. Beyond direct lead generation and "building the brand," the value of company's advertising makes it easier for its salespeople to open a sale – and eventually close it.

MAGI's marketing support resources include a good communications systems, a respectable website, its own catalog and price list and excellent lead follow-up. MAGI's advertising works well and generates several qualified telephone and e-mail leads daily as well as walk-in first-time visitors.

2. Leads are distributed among the sales force.

At MAGI, all incoming leads are "divvied" up according to the system, with each leads becoming the children of "Mommies." Discussed in more detail in Chapter 27, "Mommy" is the word I use to describe those individuals who'll nurture leads, cradle them, give them love and attention and, most importantly, can make money from leads that eventually grow up to become customers.

3. There's a full-time sales manager.

MAGI is old and big enough to have a full-time sales manager leading his troops, but he also has some personal sales responsibilities, particularly with key accounts that require someone with his advanced level of experience and sophistication. He also might handle other accounts that serve mainly to boost his income through additional personal commissions.

4. Phone lines are answered by professionals.

The incoming lines dedicated for sales are usually answered by either a customer service representative or a full-time salesperson, each of whom mans the showroom and the sales lines for one full day (and occasionally for a second or half day) on Tuesday, Wednesday, or Thursday. On each outside rep's "in-day," he or she also handles walk-ins.

The reason the company has full-charge salespeople manning the phones and the door is that MAGI wants its best salespeople attending to them. With all salespeople on site all day Monday and all afternoon on Friday, and having one on board on the other days of the week, it means prospects and customers are going to get current information on their needs, will know they're working with a pro, and be far more likely to place an order because they're being handled by a *closer*. They'll also be shown more things for future consideration.

In most apparel graphics companies, calls are typically handled by customer service personnel (the boss-- usually a good salesperson, or by whoever is available to answer the call – be it an artist, a production person, or someone other than a real salesperson (usually bad). Artists, production people, and other employees who don't work in sales are as a rule not particularly effective for handling incoming inquiries.

At MAGI, callers and walk-ins are assisted immediately by staff members. In too many companies, callers are identified as to where they're located and then told to call the rep for that territory. That's bad customer service. At MAGI, callers and walk-ins are cared for by the in-house personnel. After the prospect or customer has been attended to, the appropriate rep is then contacted by telephone or e-mail and updated on the contact. At that point the outside sales rep determines who'll handle whatever follow-up is required and when.

As in any profession, salespeople in our industry have the obligation to maintain their currency in keeping up with product knowledge and trends; product applications; current technology as well as new, advanced technology that enhances the service level, or upgrades the graphics, customer appreciation, and overall value of the product to the buyer

5. Territorial Assignments are awarded to each rep.

Each rep has an assigned territory, from which he earns commissions on all accounts located in his territory except for those covered by reps with special market territories (see 6. below), which supersedes the geographical areas where each rep normally rules the turf. The reps, themselves, are authorized to mutually agree, if they choose, to trade accounts or work out individual accommodations with one another regarding accounts and referrals.

6. Reps are Also Assigned to Handle Special Markets.

Each MAGI rep "owns" one or more areas of account specialization, which supersede the restricted geography on general sales. One rep specializes in schools, based on his previous years as a sporting goods and teamwear rep. Another handles the trucking industry, given his earlier position career as a truck driver with a delivery route. Another, a former U.S. Marine MP, specializes in police, fire, and EMT organizations. Each rep's specialty markets reflect special expertise and experience the reps bring from their previous careers, personal connections, hobbies and personal interests, and/or other individual considerations

7. The Salespeople are Employees.

Each rep is an employee of the corporation and receives those benefits, privileges, and perks all employees receive -- including subsidized healthcare, voluntary 401(k) pension participation, paid holidays, vacations, and personal days.

The fact that MAGI's outside salespeople are defined as employees, not independent contractors, doesn't derive from altruism, but because the IRS and Revenue Canada would view similar non-employee arrangements as an employee-employer relationship anyhow, since each rep earns virtually all of his/her income from MAGI sales. MAGI provides each outside rep with desk space, and business cards (which show the company's phone number, web address and street address), samples and sample kits, sets policies, and issues each rep a company-paid cell phone.

Many business owners see having to pay their share of mandated employment taxes and benefits as onerous when it comes to salespeople. They'd prefer to work through an independent contractor relationship and unknowingly conclude straight-commission salespeople "don't cost me anything" if they don't produce. They don't realize that unsuccessful salespeople do "cost." They use up management time, they dilute the company's reputation (when customers see a procession of salespeople come and go), they don't work within the company's overall or specific marketing objectives, and they don't build the long-term relationships and loyalty that ensure a company with a stable account base.

Unlike its local competitors, MAGI views the employer-employee relationship as a plus, where management can direct the activities of its salespeople within defined boundaries and goals, discipline its personnel when necessary for non-performance, can impose restrictive covenants (such as non-compete contracts), and essentially be free to operate its sales force as a business, not a luxury or a plaything or letting the lunatics run the asylum.

Dumb Mistake No. 21
Discounting the salesperson's commission when
selling directly to customers

---

8. MAGI reps' work schedules are set by management.

Every Monday, all three outside reps spend the entire day working in the office preparing quotes, doing research, making appointments via phone and e-mail, and checking on the status of their orders and outstanding quotes. The sales manager is available to work with each on more challenging orders and new opportunities. They all have lunch together and have become "family" with one another. There's an atmosphere of competitiveness among the reps in the sales "bullpen," but it's all friendly because the reps rarely bang heads on specific accounts given the defined territories and special markets each has unto himself or herself.

Each rep has a small desktop Liberty Bell, which he or she rings every time each finishes writing an order. It called "the happy noise," and seemingly every time the other reps hear a bell, you'll see them reaching for the phone to stir up or close another sale. (The tradition derives from the author's roots in Philadelphia).

At 3:30 p.m. on Mondays, everyone attends the weekly sales meeting, which is dedicated to satisfying overall company sales and marketing goals, addresses an ongoing agenda to improve performance, and includes training sessions and interaction with other company departments to keep everyone on the same page. The meeting usually lasts about an hour.

All reps work inside again from 1:00 -5:00 p.m on Fridays. During this period, each rep will have a one-on-one session with the sales manager to review call reports, individual performance, and whatever individual agenda both feel is important. Each weekly conference runs

20-30 minutes, which is more than sufficient time for the manager and the field rep to stay plugged in to one another's radar screens. The rest of the day is devoted – just as on Mondays – to preparing quotes, doing research, making appointments, and checking order status and outstanding quotes.

When manufacturer's reps call on MAGI, they've learned to do so on Mondays or Fridays so that they can use the opportunity to meet with the salespeople to personally show them new products, teach about field applications, and review their lines. From these presentations, the salespersons' opinions on what their company should carry and promote is incorporated into management's planning.

Several times during the year, MAGI salespeople attend seminars, workshops, and clinics offered in-house, at local venues, or at trade events.

9. The Compensation System for Outside and Inside Reps and How They Earn It.

Each rep earns a pre-determined (and equal) base salary, which amounts to 50% to 60% of their projected annual earnings, with years of service to the company being the means by which longer term reps earn higher base pay. Their commissions are based on *total invoiced monthly sales* -- not individual orders -- and escalate from 2% to 8% of the gross sale as each of four increasing sales plateaus is eclipsed. The reps also earn bonuses based on achieving quarterly and annual goals. Occasionally, other bonuses are offered for meeting specific marketing-related goals, such as reactivating dead accounts, selling a new category of garments, or selling accounts in targeted markets, such as the healthcare industry, financial institutions, and high-tech companies.

A few sales contests held from time to time during the year are designed in such a way that each rep has the ability to win. Ideally all the reps win all the contests. There are never any winner-take-*all* contests.

Each rep is required to have his own vehicle, and provide evidence of insurance that covers business usage of the vehicle. Each receives a fixed monthly car expense allowance, keeping the burdens of record keeping and insurance liability on the salespeople, not the company. When more costly travel is warranted, MAGI covers additional fuel, lodging, meals, tolls, and other trip-related expenses.

MAGI's compensation system evolved from what began as a straight-commission arrangement, which never succeeded in its main objective of building a loyal sales force. The ultimate failure of these straight-commission arrangements is due to the inherent weaknesses of such a system in an industry with peaks and valleys and lots of competition. For a while, the company engaged its reps via a commission-draw arrangement, which essentially is a straight-commission system that irons out the reps' income over the seasonal peaks and valleys. Often-times, though, the rep that still "owes" the company for unmet sales projections leaves for greener pastures. The percentage of companies that recover commission balances due *from* the salesperson is nil.

I can tell you from decades of intimate involvement in this industry, the turnover rate in sales is 90% within six months; three-quarters of those who fail within this window do so within the first 90 days. Of the 10% who survive the first six months, 90% of them will be gone by their two-year anniversaries.

MAGI's track record wasn't any better, which eventually spurred the firm to implement a system that recognized the realities of the selling cycle, the cash flow needs of the salespeople, and how a better system would cost less and earn the company and the reps more money in the long run. What MAGI has built over the years is -- finally! – a pro-ductive, successful, confident team of sales professionals. Its warriors are fairly compensated and well managed, get regular doses of train-ing and retraining, and have sufficient support to continue performing the sales volume levels they're capable of, committed to, and need to achieve to stay in the game.

To remind salespeople of how they're doing as individuals and as part of the sales department "décor," there's a chart in the sales manager's office (which customers can't see) tracking each rep's sales volume through the month and it's visible to all salespeople.

Part-time salespeople? Oh, there are a few here and there, but the company really doesn't need them nor does it focus any management energy on them.

One other individual, a customer service representative, works in the sales department. Her title at MAGI is "Sales Coordinator," which gives her a little more respect and clout when working with customers. She's paid hourly, but also receives additional compensation for bringing in new accounts as well as a performance-based incentive when the sales force validates its monthly sales target.

While the senior-most sales rep came to the company four years ago when her former employer went out of business, one was recruited by the company's owner, and the other rep started as a Sales Coordinator where three to six months on the job provides ample experience, understanding of the process, and motivation to move into outside sales. This entry path is now MAGI's most favorable means of recruiting, training, and testing new candidates for outside sales positions. The sales manager feels the company can add at least one full-charge salesperson per year through this channel, though he's always on the lookout for qualified additions to the sales force. Right now he's trying to convince a cable television salesman who calls on MAGI to switch teams.

The Sales Coordinator handles walk-ins and callers when no one else is available (which is uncommon under the system), coordinates art approvals and proofs going between the customers and the company, takes messages and tries to handle whatever matters she can for the outside reps. This sometimes can include filing paperwork, distribution chores, and other sales support activities. If and when this Sales Coordinator moves into full-time sales, she'll be given some existing accounts, earn her fair share of leads, have a territory and market specialties assigned, and be phased into the sales compensation plan during a 90-day transition period. She'll be given every opportunity -- and sufficient time -- to succeed, while earning a reasonable base income to enable her to meet her personal financial responsibilities.

10. The company requires salespeople to network.

Among the company's weapons is its requirement that each salesperson be involved in at least two ongoing networking opportunities. One is usually a membership in a community-oriented group such as a parent-teachers organization, scouting, a civic or service club, church, or business association. The other is usually as a volunteer serving on a committee that's organized around a community event, a charity, or some other function that enables the salespeople to meet a broad cross-section of individuals who are likely involved in a wide range of commercial, civic, educational, governmental, cultural and social activity --and are influential with where decorated apparel purchases are sourced or are connected in some way to those who make these decisions.

11. The sales force reflects its customers and its community.

MAGI's sales force has the added asset of having salespeople with diverse backgrounds and attributes. One is female, two have college degrees, two are married with children, and one is a single parent. Reflecting in part the area's ethnic mix, two are white, one is Asian-Hispanic, one is Jewish, and one is Catholic. Their interests range from country line dancing to model railroading, coaching a girls' soccer team, camping, skiing, and restoring classic cars, among a host of personal avocations and endeavors. Each exploits his or her interests and background occasionally to gain access to decision makers or other folks who know them.

The current sales coordinator is 24, single, African-American, female, speaks fluent Spanish (which she learned as an exchange student in Argentina), attended college for two years and is taking night courses toward completing her degree. She's an avid fitness enthusiast. Her brother is a well-known local TV weatherman, and her father was a restaurant equipment salesman for 30 years and still has lots of good contacts. She's great with the customers and vendors, is dependable, learns fast, and is a wizard on the company's computer system. Though she has brought in only a few orders on her own, she's anxious to start her sales career in the field. The odds of her success, given both her attributes and the company's support for new reps, are quite good.

Starting a sales force is by no means easy, and when attempted by people with no real background or feel for it, it's usually a losing proposition, especially when it's premised on a straight-commission compensation system. So, some serious homework should be undertaken to learn about the rigors of structuring a sales force, recruiting and hiring considerations, compensation systems, and on the leadership and management of salespeople. There's also much to be learned about the importance of non-monetary (psychological) compensation of salespeople. The failure to investigate these far-reaching aspects of organizing and maintaining a sales force virtually ensures its malfunctioning and collapse. A treasure trove of literature on the subject awaits you. Start by Googling the term "sales management" and soliciting the wisdom and counsel of successful sales managers and sales pros.

The two dumbest questions I get when teaching programs on developing a sales force are:

Question 1. *"Should I pay a salesperson the same commission for a reorder that I pay the salesperson for his first order from a new account?"* I answer first: "No, unless you want the salesman to quit immediately!" Followed by: "Yes, absolutely! You should pay the same commission rates because you want the salesperson to continue calling on the account and growing it." This question reveals that the person (usually an owner) asking it thinks salespeople don't work to get reorders, which also reveals the inquirer has never been employed as a salesperson. Re-orders serve as the salesperson's annuity system. The rep works to build his account base to build his income year after year. If the rep earns a reduced commission on re-orders, it's a disincentive that will result in his looking elsewhere for a place to hang his hat – and likely take his accounts with him.

Question 2. *"If I sell an order directly to a customer and no salesperson is involved in bringing in the order or the account, can I discount the sales by the amount that I would have paid a salesperson?"*

I answer first: "Yes, if you want to see *all* your salespeople quit immediately!" Followed by: "Were you to do what you're suggesting, you in essence are competing with the salesperson – unfairly, I might add. And, over time, you are training customers NOT to place orders with salespeople, but rather to call the sales office or e-mail orders, eliminating the rep from the process. What salesperson would want to continue selling for your company after losing a sale to the owner who cheated the rep out of what he gets paid to do? You can screw the salesman out of a commission ONCE. You won't get a second chance."

CHAPTER

THE TYPES OF PEOPLE YOU MIGHT LIKE TO HIRE FOR CUSTOMER SERVICE, INSIDE SALES AND OUTSIDE SALES POSITIONS

If you're contemplating starting or upgrading a sales force, you must determine the types of people you might want to hire.

Certain personalities and personal proclivities are better suited to careers in sales than others, yet the uninformed assume being a good talker is the key to success. Far from it. I'd rather have a good listener any day of the week, because the profession today has moved toward a consultative selling relationship. Today, "assertive" is good, "aggressive" is not. Aggressive salespeople aren't listeners.

I'll share a tip-of-the-iceberg glimpse into the type of people who might find success in sales. Based on extensive, empirical, psychographic research by social psychologists, these are the indicators you should be looking for when evaluating new candidates for sales positions in your company. There's also a scoring sheet for your use in rating applicants (see Figure 16).

Figure 15: **The 11 Characteristics of the Ideal Salesperson**

1. High self-esteem – The person likes him/herself and is proud of his/her accomplishments and abilities

2. Fair-to-high self-confidence – The person exudes a strong belief in his/her abilities

3. Highly self-motivated – The person is a self-starter and needs little outside encouragement to succeed

4. Achievement-oriented – The person desires to complete tasks and proactively seeks new challenges

5. Need for recognition – When reaching his/her goals and achievements, the person wants others to know of his/her success

6. Goal-oriented – The person sets his/her own level of achievement and works toward accomplishing it

7. Better-than-average math skills – Not a genius or a wizard, but better at math than most folks

8. Better-than-average verbal and writing skills – Speaks and writes well as viewed by others

9. Enjoys being with and working with people – Gregarious and thrives on interacting with others

10. Enjoys learning new skills – Welcomes insight and training and seeks it out

11. Enjoys money and material things – The person likes exercising the benefits of his/her success.

When interviewing salespeople, I look for evidence of how the individual cares about his/her attire and grooming, wears distinctive or showy jewelry, tie, scarf, fashion accessories.

If you find a candidate with all 11 characteristics, you've found – theoretically -- "The Most Perfect Salesperson on Earth!" There is, however, no such thing as a perfect candidate. But these attributes do make sense and finding candidates who tend to reflect more of this ideal profile gives a company a sales rep who's more likely to succeed than candidates whose attributes deviate substantially with the "ideal." Think about some of the successful salespeople you've known and you'll see things that mirror much of the ideal profile. By the way, should you find the perfect 11-for-11 candidate, please be advised the score is by no means a guarantee of success.

I've included a *Score Sheet for Evaluating Candidates for Sales Positions* (Figure 16), which is an evaluation test for helping you gauge the potential for success of sales candidates. While the data for the research was compiled on outside salespeople, the findings largely hold for inside sales reps and customer service people. Scores for the latter candidates are, however, measurably lower than those for outside salespeople. The areas are categorized and the values are given for each of the 11 components, each of which requires the interviewer to make a subjective judgment. A 12th component was added by this researcher for the benefit of management to input a value assigned by the interviewer as to the comfort level one has about the candidate, his/her demeanor, and other hard-to-quantify characteristics. I've designated that this area is 15% of the overall score and it introduces more flexibility for management in scoring candidates.

Strong, positive, motivated salespeople transfer their personal attributes to the company, deserved or not. The representative's manner is -- and by extension, the company's -- friendly and knowledgeable, his/her best feet are put forward, and there's a smile on both sides of the equation.

Whether the enterprise elects to go with customer service representatives, outside salespeople, or both, along with sales support people or sales coordinators, the people who have direct contact -- in person via Internet communications, or over the phone -- are the embodiment of everything a company claims itself to be. Given the tools, the training, the financial support, the systems, and well-defined management structures, the good people who'll venture forth on the company's behalf into the marketplace will radiate with professionalism. Given what's at stake, why would any company want to build its identity and its future with salespeople who project anything less than confidence, authority, friendliness, and professionalism?

Figure 16: **Score Sheet for Evaluating Candidates for Sales Positions**
© *2001 Mark L. Venit / Roundtable Management Systems LLC*

Subjectively score each attribute per the range indicated. Circle the point value. (0 = the lowest, 10 the highest)

Part I. Self-Actualization   **(maximum is 40 points)**

1. Level of Self-Esteem (score 0-10)   0 1 2 3 4 5 6 7 8 9 10

2. Level of Self-Confidence (score 0-10)   0 1 2 3 4 5 6 7 8 9 10

3. Level of Self-Motivation (score 0-10)   0 1 2 3 4 5 6 7 8 9 10

4. Need for Achievement (score 0-5)   0 1 2 3 4 5

5. Need for Recognition (score 0-5)   0 1 2 3 4 5

Part II. Skills & Attributes   **(maximum is 45 points)**

6. Goal-Oriented (score 0-5)   0 1 2 3 4 5

7. Math Skills (score 0-5)   0 1 2 3 4 5

8. Language Skills

   a. Verbal skills (score 0-10)   0 1 2 3 4 5 6 7 8 9 10

   b. Written Skills (score 0-10)   0 1 2 3 4 5 6 7 8 9 10

9. People-Oriented (score 0-5)   0   1   2   3   4   5

10. Learning-Oriented (score 0-5)   0   1   2   3   4   5

11. Materialistically-Oriented (score 0-5)   0   1   2   3   4   5

Part III. The Intangible Factor   (maximum is 15 points)

12. Vibes & Chemistry (score 0-15)   0   1   2   3   4   5   6   7   8   9

                                              10   11   12   13   14   15

© 2001 Mark L. Venit / Roundtable Management Systems LLC

In case you were wondering if there's a certain type personality, yes there is a "zone" where you'll find the bulk of successful salespeople travel. The chart in Figure 16 was developed from research data from 880 outside salespeople in the advertising industry who completed personality tests (The No. 2 pencil type) surveying a range of variables. The diagram in Figure 17 identifies candidates vis-à-vis a *Psychosocial Profile of Successful Outside Salespeople.*

The chart is divided into four sections horizontally indicating Communications Orientation (in speaking with others) from Reticent to Passive to Assertive to Aggressive, as defined below:

- **Reticent**: quiet, relatively uncommunicative verbally and non-verbally, speaks when spoken to

- **Passive**: quiet but not comatose; will communicate adequately when something or someone interests him/her; often yielding or submissive when challenged or confronted

- **Assertive**: eager to communicate one's thoughts or to prove a point; nonetheless a good listener who knows when it's his/her turn to speak again and does

- **Aggressive**: poor listener; always on the offensive, bold, energetic, classic "Type A" demeanor; at times generates alienation

The chart is further divided by Emotional Orientation vis-à-vis Customers (and people in general) by empathy and egocentrism, defined as:

- **Empathetic**: understands where someone is coming from; able to psychologically put himself/herself in the other guy's shoes; able to relate to the person, thing, or event

- **Egocentric**: relates to stimuli as it affects him/her personally; perceives no need to relate to the feelings of others except as an opportunity to benefit from the situation or individual; has little no need to walk in the other guy's shoes and would have difficulty doing so because his feet --and often his head and his mouth -- are too big.

Certain personalities and personal proclivities are better suited to careers in sales than others, yet the uninformed assume being a good talker is the key to success

To appreciate what the results tell us, in a nutshell, the best candidates for outside sales are assertive but not aggressive. They are empathetic to the extent that they can understand the customers' and prospects' needs (and are skilled at finding out what they are) and egocentric to the extent that they want to – and do -- close sales wherever possible. The football-shaped area shown on the diagram (Area F) is where you'll find the best candidates for outside sales.

Good customer service candidates tend to be in the box-shaped area (Area E), where candidates range from somewhat passive to somewhat assertive and have a good balance on the empathetic-egocentric axis, though skewing above the middle line. Good inside salespeople tend to shift toward the assertive-aggressive zone and are slightly more egocentric than empathetic. Remember, this diagram is based on aggregate data, which has ample examples of exceptions to the rules. On the other hand, it has been quite useful as a predictor of success as applied to decorated apparel salespeople (and inside salespeople in general).

As for some of the other sections of the chart, here's what you can learn from it:

▪ Don't hire people in the corner area marked "A." They tend to be very quiet, generally inarticulate, and not money-motivated. Think of them as folks who are addicted to soap operas and relate to the protagonists as if they are real people.

▪ Don't hire people in the corner area marked "B." They're not happy with themselves, blame other people or unfortunate circumstances for their troubles and act out their frustrations on others.

▪ Don't hire people in the corner area marked "C." They're uncommunicative and live only in the present, not looking to build a future or improve their stations in life – except in their dreams.

▪ Don't hire people in the corner area marked "D." These are very angry people – angry with themselves, strangers, their loved ones (or former loved ones), the government, the world – and sometimes everything and anyone. They are extreme in their beliefs -- be it politics, religion, and whatever causes that turn them on – so much so that they're also capable of violence against their perceived enemies. They and the groups they might belong to could be solicited for custom-imprinted bomb vests!

Figure 17: **Psychosocial Profile of Successful Outside Salespeople**

	Reticent	Passive	Assertive	Aggressive
Empathetic Emotional Orientation (vis-à-vis customers and prospects)	**A.**		E. F.	**B.**
Egocentric Emotional Orientation				
	C.			**D.**

© *2001 Mark L. Venit / Roundtable Management Systems LLC*

When interviewing candidates for sales positions, refer to the candidate's resume and ask open-ended questions about the person's skills and experience. It gives the candidate an opportunity to talk about himself/ herself – and give you an opportunity to listen and observe. The candidate should be the one who does most of the talking in the interview.

Do let the candidate show his stuff in role-playing (as the salesperson) with you (posing as the customer).

Dumb Mistake No. 21
Taking the high failure rate of rookies hired on a straight-commissioned basis won't apply to your company.

As I've been interviewing sales candidates throughout my entire career and still do so on behalf of clients, allow me to give you a some advice: Observe the "little things" -- grooming, neatness, speech, and your own special considerations, such as health issues (it's legal to ask these questions if they are directly job-related), personal habits, vices, day/night orientation, civic/community activity, and other factors that will influence your decision.

A final comment here must be directed at ALL the other people in your company that work in positions outside the regular sales and marketing loop in your company: they're ALL in sales, too! They need to be told this and they need to be shown how their participation in sales goes into every design they execute, every screen they image, every graphic they digitize, every garment they print or embroider, every garment they count, right down to how they put the garments in boxes and how the label looks on the box. They have impact every step of the way.

If one member of the team screws up, gets sloppy, takes unnecessary shortcuts, or leaves evidence of his negligence or disinterest, that one person can blow to smithereens all the good efforts of everyone else who played a role is producing the order. Employees need to fully understand the ramifications of an "attitude" and how that one bad apple might cost the company its most valuable revenue-producing asset: the customers who pay the production crew's wages, the salespeople's commissions, and the boss's salary. And if the bad apple proves to be your lowest-paid employee, he might very well be viewed instead as one of the most expensive.

If accelerated sales volume is the payoff of your marketing strategy, the hard work that goes into it and the fuel that makes everything else possible in the company, senior management must make sales, selling, and salesmanship primary responsibilities of the individuals who perform these functions. Those who do the front-line selling must want, understand -- and receive -- the rewards for successfully closing an order and opening up a new account.

You'll recall some of the questions posed in the previous chapter regarding your options of how to pay outside reps – straight salary, a base salary plus commissions and other financial incentives, straight commission, a draw-against-commission, and, in some companies, a percentage of gross margin or a percentage of net profit.

Each methodology for compensating outside salespeople has its advantages and limitations. I'll review them here briefly.

Straight Salary – It's done in extremely rare cases in our industry. It offers little incentive for reps to maximize their potential income. In the few companies I know that have salaried salespeople, the reps tend to be over 50, have been at the business for several years, don't solicit new accounts, and spend most of their time at a desk, though the good ones work the phones well. Most salaried reps are content to trade potential for security and stability.

Straight Commission – This is what's favored by most companies and, given the industry's seasonal peaks and valleys, is the reason why so few reps succeed. As a rule, reps paid on straight commission don't last long and tend to move on to positions with other companies, sometimes competitors, that provide a base salary they can count on during the valley periods, especially first quarter and mid-summer. Those who succeed on straight commission arrangements have many years of experience, bring a strong book of accounts, and manage their acorns well – the ones they put away for winter and the ones they sow to grow new accounts. They work mainly on their own accounts and are skilled at earning referrals and closing them. Rookies who work on straight commission rarely last beyond 90 days in the custom decorated apparel business and gravitate toward selling orders, not accounts, a practice that is both understandable and one that becomes a self-ful-filling prophesy.

Draw-Against-Commission – This works mainly for experienced reps with strong followings. For rookies it keeps them on board longer than straight commission will, but it rarely endures more than six months. When reps get behind (they owe the company sales against advances), they look for greener pastures. At the same time, the boss loses confi-dence in the rep and soon enough cuts or significantly reduces the draw. There are few winners in this system over the long haul.

Percentages of Gross Margin or Gross Profit – These arrangements see their greatest success with experienced reps and with some highly successful independent reps. But as it usually entails intimate under-standings by the rep of the company's cost structures, it tends to draw in orders sold at low margins -- which help the rep more than company. It's the most prevalent system used in the promotional products indus-try, especially with independent reps and part-timers.

Base Plus Commission (plus other monetary incentives) – Of all the systems I've observed and directed in the industry, this is the one with the most success in terms of keeping good reps on board, keep-ing them motivated and well paid, and retaining them for the longer term. It softens the slow times, increases the reps' efforts and returns in strong seasons, and assures the rep some income stability, security, and a comfort level with the company. In companies that have outside sales forces, especially those in which I'm retained for screening, hiring, training salespeople and sales managers, this route is the one that provides the best return on investment for the company's owners and the greatest overall performance by the salespeople. If you decide to upgrade or initiate an outside sales force, it's the only arrangement I wholeheartedly endorse and recommend. Period.

As with that very unambiguous opinion, if you choose to sell through reps, I recommend doing so only with salespeople who are employees of your company, not straight-commissioned independent contractors.

Whatever base salary and standard fixed commission rates you pay, you should state the circumstances and products where commission rates are variable (usually on very low or very high margin products) and certain areas of endeavors that are strictly conserved for the house (oftentimes for government bids and tenders). And be sure to state your policies about when checks are issued to reps.

Now, having said everything I've said about sales forces and salespeople, do I recommend that all custom apparel graphics companies have outside salespeople? On the contrary, most custom apparel graphics companies can sidestep having a cadre of outside salespeople, by focusing on establishing a solid lead-generation function. That's the end product of effective, productive, proactive advertising investments and a well-rounded proactive marketing program. While having one or more good salespeople is a powerful weapon for generating business, the industry's track record and turnover rates for finding and keeping good salespeople leave much to be desired. Should you be reticent to start an outside sales force, a considerably more viable alternative to this option is building a solid core of customer service representatives, coming up in the next chapter.

CHAPTER

TRANSFORMING CUSTOMER SERVICE REPRESENTATIVES INTO CUSTOMER SERVICE SALESPEOPLE

There are several alternatives to starting a sales force, and some are better and more effective than others.

Three very low-cost options are networking, conducting public relations campaigns, and telemarketing. Networking should be done on ongoing basis whatever options you choose, and is discussed further in Chapter 34. Public relations campaigns, also discussed in Chapter 30, rarely work over the long run unless you are or become skilled in its ways, and tend to be short-lived in the vast majority of cases. Telemarketing for appointments is an effective means of soliciting business, even thought it's a numbers game where, if you're committed to doing it, it means you can handle a lot of rejection. For every 100 calls you make, making actual contact with at best half the folks on the other end of the line, you will land a few leads and a handful of appointments.

But are you cut out for telemarketing? Do you enjoy doing it? Do you like being solicited over the phone? Most people, including most entrepreneurs, will answer no to all three questions. You can, however, contract the services of professional telemarketers and telemarketing agencies, and will get leads and appointments. But a high percentages of the leads from these sources aren't well qualified for follow-up selling and a high percentage of the appointments booked aren't honored. The cost for these individuals and agencies, who work on soliciting locally, regionally, and nationally, average $20 to $40 per hour (and usually include all long-distance charges).

Engaging the selling services of independent manufacturer's reps and rep groups, promotional products salespeople and distributors, and other sales agencies presents opportunities. But they are casual in nature, rarely offer your business any exclusivity arrangements, are fraught with constant pressure for you to discount already discounted or commissionable pricing structures, and rarely prove long term.

Sampling (sending finished garment samples or finished graphics to pre-qualified prospects) is another alternative to starting a sales force, but its effectiveness is limited primarily to selling preprint lines (apparel products for resale at retail). Aside from the fact that this sector isn't covered in this book, it's an area within the decorated apparel industry with a failure rate of more than 90% within six months and very challenging barriers to entry for beginners and veterans alike.

Yet another alternative to starting a sales force is exhibiting at consumer and trade events. Most apparel graphics veterans and beginners fail miserably at this due to matters of cost, lack of experience or proper positioning, and other factors such as climate, geography, and competition, among others. Exhibiting is a cost-effective option only when it's part of an overall marketing program, not the "be all and end all" of it.

The best alternative to hiring outside salespeople and one with greater likelihood of success is building a team of well-trained, money-motivated customer service reps.

This lower-cost, lower-risk alternative to putting too many eggs in the sales force basket is most effective in conjunction with a lead-generating system that produces enough action to keep good customer service representatives busy handling inquiries from qualified prospects and satisfied repeat customers. With more inquiries coming in from prospects, the outside rep's efforts at stirring up business are supplanted to a large extent by the lead-generating process. With more people looking for your products, asking about pricing, availability, and turnaround time, the task of qualifying the leads becomes the focus of the customer service people. Properly motivated by money and trained to do more than simply answering questions – but becoming skilled at asking good ones -- the customer service person's role transforms more to selling and closing orders than simply servicing leads and being pleasant. I'll look at a lead-generating model in Chapter 28.

The process doesn't end when the phone call is completed or an e-mail inquiry has been responded to.

It moves toward a higher-level marketing effort, one designed to stay in contact with the prospect, ascertaining needs, and offering solutions until the prospect places a first order.

But to make the system work well, there are a few caveats that go beyond hiring order takers and order administrators.

1. Customer service employees all need training.

Seeing to it that customer service as well as all administrative employees really understand the process of selling and producing decorated apparel and other categories the company deals in doesn't happen by itself. Without training, mistakes come with the territory. That's why it's incumbent on management to proactively take the time to teach, show, and explain what the company does and how it does it. The training process should be planned in advance. Taking the time – or more precisely, *making* the time -- will pay big dividends in saving time and money, reducing or minimizing dumb mistakes, and educating your employees to fully understand that *everyone is in sales*. As mentioned before, it is imperative that all employees know that each person in the organization plays an important role in the completion of an order and the satisfaction of the people who really pay their salaries – the customers.

Training should encompass all the workflow phases: call-handling techniques, data mining (for caller data), and gaining a cogent understanding and command of the entire process. This includes taking the order, processing it through the system, and knowing about purchasing and receiving, how the art and digitizing functions rely on accurate and complete data, what's involved in preparing art and digitizing, pre-production operations (screen making, machine threading, setting up machines for CAD-CUT®, digital printing, direct-to-garment printing, etc.), production operations, and post-production tasks (quality control, counting finished garments and other items, folding, boxing, labeling, and shipping).

Each customer service employee should be required to spend time – from an hour to several hours – in each area to see it first hand. The hours or the few days it'll take to experience an order from order entry to completion will cut months off the learning curve and preclude otherwise inevitable mistakes.

Unless and until the staffer has sufficient knowledge of the workflow system and a working command of the parts of the system -- and how they all interact with one another – the company has a weak link that's certain to hamper both efficiency and profitability. Understanding why the system works engenders an understanding of why the employee's job exists to begin with, and why it needs to be done well.

The training of the customer service support personnel doesn't end with the initial orientation process. It needs to be reinforced and upgraded from time to time – once a month or quarterly on an ongoing basis. In most companies, such follow-up training tends to happen only when a crisis has occurred and finally spurs management to act. Continuous training is the antidote to continuing crises.

2. Customer service employees need incentives.

In most companies, customer service personnel are paid either hourly wages or a salary, and without regard for sales performance. Without some small carrots, the best that management can expect is that its employees will do a good job, which is usually characterized as relatively few mistakes, generally accurate work, and pleasant, efficient order processing. These things are, of course, highly desirable, but what management doesn't get without incentives is an employee who is proactive in returning calls, diligent on making following up sales calls, and motivated to do suggestive selling (as in, "You want fries with that?").

Point 11 in The 11 Characteristics of the Ideal Salesperson was that successful salespeople enjoy money and material things. Good customer service people don't necessarily have to be money-motivated, but money-motivated customer service representatives do more than simply field calls and e-mail inquiries and take orders as instructed. Money-motivated customer service people care about closing the sale, selling additional products and services, deflecting discounts, and making sure the company gets paid.

What types of incentives work best? The most effective incentive is: money. It can be paid in the form of a small commission or "overage" on orders written, for soliciting and bringing in new customers, and for creating sales on specific products and services specified by management.

First, I'll look at commissions or "overage" incentives for customer service representatives. It doesn't take much. In the incentive systems I introduce to clients, I refer to "peanut points" – fractional percentages ranging from .25% to 1% on orders written or orders handled and shepherded through the system on behalf of an outside rep. In some cases, such as when a customer service person is teamed with an outside rep, the outside rep pays the small commission by accepting a commensurate reduction is his own commissions. In most cases, however, the company pays the small amount without asking for the money from the outside rep. The small actual dollar amount paid this way tends to be a means for the company to make additional money and shouldn't be character-ized as an expense. The main objective of this form of incentive is to free the outside rep to do more business while relying on the customer service person to handle the details and legwork wherever possible.

In the case of a company without outside reps, the customer service receives these peanut points as an incentive to be more proactive with customers than simply reactive in handling orders. In handling $10,000 in orders, the customer service person earns $25 to $100 (.25% to 1%) for her effort. What makes the incentive worthwhile for the company is that, in theory, the money-motivated rep doesn't waste time on unpro-ductive tasks, being idle, or waiting for her next assignment. She knows when she's caught up on her other assignments that she can pick up the phone and solicit a customer or contact a prospect – or an absolute stranger -- to try to generate some interest or some action. If she initi-ates two calls a day (10 a week), that's 500 or more potential income-generating calls per year.

With even very limited effectiveness, say 3% of those 500 solicitations from customer service/sales reps, the company probably opens 15 new customers and her efforts generate dozens of new orders and re-orders from existing accounts. If she's talented, she probably gets a few good referrals, too. Add it up and it's probably $7,500 a year or more from the new accounts, a few grand more in new orders from existing accounts, and a few grand more in orders from the referred accounts. Add it up and the extra effort of the customer service rep hustles $15,000 in brand new business and generates net profits of several thousand dollars for, what, 50 total hours of work in the course of a year?

Paying her .25% to 1% on the business from existing accounts gener-ates only $18.75 to $75 in peanut points of the $7,500 cited above, and at, say, 5%, earns her $375. That's about $400-500 in extra income for doing her job plus working a little harder to pocket the extra money.

As for what my own clients tend to pay in commissions and overages to customer service reps who spend the extra minutes to go the extra mile, it averages 1.0 to 2.5% for servicing accounts. That is in addition to a base salary or hourly wages, plus 5% to 10% on generating new accounts from proactive solicitations to customers not walking in, calling in, or e-mailing to place orders. Of the $15,000 cited two paragraphs earlier, that's $75 to $187.50 on selling to existing accounts and $375 to $750 on bring in new business in the course of a year – more than $1,000 in earnings from the company's gross profit of about $3,000 to $4,500, based on modest margins.

Next, I'll discuss using point systems as an incentive. An alternative to tracking sales volume is to institute a point system whereby customer service personnel are rewarded through selling units, not dollars, of decorated apparel. Regardless of the dollars involved, the number of imprint colors, stitch counts, and the number of locations of decoration on the garment, salespeople earn their rewards by focusing on closing the sale and putting "points on the scoreboard." This system works well with new customer service reps who've yet to learn the skills and nuances of "upselling."

Money-motivated customer service people care about closing the sale, selling additional products and services, deflecting discounts, and making sure the company gets paid

In these arrangements point values are assigned to products with some relationship to their selling prices. Below is a typical model for assigning values:

- T-shirts, caps, and tote bags are set at 1 one point each.
- Shorts, aprons, and barrel bags earn two points per unit.
- Fleecewear, athletic tops, and wind shirts earn three points each. Names and/or numbers on those team arments score one additional point (varying from per order or per dozen units).
- Golf/polo shirts and denim and poplin shirts are set at four points each.
- Jackets command five to 10 points each, according to price levels of various styles.

You also can establish point values for different types of signs and banners, fan hands, scrubs, and an array of other items you offer. Setting point levels for unspecified items can be done on a case-by-case basis, with the point values reflecting basic cost of the item relative to the values of already specified items. The determination of point values is set solely by management.

The system works for handling routine orders for the company from

244 THE BUSINESS OF T-SHIRTS: *A Textbook for Success in Marketing and Selling Decorated Apparel*

existing accounts and for new business that arrives by the usual channels – walk-ins, call-ins, and e-mails.

In creating new accounts through personal efforts, point values are amplified.

Dumb Mistake No. 22
Believing cash incentives for customer service reps is an unnecessary expense.

Rewards for achieving various levels of performance come in the form of dollars, prizes, or perks or in a system that provides for both cash and prizes.

Now I'll look at some of the considerations for constructing your own system. At 1,000 points, probably in the range of $4,000 to $5,000 in volume, the award can be $50 in cash or prizes. These could include a car wash pass good for five washes, a restaurant gift certificate for $35 plus two tickets to the movies, a free tank of gasoline (up to 18 gallons or so), or other rewards that the recipient will use, usually tell friends and family about, and share with a friend or loved one.

At 10,000 points (about $40,000 to $50,000 in sales volume), the rewards can be exchanged for multiples of the 1,000-point choices or for something much grander. Consider giving an all-expenses-paid weekend for two at a respectable hotel, a laptop computer or other electronics, dinner for two at a nice restaurant along with tickets to a Broadway show or rock concert, or something else that the employee will enjoy, work toward, tell friends and family about. Another idea is to award a $500 shopping spree at Home Depot, Lowes, Sears, Macy's, or other department store. And when presenting the cash or prize, do it at a sales meeting so everyone else can share in the celebration and, more importantly, realize that performance pays.

I remember when a client observed that, "It seems like you're telling everyone they're in business for themselves!" To which I responded, "That indeed is a key goal of spiffs along with commissions, bonuses and other incentives that encourage and stimulate money-motivated people to run with the ball when it comes to taking advantage of all their opportunities to earn more by doing more." In part it's a game that all participants can enjoy playing and that everyone can win – and the biggest winner is the company, itself, that should relish the obligation to pay lots and lots of commissions, bonuses and spiffs (special incentives) to as many – hopefully all – customer service and salespeople. That comment derives from my own career in which I've found writing a commission check to be the most pleasurable expense I'll ever have!

Over time, each spiff teaches a seller he or she has the ability to benefit personally from extra effort and that every sale can be intelligently and ethically expanded to generate more revenue and profits for the company, more renewable orders for the sales staff, and develop more customers who'll buy more products more frequently. So that you don't gum up the works, don't attempt more than one or two spiffs per month, but do change the games and incentives monthly to develop broader skills as your sellers will learn different techniques and the selling nuances of different products from each spiff you put on their plates.

From the examples shown, take what you want, mix and match, and come up with spiffs that get you where you want to go.

By posting the monthly spiffs with the names of each participant, you'll create a competitive atmosphere. But it's a healthy one, because unlike contests that have only one winner, each seller can earn as many spiff benefits as possible.

3. Customer service personnel need clearly stated goals and clearly defined expectations from management about what constitutes acceptable performance.

The third caveat, dovetailing with those calling for effective training and smart incentives, is setting goals for your staff. These are goals that motivate customer service and sales employees to earn more money by working smarter and more efficiently. These goals state minimum sales volume performance and/or the sales volume to be handled administratively. These figures should be carefully projected to be both realistic and attainable, and individualized if appropriate to your system. Setting goals that are all but impossible to achieve breeds contempt and frustration, attitudes that actually hinder good performance.

At sales meetings, make the payoffs and rewards to those who've met or exceeded their goals a cause for recognition and celebration. Let the occasion serve as a reminder that every sales and customer service employee can reap what he or she sows through conscientious, diligent efforts.

The goals for outside salespeople, inside salespeople, and customer service reps will reflect differences in the skill sets and challenges of these different positions in the company. But without setting goals, performance is usually hampered by the undefined expectations and aspirations of both your sellers and the company's management.

Be sure also to clearly state – in writing -- the company's other expectations of staff members, including workplace behavior and etiquette, who backs up whom when and how, standards and policies regarding how calls and e-mails are handled and responded to, and how customer complaints are managed and ameliorated (as an opportunity to keep a reasonable customer and prove you stand behind your products and services). These special sales-related understandings and commitments all are in addition to the company's stated general workplace and employment policies, procedures, culture, and prerogatives of management (essentially the stuff that's in your employee manual).

One should note that the laws regarding sales policies and wage/salary rules discrimination clearly mandate that employees, by job classification, cannot be discriminated against. When it comes to commission schedules, customer service people all earn the same type of compensation and commissions. Likewise for outside salespeople. One full-time customer service representative cannot be paid higher or lower wages and incentives than another, though the law does allow for different wages or salary considerations based on an employee's skills, experience, and longevity with the company.

Commission rates for outside salespeople must be based on sales performance, though as mentioned above, differences in experience, skills, and longevity enable the business to pay more to more specially qualified salespeople. A big exception includes additional compensation to reps who hire on and bring with them a "book" of loyal customers. This is an asset that most companies are willing to compensate at higher levels or added incentives due to the extra benefits and revenue the company gains as a result of hiring such well-equipped – and uncommon – sales professionals.

An underlying assumption in good sales and customer service organizations is that the cost of keeping a customer is a lot cheaper than creating a replacement account. Keeping customers on board isn't just the sales reps' job, it's everyone's job – from customer service, administrative personnel and your creative crew to your production people, all the folks in management, and the soldiers in shipping and receiving.

(Another underlying assumption in good sales and customer service organizations is that the cost of keeping a good customer server rep is usually a lot cheaper than recruiting and training a replacement).

In a presentations I make to employees at general staff meetings entitled, "Everyone is in Sales," I explain that everyone can do his and her job to perfection, but if the person who puts shirts in a carton without caring how the goods will travel or look when the box is opened by the recipient, can damage the whole organization's reputation. Perfect counts, perfect decoration, and perfect paperwork followed by the wrinkled, creased garments seen on their arrival suggest the company and its staff are anything but conscientious. Everyone's effort in every phase of the order's execution is important in doing the order accurately, with great garment graphics, and on time. The one bad apple -- the employee who misorders the inventory or misspells a word or doesn't inspect the goods thoroughly or fails to check registration or thread tension or does his or her job poorly -- spoils the entire company's professional reputation, jeopardizes a customer's loyalty, and diminishes the bottom line. That's why everyone is in sales, everyone is responsible for checking the work in progress when it reaches the next phase of execution, and everyone has a role to play in keeping customers coming back for more.

Customer service and sales representatives are the company's front line troops, the public face of your business, and the people who have to get the order right the first time – or that order has nowhere to go but down. Their demeanor, responsiveness, courtesy, perceived sincerity, knowledge, and friendliness are critical to positioning your company as professional, helpful, and worthy of a customer's patronage.

With all that at stake, why would any businessperson in his or her right mind want to settle for mediocrity?   Or not find investments in their staff's training and success worthwhile?

Everyone needs to fully understand that assisting prospects and customers at your sales counter and answering the telephone to talk to prospects and customers cannot be viewed as interruptions or nuisances nor taken lightly. There are lots of reasons why customers abandon one vendor for another – competitive (mainly price) advantages, mistakes, untimely delivery, and quality, among other causes. But the leading cause of businesses losing customers, for more than three-quarters of those who change suppliers, is the rudeness, discourtesy, inconsideration, and attitudes of salespeople or other employees.

[Source: Surveys conducted by the United States Chamber of Commerce]

CHAPTER

THE VENIT LEAD-GENERATION AND LEAD PROCESSING MODEL

I've explored many aspects of marketing and selling decorated apparel and related products beginning with an examination of the marketing process, intelligently positioning your enterprise, and looking at naming or re-naming your businesses. I've also discussed sorting out various markets, the primary applications of apparel graphics products, leapfrogging your way past the competition, reviewing 24 ways to get customers to love you, and addressed several different angles on the people who do the selling and how they do it.

Now I'll construct a model that organizes many of the theories, strategies, tactics, issues, and techniques I've been presenting into a comprehensive system for generating leads, capturing the leads, servicing the leads, following up on them, assigning them to people who'll develop relationships with them, and building in a function for managing, maintaining, and improving the system. Advertising is the only part of the system I've yet to discuss as to what works and what doesn't work for decorated apparel marketers, but that's the subject of the chapter immediately following this one.

In The Venit Lead-Generation and Lead Processing Model (Figure 18), there are 10 Elements for Success in processing your leads into a comprehensive system that 1.) prescribes how to handle leads to maximize your ability to convert prospects making inquires into customers placing orders; 2.) converts those customers into long-term clients; and 3.) keeps the clients you earned while you continue to generate more leads and more customers. Some of these elements have been covered already and some new ones will be introduced in this chapter. But the mission here is to implement all 10 elements so that they can all work together, reinforce one another, and facilitate the company's growth by expanding your account base, retaining your accounts, and gaining market share at your competitors' expense.

Figure 18: The Venit Lead-Generation & Lead Processing Model: The 10 Elements for Success

> *I: Effective Lead Response*
>> *II: Efficient Communications Technology and Procedural Protocols*
>>> *III: The Showroom Advantage / The Website Advantage*
>>>> *IV: Effective Lead (& Account) Management*
>>>>> *V: Efficient Data Management*
>>>>> *VI: The Express Catalog*
>>>>> *VII: The Express Price List*
>>>>> *VIII: Motivated Sales Professionals*
>>>>> *IX.: Fair Management*
>>>>>> *X: System Maintenance and Revitalization*

First, I'll look at a model for the system that I've been introducing to clients throughout my career. While the system has been tweaked over the years, its functions and key structures haven't changed at all. Please note that there are 13 components (letters A through M) displayed in the model to show you the mechanics of the 10 Elements in the system, as some elements show variations.

In the top half of the model (*see next page*) you see the Lead-Generation function beginning with an advertiser (your company) shown as item A. The business sends a message through an advertising medium or several media, letter B in this diagram. These media include print media, electronic media, telephone directories, direct mail, exhibiting at trade and consumer events, signs, billboards, vehicle signage, and a wide range of e-commerce applications (websites, web marketing programs, social media networks, etc.). The message is seen and/or read and/or heard by a targeted audience or several target audiences, C in this diagram, and/or audiences not targeted but that receive the message anyhow. The advertiser receives a range of responses, labeled Feedback, item D., which comes in may forms: a.) nothing, as in absolutely nothing happens; b.) opinions and comments about the message and/or the advertiser; c.) requests for products you didn't advertise and don't want to sell (e.g., your ad is directed to businesses for ordering embroidered shirts for their employees and a person enters your show-

Figure 19. **The Venit Lead-Generation & Lead Processing Model**

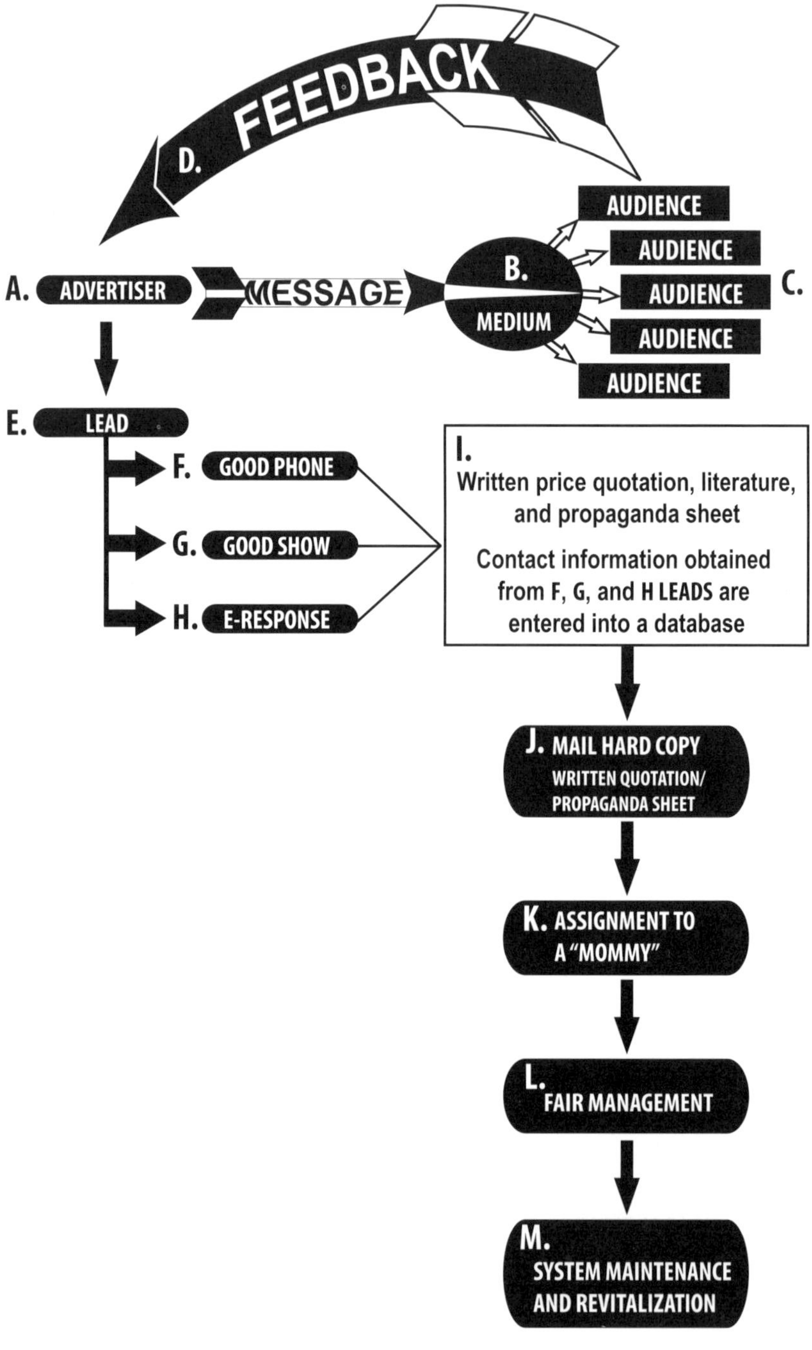

room asking to purchase one shirt -- with her boyfriend's initials on it); d.) legitimate inquiries; and e.) orders.

Feedback that comes in the form of actual orders is possible with certain web programs featuring sophisticated interactive websites with user-generated art and copy generated through direct uploads or via graphic design software programs integrated into the website (such as those offered by some web marketers as mentioned in previous chapters).

For most readers of this book and most apparel graphics market-ers, the desired feedback comes back to the advertiser in the form of a LEAD, E in the diagram. Leads are defined as inquiries regarding price quotations, availability of goods and colors, production turnaround time, requests for a salesperson to call or visit or for directions to the advertiser's place of business, or a request for other information. All represent buying signals, though the level of interest can range from casual to intense. That's where Element I, Effective Lead response, through whatever mechanisms are germane, beginning with F, G, and H., become critical.

E-mail inquiries, shown at letter H, oblige the advertiser to respond as requested, and for maximum effect, as quickly as possible. Replies could include the quotation or information sought, or a telephone call or, where feasible and appropriate, a response by a sales representative to schedule an appointment.

Element II: Efficient Communications Technology and Procedural Protocols essentially encompasses the company's technical resources from its telephone systems to its computer hardware and software -- and the company's defined – and written – procedures about how manage-ment wants leads handled.

An effective website and an effective showroom are the resources in Element III (The Showroom Advantage/The Website Advantage) that help move would-be buyers one step closer to a positive decision to do business with you. How prompt and effective your response is can reinforce the prospect's initial opinion or reverse it.

Walk-in customers are, of course, easily served upon entry. Unlike the short amount of time a prospect spends on your website, a prospect that drives to your showroom is devoting more time and effort to visit, indicating a much stronger level of interest to buy from you. As noted earlier, if your showroom confirms in the prospects' minds the "I'm-in-the-right-place" reaction, the sale is essentially a done deal with just the details remaining.

Telephone inquiries are where I separate the proverbial men from the boys in terms of advancing a casual inquiry about price or other information into a potential sale to a qualified buyer. It takes practice and it takes management's commitment to define its protocols for call handling into policy and enforcing it. Effective telephone handling is what I affectionately refer to as "Good Phone." Does YOUR company give Good Phone?

Good Phone presents your company with a wonderful opportunity to clearly differentiate your business from its competitors, enables to put your positioning efforts into motion, and dramatically improves the likelihood of getting a sales or at least retaining a qualified prospect for future solicitations.

Let's eavesdrop on a few conversations below and you'll see what Good Phone is.

Call 1. – ShirtStop
R-R-R-R -I-N-G . . . . . . R-R-R-R -I-N-G-----R-R. . .

ShirtStop: *Hello?*

Prospect: *Yes, I'd like to get some information and prices on* [custom decorated] *T-shirts.*

ShirtStop: *Uhhh, well, can you call back in an hour or two?*

 Prospect: *Can I just get a few prices?*

ShirtStop: *Uhhh, well, I'm just the shipper. You needa talk wit' Tony and he ain't in right now. But lemme check . . . (Yells out) Yo! Anybody know what time Tony'll be back? (No response heard).   Uhhh, he should be back pretty soon, so you can give him a call later, OK?*

Prospect: *OK, thank you.* CLICK.

If this call sounds anything like what might occur on your company phone, you've got your work cut out for you. Do you think this prospect, a typical Internet or Yellow Pages lead, will bother to call back?

Let's eavesdrop on another call -- to someone who can at least quote a price over the phone.

Call 2. T-Rex Screen Printing & Embroidery

R-R-R-R -I-N-G . . .

T-Rex: *T-Rex.*

Prospect: *Yes, I'd like to get some prices on [custom decorated] T-shirts.*

T-Rex: *Sure, how many you lookin' for?*

Prospect: *Well, about 50, maybe 75.*

T-Rex: *Would you prefer 50/50 or 100% cotton?*

Prospect: *All cotton.*

T-Rex: *And what color shirts would you like?*

Prospect: *Plain white.*

T-Rex: *Do you know how many colors will your design be printed in?*

Prospect: *Our logo is navy blue and red.*

T-Rex: (Quickly calculating a price for this caller) *OK, for a two-color print on a 100% heavyweight cotton T-shirt, it's $5.75.... plus set-up charges.*

Prospect: *OK. Thank you very much, we'll get back to you.* CLICK

T-Rex: *No problem...* (Among the dumbest responses we hear regularly)

T-Rex's response represents the prototypical call-handling from most apparel graphics inquiries – courteous, efficient, and the prospect gets the basic information he was requesting, no more and no less. But did T-Rex get its fair share of information from the caller?

Now I'll present an example of a more effectively handled exchange. It's "Good Phone" executed as it should be.

Call 3. Master Apparel Graphics, Inc. (MAGI)

R-R-R-R -I-N-G ...

Gina/Master Apparel Graphics, Inc. (MAGI): *Master Apparel Graphics, Gina speaking . . .*

Prospect: *Yes, I'd like to get some prices on* [custom decorated] *T-shirts.*

Gina/MAGI: (Bright, friendly) *Great! I'll be happy to help you. My name's Gina D'Angelo and yours is...?*

Prospect: *Lou Charles.*

The first three things Gina has already done right are a.) stating she's happy to help, b.) giving her name to quickly establish cordiality and rapport, and c) obtaining the prospect's name. She'll be entering all the information she's going to get during this call -- while she has the prospect on the line! -- into her contact management program (be it a special software program, an MS Word form created internally, or a handwritten form).

Gina/ MAGI: *Lou, when will you need this order?*

Were this a rush order, Lou's answer might have some bearing on the price, but the real reason Gina asks the question is simply to engender a little bit of conversion beyond just the facts and the numbers. Gina can safely presume none of her competitors will ask him questions beyond the perfunctory ones. Her pleasantry and perceived interest is certain to stand out in the prospect's mind.

Lou: *No hurry, about a week or two.*

Gina/MAGI: *I can guarantee delivery by then! And is this for your company or an organization?*

Lou: *For my company.*

Gina/MAGI: *So that I can enter this quote on my call report, Lou, may I have the name of your company?*

Lou: *Sure, Metro Dee-Jays.*

Entering this data, she'll proceed to ascertain the particulars of her caller's potential order. In the course of the conversation, Gina will ask, "How'd you hear about us?" She'll record the lead source, be it identified as being from the Internet, a business directory, newspaper ad, a business-to-business event, radio, direct mail, word-of-mouth, etc.

After giving the caller the pricing he requested, Gina now moves into high gear to get other vital data.

Gina/MAGI: *I sure appreciate the opportunity to -- hopefully -- do business with your company, Lou, so I'd like to confirm this in writing to you. What's your e-mail address? Most legitimate callers will usu-ally give it and then, when asked for other information, will continue cooperating. Then Gina explains "I'd also like to send you our cata-*

log and price list, along with some promotions we're currently offering and some other information top help you save money and buy better. What's your zip code? Followed by *" . . . And your mailing address?"*

Having gotten everything she's asked for so far, she proceeds to get Lou's phone number, confident he'll give it. It's critical to <u>ask for the data in the order outlined above</u>. With practice, doing so almost guarantees you'll get all the data almost all the time.

After the call ends, Gina will prepare a written quotation via a pre-programmed computer-generated form. or, if for a company that lacks this resource) a fill-in-the-blanks (by hand) standard quotation form. The quotation, shown on the diagram at the letter I, should be on its way via e-mail (or fax) within minutes. Literally. (My own clients are admonished to send it within two minutes of terminating the call).

Whether this particular call results in an order this time isn't critical within the context of a strategic marketing system, in which the harvesting of the data is of far greater importance. That's because Lou will receive several pieces of MAGI propaganda online and via snail-mail during the next year along with follow-up calls from Gina or from an outside salesperson who'll be assigned this lead. The company's game plan is to first convert Lou from a prospect into a customer, then work on getting re-orders or orders for additional products and making relationship-building contacts from time to time to see to it that he becomes a loyal client. His account will be worth several hundred to several thousand dollars a year, year after year. And he'll be a good source for referrals.

You're seeing **Element II -- Efficient Communications Technology and Procedural Protocols** -- in action.

The company has a good phone system to begin with, good computers, good software, and procedures all callhandlers follow – how they greet, the questions they ask and in what order, harvesting caller data, and more.

An important principle here is to make every inquiry count for something -- if not an order, at least to enhance your company's reputation as professionals, and moreover, to harvest data for subsequent proactive marketing and solicitation.

Because few companies in our industry ever send a written quote, when Gina sends it, it'll scream out to its recipient how differently

MAGI does business than the other companies the prospect has called. The prospect receives it in neat, clean, user-friendly form along with MAGI's Propaganda Sheet. Everything Gina is doing is a good representation of MAGI's professionalism and its focus on customer service. Gina's quote states all the particulars and arrives with a link to the company's website.

The process of giving "good phone" doesn't end here. It's just the beginning of the process. The ball's still in play. Now what?!

Good Phone presents your company a wonderful opportunity to clearly differentiate your business from its competitors, enables to put your positioning efforts into action, and dramatically improves the likelihood of getting a sales or at least earning a qualified prospect for future solicitations

1. Mail

Make sure all walk-ins are sent away with a written quotation and the sales materials you'd mail to callers. E-mail respondents, unless you've qualified them over the phone and their interest level convinces you they're worth spending some money on, need no further cost-intensive follow-up. Prospects you've quoted over the phone, having already received a prompt e-mail follow-up, in your prime trading area deserve to get a package in the mail, shown at letter J on the diagram. In it they should find:

a. Hard copies of what you sent via e-mail or fax

b. Your company's express catalog and price list of your most frequently ordered items

c. Incentives. Whether on a sheet or as coupons, incentives can include things such as:

1. a free second-or-additional color imprint with an order of X items;

2. free digitizing with an order over $X;

3. one-dozen free printed-or-embroidered caps with an order for X-number of specified-type items;

4. free sketch sample of art;

5. complimentary car wash, movie tickets, etc. Think of the incentives you offer to a first-time prospect as spiffs for customers. You get the idea. These same incentives can, of course, be given to worthwhile walk-ins, and forwarded to those who found your company online.

d. A promotional product – something flat such as a magnet, calendar/ calendar card or perhaps a more three-dimensional item. Practice what you preach here. And avoid cheap or cheap-looking stuff such as a low-end stick pen or key fob which your prospect won't value. A $1.00 (net) item with your imprint will help get your identity and message across quite affordably.

e. A business card

f. A short handwritten note on a Post-It Note™ or a small sheet of paper, indicating you look forward to serving the prospect, hopefully doing business, or welcoming the chance to answer questions or to make helpful suggestions. Signed -- with the sender's first name.

The package will be mailed after work or the following morning. The prospect will be receiving it in a day or two. Your logo and address on the outside makes a solid advertising impression. Your logo and name on the hard copies, on your business card and other materials inside the package generate additional advertising impressions, helping your prospect remember your company for future reference.

When the packet is received, the company's name and professional standing are amply reinforced, and the prospect has more information, more reassurance, and more reasons to award his business to your company now or, perhaps, down the road.

Dumb Mistake No. 23
Spending money to generate leads – and getting them! – but having no game plan for following them up and converting them into customers!

At this point, letter K in the diagram, it's time to assign a "Mommy" to the account, though Mommy can be assigned as soon as the lead is generated, depending on the system you determine will be the protocol for lead management. Whether an outside salesperson or inside sales/ customer service representative, the Mommy's job is to take care of the lead, nourish it, caress it, and tell the lead in the Mommy's own special way, "You are beautiful, you are loved and cared about and Mommy's there whenever you need her – or before!" Mommy has a vested interest in seeing the lead grow up and to become a customer, one that Mommy will hopefully bear you healthy "grand-leads," my affectionate term for unsolicited referrals that just start to come your way.

That vested interest is in the commissions, bonuses, spiffs, and perks the Mommy gets from the lead – but not unless and until the lead becomes a customer.

Mommy's designated responsibilities are to perform very specific follow-ups to the lead once the package is in the mail, if not sooner.

2. The First E-Mail Follow-Up

The day after fielding the prospect's call, the Mommy sends an e-mail...

a. asking the prospect if your e-mail quote and propaganda was received;

b. offering to answer remaining questions or provide suggestions and alternatives; and

c. informing the prospect you mailed a package with additional information.

3. First Telephone Follow-Up

Two to three days after the package was mailed, call . . .

a. asking the prospect if your company's package has arrived and whether it has been opened and reviewed;

b. offering again to answer remaining questions or provide suggestions and alternatives; and

c. informing the prospect you'd welcome the opportunity to do business

Given the initial e-mail, the first e-mail follow-up, the informational packet sent and the first telephone follow-up made a few days earlier, your prospect will certainly know the name of your company, the rep's name, and what your company has to offer. If no response to e-mails is made and if the rep has been unsuccessful in reaching the prospect by phone after repeated attempts, it can be assumed the prospect is no longer interested in hearing from your company or the rep. For now.

The out-of-pocket cost to do everything above, including the postage, printed materials, and a promotional product is about $10 or less. For this investment, you've cultivated a new or future customer, or a referral to someone else down the road. For $10, it's a bargain in qualitatively building your account base. But if your Mommies are good at what they do and are sufficiently motivated to work their leads, there's a good chance the rep's batting average will be respectable and improve over time.

4. Future Follow-Ups

In the next month, the outside sales rep or customer service salesperson sends the prospect another e-mail and/or another piece of real mail, and calls once or twice again. And, if it's part of the rep's responsibilities, a personal visit to the account is warranted, if feasible.

During the coming year, send appropriate e-mailings every six to eight weeks, and a snail mailer (of any type) three to four times. Within the year, you'll have likely earned the patronage of this prospect with a first order and hopefully more.

To understand Elements V through X and where they impact the model (Figure 19), I'll review each of them briefly.

Element V: Efficient Data Management

Once a lead has been obtained, regardless of whether it walked in, called in, or e-mailed in, the contact data is entered into a database of new prospects, recording:

a. All contact information (name, company/organization/event, mailing address, e-mail address, telephone numbers, type of account, and other pertinent information. The type of account can be defined broadly (e.g., business, organization, schools, teams/leagues, government, etc.) or narrowly (e.g., business – retail, business – manufacturing, business – construction trades, etc.; school – pre-school/kindergarten, school – elementary, school – middle, school – high school, school – vocational/technical, etc.). The categories and sub-categories discussed in Chapter 13 will help you decide how detailed you want to make your choices. But keeping the data on the type of account will enable you to develop specific marketing and advertising agendas for the key categories.

For example, you have a category for marinas with only 23 entries, but this type of business caters to people with boats, an audience with higher incomes and a passion for their boating-related activities. These could include deep sea fishing, fly fishing, lake or bay fishing, cruising, and partying. If you want to market a program for soliciting boat owners to order custom shirts, caps, promotional products, markings, and other items and/for their vessels, you can easily segment the products and the packages and do e-blasts, direct mail or telemarketing to this relatively small but elite group.

b. What medium (or media) attracted the lead if it can be ascertained (as in, "By the way, how did you hear about us?" being a part of the company's call-handling procedures) and identified (e-blast, trade show, county fair booth, radio., etc.)

c. The type/nature of inquiry (price, rush order, availability, please send a rep, etc.)

d. Action taken – quoted price, sent a catalog, sent a rep to see them, added to mailing list, etc.

e. Account specifics – does the firm have an annual company picnic, exhibit at trade shows, require counter people and delivery people to wear embroidered golf shirts, etc.?

f. Other helpful information – the caller owns an airplane, is the union steward, head of the local AARP group, former paratrooper – miscellaneous information that can help a rep hit hot buttons, generate a conversation or find common interests, etc.

g. Prior purchases – listed by date, quantity, item, order number, etc.

There's a simple title for what you're compiling here: A Lead Log. "Lead" here is pronounced l-e-e-e-e-d. If you create a lead log but forget to use it or keep putting off entering your data, lead is pronounced "led" – as in lead weight.

Over time, with constant updating by your sales personnel, you get a well-rounded view of each account, the person in charge of ordering, order frequency, and other data.

Though some folks might still want to enter the information on 3" x 5" index cards in a tickler file, the recommended path is to do so in a system where you can locate and easily retrieve your data. Spread sheets and Word files can accommodate some of the information, but ideally you want a user-friendly contact management software program.

Think of Efficient Data Management as having your own company "think tank," but one that doesn't just think, it remembers! Higher-echelon, industry-specific software includes a contact management function, but managing data with better resources means you not only keep a pulse on prospects and customers, you can track marketing costs versus results, track sales and salespeople's performance, and generate data as requested by management for further evaluation and analysis, including the ability to track trends as they're happening. The Efficient Data Management element provides the company with ratios and other data that management deems necessary. This can include cost-per-lead and cost-per-sale figures, data concerning (legitimately-obtained) espionage on competitors, and results of surveys of prospects and customers about the company's level of performance in customer service and product quality. You also can learn about products and services your company should consider adding or dropping.

Every smart businessperson would agree data management has great potential value to the company in many areas. But not insisting that sales and customer service personnel input the data as it's obtained or not enforcing the policy can create a potentially hazardous management disease. I call it the "Creeping Dinosaur Syndrome" – a condition where data gets lost in the shuffle or disappears completely. This can cause the company to spend untold time and money trying to figure things out that should be available at will and with up-to-the-minute accuracy.

Elements VI and VII: The Express Catalog and Express Price List - They're discussed at length in Chapters 16 and 17.

Element VIII.: Motivated Sales Professionals -- See the previous three chapters.

Element IX.: Fair Management -- In this element, I refer to management being fair specifically to salespeople and customer service staff, though I'd like to think the principle applies to all employees. Too often I've learned where management conveniently forgets its own rules about territory and commission structures, treating some salespeople kindly and others with disdain without logic or reason, approving one deal for one salesperson and denying the exact same request to another, among a host of leadership and ethical failures. If there's a surefire way to alienate the people who sell and destroy their motivation, it's management playing favorites, changing rules in the middle of the game, and leading by caprice, along with mercurial temperament, especially when it provokes brow beatings, name calling, public embarrassments and humiliation of salespeople. Those who treat their salespeople as such can generally be counted on to treat other staff equally foolishly. You can implement the other eight elements to perfection, but motivated sales professionals and fair management go hand in hand; you have both or you have neither.

Element X: System Maintenance and Revitalization

System maintenance simply means there's sufficient leadership in the sales department to see to it that the policies and procedures are being followed every day by every person who has contact with prospects and customers. See to it that the data is entered regularly accurately; and see to it that your company is getting a favorable return on its investments in its people, its technology, and its lead processing system.

System revitalization is that function of management that reviews what's working, what's not and needs to be improved or modified or changed altogether. It shows who's working and who's not and what needs to be done to effect better performance; and it recognizes when changes in the dynamics of the marketplace, the audiences, technology, and the competition mandate the system needs re-thinking and revision wherever necessary to maintain positive results.

Each element is a fundamental component of the lead processing system, not an option to be chosen or rejected. How you tailor each one to your circumstances leaves ample room for modification and adaptation. Each element carries its weight on its own and synergistically helps every other element work more efficiently.

The biggest lessons here are that every lead is important and the people who handle it and how they handle it are critical. Consider making a sign for decorating your sales office that reads:

MAKE *EVERY* LEAD COUNT!

CHAPTER

29

ADVERTISING MECHANICS AND STRATEGIES

The title of this chapter is broad enough to fill volumes of text, but what I'll discuss here focuses on advertising *custom* apparel graphics products and services. As a marketing consultant in this industry, I've been directing other people's advertising for more than 30 years. In doing so, I've personally designed and executed literally thousands of print ads for newspapers and magazines, hundreds of direct mail pieces and Yellow Pages ads, and written, produced, and voiced more than 2,000 radio commercials. Beyond learning first hand what works and what doesn't, I developed a very specific set of advertising options that'll help make building your own advertising strategies work more efficiently and more cost effectively. Knowing which weapons work best and when to fire them means you'll save a fortune on ammunition and score bull's-eyes more often.

Good advertising doesn't happen in a vacuum, nor by accident; and it's much more complex than simply creating attractive ads, coming up with some clever copy and slogans, and throwing some money at the media. Good advertising is the product of planning, targeting, evaluating feedback, and timing. You can do virtually everything right in developing a campaign, but if you make one critical error, your entire investment probably will be squandered.

In some earlier chapters I've looked at the importance of companies in our industry to better define themselves, properly position themselves vis-à-vis their marketing objectives, and differentiate themselves by creating an overall identity.

With such matters well in hand, a company's advertising dollar will go much further if it's supported by an effective lead-response agenda, efficient communications technology, the showroom advantage, a smart express catalog and price list, and motivated sales professionals. I trust by now you'd agree it makes a whole lot more sense to have these things going for you *before* embarking on any advertising campaign than not having them ready in time or never getting to them at all.

Reach, Frequency, and Continuity

Were you sitting in an Advertising 101 course right now on the first day of class and I were your professor, today's lecture would be on a.) the three functions of advertising: to create or maintain awareness, covey information, solicit business; and b.) "Reach, Frequency, and Continuity," three components critical to the success of any advertising understanding.

"Reach" means how many people get your message at any given time. "Frequency" measures how many times that same audience gets the same or similar message within a designated time frame. "Continuity" means that your advertising message spread across the various media maintains consistent thematic integrity throughout its execution in the ways your message is seen, read, or heard.

To understand continuity a little better, say your company runs a print ad in the local business journal with a bold border and a picture of your company's mascot, a cartoon pelican wearing a T-shirt. It follows that your ads in the Chamber of Commerce Gazette, the Yellow Pages, and every other print medium maintain the look, the typography, and the mascot to reinforce the association of those images with your company's identity. If your logo is a dolphin wearing sunglasses and you proudly show it in all your print ads, it would be inadvisable to have a James Earl Jones (Darth Vader) voice represent the character in your radio spots, and then a poodle wearing a T-shirt and cap in a cable TV spot. As an advertiser, your company's consistent *continuity* is the factor that over time builds a consumer's ability to associate your company with specific attributes about your products and services, your positioning statements and themes, your people, and whatever other elements you incorporate into your message. Mixing up the consistency of a female dolphin with a deep male voice and then a poodle would be the antithesis of continuity.

Good continuity is the Golden Arches™ on everything associated with McDonald's™, NBC's peacock logo branding of all its programs, and the melody of "I wish I were an Oscar Mayer Wiener" -- with or without words -- every time Oscar Mayer™ hot dog products are advertised on television and radio.

(OK, you can stop singing now.)

Whether it's your "Guaranteed 3-Day Turnaround" or "Get the good stuff!" tag lines, using the same positioning statement in all your advertising makes it recognizable more quickly each time you put your message forward. Change it each time in each different medium and you'll damage the quality and the effectiveness of your advertising program. Why spend more to do less?

Good advertising doesn't happen in a vacuum, nor by accident; and it's much more complex than simply creating attractive ads, coming up with some clever copy and slogans, and throwing some money at the media.

Your advertising message, which you get to create yourself or hire a specialist to create for you, must contain one or more of the three objectives above. Advertising by objective helps you determine what your message needs to say.

► Does your targeted audience member know your company exists? If not, your message has to establish your identity to *create awareness* of your enterprise.

► Does this audience member know about the products and services you offer and why he should buy from you and not someone else? If not, you need to convey information to him about what you've got, your business hours and other pertinent details about your company.

► Does the audience member understand you're looking for his patronage? If so, make it easy for him to see your phone number, website address, and physical location along with a direct invitation to "Visit us today!"

► Making the solicitation for his business clear and friendly.

Class adjourned. Next, I'll turn to budgeting your advertising dollars.

Budgeting Your Advertising Dollar

The next step in preparing an advertising campaign is to organize an annual budget for it. Most industry companies that even attempt to make a budget address this activity by allocating "arbitrary appropriations" or "affordable funds." The former refers to pulling a dollar figure from the air and the latter is a haphazard guess at what a company can spend without any reference to what's really needed in terms of setting or meeting objectives.

A profile of the standard advertising program done today by the average apparel graphics company has, at best, only three components and none is part of any annualized budgeting process:

1.) Internet advertising in a variety of methodologies. But in most apparel graphics companies it's done on the cheap and with little serious forethought.

2.) Telephone directory advertising. Though I'll review key considerations of advertising in phone books in this chapter, this medium is in rapid decline and has been largely supplanted by the web component of directory advertising.

3.) Something else done every so often, on an ad hoc agenda and on a "Well, let's-give-this-a-try, too" basis.

The typical advertising profile of industry firms would further reveal there is no overall strategy nor an overall budget, and whatever is actually done isn't executed with any regard for positioning the company. What's worse, the ad hoc nature of how a typical apparel graphics company handles its advertising exhibits virtually no thematic, consistent approach over time. Every ad seems unconnected to what ran before. And when the company's "campaign" fails, the advertiser is quick to blame the failure either on the medium, the rep, or the idiots who didn't respond.

Dumb Mistake No. 24
Advertising on an ad hoc basis, trying this and that, throwing money at it, and doing it all without an overall strategy or an annual budget is a fool's errand

---

Another budgeting approach that many companies follow is the "competitive parity" approach. Simply put, it means if the other guy does it, you should, too. If he puts in a bigger ad, you must, too. If he does a billboard on Route 50, you will, too. The outcome of this method is that unless the two companies have identical marketing agendas, copycat tactics won't – and don't -- work for the follower. Who's to say the first guy's concepts are all that well thought out to begin with?

So, why follow his lead?

What's effective and realistic in determining a budget is to tie your advertising dollars to total sales revenue for custom decorated products.

Excluding any revenues from preprints, contract work, promotional products, or other revenue streams, I recommend a spending level that's 2.5% to 3.5% of the *total revenue from custom apparel* for companies in business for several years, 3.5% to 5% for younger companies, and 5% to 10% for start-up companies or even more, depending upon their target audiences, geography, and sales goals.

An alternative for start-ups is to establish a per-unit (meaning per-garment) budget based on a projection of first year sales. A good guess here is to allocate 25¢ per unit for T-shirts and a pro rata amount for higher-ticket items, say, 50¢ for sweatshirts, 75¢ for golf shirts, $1.25 for jackets, and so forth.

What media work best for custom decorated apparel products? For most companies it's Internet advertising, targeted direct mail, business-to-business events, and radio. Following these are, to one extent or another, print media, telephone directory advertising, television and cable television, promotional products, telemarketing, outdoor advertising (billboards), signage, and vehicle graphics.

Next, I'll look at your advertising media options, which begins in the next chapter: Websites and Internet Advertising.

CHAPTER

WEBSITES AND INTERNET ADVERTISING

E-Commerce today includes a variety of mechanisms: websites, web advertising, e-blasts, and social media. And these are your choices only as of today. Experts writing just a few years hadn't contemplated the phenomena of social media *today*, as it didn't even exist as a mass phenomenon! (Given the rapid advance of Internet technology, I, myself, contract web advertising assignments to experienced high-tech specialists). With ever-advancing innovations in technology, the boundaries of telephones and the Internet have been blurred to the point where the two technologies completely overlap. While predicting what will transpire in the years ahead are matters of conjecture and imagination, one can very safely predict there'll be yet new applications and opportunities for marketers. Nonetheless, I'll look at what's in your e-communications resource pool as of 2011.

Websites

For small businesses, websites once were the province of geeks, among whose chief responsibilities was learning enough about the customer's industry, products, and pricing to begin to develop a website.

Many fell short of that mark and were costly, so the industry's main wholesaling powers developed their own sites for use by their customers and their customers' customers. With their extensive experience in the field, the wholesalers' web marketing programs are excellent sourcing tools and relatively simple to initiate. Simply contact your favorite wholesalers to learn about their available web products, set-up charges and monthly hosting fees.

And as the wholesalers have characterized these endeavors as marketing support assets, you'll find them exceptionally competitive and affordable (and some are absolutely free!). More importantly, they've taken care of much of the thinking and the code writing, making this tool almost irresistible. The major downside is that they're limited to merchandising their own lines, though some can be customized to include some other offerings of your choice. Anything regarding custom decorating services is left to the advertiser to insert. The general parameters of websites are well known and explaining the basics to you would be as unnecessary as explaining why you need to own a telephone. What matters here is developing your web presence as part of your positioning strategy and differentiating your company from your competition. Your website is a cost-effective means of educating and updating your prospects and customers about your business, your product and service offerings, and pricing.

While websites can indeed bring new business to your company, the cost and sophistication of attracting qualified or even semi-qualified leads can prove expensive and daunting. Just because you find the solutions to getting hits on your site doesn't equate to bagging orders and gaining serious opportunities to quote potentially viable customers. Why would a shopper in Oslo, Norway, searching for embroidered caps elect to buy from a provider in Ogallala, Nebraska -- when he can buy the same item in his own town without having to wait longer for and pay shipping for overseas delivery? Unless you hold sway in a particular niche market, have a unique product, or have some esoteric technical capability, much the same can be said for servicing leads from shoppers distant from your facility in the U.S. or Canada.

Beyond some of its general selling advantages, what makes a website for your company a must is its value to you and your customers as imperative marketing support for your customer service and sales functions. Oftentimes, routine answers to frequently asked questions and frequently sought items and pricing is a just a few clicks away and on demand 24/7. How easily your customer can find answers can be a huge factor in differentiating your company from competitors. Ergo, if you're going to have a website, it ought to be a good one!

A good website increases customer confidence and loyalty. More sophisticated customers can glean a good deal about a company from the design of a website. A site that's difficult to navigate, is poorly organized, and devoid of pricing is a turnoff to would-be buyers looking for *useable* and *desired* information. I personally like websites with "personality" and a flair for design. But how well the site satisfies the user's basic need for information will have more bearing on where he'll place an order than how many gazillion styles and colors he can buy from a given vendor.

When developing your website, endeavor to make it more interactive, inviting, and easy for your visitors to place orders, sign up for newsletters, special offers, and "hot deals." It also should provide customers with forms they can download. Doing so not only allows customers to do their thing on their own schedules, it reduces your administrative costs and your customers' dependence on having to request assistance and pricing on basic items.

While I can point to many successful online marketers in our industry, the fact of the matter is that few firms can count on getting much web business. The challenge is the expertise and the size of the war chest necessary for marketing your company via the web.

Virtually any company with a website will be found by search engines. But to what avail if your company is one of the hundreds of thousands of items found by someone doing a search if you're not on the first page or right behind it? Getting to the very top or anywhere on the first page takes extensive expertise, talent, effort, and ultimately money. This money buys some of the expert's time (unless you plan on becoming an expert quickly yourself), pays a company such as Google to put your site where it's more likely to be seen, or secures lists of prime prospects for your lines.

Optimization is the key word here (pun intended). Optimization is the process by which astute web marketers find the keys to the key words and phrases that'll garner a high-priority listing.

The process of search engine optimization (SEO) is designed to increase the volume and/or the quality of traffic to a website or a web page via "natural" (unpaid) or "organic" algorithms. Algorithms are complex mathematical operations used in determining the location of sites and popularity in terms of "hits." SEO explores what people are searching for and involves distilling the content and coding to help web marketers ascertain the best key words that attract those looming for a given topic. Unless you are an Internet wizard or have one on staff, my strong recommendation is to engage experts or consultants specializing in optimization.

Search engine optimizers work on specific projects or can assist in developing entire marketing campaigns, including building in factors that skillfully manipulate a site page's wording to help boost its results in the placement of a client's material on web searches. Among the many special skills some optimizers possess is knowing how to write copy that gets more attention from search engines as well as writing persuasive content for the website's visitors. Though there's considerable "art" that goes along with it to produce the results clients seek, optimization is an advancing science. What all this means to you is that if you believe your company can prosper primarily based on business you can generate online, you're bound to be very disappointed without having an optimization expert on your payroll or under contract.

Google and the other major search engines will help you sort out all this. But the design of your site and constantly monitoring it for what's working or isn't and why or why not it's working oblige e-commerce marketers to make the necessary investments in having people who understand it all advising you on a regular basis. You have a variety of web marketing plans offered by the big names that minimize upfront outlays by charging you on a pay-per-click basis and/or for a percentage of sales generated online. But one can safely predict that the various plans, fees, and options available to you will constantly evolve, so whatever might work today cannot be guaranteed to work tomorrow – not without staying in the loop and hopefully well ahead of it.

It's important to understand that search engines look at more than just key words when determining search results. They also look at the content of web pages to find more information to satisfy search requests as well as alternate text terminology. As crucial as key words are, if they're not relevant to the page content, your results will be adversely impacted when prospects click on key words and then find the content has little to do with what the information they're seeking. The challenge then becomes one of developing key words for each page of content making each page, itself, searchable.

E-Mail Marketing

E-mail marketing is perhaps the most affordable advertising medium of all. You can send straightforward solicitations, convey new information, issue newsletters, handle online registrations for events and webinars, collect feedback, conduct surveys and questionnaires, collect payments, or simply touch base with and keep your company visible to customers and prospects. You also have the unique ability to link your message – as in "Click here to order" or "Click here to learn more" – to your website or other sites to enable those interested recipients of your messages to take the next step at will. Responses to your advertising message generally occur within 48 hours of issue, after which the response rate drops to nil.

Dumb Mistake No. 25

Thinking that by simply creating a website, your mailbox will be stuffed with orders every morning when you arrive at work.

Increasing the "open rate" of your e-mail (the metric used for the percentage of recipients who actually open your e-mail) and click-through rate (the percentage of recipients that followed a link to the touted website) are yet other challenges that experts are skilled at facilitating for you and teaching you the ropes.

When contracted through third-party services, such as Constant Contact (constantcontact.com), e-mail marketing gives you enhanced abilities to segment your lists by various criteria or key interest groups.

This allows you to send your messages and promotional offers to those individuals who are more likely to respond to or forward your e-mail to others they may determine might be interested in it, further extending the reach of your message. E-mail marketing companies also provide templates for professionalizing the look of your e-mail message.

Among the advantages of using third-party e-mailers are that they can easily segment your e-lists by customer type, maintain and cull multiple lists, keep you in compliance with spam disclaimers, capture opt-ins from offers in a registry for tracking, issue instant thank-you e-mails, post newsletters, handle opt-outs/unsubscribes, and perform a range of other services. Fees are determined by the size of your lists not from the number of mailings; the cost for most decorated apparel firms typically ranges from $15 to $50 monthly. There's a learning curve that comes with the territory, but your service provider will help you master it and keep you in the loop on new developments.

E-mail marketing is perhaps the most affordable advertising medium of all

Just as any commentary about direct mail should include some atten-tion to the term "junk mail," a serious discussion about e-mail market-ing should in my opinion include mentioning the term "junk e-mail" or "spam." We all know what it is and most of us spend time every day hitting the delete button for messages we have no interest in and often despise for a variety of reasons. How much is the correct frequency for e-mail to your customers and prospects. My counsel to clients is once every 6-8 weeks in general, and never more that once or twice a month. My experience is that for my clients sending daily and weekly e-mails proves detrimental to their overall marketing efforts. Lesser frequency appears to be much more effective in generating quality leads and orders.

Social Media Marketing

Emerging in the 1990s, social media in the first decade of the 21st Century catapulted the evolution of the connectivity potential offered by the Internet. And its subsequent and continuing growth has been nothing short of exponential. From the early days where online con-nections among individuals and companies of similar interests took place via basic e-mail, forums, and public or private chat rooms, social media (or Web 2.0) began to arrive on the scene. Not only did Web 2.0 make it easier for individuals and companies to connect, it also made the experience richer, particularly in conjunction with the spread of high-speed broadband Internet connections now available in so many parts of the nation and the world.

Though there are many sites providing a platform for social network-ing, today four major networks rule the roost: Facebook.com, YouTube.com (owned by Google) Twitter.com, and LinkedIn.com (a more pro-fessional network than a social network). MySpace.com, the Web 2.0 pioneer launched in 1993, attracts about half the visitors Facebook does.

If you're wondering if social media should command a place in your company's marketing agenda, consider the history about Face-book and Twitter.

From its founding in 2004, Facebook.com eclipsed the 500 million mark of active users worldwide in 2010, with more than 120 million in the U.S. alone. Fifty percent of these active users log on to Facebook on any given day and, on average, spend nearly an hour a day on the site.

Also in 2010, Facebook passed Google.com as the most visited site on the Internet and more than 100 million unique visitors looked in on YouTube. A "unique visitor" is a unit of traffic to a web site, which counts each visitor only once in the time period being measured through the use of "cookies" that are placed in a computer when a visitor first registers for a site. In other media, this term for "unique visitors" is called "reach" – as in how many people a message reaches.

Early in 2010 YouTube enjoyed more than 400 million unique visitors from around the globe with more than 100 million logging on in the U.S. Twitter in 2010 reached more than 50 million participants in the U.S.

These numbers should grab the attention of any serious marketer as to the reach of Web 2.0. But understand one important fact about all of these platforms: While any person or company can create a Facebook page, post videos on YouTube, open a Twitter account, or join the LinkedIn network, the key to making it work is to generate "subscribers," "followers," or "fans." This is the social media equivalent to "permission-based marketing" for e-mail. By subscribing to a social media network, the individual is declaring he or she wants to hear from you on a continuing basis; the posts or uploads an individual makes on his/her account are then automatically distributed to all subscribers. How do you gain subscribers, followers, or fans? It's simple. You have to give them information that they're interested in hearing or learning about.

A second key to using social media marketing effectively is to understand that while it's free in its basic form, there's an evolving variety of paid advertising methodologies. It also carries a cost in the time and effort you must devote to it on a regular basis. Posting to a Facebook page, or YouTube or Twitter account once every month or two isn't going to get you any results. Weekly is better. In most cases, daily (or several times per day) is even better. Just as with any other marketing initiative, it requires dedicated effort on a consistent basis. Without that, you won't get results.

A final key to using social media effectively is to understand your markets and which media outlet or combination of outlets might be better at reaching your prospects. For example, if you're selling business-to-consumer, you'll be able to see much better results with Facebook, YouTube, or Twitter than you will with LinkedIn. But for business-to-business marketing, LinkedIn provides you with connections through friends and friends of friends of friends to obtain an introduction to that purchasing manager at one of your targeted corporate prospects. Don't ignore the other three in business-to-business marketing, but do your homework on all these (and other) Web 2.0 platforms to identify the best routes to your prime prospects in your desired market segments.

Online investigation will yield information on books, newsletters, webinars and other classes on social media marketing, and isolating key words that drive up your response rate.

And as social media continue to expand and new media are being invented constantly, whatever figures and rules of the road you read about above will likely be dated by the time you finish reading this chapter.

CHAPTER

DIRECT MAIL, BUSINESS-TO-BUSINESS EVENTS, NEWSPAPERS, AND TELEPHONE DIRECTORY ADVERTISING

Direct Mail

Direct mail gives advertisers an efficient means of targeting audiences as broadly or as narrowly as the sender deems appropriate. With proper planning, you can determine your own deadlines. And without many of the legal restrictions that you might encounter with newspaper, magazine, or radio advertising with regard to making superlative claims, direct mail lets you say just about anything you please, (including the virtual right to lie). You've also got lots of room to show off your staff and satisfied customers and tout your products, services, convenience, and other reasons why people should buy from you.

Direct mail is often referred to as junk mail, because so much of it is. But intelligently targeted and executed, direct mail is among the most cost-effective vehicles there is for generating leads from custom apparel decision-makers. If you don't want your advertising lumped in with the term junk mail, make your direct mail pieces attractive, colorful, and easy-to-read and understand. Testing your message before you mail to make sure it's understood clearly is a critical exercise. Don't test it on employees, friends or relatives unless they have some expertise in these matters and can be expected to be candid, not gushy about it because it's you -- their boss, son or daughter, or best bud – who's sending it. Test it on good customers, or, for a mass mailing of thousands of pieces and funds permitting, with a focus group comprised of absolute strangers who reflect the profile of your targeted audience(s).

Given the realities of his or her own time and interest, know that the recipient of your direct mail will decide in a matter of seconds as to whether to even open your propaganda. So make it easy to open by keeping it to a self-mailer (no envelope) for most applications. Use an attention-getter to arouse the recipient's interest. Effective attention-getters are a powerful statement ("For the best dressed team in town…"), a thought-provoking question ("Does your company's T-shirt have to be boring?"), an attractive offer ("No set-up charges and free artwork when you order before March 1!") or an eye-catching graphic, photo, or other strong visual hook.

Given that you're in the graphic arts business, it would be nice to think apparel decorators also can turn out mailers that reflect your creative prowess. But by observation, that's rarely the case, due to the fact that most of the artists in this business are clueless about what constitutes good advertising art. Just because your artist can do great T-shirt art or your digitizer can create killer embroidery doesn't mean he knows how to get into a prospect's mind by creating an effective attention-getting message with commensurably appropriate art and layout. The admonition here is to hire a professional who knows advertising even if he or she doesn't know about apparel graphics or this industry.

Consider the case that your direct mail campaign will cost X amount of dollars for development, printing, and postage -- say $1,000 or more. If a talented pro charges you $250 for designing a mailer than generates $12,000 in orders, wouldn't that make more sense than saving $200 by letting your staff artist create a piece that generates only a $5,000 return? If you purchase a high-tech CD sound system for $1,000, would you consider playing it through two plastic bookshelf speakers that you bought at the local mass merchandiser for $29.95? For anyone who might think a direct mailer is a commodity or that relying on inexpensive composition can save money, think again. Yes, you can measure the *perceived* savings, but you'll never experience what a better, more effective, more attractive mailer would have earned in new business and from sophisticated buyers. Whatever that figure is, it would most likely dwarf whatever "savings" an ineffective mailer produces.

Writing your copy is a matter best left to experts, but for do-it-yourselfers there are several copywriting formulas that apply across several media categories. One formula I'll recommend to you that's easy to work from is the AIDA (pronounced "Eye-EE-da", as in the famous Giuseppe Verdi opera) formula. A=Attention, I=Interest, D=Desire,

A=Action. Not just a formula for writing direct mail copy, this formula also applies to writing e-mail blasts, radio and television commercials, for many types of newspaper and magazine advertising, and to a limited extent, billboards. For display ads in telephone directories, since the prospect already demonstrates interest and desire, the most salient feature should be the attention-getting function.

Attention is the part of the ad that "hooks" the prospect with a thought-provoking statement, question, challenge, or with an eye-catcher or ear-catcher. *Interest* is explaining something about the product and why someone would want to buy it, especially from your company. The interest component can be done effectively in direct mail and other advertising with "bullet copy" (short phrases, frequently preceded with bulleting) and is usually preferable to paragraph copy. It's OK to supplement the bullet copy with short sentences. In the *Desire* aspect, the object is to make the pitch directly *relevant to the prospect*, particularly with regard to what's in it for him and right now. Once again, bullet copy is effective in the desire part, and where appropriate, with a sentence or two to help in getting the message across more completely. The *Action* part of the AIDA formula is where you ask for the order or the lead via a telephone number, a web link, a reply card, a coupon to be brought in or used online, or other device that enables and invites a prospect to keep the ball rolling. Reply cards, or more accurately, a perforated tear-off section of a mailer, are important because many prospects will review their admail after hours, when your phone isn't being answered. Of course, getting the prospect to visit your website usually is a more immediate and practical solution for the prospect Practicing writing ad copy using the AIDA formula is the best way to learn it. As a courtesy to readers of this book, I invite you to e-mail me your copy for my personal review and I'll endeavor to write back to you my suggestions for improving your ad and/or message.

For some important words and phrases for use in your direct mail, refer to Chapter 35, "Magic Words in Advertising Custom Decorated Apparel."

Timing is absolutely critical in direct mail campaigns. Send your message at the wrong time of year and you'll throw your money away. Very specific audiences such as schools, organizations, events merchandisers, souvenir accounts, ski lodges, and summer resorts are best reached at different times of year based on their own seasonal buying cycles and particulars. It's beyond the scope of this chapter to itemize the ins-and-outs of each special market. There are, however, predictable optimum windows for sending *general* mailings to a general business audience, and these same seasonal windows work to some extent, for campaigns directed to athletic buyers, schools, and organizations as well.

There are two best times to send a general mailing: 1.) two weeks before the psychological start of spring, and 2.) in mid-September. The psychological start of spring has little to do with the Vernal Equinox, which usually occurs around March 21. Draw a line from mid-Florida, across South Texas, to Southern California, and you'll see the geography where spring registers psychologically in early February. Flowers are in bloom, Little Leagues are being organized, and the birds and bees are back -- and busy. Draw another line from the Carolinas to Northern California and you'll see the next territory where spring is happening in the mind from late February to early March. North of that line, for the rest of the U.S. and from the border to 200 miles north of it in Canada, the psychological start of spring occurs from late March to early April. Yes, the northern U.S. and southern Canada can still experience an occasional blizzard until mid-spring, but the mental predisposition to look forward to spring has already taken hold. As for mailings for the remainder of Canada, well, hang in there for a few more weeks.

Your first major window for sending direct mail to custom apparel buyers means you should plan your mailing to arrive about two weeks ahead of the psychological onset of spring. Mailings received prior to this generally won't give you a cost-effective response. Other than folks working out at the fitness center, who in your town is thinking about buying T-shirts when mounds of snow are still piled next to the highway? The phenomenon happening here also can be appreciated in early July, when whatever incentives you might offer on heavyweight sweatshirts will be heard as a resounding thud.

The second major window for apparel decorating direct mail material to arrive is in mid-September. Though some schools and colleges resume classes in late August and the Autumnal Equinox doesn't occur until around September 21st, for most of North America the psychological last day end of summer is Labor Day. Conventional wisdom suggests that advertising mailings should already be waiting for teachers, club officers, and businesspeople when they get back to work on the day after Labor Day. Well, since that's what most people in our business and hundreds of others think, the people who fall into the targeted audiences end up with a ton of mail waiting for them with more admail pouring in every day.

As a result of what I've learned about fall mailings, my counsel to clients is to plan their fall mailings for arrival a week or two after Labor Day, when it will hit mailboxes with considerably less company from competitors. There's a good likelihood that prospects will have gone through the other stuff by then, so that when your mailer arrives, it will likely get a bit more attention and a more through perusal.

I recommend that if you're going to commit to a direct mail advertising schedule to generate leads, do it at least three times a year and commit to doing it for two years running to the same audiences to build stronger awareness and frequency – and results. I also recommend sending an occasional postcard at key intervals in between your major campaigns to keep your name in front of your customers and prospects. Do this in late spring for summer buys, early August for advance fall buys, early November for holiday-oriented buys, etc., and offer small incentives to help the low hanging apples fall from the tree.

Allow me to introduce a concept here that I call "pushbutton marketing," an effective mechanism for generating a quick mailing from the company's customer and key prospect lists. It's good for marketing to a narrow sector of your account base and prospect list. For example, you attend a trade show and see a particular item that stimulates a promotion of interest to a special audience. In this example it's an apron with wide horizontal bands of red, white, and green -- a "natural" for marketing to owners and managers of both Italian and Mexican restaurants for outfitting their servers. (These colors also work for restaurants featuring the culinary delights of Oman, Bulgaria, Iran, Madagascar, and Tajikistan).

When you get back from the show, you design a quick mailer featuring the item, generate your mailing list and within an hour you've printed out colorful, well-targeted mailers and user-specific labels. Fold \up your flyers, stick on the labels and a first-class stamp, and head to the post office. (Yes, of course, you can do this online as well). In a few days, follow up the mailing with a phone call. That's pushbutton marketing! Think of how many specialized audiences you can access with such highly targeted mailing campaigns and how by doing small mailings like this on a weekly basis, you can bring in a few new accounts with every mini-campaign.

"Card deck" direct mail programs, where your advertising piece is inserted in an envelope or shrink-wrapped with several other advertisers' by a third-party direct mail marketing company, can be an effective, money-saving vehicle. For 15¢ to 25¢ per insert, you can reach a selected local, regional, or national audience without having to worry about addressing, stuffing, and sealing envelopes, or renting a mailing list. These programs are everything they're cranked up to be, but there are limitations you should be aware of before buying into one. The fact that your ad sheet (usually 5½" x 8½") may not give you as much space as you could dedicate in your own direct mail program and is grouped with other ads isn't necessarily a disadvantage, given the very low cost of the program. But when more than 20 adsheets are jammed into an envelope, their documented effectiveness is significantly reduced. A bigger impediment is the scheduled delivery date as determined by the vendor. If it works within the timelines cited a few paragraphs ago, the vehicle can be considered viable for your objectives. If, however, the mailing occurs in December or January or during late June to July, pass on it.

Be sure to confirm whether the program you're looking into will be mailed to residences (consumers) or to businesses. If you're targeting businesses, a mailing to residential addresses will have an unacceptably high waste distribution factor. However, if you're targeting individual decision-makers who are active in schools and organizations, especially as volunteer leaders, a consumer mailing may prove quite productive.

Mailing wholesalers' catalogs can be a highly productive, high-impact investment, but it can also be an expensive proposition. *Consider such an undertaking only if you have sufficient budget, a qualified list, and an express catalog* with an easy-to-read price list that accompanies the wholesalers' catalog. Counting the costs of the catalog and price list, an envelope, a small 3-dimensional promotional product, and postage, you'll be spending anywhere from $1.50 - $2.50 per recipient via bulk mail, about a third to a fifth of the cost mailing the wholesalers' standard fat, colorful tomes.

Dumb Mistake No. 26
Mailing out mailing materials without having first tested the message, the offers and incentives to see if they'll generate a response to justify the cost of the effort.

If you forecast that you'll be mailing at least 1,500 to 2,000 pieces annually, consider applying for a bulk mail permit from the United States Postal Service (USPS) if your effort will meet the post office's current minimum of at least 125 pieces or 15 total pounds per mailing. (The deal is quite different in Canada). You'll find the USPS's rules and regulations must be observed scrupulously, but the effort is worth the savings if you're going to be a regular direct mail marketer. Said permit entails paying a one-time fee of $185 (to be allowed to use and print the permit number) and an annual usage fee of another $185. But you can mail up to 3.3 ounces typically for 31¢ to 37¢ (2010), depending on how many items are going to how many zip codes, though as much as 51¢ cents for larger-size mailers. First class mail for 3.3 ounces is over $1 per piece. Pre-sorting your admail by zip code saves a nickel per item instead of asking the postal service to do it for you.

Beyond traditional direct mail programs, there are other approaches that include sampling your products to key targeted, pre-qualified prospects by creating speculative -- actual-production! -- samples with the recipient's imprint or embroidery on the garment or other merchandise.

Whatever form your direct mail program takes, endeavor wherever possible to address your materials to specific individuals. A phone call to some of your intended recipients usually can help get you the information you seek. But where you can't or it's impractical, address your mailings to someone who might actually have an interest in seeing it and to reduce the barrier of "mailroom clerks" in big companies or big organizations not knowing where to direct your envelope. This is accomplished with a title of a department or a real person who wants mail such as yours: "Attention: Director of Human Resources," "Attention: Human Resources Department," "Attention: Marketing Director" (or Dept.), "Attention: Director of Athletics," "Attention: Senior Class President," etc. When all else fails and you're at your wits' end: "Attention: T-Shirt Buyer!"

I'll share a secret with you about getting attention for your mailer and improving your chances of getting it to the right recipient: Be clever with the title of the intended recipient! As in: "Attention: Highly Creative Buyer of Custom Apparel," "Attention: Highly Intelligent Buyer of Great-Looking Custom Apparel," and "Custom Decorator Apparel Buyer Who Wants to Do Business With a Local Company." I'm sure you'll come up with other good ideas to get your piece delivered and read.

Allow me to preach a moment about proofreading your advertising, especially catalogs, price lists, web sites, and direct mail promotions. GET SOMEONE ELSE TO PROOF YOUR WORK. Repeat: GET SOMEONE ELSE TO PROOF YOUR WORK. Maybe TWO someone-else proofreaders. Finding out your mistakes can be costly, and if not in money, in embarrassment. No one is exempt here, including this author, from goofs we wish we hadn't made, but did, and beyond the usual excuses of pressing deadlines, "Hey, isn't that what editors are for?," "too much on my plate that day", and "the dog ate my homework!"

Whatever I might say positive about direct mail programs, the rising cost of postage vs. the minimal cost of e-marketing both are cogent factors occasioning the decline in snail mail advertising and the boom in e-marketing.

Business-to-Business and Other Targeted Audience Events

As discussed in Chapter 18 in conjunction with the discussion of showrooms, displaying your lines to prospective business buyers present highly qualitative marketing opportunities. In addition to business-to-business events, similar exhibition at venues for coaches, teachers, organization leaders, and other special target audiences present huge opportunities to move your company forward.

Selecting appropriate trade and professional events at which to exhibit can be done by researching trade publications online to see schedules, projected attendance, and booth details for exhibitors.

In some instances, membership in the sponsoring organization is required, a detail that's usually simply a matter of completing an application and paying dues and sometimes an initiation fee. While becoming a member firm may be a formality, utilizing the membership may have additional longer term benefits – such as being able to advertise in the group's publications and online newsletters, getting press releases included in the group's membership communications, purchasing/renting membership lists, accessing exhibit space at regional events, attending meetings and conferences, and being listed in the organization's directories. Many industries offer "associate" or "affiliate" membership status for individuals and groups; such status enables the associate member to gain access to the group's members and to network with them as well as other vendors to the audience. For example, you don't build houses, but you can join local, regional, or national construction trade groups as an associate member and receive a wide variety of the organization's membership benefits as well. These can include discounts on a range of services and products -- from credit card processing and freight to insurance coverages to web hosting.

Your budgeting for an event begins with the rental fee for space, which can run $100 to $500 for a table at a local event, to several thousand dollars for a booth at a national convention or conference that attracts thousands of attendees. In the U.S. and Canada, booths are usually 8' to 10' square. FYI, a four-booth space at an ISS costs upwards of $10,000 per show in rent for the exhibitor. In many cases you'll also be charged for drapes, electricity ($200 and up), and contracted fixtures (tables, chairs, table draping, carpeting, additional lighting, etc.) and services (carpenters and laborers to help set up your display, attendee badge scanners, and booth cleaning, among other things). Unless you'll be driving your display, booth materials, samples, and literature to an event, your freight bill will be at least several hundred dollars each way. And if the event is held at a venue where you're restricted from personally carrying in your own stuff, expect to pay a few hundred dollars more for having your stuff moved from the loading dock to the booth.

What often costs more than your booth when exhibiting at an event distant from your home base is travel, meals, and lodging for your crew, excluding any payroll costs. Don't forget to budget for cabs, parking, other incidentals, and surprises.

To give you some idea of the overall cost of exhibiting, here are some real world figures for exhibitors showing at three-to-four day events you're familiar with (or will be soon enough):

-- At a regional event such as an Imprinted Sportswear Show or a national event such as the SGIA Expo or the PPAI Expo, the budget for an exhibitor with one booth and two staffers: $6,000 to $9,000. For four booths and staff to man it, $20,000 to $25,000.

For a 10-booth island and a crew of 12, you're looking at $50,000 to $70,000.
-- At a state athletic directors'/coaches' conference 200 miles from home, for a one-table display, expect   to pay anywhere from $1,000 to $2,000, plus membership fees, sponsorship fees, and incidentals.
-- At a state fair or local rodeo, costs for the booth and expenses will run from $2,500 to $5,000.

And the figures above do NOT include pre-show promotion by your company to prospective attendees, payroll, materials and samples distributed in your booth to attendees, liability insurance, and hosted receptions, among other things.

To help you plan and organize your efforts for exhibiting, here's my recommended course of action, "The Six P's:"

1. Project Your Costs. Budgeting for the event should cover everything you can think of – and then some! Be aware that in most cases, your booth rental and fees associated with exhibiting (electric, fixtures, etc.) likely will oblige you to pay in full, in advance.

2. Plan Your Booth. What you'll need will hinge on where you'll be exhibiting in terms of distance, the type and sophistication of the event and the audience, the lines you'll be selling, and your experience as an exhibitor. What you need to do for a national event attracting thousands of buyers is a far cry from readying a tabletop display and peripherals for a regional teachers' conference. You can spend several thousand dollars for a lightweight, portable professionally manufactured booth complete with knock-out graphics, lighting, and a coterie of whistles and bells from video monitors to live models. You can, of course, build your own displays, which in time will tell you your subsequent needs. My counsel is to start small, test the event with a small presence at first, or better yet, visit the event to see the level of commitment you'll need to make to be seen as "a player." Then, wait the necessary time – a few months to a year – before taking the proverbial plunge. Do discuss your plans with experienced exhibitors to get their input before embarking on a firm course.

Also plan what you'll need to distribute in terms of literature, samples, and freebies. Plan the activities you'll be doing in the booth from product demonstrations to handling leads and everything in-between.

3. Position Your Company. Who your competition will be at the event usually can be ascertained well in advance by asking the event sponsor about companies who've exhibited at the venue in the past as well as those signed up for the next round. Learn about what the competition does at the event.

Whether you'll be doing the same things as they do or working hard to differentiate yourself from them are matters best determined from your research, not conjecture. First impressions are indeed lasting ones at events and passers-by who ignore your booth or stop only for a few seconds and then move on often are lost for the duration of the event and probably beyond. Ergo, it pays to look like you know what you're doing. If you don't get to stop the attendees at your booth or table, nor meet them, nor tell them your story, nor get their "vitals" (contact names, addresses, phone numbers and email addresses), your investment and efforts all will be for naught.

4. Present Your Company and Its Story. You'll only have brief moments to open a dialogue when traffic comes to call, so make certain you can explain to attendees who you are, what you can do for them, and why they should consider buying from your company – all in about 30 seconds, à la "an elevator speech." Word to the Wise: Don't wing it, script it. And then make sure every staff member in your booth or at your table can recite it. Strongly recommended for first-time exhibitors is a healthy role-playing session with your team before the event – or in the mirror. What you'll wear working your exhibit also speaks volume about your professionalism. Given the business you're in, why you wear anything other than decorated apparel showing your company's name and logo?

Nonetheless, for venues and audiences where professional dress may be more appropriate, that admonition can get a bit tricky. As I wear suits when working the ShopWorks booth and conducting seminars and workshops at trade events, my own solution to demonstrating my connection to my industry is with custom embroidery on my shirt cuffs and a 24k-gold T-shirt pin on my lapel.

Social skills matter when exhibiting. Those individuals representing your company and having contact with attendees in your booth, on the event floor or nearby should be "people persons." Folks who are uncomfortable in such settings and who don't do the "eye-contact thing" well are liabilities at business-to-business venues. Booth etiquette enters the equation here, too, and a little research on do's and don'ts might go a long way to earning a lead or sending one away. Among the basics here are good grooming, looking interested, not whining, not reading, and having fresh breath and dry hands.

5. Participate in the Event. More than simply exhibiting your wares, endeavor to become a participant in the industry or group at hand by involving your company in sponsorships, seminars and workshops, on planning committees and advisory boards, and other avenues of value-added effort. It's a low-cost (and sometimes *free*) way to demonstrate your company's leadership, accelerate your ability to network with key companies and individuals on the scene, and earn added recognition for your company and your product lines.

6. Promote Your Company's Exhibit. Promote the fact that you'll be exhibiting in advance of the event via e-mail or direct mail to registrants and include an incentive to visit your booth or table to boost your traffic. Promote your company after the event with follow-up phone calls and e-mails, especially to those who visited your booth or table. Keep notes during the event as to who asked about what, who expressed an interest in this or that, and personal information gleaned by chatting with them (about their hobbies, town, favorite teams, a child's success, a cause they work for, etc.). Most of us have limited brain capacity to remember and sort out who said what, who's into whatever, and what what's-his-name's name is! With each day that passes after the event, the information gets blurrier.

A company's goals for exhibiting at a particular venue can vary quantitatively and qualitatively. In most cases the objective of exhibiting is to garner qualified leads, as actually ever writing custom orders at an event is rare. Though your results from a particular show might seem disappointing at first, there may be other long-term benefits that don't manifest themselves until weeks or months after the event. These can include attracting good reps or gaining a huge account from a buyer who spent only a few moments in your booth.

Veterans also can attest to the realities of exhibiting that beginners don't learn right away and often learn the hard way. What could have been a good venue -- and one where some competitors may have done very well -- can be wrecked by a poor booth position or because turnout was impacted by bad weather or another factor over which you had no control. Or the fact that you weren't as prepared for the event as you should have been. In many cases you won't see the kind of results you hoped for until you've exhibited again and again at the same venue. The good news is that if the particular audience is in fact worth your efforts, you'll see over time that the event will become better for you each time you present your wares. It's because the audience becomes familiar with your company as well as the fact that you get smarter about how and where and what to exhibit each time you show.

Though your results from a particular show might seem disappointing at first, there may be other long-term benefits that don't manifest themselves until weeks or months after the event, such as attracting good reps or gaining a huge account from a buyer who spent only a few moments in your booth.

Newspapers and Other Print Media

Advertising in local newspapers can be an effective means of creating awareness of your company and keeping your name visible. That said, be aware of the downsides.

1.In the overwhelming majority of cases, advertising on a daily basis is a prohibitively expensive investment for most decorated apparel businesses. If you believe your local newspaper nonetheless merits your advertising commitment, it's advisable to advertise in the newspaper only once a week, in a particular section, to build frequency with the same audience. If you're targeting the athletic or school markets, the sports section is an obviously more advantageous choice. To reach women, the lifestyle and food sections are where you'll gain the highest concentration of them. (Please note this is not a sexist opinion, it's a well-documented fact). The business section is the logical choice for targeting business decision-makers. And if you seek a broad audience, consider being in the front section, generally the one dedicated to news.

The most effective newspaper advertising for most custom decorated apparel companies is a "tombstone ad," a trade term for an ad that rarely charges. It gives a basic message of who, what, where, hours, a phone number, and a positioning statement or tag line. "Sale" ads generally don't work for apparel decorators, because buyers of our product categories tend to buy primarily near the time when they'll need them.

Incentives to prospects to buy before they're ready really don't trigger any emotional hot buttons. Don't bog down your ad with "free screens," "free digitizing," or other hype unless it's part of your everyday offerings. And touting ridiculously low prices is of highly questionable value, except for those operators who specialize in bait-and-switch tactics.

If the newspaper offers a weekly "professional directory" or "business card" section, having a weekly presence in it will build recognition over time. And when someone makes an inquiry over the phone and responds to your question about where he heard about your company, the answer at the moment might be "on the Internet." The fact that the caller saw your ad regularly in the newspaper (or in other media) or heard it on the radio may be the real underlying factor in generating the call.

While a major advantage of newspapers is being able to run an ad on short notice, apparel graphics marketers are advised to use newspapers only for long-run exposure, not last-minute whims. Sure, for those occasions when you might want to blow out your stockpile of misprints, rejects, headaches and overruns, a one-shot local ad is OK. But for generating custom leads in the context of a well-organized campaign, use newspapers to build awareness over many months and only when the targeted audience is local.

If you're targeting local or regional businesses, publications specifically directed at these audiences are a far better investment. Most of these vehicles are published weekly or monthly. Advertise in these media on a regular basis – nine to 12 monthly issues or at least 39 weekly issues a year -- to get the most effective reach and frequency. Keep your ads here, too, in the "tombstone" mode and avoid price hype. Advertising in these publications is an excellent means of positioning your company to the commercial marketplace. And if your company is a member of any local business associations or the local chamber of commerce, do put their logos in your ad.

Magazines, a term often associated with slick paper and heavy-on-color photography, targeted to special interest groups are often good advertising investments. These include publications addressing a specific business community (the food service industry, trucking, broadcasting, ski operators, etc.), leisure activity enthusiasts (runners, off-road enthusiasts, model railroad hobbyists, etc.), and other well-defined user or participant groups. As these media usually are published on a monthly basis and today also are combined with online versions, they offer good opportunities to create awareness and build frequency. For these types of publications, commit to at least four months of consecutive exposure before making any qualitative evaluations of their effectiveness in generating leads or accounts. These things take time to gel, and thinking you'll be able to see a return after one or two issues is very unrealistic and a disservice to your budget. Note nonetheless that many of my clients have maintained their presences in these vehicles for many years.

When buying print media, be sure not to buy on the "open rate," the price charged to occasional or one-time advertisers. Buy a contract based on a commitment to a minimum number of weekly or monthly insertions or in the case of newspapers, a *lineage* contract (derived from the total number of lines you'll run annually) or a *column inches* contract (based on the total you'll commit to over a year). When you buy on a frequency contract, rates always will be significantly lower than whatever you'd pay for one-shot deals. Investigate what you think will be best for your company and then incorporate it into your annual budget.

Aside from any other details you need to know about newspaper advertising, especially in major metropolitan areas, it's a fact that most traditional daily newspapers are struggling to survive, to maintain ad revenues, and to maintain readership. Those that are surviving do so on matters that go well beyond traditional news coverage, since most people know the news well before tomorrow's newspaper is being printed. Newspaper readership is in decline and statistically aging as newspapers continue to lose their younger readers to the Internet and the gamut of their subscriber base to cable news networks. If you're considering making any commitment to print advertising, my strong recommendation is to do so mainly in publications with much more narrowed, more focused audiences.

Telephone Directory Advertising

In the industry's youth in the 1970s and 1980s, telephone directory advertising was an affordable ticket to steady lead-generation. It was the one medium that virtually all custom apparel decorators used in their advertising programs, and for many of them, the only medium. With the deregulation of the telephone companies in the 1980's, most areas in America saw a proliferation of telephone directory publishers, a situation that still prevails and makes budgeting for this medium a continuing challenge.

The primary strength of telephone directories also is their greatest limitation. Their advantage always has been its value to those close to making a decision about where to buy -- not in reaching out to people who either aren't currently interested in buying, are satisfied with their current situation, or haven't thought much about buying your products as opposed to others'. It is strictly a reactive medium and the antithesis of a *proactive* form of advertising.

As a general rule, telephone directory usage is declining and most people under 40 rarely consult a hard copy telephone director at all. In our industry, the number of companies relying on such directories for leads shrinks year after year. Meanwhile, advertising rates continue to escalate and the pitch from Yellow Pages' vendors today is geared to touting the directories' online presences and features.

For those apparel graphics firms that nonetheless find themselves in a position to use telephone directories in their advertising plans, their place should command only a small portion of your advertising budget, rarely worthy of more than a 15% to 20% share at best.

Keeping in mind my rather unenthusiastic admonitions about the Yellow Pages, I'll look at how to make whatever investment you make in directory advertising yield better results.

Bigger isn't necessarily better, it only costs more. Making your ad get more attention and providing prospects with more reasons to call are the objectives here, and there are cost-effective ways to achieve both goals without having to unload your company's treasury in the process. Graphics and text rule in whatever heading your listing appears. Below is a rundown on the specifics on how to improve your telephone directory ads. But you'll find many of my comments will apply as well to ads in other print media and online media.

Graphics

As the rules and regulations for small listings and in-column ads preclude the use of graphics or limit you to one small logo, we're talking strictly display ads for using any real graphic prowess. Here are some tips on maximizing your impact:

► **You Do the Art.** The folks who do ads for the publisher are nice and all that, but none of them went to art school dreaming of the day they'd be sitting in a cubicle doing Yellow Pages ads. They crank 'em out by the hundreds, and browsing through any directory, you'll see they all kind of look the same, don't they? These artists are working under serious time constraints, but you shouldn't, given the amount of money you'll spend for your ads. Create your own ad (or hire an expert) to make it be the best it can be, not one that looks like all the rest.

► **Borders.** A bold, thick, rounded border helps an ad stand out. Or create a border using words spelling out your products, services, or other pertinent information.

► **Typefaces.** The most prevalent typeface in directories is what I call "skinny stick." It comes in boring and boring italic, and can occasionally be done slightly thicker. Big deal. Use different type than what you see everyone else using. Use typefaces as they were intended -- to give words personality, be it masculine, feminine, modern, traditional, high-tech, folksy, whatever.

► **Reverses.** Use reverses (white or the paper color emerging from a black or dark ink background) to call attention to the most important aspect(s) of your ad -- especially your phone number.

► **Logos.** Yours is important, but don't waste valuable real estate overemphasizing it. Prospects want reasons to call you, and your ego isn't one of them. If your company is a member of respected local or national organizations (SGIA, the Chamber of Commerce, etc.), show it.

► **Color.** The directory publisher's upcharge for the first additional color (after the standard black) is substantially higher than the base price. Color's nice if you want to spend the money, but if you can afford to do it, I'd suggest your money would be better spent going with a bigger one-color ad, not enriching the publisher by buying color. A smaller ad with good graphics and reverses will accomplish more than a larger, mediocre ad in full color.

Text

Command attention! The first word in the AIDA formula is attention, so use a phrase that hooks the browser and hopefully causes him to read on as to why he should call you. The seven most effective headlines (and campaign themes) I recommend are:

1. *"Call us first!"* This phrase is part of a general campaign, but is especially powerful when used in the Yellow Pages. It's quite effective in and of itself in generating calls. For companies skilled in effecting "Good Phone," there's little doubt that if you can get the first call -- or any call -- from a Yellow Pages' shopper, you've got a better shot at converting that caller to a customer than the other guys. (They lack the game plan, the tools, and the skills to beat you at fielding inquiries).

2. *"Get a second opinion."* This is a variation on the point above. I recommend this in areas where there's a single dominant player who needs to be brought down a peg in size.

3. *"We wrote the book on custom screen printing and embroidery in* (town, area). *For your free copy, call* (phone number)." Unlike most of your competitors, you have a user-friendly express catalog and a price list working for you. More important to the purpose at hand, though, is giving a caller a very good reason to contact you.

4. *"Buy Factory-Direct."* If the competition includes several sales agencies and you decorate in-house, this differentiates your company and gets the message across.

5. *"Visit Our Showroom."* Many prospects want to see and feel the merchandise and this invitation assures them you've probably got what they're looking for. Given that most of your custom competitors don't have a real showroom (or even a good set of samples!), your showroom now is more than just a great selling tool, it's a practical advertising hook as well.

6. *"We understand budgets and deadlines."* While it doesn't necessarily mean you can do anything about their budgets and deadlines, this line does, however, generate calls. The message speaks to the hearts of your callers and because it's in print, they tend to believe you mean it!

7. *"We sell attention!©."* What customers buy from you is much more than apparel graphics products and services. They buy your talent, your expertise, your experience, and your professionalism. If you're good at what you do, people will come to you for advice as to what they should buy, what's most affordable, what's the latest in style and color, or what would look best. "We sell attention!" (a copyrighted phrase available for license from the Apparel Graphics Institute) gets their attention for any apparel graphics company as well as for promotional products distributors.

Note that though you see quotation marks in these headlines, don't use them in your ads.

What matters most in your Yellow Pages' advertising should be giving the prospect information that entices him or her to call you, not repeating what everyone else is saying, which usually includes space wasted on listing products and telling that you sell to schools, organizations, and businesses. (Said audiences are already looking in the heading, so why waste space on it?) If you absolutely insist on listing products, save valuable real estate by recapping your offerings in very small print. Give your hours, your website, and your address if your business is located in a commercial property. For more items and terms that'll help your ad get better results for your company, consult Chapter 35 - "Magic Words in Advertising Custom-Decorated Apparel."

The heading your ad is listed in can make all the difference in the world in terms of results. Think of it as the "key words" for telephone directories. Certainly you already know the most well-known headings – "Screen Printing," "Embroidery," and "T-shirts." If you do apparel decorating in-house, consider listing your ad under "Screen Printing – Wholesale & Manufacturers," "Embroidery -- Wholesale & Manufacturers," and/or "T-shirts -- Wholesale & Manufacturers." If these headings aren't yet offered in your area, being the first to initiate the "Whol. & Mfr." (as it's done in print) suffix to the heading will give you a year's head start on the competition, which you can expect will join you there the following year. The addition of "Wholesale & Manufacturers" suggests to readers (hopefully honestly) that your company isn't simply the middle man in the equation, but rather the direct source and thought of as offering lower prices.

There are other headings that also may prove beneficial, depending on your area and your competitors. These include: "Sporting Goods" (if you specialize in teamwear and sell names and numbers), "Promotional Products," "Fundraising" (good for schools and organizations), and "Uniforms," where decorated apparel products now command a sizable share of the uniform market.

Explore with your directory salesperson buying space in additional directories – and related package deals -- in areas adjacent to yours or in nearby towns where you have field representation or can serve these customers effectively from your location.

CHAPTER

RADIO, TELEVISION, BILLBOARDS, SIGNAGE, TELEMARKETING, AND PROMOTIONAL

Radio

In an earlier life I was a disc jockey and newscaster, and learned first hand the power of this medium to work for its advertisers. So while my bias is admittedly strong and personal, the overwhelming success my clients have had with radio is too great a story to keep from readers of this book. My experience with using radio for apparel graphics marketers extends to creating radio campaigns in more than 100 U.S. and Canadian markets, and everywhere it has been executed, it proves time and again to be a powerful, cost-effective lead generator.

In our industry, at best a very small percentage of apparel graphics companies has ever used radio, and only a tiny percentage uses it successfully as an integral component of its marketing effort. Those for whom radio has failed blame the medium, although the real cause of the failure was probably something else. Why the high failure rate? You'll understand why very shortly.

What makes radio so effective begins with its very nature as an *intrusive* medium, one that reaches listeners wherever and whenever they might be listening. Contrary to the ill-founded idea some might advance that people dial out commercials, the fact of the matter is a.) they generally don't, and b.) many listeners actually *enjoy* good commercials! (Emphasis here on good.) Another challenge to the validity of using commercial radio is the market segment that listens to subscription-based radio, which I acknowledge, but don't consider a major segment. Not statistically, anyhow.

Radio reaches and tells people about your company and your products whether they want to hear it or not. And, if the messages are good, it recruits prospects who wouldn't have thought on their own to initiate an inquiry, former users who haven't bought in a long time for a variety of reasons, and current buyers who'd like to compare what they're getting now with what the radio advertiser has to offer.

The biggest limitation in this business to using radio is the population in your primary marketing area. For apparel graphics firms located in North America's top markets, you probably can forget about using radio altogether or at best can afford to buy time on just one station. Sixty-second commercials (or "spots" in the vernacular of radio) in major markets typically range from $100 to $500 per spot on the low side from 6:00 a.m. to 7:00 p.m. to a few thousand dollars per spot for top stations in New York and L.A. And while 30-second spots cost 30-40% less than "sixties" or ":60s," my experience is that the shorter spots are wholly ineffective in presenting the information necessary to sell custom apparel graphics products.

For advertisers in markets of one million persons or less, radio can, however, become a viable option.

For markets of 250,000 to 500,000 people, radio becomes very affordable, where :60s go for only $25 to 50 per spot when bought efficiently. For that money, on a popular local station, you can reach thousands of listeners waking up, going to work, and to a lesser extent, on the job. For a high rate of $50 on a station with 5,000 listeners in a given day part, the math works out to *a penny a listener*! Even at twice the price, it's a bargain.

Why so many apparel graphics advertisers have bad experience with radio is the fact that so many advertised on radio without knowing how to buy air time or worse, on a trade-out for shirts or caps. Was the trade with a station that had the right format to attract buyers? Were the spots aired at the best times of day? (Or wasted by being broadcast in the evenings or on weekends?) Was it a *good* commercial, as commercials go? Was it written by a pro who really understood the firm's objectives, its industry and its buyers? (Chances the spot was written by the rep who handled the account but *doesn't earn commissions on trades*). Did it sound like so many other commercials on the same station, done by a staff disc jockey who records a score of other commercials every week? Was the campaign broadcast at the best time of year for the products advertised? If the answer to any one of these questions is "no," the campaign is destined to fail. If the answer is "no" to two or more of these questions, the campaign is guaranteed to fail!

What type of stations work best for generating leads for custom apparel graphics products? Which don't work at all? To understand which type of station formats produce the best results, start with the facts that the primary demographic of buyers of custom orders is between 25 and 49 years of age, tends to show higher education and income, and is distributed about 60:40 females. The closer a station's primary listening audience comes to this profile, the better the station for your lead-generating purposes.

Here's a round-up of formats, both the productive and the not-so-productive:

► **Soft Rock/Light Rock**: Perfect age demo, skews toward the female side. Good on-the-job listenership, especially in offices and stores. I highly recommend it.

► **Adult Contemporary**: Listeners fall in the 18 to 35 age demo. Skews female. Best used in markets where there's no soft rock station. These stations tend to be pricey because their audiences are huge. Lots of waste here. I rarely recommend buying time on them for selling custom decorated apparel.

► **Country or, more precisely *Contemporary* Country**: We're talkin' Brad Paisley, Taylor Swift, and other hot country artists. Country delivers a good age demo, but listeners stretch both younger and older beyond the 25 to 49 demo. Men and women. Income demos tend to be higher than national averages. Excellent listener strength in all day parts. More importantly, country listeners are highly loyal; they rarely change stations compared to other listener groups. I find country stations to be excellent sources for qualified buyers and solid lead generation. I highly recommend it.

► **Oldies**: First, it depends on just how old the oldies are. If they're playing hits from the 70s, and 80s, and 90s, it's good. Too much from the 60s, not good. Skews heavily male. Recommended in some markets, but not all. I rarely buy time on oldies stations.

► **"Best Mix" Music**: With some current tunes and some older, these include stations whose positioning liners say, "We play anything." I listen to this format at times and like it personally; but I rarely recommend buying it.

► **Classic Rock**: Somewhat older audience, 35 to 65, and skews toward males. Excellent in yielding qualified leads from boomer decision-makers, particularly for blue collar buyers. Recommended in some markets, not all.

► **Modern Rock**: Great music, but listeners are way younger that what the demo calls for to reach decision-makers. College campuses? Perfect audience, but there are much more cost-effective ways to market to on-campus decision-makers. Not at all recommended.

► **Middle-of-the-Road (MOR), Music of Your Life, Other Older Listener Formats**: Basically worthless for selling custom orders as the youngest part of this audience is usually 60 or older. Not recommended.

► **News & Information**: Tends to skew 35+ and heavily male. But education and income are much higher than most other listener groups. OK for drive times, but not good for mid-day. Usually expensive, too. I recommend it only in smaller markets and toward stations focusing on local news, local sports, and weather in the morning.

► **Talk**: Talk radio is huge, but talk show aficionados skew older. Great for reaching businesspeople who listen during the day. Top draws such as Rush Limbaugh can be pricey, but my experience has been that the loyalty of the audiences and the frequency of their listening make buys on Rush and other conservative-oriented programs worth the added premium one pays to air spots on them.

► **Hispanic**: Very important in some key markets and growing by leaps and bounds. But weigh local factors. If Hispanic decision-makers are tuning in, your company should consider buying on Latino stations, especially if your company has Spanish-speaking salespeople on your team. Listenership is 18 to 54 overall and very loyal. In major markets, there are usually several Hispanic stations, however, and the most popular one can be rather pricey.

► **Inspirational/Contemporary Christian**: Very loyal audiences, but usually just a small percentage of total listenership. Effective for generating what tend to be smaller orders, but you know the customers will honor your invoices – or potentially face eternal damnation. Weight local factors. Good value for the money in most cases.

► **Sports**: Overwhelmingly male and draws spectators for the most part, not the players. Good for creating awareness, but my experience is that these stations are iffy in terms of generating orders for businesses, \but OK for drawing leads from the athletic market.

▶ **Urban/Hip-Hop**: Very loyal audiences and effective for getting frequency, but listenership skews too young to include a big percentage of decision-makers. The orders that are generated tend to be smaller ones. Often expensive, too. Not recommended.

Other formats, including classical, heavy metal, and hybrids, won't get you cost-justified leads. I rarely recommend buys on these stations broadcasting these formats.

Which day parts work best? Decidedly not the cheap ones, which are evenings and overnight. (And never buy radio on price. Buy it on the size and strength of the primary listening audience). Radio listenership is mainly a daytime phenomenon. All my radio campaigns concentrate the "buys" from 6:00 a.m. through 3:00 p.m. Never later. The object here is to reach people during most of the hours when they're in a position to respond to your advertising by calling you. I've learned from long experience that late afternoon spots and evening drive time spots don't generate leads. I won't buy this time slot (3:00 p.m. to 7:00 p.m.) and neither should you. Ever.

Which days work best? Mondays, Tuesdays, and Wednesdays for sure. Weekends are worthless due to lower listenership and the fact that most people are doing leisure activities. Fridays are generally weak days for generating incoming leads. Thursdays are generally unnecessary.

My secret formula for buying radio is to buy the "front" of the week. Not only has it proven to perform well for business-to-business campaigns, but because early week times are lower in demand from other advertisers, it means you usually can get better rate flexibility for airing your company's spots on these days.

Another part of the secret formula is the frequency factor. It's three to four spots a day (I use only "sixties"), three days a weeks, for eight to 10-week "flights." Virtually all the radio campaigns I direct coincide with the seasonal windows discussed in the section on direct mail (going into spring and after Labor Day). Never run your spots in afternoon drive time or evenings. Overnights? If they're free, take 'em.

Radio rates usually are negotiable. How negotiable depends first on your skill at negotiating and then on the variables of how much you're spending, what times of year you'll be advertising, how well you pay your bills, and how much the station wants your account.

As with direct mail, radio is an area where getting professional help usually will pay for itself many times over. You'll learn about understanding Arbitron™ ratings, buying sponsorships (weather, news, features), and how to get added value for a buy. You'll often get better rates and extras such as bonus spots, on-air "mentions," and additional promotion. (As a service to readers of this book, the Apparel Graphics Institute offers telephone consultation at no charge to industry firms interested in advertising on radio. 410.641.7300).

Dumb Mistake No. 27
Trading shirts for air time without having first negotiated the rates for the air time and the hours during which your commercial will air.

Because the apparel graphics industry sells products that almost every radio station wants for its listeners, advertisers, and staff, apparel decorating firms are excellent candidates for them to trade air for cloth (or what I affectionately refer to as "airables for wearables"). But don't trade for anything that's outside the recommendations here on time slots, seasonal windows, frequency and formats. Endeavor to exclude a portion of the trade (half of it or more) so you can get some cash in the deal, hopefully enough to cover your out-of-pocket garment costs. Well-executed promotional programs for stations using decorated apparel can work well, especially for your company when what you design and sell is in such demand that the radio station wants more shirts more than you want or need more advertising. When this wonderful situation occurs, do not continue trading goods for time and don't use more radio time than you need. You can be certain the stations will try to trade more air time in exchange for more shirts. Don't fall for it. Sufficiency is the rule here, not overkill.

Good commercials come in lots of flavors: humorous, straight, clever, and serial campaigns. When well-written, well-produced, and coupled with smart buys, radio delivers the lowest cost-per-lead for any medium I've ever used in this industry except for successful e-commerce campaigns. My experience also is that the ratio of dollars spent on advertising-to-*sales* (not leads) shows the highest level (lowest cost) of performance efficiency, too.

There are yet other media beyond those previously discussed, which can be effective in satisfying one or more of the three key objectives of advertising. But their usage is usually limited by circumstances and doesn't have the same level of universality as the ones I've reviewed. That admonition notwithstanding, here's a rundown on the other media and my read on each.

Television & Cable Television

Few people watch broadcast television anymore on a signal they receive through an antenna. Most view it via cable along with dozens of other channels that have segmented the audiences for television much as radio has segmented audiences by music preference and specialty formats. Except for companies in markets of 50,000 to 100,000, broadcast television is prohibitively expensive and even then, your ability to target specific audiences on broadcast television is difficult. By definition, it's a *mass* medium, which for *custom* decorated apparel companies means lots of waste distribution (read: wasted dollars). Moreover, TV is something most adults watch mainly in the evening. This fact makes it a poor candidate as a lead generator. TV, however, has few equals in creating awareness for key target audiences of custom apparel. In the many campaigns where I've used television in the media mix, the decision always is to go with well-targeted cable channels. For some athletic-oriented apparel decorating companies, though, I have on occasion bought prime time entertainment and sports programming on broadcast channels.

Where TV works best for apparel decorators is limited to the function of creating awareness, especially so when your commercial showcases your facilities, your equipment (in operation), your personnel, and your work (show close-ups of your best screen printing, heat printing, and embroidery).

Cable TV can, however, frequently be bought on a much narrower geographical basis than either radio or broadcast television. This makes it easier to target audiences with higher levels of income and home ownership, demographics that dovetail with those of the decision-makers you're trying to attract. "Narrowcasting" also is much more affordable than *broad*casting. The best choices on cable TV for advertising custom apparel decorating are not mass entertainment channels, but cable news channels, Discovery, History, and A& E, because that's where you're much more likely to access the audiences that include the decision-makers who buy your product categories. ESPN and other sports programming channels are good for reaching men, but there's a great deal of waste distribution. Rates for cable TV tend to be in the same affordability range as radio.

Billboards

Like TV, billboards are better for creating awareness than for generating hard leads. Their usage usually is prohibitively expensive for most companies, especially if the boards are located on overcrowded main arteries. In major markets, billboards on Interstate highways can run tens of thousands of dollars – *a month!* Note that when cruising at 55 mph on a straightaway, a driver has all of six to seven seconds to read and digest your entire message on a billboard.

Aside from wonderfully creative campaigns for companies with huge advertising war chests, mainly use local billboards for posting directions or arrows to your shop. Consider those at intersections with traffic lights, where people have more time to read more text while they're waiting for a light to change. The biggest downside to billboards is that they are a mass medium that, while they reaches a large number of people – literally millions of views on an interstate -- only a small percentage of them are decision-makers who buy your products.

Signage

A no-brainer, eh? A good sign is a great way to broadcast your business and your location and very inexpensive as a long-term investment. If your company is, however, located on a major thoroughfare, use it to your advantage and spend as much as you can afford on high-visibility signage, making your location plainly obtrusive.

Allow me to digress a moment. The value of an attractive sign on a building with frontage on a busy thoroughfare is obviously considerable and begs the question of whether you should ponder moving your company to a location with better visibility. My answer is that if you can find an opportunity to do so and pay rent (to a landlord or to yourself if you own the building) commensurate with other light industrial rentals, it's a matter for further exploration. As a general rule and barring the deal of the decade, paying twice or more for space than typical commercial/light industrial rates should be evaluated vis-à-vis what the additional rent would be vs. how much advertising budget it would take to generate significant additional revenue to a level approaching the guesstimated benefit of a better location.

What I've seen all to often, though, is most companies that opted for more visibility at a higher rent or mortgage don't generate the additional volume they anticipated simply by moving to a busier location. My observation here is the rule, not the exception. In other words, the decision to move is a seemingly easier way to generate greater sales compared to increasing a company's marketing efforts and advertising commitments to gain the additional sales.

Nonetheless I can cite a few exceptions to my own comments here, but it wasn't solely a better, more visible location that did the trick. And in each case, it encompassed *much better* signage, a great showroom, enhanced customer service for walk-ins, and *increased* advertising to ensure more visitors. Anyhow, you've gotten my opinion, based on my own industry experiences, and I acknowledge there are other ways of seeing the equation. I'll leave the ball in your court on this issue.

What constitutes a good sign, though, is one that has the following attributes: It attractively displays the company's name and logo, hopefully with sufficient space for a tag line and appropriate descriptors, and with reasonable visibility. Said visibility is a matter of how big the signage is – and perhaps the landlord's permission and/or the municipality's signage ordinances and building codes – and the distance from those who're able to read it without a pair of binoculars handy.

A good trick is getting your message across is, providing you've got everyone's permission, is to put large (3' to 5' tall) silhouettes of your most popular products – T-shirts, caps. hoodies, etc. – on the walls of your building, on your shop's windows, or on the signs for your company.

Vehicle Graphics

This is another no-brainer, especially if your company has its own vehicles. When parked in a visible location and when on the road, thousands of people will see the vehicle's graphics, making it an affordable means of advertising, especially on a per-impression basis. Where your staff -- especially salespeople -- are on board and cooperative about putting magnetic (removable) signs on their cars and truck, you can multiply the advertising impressions your company can generate around the community.

Telemarketing

As a form of advertising, it does have its advantages. I'll ascribe its greatest effectiveness as a proactive advertising medium in this business as being limited to making appointments, not selling orders, over the phone. Many readers of this book are right now gagging on the mere thought of making telemarketing calls. Nonetheless many companies in this industry have become successful thanks to salespeople using tele-marketing for opening doors and closing sales. Few people, however, like to do telemarketing, and even fewer are skilled at it.

There are professional telemarketing firms, however, throughout the U.S. and Canada that you can engage to make appointments for outside salespeople. These firms work on a per-hour fee basis and/or for com-pensation linked to securing firm appointments. Having been a good telemarketer, myself, when it was about all I could afford when start-ing my ad agency, I can honestly say I enjoyed making the calls and it certainly paid off. For me. (Hmmm, now you're thinking I was voted "Most Likely to Take A Life" in my high school yearbook?) But that was a long time ago, when telemarketers were at worst considered mere nuisances. I mention telemarketing in this chapter as a viable advertis-ing medium for your consideration only because I have a professional obligation to do so, despite knowing most people will peremptorily rule out telemarketing.

Promotional Products

They're effective and appreciated as thank-you's and goodwill gifts. But as an advertising medium, they're most effective when used in the context of a campaign conducted directly by your salespeople or in conjunction with a direct mail program. The addition of a promotional item inserted in a mailer is tantamount to the assurance your mailing will be opened and at least glanced at. The better the product you give, the better your response will be. A high-quality promotional product (with your advertising imprint on it, of course) placed inside a carton of finished goods or delivered to the decision-maker will remind him that you value his business and do want to be remembered.

The various advertising categories cited in this and the previous two chapters cover most of what really matters for apparel decorators. Lest I be accused of forgetting to mention balloon and banner displays to attract attention, bench advertising, restroom ads, placemat advertising in diners, including this sentence gets me off the hook. But if you have a friend who'll let you borrow his blimp for a few years without charge, take him up on the offer and have at it!

CHAPTER

CREATING A MEDIA PLAN AND BUDGET

Having preached about the need to project a budget for your annual advertising commitments and about developing an advertising plan, I'll now present a sample media plan and budget to help you visualize creating one for your company.

The hypothetical company, Capitol Custom Clothing Company (CCCC), using this plan is located in Springfield, Illinois, an area with a population of the city and its suburbs of just over 200,000 people.

The company is entering its eighth year in business and projects $800,000 in sales for the coming year. Its core business is custom decorated apparel sold mostly in the local area to businesses, schools, organizations, and government agencies. But the company added CAD-cutting and laser-engraving two years ago to augment its production capabilities and has seen its investment produce over $100,000 in annual volume. Projected annual sales volume (figures are rounded for your convenience) by product category is:

Figure 20: **Capitol Custom Clothing Company's Revenue Sources**

Decorated apparel	–	$600,000 (75%)
CAD-cut signs	–	80,000 (10%)
Laser-engraved executive gifts	–	40,000 (5%)
Promotional products	–	30,000 (4%)
Contract work	–	50,000 (6%)
TOTAL		**$800,000 (100%)**

The company has budgeted 3.25% of its gross revenue for all its sales except for contract work, or $24,375, for advertising. Note that the contract work gets no advertising budget at all, because CCCC isn't looking for any more contract work. The three companies for which CCCC still does contract work allow the company to make a fair profit on the service, present no impediments to its local sales efforts, and have relationships with the company that date back several years. CCCC would rather get out of contract work altogether, but it has grandfathered these accounts and if and when these accounts elect to take their work elsewhere, the company won't seek replacement accounts.

Here's how the ad budget is divvied up along with some insight as to what the company will be doing to enhance its direct expenditures.

Figure 21: **A Sample Media Budget**

ANNUAL ADVERTISING BUDGET

1. Radio	$ 9,000
2. Catalog Mailings	4,000
3. Supplemental mailings	1,000
4. Web Marketing	3,000
5. Promotional Products	1,200
6. Christmas Promotion	1,000
7. Yellow Pages $125/month	1,500
8. C of C newsletter	500
9. Business Weekly	1,000
10. Church Bulletin	100
11. Business-to-Business Event	1,000
12. Chamber After Hours	500
Unallocated funds	575
TOTAL ADVERTISING	**$24,375**

Next, let's take a closer look at the expenditures and their objectives.

1. Radio – The $9,000 figure shown is actually for a $12,000 annual buy for two eight-week flights, one beginning in mid-March and the other beginning in mid-September. Half of the $12,000 is done on trade with the stations involved; the total cash outlay for garments is about $6,000 plus about $3,000 in labor, materials, and overhead. That's why I've shown $9,000 for the cost of radio, even though CCCC is getting $12,000 of advertising. Using :60 spots at between $15 and $45 across three stations – country, soft rock, and talk -- the contracts total just over 400 spots. CCCC earns about 100 bonus (no charge) spots on a 1:4 ratio (one free spot for every four contracted). All the commercials are aired from 6:00 a.m. to 3:00 p.m., including about 20% of them run during morning weather checks. CCCC runs an online store for the station, the stations buys shirts over and above the trade, and the company gets lots of value-added perks (concert tickets, among other things). Its relationship with the stations has gained the company relationships with other advertisers on the stations, which translate to further sales.

The functions of CCCC's radio advertising are to create awareness and reinforce it, inform customers and prospects about the company's offerings and capabilities, and to solicit inquiries.

2. Catalog Mailings – CCCC publishes its own express catalog and price list and mails it to its customer base of about 400 companies twice a year, in mid-September and mid-March. It also mails catalogs to an additional 200 prospective buyers in schools, government agencies, and major employers in the area. Additional catalogs are distributed to prospects seen by the salesperson, to walk-ins, and at an annual business-to-business event, hosted by the Chamber of Commerce each year in spring. The $4,000 budget for this includes the cost of printing, mailing, catalog envelopes, and labeling.

The functions of CCCC's catalog and price list efforts are to make it easy for its customers and prospects to buy its core products, and hopefully retain the materials for immediate or future reference. It also reinforces relationships, builds new ones and helps differentiate CCCC from its competitors, few of whom, if any, will publish their own catalogs and price lists, much less distribute them.

3. Supplemental mailings – Approximately two or three times a year, CCCC sends additional small single-page flyers or postcard mailings to its customers and occasionally a mailer to a targeted new audience (the company always is experimenting). A mailer for Christmas-oriented orders for employee apparel or promotional products usually is mailed around the third week in October and a mid-spring mailer is sent to shake some additional apples off the trees in peak season. CCCC budgets $1,000 for these efforts.

The functions of these additional direct mail efforts are to remind buyers that CCCC is busy looking for business, reinforce its other advertising, and bring in some extra business.

4. Web Marketing – CCCC promotes itself online through a variety of programs and does e-blasts to customers and prospects in a variety of markets, using different angles for different audiences. While its web hosting expenses are handled for accounting purposes under "Communications" (for house phones and cell phones), its other costs average $250 monthly, including operating a few online stores for key accounts. Ergo, $3,000 is budgeted. Fortunately CCCC's art director doubles as the company's webmaster.

The functions of CCCC's web marketing and advertising are to create awareness for prospective buyers, make it easy for its customers and prospects to buy, inform customers and prospects about the company's standard offerings and capabilities as well as product lines and services these buyers might not be aware of, and to build and reinforce the company's credibility.

5. Promotional Products – Excluding its membership in PPAI (Promotional Products Association International), which is handled for accounting purposes under dues and subscriptions, the company keeps a supply of attractive imprinted promotional items on hand, all of which are purchased at deep discount from PPAI-accredited vendors. The company budgets $1,200 annually to meet its estimated usage of abut $100 a month in "stuff."

The functions of these products essentially are to build goodwill and make it easy for its customers to find CCCC's phone number and website.

6. Christmas Promotion – In early December, the company sends its customers an annual commemorative item featuring a framed screen printed winter motif on Pellon™ with an embroidered highlight. There's no mention of the company on the product except for a microscopic imprint below the design, if on it at all, or via a sticker on the back of it. Some are sent via FedEx Ground, while most are hand-delivered by staff. $1,000 is budgeted for this annual ritual.

The function of this effort primarily is to reinforce CCCC's position in the minds of its customers as being a company that's creative, smart, provides value in all its endeavors, products, and services, and is worthy of the recipient's continued loyalty and patronage. The Christmas promotion also is distinctive, appreciated, and serves to strongly differentiate CCCC from its competitors.

7. Yellow Pages – CCCC has significantly reduced its telephone directory advertising from a decade earlier. It runs small in-column ads and some bold listings in two local directories under the headings "T-Shirts – Whol. & Mfr.," "Embroidery – Whol. & Mfr.," "Promotional Products" (mainly to tout CCCC's laser-engraved products), and "Fundraising." Along with getting listed in the publishers' online directories, the Yellow Pages commitment is held to $125/month or $1,500 a year.

The functions of its directory advertising simply is to create awareness of CCCC for potential new customers. It gets some value-added differentiation by being listed as a direct "wholesale" source for its categories.

8. Chamber of Commerce newsletter – The C of C publishes a quarterly newsletter for its membership of several hundred companies. The company runs a display ad in each edition and gets a free one-page insert once a year, which CCCC uses for its spring campaign. Annual cost is $500. CCCC is active year 'round in the organization, too. The owner attends nearly every one of the group's 10 meetings a year, and there always are at least two CCCC faces at the "Chamber After Hours" social event (10 times a year)– the owner and/or the sales rep and/or the customer service rep – and at the annual banquet. The owner always is serving on a C of C committee, usually the one that plans the annual B2B show or the parks department's free summer concerts in the park, which the chamber underwrites. Once a year, the company hosts one of the after-hours events, usually in September, which brings some 300 people to CCCC's facility for an hour or two. (See Item 11).

The functions of its ads in chamber publication are to build awareness of and credibility for CCCC as a worthy colleague to local businesses. Its helps build and strengthen awareness with its frequency.

9. Business Weekly – A weekly tabloid-size publication that goes to a several thousand area businesses is the only regular print medium CCCC utilizes. It advertises in 38 of the publication's 50 issues, dropping out from mid-December to mid-February and for the month of July. CCCC's business card-size ad runs in the paper's "Executive Directory" section under the heading "Customer Apparel & Promotions" and rarely changes during the year. The deal also includes four quarter-page display ads that run once a quarter. The modest budget for this is $1,100 annually. As an advertiser, CCCC can count on the publication to run several press releases a year from the company.

The functions of this advertising are to build awareness of the company and solicit business.

10. Church Bulletin – $100 for an annual sponsorship in a monthly church bulletin gives CCCC a business card-size ad in the publication each month to let the owner's fellow members know he'd be pleased to provide decorated apparel and other items for their businesses, schools, and events. The function of this item is more a charitable contribution than serious advertising.

11. Annual Business-to-Business Event – The Chamber of Commerce sponsors a two-day B2B event each year in late February, drawing some 3,000 attendees from the metro area and beyond. CCCC takes two booths ($250 each). The owner, the sales rep and the customer service rep work the event to meet their customers and new prospects, build their mailing lists, and stay "wired" in the business community and with local politicians. They also do this via after-hours networking at the social events held the night before the event opens and after close of business on the first day. Including partial sponsorship in some programs at the event, incidentals, and some give-aways, the event is budgeted at about $1,000.

During the event or immediately before it opens, CCCC staff visit the booths and tables of exhibitors they feel might be candidates as good prospects. When you exhibit at events, your paid participation in the event gives you the right to solicit other exhibitors, so do take extra advantage of your position as an exhibitor.

In addition to serving the basic advertising functions, this event's primary goals are enhanced positioning, developing relationships for subsequent solicitation, and a powerful dose of differentiation.

12. Chamber After Hours – The Chamber of Commerce's monthly social get-together at a sponsoring member business draws a big crowd. With a cash bar, light munchies offered by local restaurants and catering firms, and a disc jockey furnished by a local radio station, it's a popular local happening for the business community. Once a year CCCC volunteers to host the September edition of the event. While the event is going on, CCCC runs production orders in the embroidery department and runs a "local pride" seven-color T-shirt design on its automatic press. To do so, the company avails itself of the generosity of its primary gar-

ment distributor for 288 free white cotton tees for distribution to attendees. The firm trades out custom shirts for a big tent and folding chairs
from a local rental company and hires a balloon artist and a magician
to work the crowd. Virtually everyone in attendance will spend some
time wandering throughout the shop seeing production being run and
the art department busy on new designs, and picking up a free T-shirt
as it comes off the dryer. CCCC will go out-of–pocket for about $500,
or more. CCCC employees are, of course, all proudly wearing a variety
of embroidered or screen printed company garb.

In addition to serving the basic advertising functions, this event's
goals are to reinforce relationships and develop new ones.

Dumb Mistake No. 28
Scheduling advertising when there's little or no demand for
your product – such as promoting sweatshirts in mid-July!

You'll note in Figure 21 there's $575 in "unallocated funds." Yes,
there's some money left over – on paper, anyhow. The reality is that
while the budget will largely be executed as planned, there's always
the likelihood something will go over or under budget, a deal will be
revised, and surprises inevitably will occur. The exercise of media
planning and budgeting isn't as much about precisely calculating every
penny in advertising as it is in providing a game plan, a schedule, and
organizing the company's thinking and strategies. It also creates a roadmap for its staff to see to it that preparations are made at the appropriate advance intervals and that everyone stays on the same page. CCCC
knows from experience its budget will undergo some modifications
during the course of the year, but overall it will be largely executed as
outlined. Also, the firm is assured its messages will get out to its audiences, its presence will be visible in its core market, and that its sales
volume *should* come in somewhere in line with projections.

In Figure 22 (next page), showing Monthly Distribution of Advertising Dollars, the company is able to see its whole year outlined and
budgeted, making it far easier to stay on track executing its game plan,
knowing its next moves and what needs to be prepared and when it
needs to be ready.

Figure 22: Monthly Distribution of Advertising Dollars

	JAN	FEB	MAR	APR	MAY	JUN	JUL	AUG	SEP	OCT	NOV	DEC	TOTAL
Radio	--	--	1400	2200	900	--	--	--	1400	2200	900	--	9,000
Catalog Mailings	--	--	2000	--	--	--	--	--	2000	--	--	--	4,000
Supp'l Mailings	--	--	--	--	300	--	--	--	400	300	--	--	1,000
Web Mrkt'g	250	250	250	250	250	250	250	250	250	250	250	250	3,000
Promo. Products	100	100	100	100	100	100	100	100	100	100	100	100	1,200
C. of C. Newsletter	50	50	50	50	50	50	--	--	50	50	50	50	500
Business Weekly	--	100	100	100	100	100	--	100	100	100	100	100	1,000
Church Bulletin	100	--	--	--	--	--	--	--	--	--	--	--	100
Yellow Pages	125	125	125	125	125	125	125	125	125	125	125	125	1,500
B2B Event	--	1000	--	--	--	--	--	--	--	--	--	--	1,000
Ch. After Hours	--	--	--	--	--	--	--	--	500	--	--	--	500
Cristmas Mailing	--	--	--	--	--	--	--	--	--	--	--	1000	1,000
	625	1625	4025	2825	1825	625	475	575	4925	3125	1525	1625	$23,800

Figure 22 is a month-to-month tally of advertising expenditures. The advertising outlays tend to reflect approximate cashflow peaks and valleys during the year. This phenomenon is decidedly not accidental, but quite deliberately engineered to help the company be in a relatively good cash position to pay its advertising bills when the advertising is doing its heaviest lifting – successfully.

Note also the June to August lull in advertising. It, too, is deliberate, reflecting the reality that while summer business can be is steady, in the general custom apparel arena it's a period of relatively soft demand – with the spring peak over and the fall peak not yet emerging. And hardly anyone in the company wants to work extra weekends in summer.

The budget above is for a larger enterprise. It is a hypothetical exercise to give you a picture of the task at hand and it's a budget for a company selling custom decorated apparel to general audiences. Were this company focused on special or niche markets, its configuration, media selection, and other aspects of it would look much different, given different windows of demand, different geography, or other salient unique attributes.

A Message to Start-Up Entrepreneurs: As I mentioned in the early part of the book, I work with two start-up companies each year and developing media plans and budgets are radically different from doing the same function in a mature company, as shown above. With start-ups, my efforts focus on helping to develop a great name for the company, positioning the company to its initial audiences, teaching clients how to create their first express catalog and price list, and constructing timetables for implementation. The primary marketing efforts are distributing catalogs and price lists, usually by direct mail, and getting a website up and running. Establishing an initial account base usually is a matter of extensive networking (more on this in Chapter 34) and personal selling. All this takes from six months to a year for the owners to get the new business in gear with a small but growing account base, along with continued networking and continued personal selling in most cases. My job with start-ups has one other concrete goal: help the owners move to a position where they can actually take some money out of the business.

For start-up entrepreneurs looking at the budgets and media plans above, this exercise is academic until your company gets through its umbilical phase, which almost always entails pouring cash into the company for its catalog and web efforts, among other marketing expenses. Said umbilical phase will entail a mountain of hard work in networking, working the phones, and convincing buyers to give your start-up business an opportunity to prove itself.

CHAPTER

NETWORKING AND GETTING PUBLICITY

Networking, a process of sharing and developing contacts, information and services among individuals and groups having a common interest, is perhaps the most affordable and most qualitative means of building an account base. For newcomers, though, it's the means to starting to build an account base. Being a good networker assumes having -- or developing and sharpening -- the basic social skills involved in making contacts and meeting people. It also means, comfortable with and willing to exploit one's contacts to further relationships to a point where they'll eventually put some cash in your pocket.

Networking is a commitment to facilitating your own success, and when its initial goal is to advance your ability to grow your account base, its practitioners need to exude a sense of professionalism and proactively and constantly projecting a strong, positive company identity. And anyone investing the time to network needs to commit himself or herself to following up on the contacts they make and the information they learn.

Networking opportunities abound. If you don't know where to find them, just open your eyes! They're all around you -- from local civic, social, and service clubs (Rotary, Lions, Kiwanis, Elks and Moose Lodges, and your Chamber of Commerce and local business associations) to your church, athletic association, interest groups, and political committees and causes. Attending meetings and other functions and activities of the groups regularly will help you integrate with the membership. Of course, if you don't or won't make the time to attend regularly, don't waste your time, money and the organization's good will, as "checkbook memberships" preclude most networking abilities.

Speaking to school groups and local organizations also gives you opportunities to advance your business. Various groups always are looking for speakers – to teach lessons from the real world, about interesting personal pursuits, and life experiences. On what subjects can you share your knowledge or insight? First, it's your company – what you do, what you sell, how you started your business, and what you've learned from the experience. Second, it's your interests, particularly those that you can define as "passions" and areas where you can document expertise.

To attract invitations to share your story, mail or e-mail the group with your offer to speak, a brief explanation of the subject(s) you speak on, how long your presentation is (or can be adjusted to), and, where appropriate, include things you've published online, in newspapers, in books and articles, etc. If you've got wallpaper (degrees, commendations, awards), share it with your customers and prospects.

Dumb Mistake No. 29
Conducting a plant tour to a local school, scouting, or other group and not sending out a press release to publicize what a nice, community-oriented, friendly company you have!

If your company has a commercial location and does apparel decorating in-house, you can amplify networking by bringing your opportunities into – inside -- your business! Inviting groups to tour your facility gives you the platform to speak about your company and demonstrate its resources to lots of "witnesses."

Who wants to see your company in operation?

Start with high school and college art classes; your invitation to bring groups into your shop should be sent to department heads or classroom teachers. The benefit to the students is that they get to see what they're learning about in class being done in a real-world environment (even though we sometimes think our businesses are anything but "the real world"). They'll get to talk to the artists and see how art undergoes a transformation via screen making, digitizing, or other pre-production technologies and then executed through your company's various production methodologies on a variety of products.

Inviting high school and college business classes presents a great opportunity for students to see your business from start to finish -- how and to whom it markets and advertises, how orders are gathered and processed along with all the pre-production, production, and post-production phases of your operation.

Other groups simply want to make field trips to interesting places

– like yours! Considering the whole world wears your products, lots of people are fascinated to see exactly how they're done "live and in person." School groups, women's clubs, seniors, church youth groups, summer camps, special education students, and lots of other organizations will welcome a chance to see your business up close.

When bringing in tours, especially public school kids, advise them they'll actually get to take home an item they'll see produced on your premises. For schools, it's a parent permission slip and a notice to send the kids to school with a T-shirt on the day of their tour– or offer to provide one at $3. For some groups, you might ask the decision-makers to authorize an actual small order for the group that everyone will see produced.

In addition to sending invitations to tour your facilities, list this service to the community on your website and, where appropriate, in local ads.

Aside from meeting people, dazzling them, and having some fun, the tour generates buzz among the groups, and gets follow-up mention in their newsletters, meetings, and perhaps with photos sent to local newspapers. You get rave reviews and referrals from those who've experienced your professionalism, your enthusiasm, and the pride you take in all phases of your operation. And from all that you get business, especially from groups you've perhaps had difficulty penetrating through advertising, such as schools, colleges, senior centers, and local organizations to name a few.

The fringe benefits of hosting tours include meeting potential employees – from artists to summer help to salespeople -- and publicity. To grab a little more attention and be thanked in the process by the group your hosted is to send a press release and photos to local newspapers about the event, to post photos on your website, and to forward video footage of the event's participants on YouTube and other social media.

Another way to attract the attention of schools and colleges is to provide internships to students, especially for budding commercial artists, marketing majors, and other young people who'd like to work as interns in your business. The various arrangements may require little from your company beyond giving the student the opportunities to participate and learn, and your completion of evaluations of your interns' performance. In other cases, especially work-study programs, you're required to provide some compensation, usually at least at minimum wage.

Conducting on-site experiences and tours and providing internships don't necessarily guarantee business, but at the very least you get inside the decision-making ranks of the organizations, schools, and other groups you've served. What you should get in return is at least the opportunity -- the shot! – at doing business. And then it's your move to escalate the contact and the relationship to something gainful.

Here's a prescription for following up on networking leads to maximize their potential to become customers:

1. Enter details of networking contacts into your database -- names, email addresses, phone numbers, and other pertinent information. Whether you put the details into a computer program (Word, Excel, whatever) or old-school 3" x 5" index cards in a tickler file, the faster you enter the information, the better the chances of seeing the fruits of your labor. All too often when networkers get back to their offices, they toss the business cards and notes in their pockets onto a desk or next to the kitchen phone or in a folder -- and forget they're there. So, while doing these chores the same day or evening you get the information is best, be sure to attend to it by the end of the week.

Buying a contact management software program is strongly recommended. The software enables you to store data for easy retrieval, tracks the source of the lead, and, as long as the account activity is faithfully entered, lets you see when contacts were made or attempted, what was discussed or what action was taken or promised, and can be programmed to issue alerts and reminders about future contact dates and other types of necessary follow-up. I'll suggest you look into the ACT and Goldmine contact management systems, among many other good ones; you'll quickly understand how these resources pay for themselves many times over.

2. Refer to the follow-up agenda detailed in the latter part of Chapter 28. The section, as you might recall, outlines what to send initially, how and when to follow-up with calls, e-mails, and visits.

Getting Publicity

An old phrase from my radio days proclaimed: "The news… when it happens, where it happens, even if we have to make it happen!" It applies today about getting publicity for your business.

While it's easy to post your company's doings on the Internet and letting the world take it from there, it's another story getting coverage of your company in the newspaper or on television. But if there's something interesting about what your company is doing – or that's downright newsworthy -- you probably won't get any attention unless you initiate the process of making it happen. You get the ball rolling by sending a press release to your local newspapers and business publications; when you've got something really newsworthy and hot to brag about, make a phone call to the news department. Do likewise for notifying local television stations and a make a follow-up telephone call to the newsroom to see if you should get ready for a news crew that might be visiting your shop.

Your press release should be no more than one page in length and give the details of the story with a brief explanation of your company, its products and services, location, and any special attributes. Before you send your first press release, do some homework to learn the best ways to go about getting it printed or getting your story covered. Giving a suggested headline and sending photos along with your release always helps.

There's a great deal that could be interesting about your business. Here are a few examples of what might get your company in the news …

► **New equipment:** ABC Designs last week installed the largest screen printing press in Iowa at its plant in Carroll. Capable of printing 700 shirts per hour, the 14-color press will help ABC Designs keep up with orders for its growing line of T-shirts distributed throughout the Midwest.

► **New technology:** Presto Promotions fired up its new direct-to-garment digital printer, the only one of its kind in service in Utah. Using the latest digital graphic technology, the device can print full-color graphics and photographs on apparel in less than two minutes.

► **New location or expansion:** AdWear moved into its new 40,000 square-foot facility in St. Paul last week upon certification by city inspectors last month. Notes CEO Will Roberts, "We doubled our sales during the past two years and the new building will accommodate our projected growth for the next five to seven years." Roberts reports the company will add eight to 10 new employees this year in its embroidered apparel and vehicle graphics divisions. The former production facility will now serve as the company's downtown showroom and will expand its hours of operation to include evenings and Saturdays.

▶ **Staff Development:** Maxine Lykens, vice president of Michigan Apparel Decorating, returned from her annual trip to the Imprinted Sportswear Show in Long Beach, California, the nation's largest apparel graphics trade show. Lykens attended a workshop on strategic marketing and while at the 500-exhibitor show purchased a new CAD-CUT® technology that will help the company expand its product lines to now include signs and vehicle graphics. "MAD-Max," as she's known to her customers, comments, "This is the eighth consecutive year I've attended the event," and noted that this year she was accompanied by sales manager Joanne DuBois and staff artist Ron Richards.

▶ **A Big Deal:** Dr. Hilla Liman took office last week as President of the Third Republic of Ghana in West Africa, following the military junta's withdrawal from power. His election is due in part to help from Empire Specialty Printing Corporation in Upper Darby (PA), which provided 22,000 T-shirts to village captains of the People's National Party and The People's Vanguard, which merged for the election. The firm also provided tens of thousands of key rings, pens, and buttons that showed the logo of the merged parties, designed by ESP's CEO Mark Venit, who was also engaged as a political consultant to Liman's campaign staff. (Yes. this is a true story; it occurred n 1979).

▶ **Employee Promotion:** Peak Performance Apparel & Promotions has promoted Marge Ginovera to Embroidery Production Manager. Ginovera has worked at the firm for seven years, beginning her career there as a quality control technician and then becoming an embroidery technician.

▶ **Plant Tour:** First & Goal, Inc. welcomed Miss McVicker's 6th grade class at Amistaad Elementary School in New Haven to tour its Hamden screen printing and embroidery plant and see T-shirts being printed and baseball caps being embroidered for sailors stationed at the submarine base in Groton, CT. Both items were decorated with the U.S. Navy's official insignia. Each student received a tote bag with the same design, compliments of First & Goal. While on tour, the students watched staff artists create graphics on computers and saw how the designs went through the company's processes to end up being applied on apparel.

First & Goal also conducts tours for local scout troops and high school business classes. The photo below shows the class huddled around art director Michael Angelo as he adds text and color to a design the company is readying for the Strawberry Festival.

▶ **Presentation:** Joy Shane, owner of Pride & Joy Apparel Creations in Roanoke Rapids (N.C.) was the featured speaker at the Rotary Club's weekly breakfast meeting on Tuesday, explaining about how her business moved from the dining room table to her garage to her new shop on Route 301 within two years. Now in its fifth year, the company sells custom decorated apparel throughout the Carolinas and Virginia. It employs a year 'round staff of 14 locally and two salespeople based at the firm's satellite sales office in Emporia, Virginia.

▶ **Event:** North Star Custom Apparel welcomed more than 300 attendees to its Thunder Bay facility as host of the Chamber of Commerce's February edition of its monthly Chamber-After-Hours Mixer.

▶ **Bragging Rights:** Mardi Gras Graphic Products ran three shifts this week to keep up with demand from New Orleans Saints fans for tens of thousands of shirts, caps, and jackets celebrating the team's Super Bowl victory on Sunday night. Emblazoned with the team's logo and the words "Who Dat?" and "Super Bowl Champions," the various apparel items give the company a huge boost in business just as Mardi Gras shirts are about to hit the streets in The Big Easy next week, notes MGGP's owner Khalid Khan, he also reports "We were anticipating a strong year ahead, but we now expect spectacular sales through the next season. We just hired 11 extra full-timers and probably will add a few more in the fall."

While it's easy to post your company's doings on the Internet and letting the world take it from there, it's another story getting coverage of your company in the newspaper or on television.

I'll trust with the suggestions above, you'll find lots of excuses – nay, reasons! – to publicize your enterprise.

Do note that publicity for your business in the newspaper and elsewhere is great for creating buzz, but it's NOT a substitute for solid, intelligent marketing and advertising endeavors. The impact of buzz alone is short-lived. But by continuing your advertising program, you can keep the buzz alive almost indefinitely.

CHAPTER

MAGIC WORDS IN ADVERTISING CUSTOM DECORATED APPAREL

My intentions in providing you with my "Magic Words" list are a.) to save you time wracking your brain trying to figure out what to communicate about your company, and b.) to help stimulate other ideas about what you might like to say about why folks should buy from YOU, not the other guys.

Use this chapter to help in creating the "About" section on your web site and to compose your propaganda sheet, newspaper and magazine ads, direct mail, e-blasts, radio scripts, TV text "supers," catalogs, and anything else that serves the cause. I've organized them into categories for easy reference.

What you do and what to call it . . .

▪ **Screen Printing** – The correct and eminently more professional term is NOT "silk screening." Everyone *thinks* they know what silk screening is because they did it in high school art class, scouts, or at summer camp. What *you* do is a highly developed technology, not an arts and crafts project.

"Screen printing" is the term professionals use; so, if you are a professional, eliminate the term "silk screening" from your business vocabulary.

▪ **Embroidery** – What you do for businesses, schools, organizations, and events is NOT monogramming, the term more germane to personalizing apparel and giftware with names, initials, and decorative arrangements of initials. Use "monogramming," if you offer it, within its proper context of personalization, not commercial embroidery.

▪ **Heat Printing** – A heat transfer is the term for the paper and the ink on it that you transfer onto a garment or other substrate. The process by which heat transfers are used in a heat press to decorate substrates is heat printing. That's the word – or words – from Stahls' ID Direct, the world's largest manufacturer of heat presses, custom heat transfers, and heat printing supplies and the world leader in advancing heat printing technology.

■ **Engraving / Laser Engraving** – The terms denote the technology and the process. The official term for the industry organized around trophies and awards is the "recognition industry." Another term for awards and trophies is "Recognition Products."

■ **Direct-to-Garment Printing** – The term for what direct-to-garment printers do. It's a cumbersome term, though and is sometimes written "D2G." I personally refer to it in promotional materials I prepare for clients as "digital-direct printing."

■ **CAD-CUT® Technology** – CAD-CUT® enables you to provide signage, vehicle graphics, banners, custom multicolor names and numbers, custom decorated apparel, custom appliqués, and moreover, enables you to deliver it all quickly and with a user-friendly minimum order of *one* item!

What you sell...

■ **Decorated Apparel, Custom Apparel, and Custom-Decorated Apparel** – Use whatever terminology you like. Other variations include "apparel graphics," "graphic apparel," "embellished apparel."

■ **Promotional Products** – This has been the preferred term within the promotional products industry since the late 1970s. ("Advertising specialties" is a term created in the late 1940s and is today often a misnomer). The term covers a myriad of products, decorated with a plethora of different technologies.

Promotional products are what you sell. In some promotional materials I write, I sometimes refer to the products as "promowares." Eliminate the term "advertising specialties" from your business vocabulary.

■ **Preprints** -- This is an industry term used to describe finished decorated products sold to retailers for reselling them. It covers screen printed and embroidered garments and those decorated by other technologies as well. Everyone in the trade knows what it means. The term derives from the time-saving practice of retailers who sold heat-transferred garments on demand, whereby a customer would pick out the design and/or lettering desired and the garment and color it was to go on. As retailers found there were very predictable combinations of stock designs and garments (mainly tees and sweats), they'd instruct their store employees to produce the garments during slow hours in the store without waiting for a customer to order it. That way, the employees' time became more productive and selling garments became easier. Hence, the term "preprint." Customers appreciated the convenience and the time saved. Eventually the term came into the industry's lexicon as describing any finished (decorated) garments sold to accounts for re-sale.

What you also sell...

- **Wide Selection/Comprehensive Selection** (the latest styles and colors)
- **Uniforms for the Best-Dressed Teams in Town**
- **World-Class Graphics** (if indeed you deliver world-class graphics)
- **Money-Making Ideas** (for fundraising)
- **Other Services:**
  - **Athletic/Team Numbering and Lettering**
  - **Personalization**
  - **Installation of Vehicle/Marine/Aviation/Whatever Graphics**
  - **Design and/or Hosting Company Stores, Club Stores, School Stores**

Also mention some of the "little extras" in products, services, and conveniences you provide, such as...

- **Try-On Samples/Try-On Clinics/Loaner Samples**
- **XXL, XXXL, XXXXL, XXXXXL** sizes available

Advantages of Buying from Your Company...

- **Guaranteed Three-Day Service** (or whatever) – Given that your competitors won't be saying anything like this, your company goes to the head of the class! (Hey, these guys must have their act together!) Remember, you don't have to guarantee three-day turnaround on everything you sell, just the stuff you know you can get in – and out -- quickly. You can explain the fine print when you get the call or meet the walk-in prospect.

- **Free Catalog and Price List** – This feature alone dramatically differentiates your company from more than 95% of your competitors.

- **Buy Factory-Direct** – (Or, for sales agencies, that you are direct factory representatives for the nation's leading apparel manufacturers, promotional products manufacturers, etc.). The term "factory-direct" leads buyers to perceive they're cutting out the middleman. For decorators, it means keeping the added mark-up for themselves.

- **Visit Our Showroom** – Isn't this one of the biggest reasons people want to visit you? If you've got a good one, brag about it!

- **In-House Art Department, In-House Production of _____, In-House Digitizing** – OR – **Complete In-House Production/Production Facilities** – If you offer these advantages in-house, flaunt them!

- **Rush Service Available** – Define your policies, if possible, instead of always "winging it." Determine what your policies are for charging for fast delivery (which always can be waived for good customers and key prospects).

- **Evening Hours/Evening Hours By Appointment** – Buyers who are unable to do business with you during the day or would be inconvenienced by doing so appreciate the opportunity to see you and touch and feel your products without having to limit themselves to trying to do the same thing on a website.

- **Open Saturdays until Noon/1:00 p.m./whenver** – Once again, it makes buying from you easier and friendlier.

- **Huge Inventory** – Either you've got it on the shelf or you use "off-premises warehouses" -- such as your favorite wholesalers! The perception from buyers is that having inventory means you can deliver faster.

- **We'll come to YOU!** (Or "Have Reps, Will Travel")

- **Prompt/Fast, Courteous Service**

- **One-Stop Shopping**

Other Reasons to Buy from Your Company...

- **We guarantee our imprints and embroidery *forever*!**

- **Conveniently located at** ...If your location is a bit hard to find without a GPS or a clairvoyant, insert a map or idiot-proof directions)

- **Visa, MasterCard, American Express Accepted** (Show the logos and buyers get the message).

- **Serving the area/valley/region for XX years/Since 19XX**

- **Locally Owned and Operated**

- **Competitive Prices** (Legal and ethical limits preclude making bigger claims, using deception, and telling outright lies).

Community Involvement and Just Plain Bragging....

- **Member/Supporter** – Tri-State Chamber of Commerce, Downtown Business Association, Valley Convention & Visitors Bureau, Grant-A-Wish Foundation, Babe Ruth Baseball, Pop Warner Football.

Just about anything your company is involved in or supports goes. But think twice about listing political causes and political parties you're associated with, unless, of course, you don't mind a alienating these potential customers.

- **Honors and Awards** – Businessperson of the Year 2011 -- East of Eden Chamber of Commerce; Official Supplier to Boy Scouts of America Northeast Jamboree; Southern Heritage Council – Leadership Award 2011; First Place - Impressions Magazine Technical Achievement Award 2011

Other Words that "Sing" in Advertising...Unchallenged, Unrivaled, Friendly, Save Time, Save Money, and Free!

CHAPTER

36

CULTURAL DIFFERENCES BETWEEN COMPETING PRODUCERS AND SELLERS, ORDER PROCESSING, AND ORDER MINIMUMS

Cultural Differences Between Production Companies and Sales Agencies

A successful marketing and advertising agenda will generate leads and lots of follow-up activity the moment those leads come in – from entering the orders, getting them through the system, and finally putting them in the customers' hands. But what good is it all if a company's administration is inefficient, its production resources can't keep up with sales, money is always in short supply, and invoicing is usually behind schedule?

I'm about to explore how administration, production, finance, and purchasing impact a company's ability to deliver on its promises. This is where a serious shortcoming in any one area can destroy a marketer's credibility, drive salespeople into oblivion, and jeopardize profitability.

This book addresses two different types of companies: a.) those that produce orders in house and sell them to end users and b.) sales agencies, which include promotional products distributors, T-shirt retailers, sporting goods retailers, and independent custom decorating marketers. Decorators will read this chapter with the bias of being in the production business. Sales agencies will read it and probably skip sections that speak to decorators. Newcomers and veterans will read from their different perspectives, based on their varying degrees of knowledge, experience, and resources. Whatever your bias is here, it's helpful for each audience to be aware of and understand the processes as viewed by the other folks.

While the fundamental difference between apparel decorators and sales agencies obviously is the internal ability to produce finished orders, there are other substantial distinctions that provide each type of company with advantages and limitations.

Under normal circumstances, producers have control over their production process. (Then again, many producers in our industry -- and many others -- might sometimes see the inclusion of the words "normal" and "production" in the same sentence as oxymoronic). Control is the single, greatest advantage producers have in competing against sales agencies. And as sellers themselves, the ability to perform in-house miracles on demand enables them to close orders in certain panic-rush situations where sales agencies just can't deliver.

On the other hand, producers have all the additional responsibilities and risks of being in the production business -- the personnel business, the banking business, the warehouse business, and the overhead business.

Relative to screen printing and embroidery firms' operating costs and ratios, sales agencies usually have less overhead, lower management costs, and much smaller appetites for capital. By virtue of the fact that they're primarily in the selling business (theoretically, anyhow), their focus on selling usually creates more efficiencies in workflow and enhanced levels of customer service. These both are attributes that favorably impact the bottom lines and the scope of the marketing efforts of sales agencies.

And unlike screen printers and embroiderers, sales agencies have a special financial tool that their counterparts in the production sectors of the industry can only dream of having: predictable costs. Sales agencies know exactly what they pay for decorating, to the penny. How many printers and embroiderers can tell you that? (Virtually none!)

Only a small fraction of sales agencies have any credible in-house graphics capability, though, and this is one area in which production houses have another powerful edge, one that amplifies both their control and their creative advantages. But those sales agencies that do have internal art capability can be fierce competitors when they're able to offer art services as an integral part of their merchandising arsenal.

Luckily for printers and embroiderers, few sales agencies go this route. If they did, to a great extent the control advantage their producer competitors have would be nullified, both on the creative level and in turnaround time. But with the increasing user-friendliness of computer graphics, templated art libraries, and scanners, the distance between producers and sales agencies may one day become a moot point.

In any case, having the wherewithal to provide a customer with one-stop direct sourcing that goes from concept-to-completion-to-cartons all under one roof can be the most persuasive argument a buyer can hear. Imagine having such weaponry *and* at the same time be known for providing prompt, courteous, dependable first-class customer service. The company that can do all this represents a very significant threat to every other competitor in its market, regardless of how old, how strong, and how big the other guys may be.

Now add to this mix a company that also can construct a respectable lead-generation system, and you've got a scenario where an assertive marketer is in a position to not only drive his competitors crazy, but to drive them out of business! Competitors become forced by marketing masters to endure substantial shrinkage in market share, forced perhaps to react by increasing advertising expenditures but without a supporting game plan. And many still are clueless about how the assertive market-er has gone about rewriting the rules of engagement in his own favor. Eventually a certain key competitor or two will have little choice but to come to terms with the marketer who's causing their downfall. The victorious marketer who sees a fatigued competitor waving a white flag is in the desirable position of being able to name his price for the former rival's business and state the terms. Or he can choose to let an injured opponent bleed a while longer before going in for the kill.

So, which type of operation -- production company vs. sales agency -- is better? Both systems work well. The full-service, soup-to-nuts apparel graphics company that produces and sells is a very attractive proposition for some and a non-starter to others. The go-all-the-way option sure sounds great, and might – *might* -- yield bigger benefits and equity and income for its owners. But that route obligates those who choose to do their own production to also endure the consequences and financial risks of all the related challenges. These include the cost and frustration of the learning curves in technology, capital formation, and managing not only the technologies but the people who put them in play.

I'll admonish newcomers here -- especially those who have yet to purchase screen printing or embroidery equipment -- to consider all of the things it'll take for you to succeed in the custom apparel graphics business. Owning your own production facilities is not necessarily a ticket to success. I'll add that start-ups contemplating buying screen printing equipment should hedge their bet. My advice here is to test the waters of production by first using heat printing as the means of production and, when warranted, contracting out screen printing work as needed before investing more than $10,000 (on the low side) setting up a manual screen printing shop.

Know that what will really determine your ultimate level of success in selling custom decorated apparel isn't whether or not you're in the production business, it's how well you market and how well you deliver orders.

For those of you that do in-house production and have some credible technical wherewithal, I'll look at some of the issues germane to your in-house resources for printing or embroidering what you sell.

Order Processing

A hard-working salesperson has just gotten a commitment, a solid "yes" from a prospect who just became a customer. In its advertising campaign, the company told how great it is at art and production, how much it has to offer in product variety, how helpful its sales staff is, and how nice a company it is to work with…yada, yada, yada …you've heard it all before. How efficient and intelligent the process of actually writing the order is can go a long way in validating a customer's confidence in the company he's buying from, or proving to be the first warning sign that he's dealing with turkeys.

An effective sales order form is one that records as much information as is necessary and spells out all of the important details that the seller, the buyer, the people in the art department, pre-production processes, production, shipping and receiving, and the front office all need to know to shepherd an order from placement to completion. A smart order form accomplishes all this and serves to literally get all the players working on the same page; the rest of the process is bound to go smoother, ensuring the job will very likely be done right the first time and be ready when promised. If you're new to the industry, good order forms are easily found online. (If you need further help on designing your *first* order form, call me!)

Internal Capacity and Capabilities

How many units or sides can your company or your contractors produce in a day or a week? With how many colors of ink or thread? How big can you go in terms of outer dimensions for the decorated area? How many people earning how much payroll will it take to produce orders efficiently on your equipment? Can you produce at a competitive cost relative to both your rivals' operating costs and with real opportunity to have some money left over (you know, that profitability thing)? Do you have adequate capacity in both equipment and personnel to produce in peak season? Can you count on having ample "bench strength" if key personnel were to leave your employ at a critical moment or a peak period? (Invariably that's when most turnover occurs). Do you have sufficient staging space and warehousing capacity in your facility or have affordable short-term space nearby? These questions beget many others.

Seasonal factors, a home run order or two, and a few highly productive accounts can challenge your resources and your wits. I suspect there's some natural law that causes multiple "big hits" to happen at the same time and potentially overwhelm a company's ability to manage it all. Most of the time, though, entrepreneurs will rise to the occasion and perform near miracles to maximize resources and internal output, by putting on a second shift, renting a trailer to hold overflow inventory, robbing Peter to pay Paul, and creating other short-term solutions.

Astute producers, however, recognize there are times when there's no intelligent alternative to outsourcing some production to contractors. When a company's already-maxxed resources cannot be stretched any further and the Law of Diminishing Returns begins to take over, customers may threaten with cancellations or issue the last-straw declaration – read: "We'll never buy from your company ever again!"

Contract screen printers and embroiderers come a dime a dozen. Finding good, reliable, technically proficient ethical ones is, however, another thing. And finding the right one with a livable price isn't likely to happen so fast when you're on overload and up against a wall, scrambling for time and frantically trying to locate fill-in stock at the same time, and all this is happening in peak season!

For sales agencies, contracting printing and embroidery is all is a day's work. Successful, well-organized sales agencies, such as some of the leading promotional products distributors (who contract everything they sell, from a myriad of vendors, across many graphing imaging processes) have it down to a science.

For apparel decorators, however, contracting only is an occasional issue and usually enacted with great reluctance and trepidation. For overload situations, however, it's the prudent managerial and financial alternative, one that minimizes risk of capital, focuses on the immediate need to address turnaround, and mitigates the urgency to bring in additional and/or more sophisticated equipment.

The major concern of most screen printers and embroiderers who must turn to trade sources to handle their orders is quality, which, however, will cease to be an issue once a conscientious professional source is secured. Unlike those companies who do contract work as a sideline or beg for it during their slow months, most of the industry's leading contract printers and contract embroiderers specialize in contract work and are skilled in producing it on a predictable basis and at a realistic, premeditated price.

Quality-wise, they're usually among the best in the business because they have to be. Superior technical and managerial skills to produce efficiently and on time is what the best contractors must possess in order to maintain their enterprises' viability and profitability. Part-time or moonlighting contractors rarely have the same motivation, experience, or skill. Remember this when looking for contract decorators.

Where a trade buyer still has concerns about a contractor's quality, he can insist on seeing a production proof, especially for runs involving special color matching, high tech imprint/stitching demands, specialty processes or other complexities.

Where a selected contract source is located geographically is a matter of common sense. Warning: Don't buy from hometown sources if you have the slightest concern about the contractor's integrity, the fidelity of his employees, or about shop security. Integrity means the contractor doesn't solicit his trade customers' accounts and wouldn't dare pass along any particulars about such accounts to in-house sales reps or other contract accounts (read: your competitors). Employee fidelity in this regard means that the contractor's employees keep their mouths shut as well. Shop security in this context means that the contractor doesn't permit his trade customers (your competitors) to wander around his production department or anywhere else in the shop where your job and the paperwork for it are within view or reach.

As a rule of thumb, it's usually safer to contract from a source that's sufficiently distant from your plant or office, but no farther than one day's shipping where possible. (Farther away is OK, as long as you can accommodate the extra transit time and freight budget, and feel the craftsmanship of the contractor merits your patronage despite the distance).

Be aware that most professional contract houses mandate that your orders are subject to a waste allowance, usually in the 1-3% range, whereby the specified percentage of spoiled garments within this pre-determined limit cannot be charged by you to your contractor for reim-bursement. Over the set amount, though, the contractor is responsible for replacing the garments or, more commonly, reimbursing for dam-aged goods.

For a listing of contract screen printers, embroiderers, and other deco-rating sources, consult the Business-to-Business ads in trade publica-tions under the headings "Contract Embroidery" and "Contract Screen Printing." The companies that advertise there are telling you they want and need your work. (These ads appear in the back of our trade maga-zines, just before the classifieds).

Dumb Mistake No. 30

Outsourcing work to a contractor in your own backyard that allows its trade customers – your competitors! – access to its production areas and/or has its own local sales force. Doing so is tantamount to asking someone to solicit your accounts and steal them from you.

Minimum Orders

How many garments constitute an acceptable minimum order? The answer differs from company to company with regard to the type of equipment owned, profit margins, and how long the company has been in business. But marketing considerations also come into play here. Placing the bar for minimums too high for drawing orders from a poten-tially large account whose need at the moment -- particularly for a spe-cific use or occasion and on a first order -- may be only a dozen pieces.

This was the case for the largest account I ever handled, a coal com-pany in southwestern Virginia, with offices in Philadelphia. An old friend from high school, whose brother was a part-time screen cleaner at my company, ordered a dozen yellow tees with a black imprint of a happy-face smile and the company name arced above it. Said old friend, who was the firm's marketing director, told me her boss wanted them as part of a welcome package for executives from Japan touring the firm's mines. The following week, Randee called back and re-ordered a gross, because the boss "just liked them and wanted to keep a supply on hand" for other visitors. With an insider helping me to meet other company personnel, I eventually worked my way into the human resources department and into the safety engineer's office.

Employing more than 6,000 miners and another 1,000 support personnel, the company had very proactive safety programs, recreational programs, and community-relations programs. A dream account with thousands of employees and facilities in dozens of towns in Appalachia, the firm wanted a one-stop source for decorated apparel and promotional products. By my third year of working with the company, its annual volume with my company exceeded $240,000 a year and grew incrementally over the life of the account. All that started with an order for one dozen T-shirts. Lesson to be learned: Small orders do not necessary derive from small companies.

For many small companies, the minimum order is one piece. For most screen printing companies, though, such a minimum is absurd for reasons other than speculative work or sampling, though it can easily be accommodated by direct-to-garment printing, CAD-CUT® graphics, and sublimation transfers (or outsourced to a contractor who does this work).

A counterproductive practice of many custom apparel markers, however, is viewing minimums strictly from the aspect of efficient production. With screen printing companies, the movement to minimum orders of two, three or more dozen units begins after the enterprise as been in business for a year or so. Business is coming in and things are going well, making the producer feel confident that hiking an existing one-dozen minimum to, say, two dozen won't hurt sales and might even improve profitability.

The thinking is correct from an accounting point of view and improved efficiency in production will in fact result. As both beneficial outcomes prove true and after another year or two passes, management once again feels safe and justified in jacking up required minimums by another dozen or more.

Growing embroidery companies also manifest some of the same thinking, but to a lesser degree, owing to the higher dollar volume per order, making smaller minimums still profitable. The screen printer whose minimums are now at three-or-more dozen is guilty of "inside-out thinking." This common management pathology results from making decisions based on what may be seen as desirable from one or more internal aspects, but can be unwittingly detrimental in others – particularly in attracting new accounts.

The downsides of inside-out thinking occur because management doesn't see the unintended consequences due to its inexperience, short-sightedness, or simply a fundamental lack of knowledge about the interrelationship between marketing, sales, finance, production, and administration. Nor can they cannot fathom an holistic management approach that recognizes these other variables.

The net effect of higher minimums will indeed satisfy the goals of bean counters and production managers, but may well have adverse impact on sales and marketing efforts. For the argument that "we really don't want to encourage small, marginal orders," a higher minimum is an intelligent mechanism to fulfill the prophecy. In so doing management elects to forfeit orders from a group of hunting buddies who want to buy six custom sweatshirts and from two-man plumbing companies that want a five T-shirts for each partner. But viewed from a marketing perspective, the company stands to lose far more than just these small orders.

It loses the ability to take entry-level orders that can be built over time into larger, more frequent orders, where a small account can discover (or more accurately be shown by salespeople) over time more uses for your products and more recipients for them. It also puts these customers in a position to buy other items you might offer, such as promotional products, signs, vehicle graphics, and employee awards.

The small order that didn't happen isn't a big deal to either the buyer or the seller. But what's lost is the opportunity to learn the person who called for a quote on a dozen shirts for a sales meeting also is the president of a Little League with a thousand kids in it. A buyer who calls about getting five embroidered golf shirts to outfit employees working a local charity event is a well-wired player on the town's annual festival and parade committees and her retail furniture stores employ 70 floor salespeople, warehouse staff, delivery truck drivers and office workers. The co-chair of the charity event -- one of those prospects for the lost golf shirt order -- would have been very impressed with the seller's work and she's the HR director of a local hospital with 2,000 employees. Ouch!

The net effect of higher minimums will indeed satisfy the goals of bean counters and production managers, but may well have adverse impact on sales and marketing efforts.

An inside-out policy that raises minimums too high impacts the long-term potential of otherwise seemingly insignificant leads. Every veteran in the industry can tell his or her own stories about small orders that grew into giant orders or giant accounts, situations similar to those I've shared above.

Given the cost of an effective lead-generating program, some of the smaller inquiries it produces will have strong sales potential right around the bend or down the road and shouldn't be peremptorily shut out.

Know that establishing lower minimums doesn't mean you have to give small-quantity orders away at small prices. Charge what you have to make it worthwhile on a per-order basis – or charge through the nose if you'd like! But realize that cogent strategic marketing and market share considerations would teach that it's better to offer a low minimum at high prices than to forfeit such orders, sending the prospects off to a competitor.

My recommendations? One dozen minimum for screen printed T-shirts, sweatshirts, golf shirts, and caps. For printed jackets, six pieces, and maybe fewer if the price is right and the particular customer is worth the trouble. For embroidered garments, I advise a minimum of one dozen units for T-shirts and caps. For golf shirts, denim shirts, and jackets, I recommend six pieces, and again, for the right customer, maybe fewer.

CHAPTER

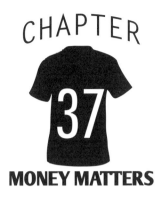

MONEY MATTERS

Being in the business of selling custom apparel graphics products means you'll need to develop a good relationship with a friendly bank as well as becoming one, yourself, to certain customers. Your landlord, leasing company, and all your suppliers need to be paid. Many of your customers will demand -- and some will certainly be worthy of – credit terms, making your company a lending institution, an issue discussed later in this section.

How do you pay your bills, your staff, yourself, and for the garments you need to fill orders? Well, money generally works best and there's really no place to wash dishes in this business.

Among the first places you might look for money, but not necessarily the best or most personally desirable sources, are investors, which can be friends or relatives or acquaintances, or "angels." What real investors (not your mother) want is a healthy return on their money via the long-term appreciation of the value of your company, or one would hope, anyhow. Investors receive a specified percentage of ownership in a partnership entity or, in the case of a corporation, common stock, preferred stock (which is non-voting stock that promises to pay a fixed dividend each year), or convertible bonds (an instrument of indebtedness that can be transformed at some point into shares of stock). Banks are, however, where most people in our industry turn to for financing. But as many veterans will attest, many bankers know little about our industry and tend to look at apparel graphics companies, especially new ones, as relatively high-risk ventures.

High-risk means you'll be paying at least 10% for loans, and probably much higher. Start-ups will, in most cases, simply be turned away and told to come back in two years.

Allow me to digress for a moment and suggest a very effective way to educate your banker is to furnish him or her first with a recent copy of *Impressions Magazine* and the show program for an Imprinted Sportswear Show. What it says to your banker is that the industry is bigger and more encompassing he or she ever imagined. Seeing all the advertising, the nature and content of the articles both technical and non-technical, and the diversity of the subject matter imparts a level of respect for what you do greater than any explanation you give will accomplish. You might also want to photocopy some of the industry data in charts and graphs I've presented in industry publications from time to time.

Relatives might be a little friendlier as investors, but if things don" go the way you plan, you know the consequences of owing money to relatives. Owing money to a bank means the most you can lose in a worst-case scenario is only your house or other worldly possessions – not your inheritance or your siblings.

How much cash or credit you'll need for your apparel graphics company will, hopefully, be much more than you ever dreamed of, in those wonderful instances where your business grows beyond anything you ever imagined. How much you can get, though, is a matter of how much you're willing to share or pledge in terms of equity and or collateral vis-à-vis the judgment of your creditworthiness in the opinions of investors, bankers, and vendors.

Financing your operations, as differentiated from financing equipment or a building, basically comes down to having cash for garments, payroll, overhead, and for production supplies or paying your contractors.

Beyond whatever financial resources you or your company already can muster, including the use of your personal credit cards, the traditional sources of money for garments are banks, factoring companies, and garment distributors and manufacturers.

Commercial banks offer money in the form of a.) short-term loans (or "term loans") or a credit line pegged to the prime rate plus up a point of two, or more if you're considered too new or too risky; you pay back the bank on an ad hoc basis, but usually within one year upon demand; b.) long-term loans, which are paid back to the bank in fixed monthly installments; and c.) receivable financing, where what customers owe you becomes the formal or informal collateral supporting this special mode of short-term financing.

Short- and long-term loans are granted only to creditworthy borrowers.

What constitutes creditworthiness and what interest rate will be charged are matters that won't vary greatly between competing banks, although if you look hard enough you'll find that certain financial institutions are more willing than others to work with small companies and even some start-up companies. In the real world of today, however, banks are subject to ever-tighter state and federal regulatory requirements about who'll qualify for loans and who won't.

Short-term loans can be used to cover the cost of your goods from the time payment is due to your supplier and the time you receive payment from your customers. The use of (short) term loans is one of the most prevalent forms that creditworthy apparel graphics companies use for financing large inventory purchases along with the use of credit cards.

Long-term loans should be used strictly for equipment, start-up costs, real estate, and, if and when necessary, debt consolidation.

Receivable financing is an arrangement whereby a traditional financial institution advances you cash for invoices yet to be paid by your accounts. Essentially you pledge to reimburse the bank when your receivable arrives. These arrangements can be, and usually are, relatively informal and with relatively simple paperwork. In some cases, though, your customer may be instructed to draft payment of an invoice jointly to you and the bank, meaning you can't cash the check without the bank's endorsement as well.

A modified form of this practice is used when you need money to buy inventory against orders you have in hand. Booked orders (sold, but not yet produced or delivered), while not a form of collateral, are documentation for the fact that you've got business on the books and need cash to turn this action into receivables and, hopefully, profits.

Of course, any transactions meriting receivable financing or inventory financing will cost you some money. As these matters go, you're basically doing short-term borrowing that doesn't involve extreme risk on the bank's part, so rates are usually affordable. Figure on an annualized interest rate of about 12%, or less than 1% per month on whatever funds are outstanding for creditworthy borrowers. If you have to pay more than 1% a month, you're probably getting hosed.

Factoring companies, or "factors," "buy" invoices and accounts receivable. Huh?! Factoring is the assigning of invoices or accounts receivable to a third party, the factor, for immediate cash. Factors that trade in our industry pay 40% to 60% of the dollar amount of the receivable when you need the money and then credit you the balance when the customer has paid the balance in full. Factors also may charge additional fees for these services.

Essentially what you're buying is cash flow. And while a number of money companies offer financing to smaller firms in our industry, few custom apparel graphics companies avail themselves of this support due to the usually high carrying costs. Those apparel graphics companies who deal with factors on receivable financing are for the most part preprint companies.

But if your bank is willing to work with you on receivable financing, it's generally made at more favorable rates. The downside, though, is that in so doing, you consume a significant portion of whatever other exposure the bank will accept on your total account.

Letters of Credit are another payment mechanism. You get them from your buyer. Letters of credit are arranged with a bank in a predetermined amount and for execution on a predetermined date; the bank exercises its customer's instructions to the letter. Letters of credit certainly are a more powerful, more definitive form of payment than a customer's promise to pay a vendor on a certain a date. A buyer and a seller agree in a letter of credit that an invoice will be automatically transacted, usually electronically, via the "LC" on a stated date between the account and your bank. Agreeing to pay (or being required by one of your vendors to pay) via a letter of credit assures the creditor of payment as specified and removes the customer's option to withhold payment, pay late, or use your receivable to pay someone else.

LCs can be transacted between banks, suppliers, distributors, factors, and producers. Occasionally you'll see the term ILC, for Irrevocable Letter of Credit. ILCs are frequently used in international transactions, whereby once an ILC is agreed upon as a form of payment, the payment cannot be canceled for any reason. With a standard LC, you can cancel the transaction "for cause," such as non-delivery.

Once an LC is transacted, you've borrowed money from the bank, which begins charging interest on the money from that date along with potential other fees agreed upon in advance.

As a buyer of garments, you might be in instructed by a handful of vendors to pay via an LC. As a seller, you might at times insist a customer pay by LC, especially for a large order that would seriously strain your finances if a customer were to pay late or not at all.

For most screen printers and embroiderers and sales agencies, the most desirable source of financing their purchases of garments comes from their preferred distributors and manufacturers. There are those who offer terms, which are usually net 30 days, or for key accounts, as much as 45-60 days, though even longer terms can be negotiated in some cases.

Where your own financial strength is insufficient to warrant direct credit from a garment vendor, some distributors and some mills can be enlisted as "partners" in certain large, profitable orders. In such arrangements, the vendor will accept your customer's purchase order as virtual collateral, in which case you pledge not only the receivable as a guarantee to the vendor, but pay the vendor a percentage of the receivable as well. Some such partners also may ask for a slightly higher price for the garments.

Dumb Mistake No. 31
Telling a customer you don't accept credit cards.

Of course, more traditional buying and selling arrangements between suppliers and buyers are the preferred standard. But when you need serious help – especially in the event you get some humongous orders from large, creditworthy accounts – you'll find your garment suppliers will work with you quite diligently. They want you to get the business and they want to be your supplier. These deals are never advertised and even most long-term industry veterans are unaware these deals exist. But I can assure you that many distributors and a few mills are happy to become involved in the sharing of your success, because everybody wins.

Who else has money for you? Your customers! After all, they're the people whose business causes you to need inventory to begin with, so let's invite them to help us all the jolly well they can. For most companies in this business, the prevailing means of directly financing orders is getting a 50% deposit from the buyer upon placement of an order and collecting the balance on delivery.

One common mistake many custom apparel companies make in asking for deposits is explaining to a customer that a deposit is required because "it's a custom job and should you for any reason decide not to accept it," your company cannot sell those custom-decorated garments to anyone else. Hey, all that's true, but it also suggests to the customer you don't quite trust him. It's better to explain nothing when you ask for a deposit, since many customers expect to pay one.

But if you're asked why you need as deposit, tell the real reason: "We require deposits because it provides us with some of the cash (or cash flow) to purchase the inventory we'll be buying for your order." And should a customer tell you not to worry about the money because his company has been in business for 35 years, respond that your company has not been in business for 35 years and that you still need all the help you can get.

Among the easiest ways to ask for money is to say upon figuring the total, "OK I need a deposit for (X-amount). Would you prefer to pay for it with cash, a check, or, your credit card?" When taking payment via credit card, as discussed earlier in this book, require the (entire) order to be paid in full.

Your customers' credit cards are a convenient place to find the money you need, but the conventional wisdom in our business is that the need to accept credit cards for payment of orders just isn't there as a competitive issue, and that the cost of accepting credit cards is an unacceptable percentage of the profit. The thinking here measures costs against benefits. Or, as I observe in the field, one where decorators measure their perceived costs against their lack of awareness of the very real benefits.

.

If you're new in the apparel graphics industry or new to owning a business, you might be singing "The Cash Flow Blues" sooner than you think. It affects small companies, particularly family-owned companies, in all businesses.

It seems when you go into business you have an optimistic, simplistic grasp on the inter-relation of sales, expenses, and profits. But in due time, you get some unanticipated, very unwelcome lessons about cash flow. Whether you learned about cash flow in class in business school or while studying at the College of Hard Knocks, learning about this subject first-hand as owners of your own enterprises provides you with an understanding of cash flow realities that people just don't get from textbooks or in the lecture hall.

In business, you learn very profound lessons in cash flow realities in the process of:

- **Experiencing a soft period in sales:** Not enough business means your overhead eats up an even greater percentage of your total revenues.

▪ **Watching your sales soar:** Times are good and you need more goods and more labor, even though you might not see your money until sometime down the road. Your increasing demand for credit means you accept higher interest charges and as they mount, it's often with a mounting payroll as well, including ever-escalating minimum wage rates and mandated benefits.

▪ **Losing track of your payables while you're preoccupied with handling incoming orders and getting them out on time:** "Yeah, I should be better at keeping my receivables straight, but there are only so many hours in a day, ya know!?, and only so many issues I can handle at one time. When things slow down, I'll have more time to attend to such things." And there's the conventional wisdom that goes "since we're busy, we *must* be making money, so we'll be able to pay our bills soon enough. " Uh, huh. And once all your receivables are in, everything will straighten out. Right?! (Well, theoretically, that's how it's *supposed* to work.)

▪ **Learning from your accountant you made some money:** Then you ask of her, as millions of businesspeople do regularly, "Great! Where is it!?"

So, is there any way out? Will there ever be light at the end of the tunnel? Or does the tunnel merge with some black hole at the center of the galaxy where the Cash Flow Monster insatiably sucks the breath out of small businesses?

Well, yes, there are ways out and in time, with proper planning and discipline, indeed there'll be light at the end of the tunnel. But the Cash Flow Monster is ALWAYS lurking, ready to pounce the minute you let your guard down.

To help you keep your creditworthiness in our industry or recover it, here are eight specific steps to avoid a face-to-face encounter with the Cash Flow Monster and to become best friends with his nemesis -- and your heroine -- The Positive Cash Flow Goddess.

1. Update your books. Get your books in order. It'll take a day or two of agonizing effort, but without a clear picture of the task at hand, you can't begin to talk seriously with vendor creditors or to your bank, not if you want a long-term solution and don't want to be clobbered with

Pay Day Loan Co. rates.

2. Meet with the loan officer at your bank. Ideally you'd like to get a credit line, overdraft protection, or perhaps a comprehensive refinancing of your business, neatly consolidating your debt into a one manageable package, hopefully for a livable term and at friendlier rates.

The goal here is to get a little breathing room through lower rates and reduced monthly payments over an extended period. Don't expect miracles. But the banker wants to work with you, considering he's in the business of renting money, isn't he? Nonetheless he has to adhere to rules and regulations. Yes, he's willing to take some risk, the amount of which will determine what he'll allow on interest rates, the term, and, of course, the size of the loan. But he's not in the fairy tale business.

If you're denied a good financing or refinancing package, insufficient to your needs or way too costly, don't give up. There may well be another bank that's more accommodating in assessing risk and more aggressive in enlisting new accounts, including yours, as long as it can be convinced your enterprise is viable despite its occasional financial acne.

3. Tighten your belt. Reduce and keep payroll to the bone. If warranted, shorten hours, lay off employees or terminate where you must. Damn right it's tough to do, but what's the alternative? Are you running a business or a social service agency? Make the tough calls. And sooner rather than later.

4. Review your expenses, shop what you can, economize. When was the last time you took a good look at your liability insurance coverage, had your unemployment compensation rates recalculated to reflect recent payroll trends, or leaned on vendors for free freight? Can you renegotiate leases or your rent? Once you start looking for qualitative savings, you'll probably find a few items worth the effort. No, price isn't everything and you don't abandon vendors who've provided good service and worked with you in the past. But you don't have to cheat yourself, either.

5. Sell off old inventory. Get a handle on your holdings, including those oddball samples and other accumulated stuff, especially higher ticket items such as boxes of wearables collecting dust. Offer them as a package to customers who are amenable to assortments if given incentives to buy them, decorated or undecorated. Conduct an in-house sale for employees and their friends and relatives, a factory sale inviting employees of nearby businesses and residents (it's great networking, too!), or head to a flea market with your stuff. Endeavor also to return these goods, if possible, to the vendor who sold them to you. (No, they don't exactly advertise the fact that they'll take stuff back, but many will as an occasional act of mercy or goodwill. Yes, even eat restocking charges, if they're reasonable. As for all those misprints and rejects you've been hording in hopes of at least recovering your cost, you're dreaming. Unload 'em -- the sooner the better and at any price. Or donate what you can't convert to cash to a charity, where the stuff will do *somebody* some good.

6. Escrow Payroll Taxes. Open a separate account for putting aside your total payroll taxes -- both your portion and the withholding you do -- *every week*. All too often I observe companies using this tax money for cash flow. Some think it's an easy way to borrow money until they learn the heard way it isn't. What with the interest and penalties the IRS or Revenue Canada is certain to assess when you're late, *payroll tax withholding money is the most expensive money you can borrow*. Forbid yourself to touch this money except when withdrawing it for its intended purpose. It takes discipline and forbearance, and the start-up is quite painful, but once you're "cleansed," you're on the road to positive cash flow recovery.

And escrowing the money in an interest-bearing account will not only earn you a few extra coins, it'll make your overall financial picture look a little better on paper.

7. Review your buying habits and policies. Except where you're already getting free freight, group inbound orders so that you receive bigger, heavier shipments, and cut the number of *deliveries* from your preferred sources by half. Advise your customer service rep there that you want your orders stuffed into the biggest cartons they can ship. You'll pay less per pound, incur fewer add-on handling charges per carton, and incur fewer C.O.D. charges. And do the kind of review on sourcing you've been meaning to do, but haven't gotten around to doing. You're certain to effect some worthwhile dividends for your effort.

8. Investigate new equipment purchases. It's likely that you've considered acquiring some new, labor-saving equipment. If you can realize measurable payroll economies with it and/or gain competitive advantages, this might be the smart time to buy, if your budget allows. How long is the payout and the payback? Industry-specific leasing companies are hungry for this business, even if your banker isn't. Weigh a possible purchase perhaps not as to whether you can afford it, but whether you can afford not to.

Regrettably, the prescriptions above do in fact treat the symptoms, not the illness that is likely to remain for the near term until the medicine begins to take effect. The correct dosage for each malady will vary from company to company. (Few companies likely need help in all the areas, but if your company really needs to address all eight recommendations, it's probably beyond help and beyond hope).

Ideally, positive cash flow should come from increasing sales. Positive cash flow won't come from praying for it or reading about doing something about it. It'll come from looking the Cash Flow Monster straight in the eyes, ending the denial, and taking corrective action.

When you finally meet up with The Positive Cash Flow Goddess, it's best to show the lady some respect. Kiss her hand, and tell her you'll be back to see her often.

Being a Creditor

As much as some apparel decorators often seem to find themselves strapped for cash to pay creditors and meet payroll, being a successful custom apparel decorator means you're also expected by some customers to be a lending institution.

Being a creditor makes it incumbent upon you to establish credit procedures and standards, enforce them, monitor accounts and credit limits, know when to take prudent risks and, of course, when to avoid unnecessary exposure. It is in this area -- being a bank -- where many an apparel decorating company can collapse under the weight of accounts receivable, credit nightmares, and taking on more business than they can handle, administer, and collect on. It's where the proverbial men are separated from the boys. If you do your homework and get good advice, however, there's every reason to expect you'll do just fine. Investigate more sophisticated accounts receivable software, especially if your computer system or existing software leaves much to be desired.

For those unfamiliar with or having limited experience in financing customers' orders -- especially for big accounts placing big orders -- you've got lots of people who'll help you establish intelligent, cogent credit procedures. These include your banker, your accountant, and advisors from the local office branch of the Small Business Administration and other professionals available to you on a no-charge basis. These include local, state, or provincial economic development agencies, as well as from the business schools at many colleges and universities. The help is there if you ask for it.

What with the interest and penalties the IRS or Revenue Canada is certain to assess when you're late, *payroll tax withholding money is the most expensive money you can borrow*.

Given the situations where there's little choice but to give terms to those creditworthy customers who insist on buying this way, the good news is that the overwhelming majority of accounts you extend credit to do pay their bills within terms or at least not unreasonably late. But it's incumbent upon you, the creditor, to do your homework in verifying the trade references supplied on your credit application and ascertaining the applicants' credit standing *before* extending the credit as well as being careful to follow the customers' written administrative procedures to the letter. And don't assume that just because an account is big or national or powerful locally, its money is "good." If you make such as assumption, you might consider investing money with Charles Ponzi, getting Bernie Madoff's accounting team to do your tax return

To help collect your larger size receivables on time, follow the suggested procedures below:

Once you've shipped the goods and sent out your invoice, allow a few days for the customer's accounts payable department to receive and enter the data. Then call the A/P department to ascertain if in fact your invoice has been received and entered. If it has been, confirm that everything is correct, that there are no outstanding issues that could cause payment to be withheld, and review any other details.

Do ask if your check will be issued within terms and request that it be made available for you to pick up in person (if the payment office is close by, if you're really hurtin' for the money). A week or so before your invoice is due, call again to see if everything's still in order. If it isn't, get crackin' to remedy the situation, not after the payment due date has already passed and you're still looking for a chcck.

Despite the financial challenges that go with the turf in this business (and most others), these are good challenges when they're proof of the fact that you're staying in the game, growing, and actually making money.

CHAPTER

HOW TO RUIN YOUR BUSINESS

You've read lots of details and recommendations about how to succeed in selling decorated apparel.

I've endeavored to give you some long-held secrets, inside information, and anecdotes along the way. Now I'll switch gears to tell you how to ruin your business by telling you how others wrecked good companies. All but one of the companies in this chapter have died from their illnesses. The one still breathing is in a condition I'd characterize as being on permanent disability, brain dead, and will inevitably succumb to infection from self-inflected wounds and refusing treatment.

Read how each got sick and understand how those things that went wrong -- by circumstance, stupidity, negligence, nastiness, cluelessness, or a combination of these business pathologies – didn't have to be fatal.

Each one of the stories in this chapter is true. I worked professionally with all these companies at some point to one extent or another. Some I gave up on, one I had to put out of its misery, myself, one will carry on for the time being until it's too late to save. Each company forfeited or will forfeit what would have been a successful, profitable future through its owners' perennial pigheadedness, solipsism, or denial.

One other true story, in the following chapter, will, however, offer some eye-opening "teaching moments." It might also inspire some struggling entrepreneurs to take bold action before succumbing to total financial asphyxiation.

Hopefully you'll learn from their mistakes.

Superior Shirts – Green Bay, Wisconsin

Superior Shirts was founded by Patton "Pat" Bell. In high school in the late 80's, Pat worked after school at a local mom-n-pop screen printing company, and after graduation, took a full time job there. After summer, with help from the Bank of Dad, he opened his own shop. A born hustler, Pat quickly earned business from local manufacturers and bars. Earning a respectable livelihood from his first day in business, he soon wanted to expand into embroidery to get control of the work he was sending out to a nearby contractor, who was consistently late on delivery and short on straight answers.

About that same time, older brother Stan was finishing up his business degree at the University of Wisconsin-Green Bay. The Bank of Dad, which financed the new embroidery equipment, got the brothers together and before long the expanded enterprise saw Pat focusing on production while Stan concentrated on sales. Business was good. The relationship of the brothers was not. Though their wives were friendly with each other, the brothers argued constantly, over seemingly everything. They saw each other only at family get-togethers for Thanksgiving, Christmas, Easter, and a few birthday events

Meanwhile, the business continued growing, and when additional space was needed, the brothers agreed to open a second location in nearby Appleton, Wisconsin, near Stan's house, which also would house the embroidery division.

Business continued on the upswing, but with personal things deteriorating, the brothers spoke only when absolutely necessary and only by phone when intermediaries couldn't solve issues. Hiring a consultant (me) helped bring them together somewhat, but only about business. With different agendas, different workplaces, different thinking about how to run and grow the business and who would be in charge of what kinds of decisions were constant irritants. After 10 years in business together, the brothers barely ever spoke at all to one another. Stan started buying things without Pat's knowledge -- including inventory – and without writing up purchase orders, which drove Pat crazy. In time, the brothers met only once or twice a year – a thousand miles away, at the consultant's location.

With sales approaching $2 million, they wanted to split the business into two separate independently owned businesses. Trying to force each other to make concessions, they couldn't agree on anything equitable, or any formula to divide the enterprise. So, Stan simply walked away, took another job, and stuck Pat with huge bills that the company couldn't pay, including long-term equipment loans. Refinancing was not an option, as neither would allow their homes to be pledged as collateral for a consolidation loan. Unable to find an investor-partner or a buyer, Pat scraped up enough to pay off his father, and shortly thereafter declared bankruptcy.

Despite its strong sales, good reputation with customers, and talented staff, the company choked on its debts and its cumbersome decision-making process and eventually lost the support of its vendors.

There could have been solutions, but the extent of the animus between the brothers made negotiations impossible, even between their attorneys, who tried diligently to resolve the impasse. But to no avail.

The assets of Superior Shirts were liquidated at auction. Stan went on to a career in real estate, but you know what happened to that industry in the deep recession. Pat opened a restaurant in downtown Milwaukee and made a lot of money, while wife Stephanie became a promotional products distributor and discovered she had a great talent for sales and networking and built her company to $1 million in sales within a few years. Pat eventually sold his successful restaurant and join his wife in selling decorated apparel and promowares.

Desert Fox Designs – Tempe, Ariz.

Bob Zimmer was a successful real estate broker and had some money to show for his 12 years in the field. His wife, Sheryl, had a good job in the admissions office at the Arizona State University. Bob and Sheryl, both ASU grads, were active in the alumni association and had good business connections throughout the area. Bob finally fulfilled his dream of owning his own business when he bought a local screen printing company, grossing about $700,000 in sales. Bob figured with his background and connections, he could build the company, make some money along the way, sell it in five to 10 years, and retire at age 50. He paid $450,000, making a $150,000 down payment with a three-year payout to the owner, who held the paper in this deal.

Bob had called me about two months before he bought the business to discuss his pending acquisition and learn more about the industry. During the conversation I offered to review the company's financials to get a better handle on its operations and its value, to do an industry-specific appraisal, and visit the company to evaluate its personnel and operations. I never heard back from Bob until six months after he bought the company. After settlement, as I learned, he had retained the sales manager and production manager he inherited and had put some money into the company's showroom, signage, and the (rented) building's exterior, which was on a major thoroughfare near the ASU campus. But, he explained, the business was struggling.

So he hired me to come to Arizona to conduct a management audit and review his marketing efforts. Seeing his financials before I arrived, I saw a company hemorrhaging with a bloated payroll, spending nothing on advertising, and paying a huge amount for the mortgage on the business. As expected when I arrived, I saw too many people in production, working at a leisurely pace, in November (when business is strong there). Meeting with the sales and production managers, I found them affable, but basically "jobholders," performing only minimum routines during their 8-to-4 vacation at "work" – no thinking, no extra effort, no appreciation of the fact they were employed by a *business*, not a social service organization or leisure activity center.

My recommendation was draconian. Either a.) walk away from the business and the mortgage, swallow his $150,000 mistake, and find another business; or b.) work on a game plan, implement it, replace the sales manager and the two salesmen ("salesmen" in name only and basically order takers), and replace the production manager with someone intelligent, competent, and knowledgeable about screen printing. Bob selected option b.) and I extended my scheduled three-day assignment by two days to develop a marketing strategy, plan his advertising program, create a catalog and price list for him, and chart an implementation schedule and budget.

In the months that followed, Bob's relationship with his sales manager and production manager soured, and both quit to start their own business and compete with Desert Fox. Meanwhile, Bob had ignored all the recommendations I had made and his salespeople absolutely refused to sell from the price list, opting to sell as they always had – negotiate, discount, sell at any price. And Bob let them do it.

Thinking he could throw money at the business and blowing almost another $100,000 in working capital along the way (in addition to the leasehold improvements he had made), Bob folded his tent two months after his former employees became his competitors. The guy he bought it from took back the business for the balance owed; he then re-hired the old sales manager and his buddy and went back to business as usual. During the year the former owner was out of the industry, a few new competitors had opened shop and had taken away more than half of Desert Fox's market share in addition to producing better quality work and selling at higher prices. Outsmarted, outmarketed, and outrun by its competition, Desert Fox closed its doors two years later.

Blue Ribbon Graphics – Anaheim, Calif.

A major force in the industry through the 1990's and into the 21st century, Blue Ribbon grew with its customers in the movie industry, recording industry, and theme park industry, winning apparel licenses from several of America's premier trademarked brands. Owing to its cutting-edge art staff and its astute and well-connected sales force, the company's sales soared to more than $12 million annually. Then the boss, Justin Romanoff, got involved with a younger woman and then, younger women. Not surprisingly upon learning of her husband's serial infidelity, his wife Jane, a homemaker who had helped build the company during its infancy and was 50% owner of the company, sought a divorce

Mr. Romanoff had a few million dollars in the bank, all under his control. So he handed Mrs. Romanoff the keys to the building, wished her good luck in running the company, and took off with a girlfriend 30 years his junior for a life of leisure in Moorea in French Polynesia, 12 miles west of Tahiti.

Referred to me by an industry colleague, Jane called me and made me an offer to run the company. Content with my lifestyle and income, I politely declined, but accepted her pleading invitation to oversee the company while she sought a CEO, find out the skinny on the loss of revenue, and attempt to breathe some life back into the company and its staff. Our game plan was to share my time between Maryland and California for a few months until the situation could be rectified or a buyer for the company could be found.

During my first week on site, I found a company that couldn't pay its bills, including for some inventory for orders the company didn't transact or that anyone knew about. There also was a bunch of other smaller but telling items of interest, such as long distance calls in the middle of the night to a phone number in French Polynesia.

Among my first decisions was to cut payroll in production by almost half, as virtually the entire staff had been retained even as sales were shrinking. That same week I had warehouse employees take a full inventory to ascertain inventory holdings, and instructed the company's CFO, hired only weeks before I first visited the company, to investigate all inventory purchases for the past two years. I also met with the company's bankers, who were about to call in some delinquent loans, and bought a little time.

By the time I'd returned, having called the phone number in Moorea from my home in the middle of the night, myself, and having been apprised by the CFO of escalating inventory "mysteries" in the warehouse, I was close to understanding the whole situation. On day one of my third trip to Blue Ribbon, I hired a computer wizard to track what had happened to some art files, who showed me where digital files had been transmitted and then erased. That week I also spoke to the company's bankers, again, and then with Jane's counsel. On day two, I made calls, posing as a shipping and receiving clerk, to lower echelon personnel from DreamWorks, Disney, CBS, and Universal Studios to ask seemingly innocuous questions about order deliveries and deadlines.

What I had learned would read like a novel about business conspiracy, fraud, deception, and a few uglier things.

My findings after my five-week mission at Blue Ribbon:

1. While Justin had left the country, he was in fact in daily communication with his nephew, Skip, who happened to be the rep who handled the company's biggest accounts. Having formed a decorated apparel brokerage in partnership with the nephew, Justin was directing all the new company's moves, which included slowly diverting sales from Blue Ribbon to the partnership. After one year following Romanoff's departure, Blue Ribbon's sales were down $2 million and after the second year, it dropped another $4 million to just over $6 million in revenue.

2. Inventory that had been ordered by a Blue Ribbon employee and billed to Blue Ribbon had been shipped repeatedly to addresses in nearby Compton and City of Industry, California, to contract screen printing companies. (I called these companies, too, posing as buyers from the big accounts to see when "our jobs" would be done).

3. Confronted by me with the threat to have him charged with criminal conspiracy, theft of property, and a few other juicy felonies as suggested by counsel, I got him to admit to what was going on and his role in it.

When the bank could be held off no longer and advised on a Tuesday morning it would call in its loans the following day, I met with counsel, who that afternoon filed Blue Ribbon's bankruptcy petition at the L.A. County Courthouse (on the tenth anniversary to the day of O.J. Simpson's acquittal).

The rest of this sad story is that the company was liquidated at auction, Justin Romanoff and his nephew got off scott free, the Romanoffs ended up with nothing. Their only child, a teenage daughter, estranged from her father for obvious reasons, was killed in a skiing accident a year later. Jane eventually met a wonderful gentleman, married him, and is now retired and living in Costa Rica. Justin Romanoff's whereabouts? Who cares?!

Crimson Creations – Tuscaloosa, Ala.

An outgrowth of the owner's part-time business while a student at the University of Alabama, where he graduated with a degree in Fine Art, Crimson Creations is celebrating its 25th anniversary. I doubt it'll be around for its 30th unless management takes a closer look at where the company's going.

Accepting the company as a client two years ago and making two visits there, I found a company with stagnant sales and profitability (which is why I got the call) in its custom division, and static or declining sales in its seven retail locations. The custom side of the business caters to campus organizations, including Greeks, local businesses, and supply chain vendors to the nearby Mercedes-Benz plant. The stores, which carry leisure apparel geared to students and to U of A alumni and fans of its nationally ranked team, are located in and around the Tuscaloosa campus, in Birmingham, Gulf Shores, Dothan, and Montgomery, Alabama, all cities and towns rich in Crimson Tide fans and alumni. The company also is a licensee for the university's trademarks and produces all of its own licensed apparel as well as its own line of branded apparel, "Bamamaniac," launched 24 years ago.

A $3 million business, Crimson has provided its owner with a comfortable income since its inception as a full-time venture. But things are changing outside the company and management hasn't done much to address them. Nor is it even aware of what's happening all around it.

The custom business has in the past year remained predictably constant in sales volume, though two new competitors have come into the market and are marketing aggressively to vacuum up leads. Meanwhile, Crimson continues selling as it always has, at whatever price it can get, and without a price list. It's a safe bet that without revitalizing its marketing – or more precisely, doing some at all – that its custom business will remain at best static, but, more likely, will begin to suffer the natural attrition of its account base.

Its retail stores are maxxed out and, having spoken with several of the store managers, I was informed few new designs are furnished to the stores. When they are, they come infrequently and look much the same as the existing crop. Crimson's retail customers walk in, see the same old stuff, and more often than not walk out, and, as any retailer would understand the phrase, "without any bags leaving the store."

My observation to the owner was that the designs on the garments are behind the times -- way behind, and that he should invite some new and younger artists to submit work or give out a few spec assignments. Learning that the designs have all been done by the same artist, the owner's brother, since the company's first forays into retailing, I commented to the client that his brother hasn't really been doing the designs for 23 years, but rather doing them "for one year, 23 times." I was advised, my recommendation notwithstanding, that said artist would remain the primary – and perhaps the sole – source of the creative component of the retail stores as long as he's alive. Seriously!

With licensed Crimson Tide™ shirts from several vendors now commanding permanent space in local department stores, at Wal-Mart, Target, and another major retailing competitor selling similar designs as well as some much hipper, trendier stuff, especially for U of A garments, the outlook isn't very bright. And the upscale competition's stores present more modern, friendlier store environments. Having seen this phenomenon all too frequently with other apparel decorators producing preprint lines, I can safely predict the retail division will continue to atrophy and that soon enough, stores will have to be closed along the way. That is, unless somehow the owner of Crimson Creatives undergoes a personal epiphany revealing to him that new retail designs will help revitalize the company's retail outlook. Of course, said possible epiphany might come too late.

Lessons to Be Learned

I'm proud to claim a rather successful track record in my professional life helping to fix companies and helping facilitate their growth and success. There are, however, situations in the consulting business where my help, my counsel, or my intervention in a company went for naught. If I'm guilty of anything, I'll acknowledge my mistakes in sometimes accepting work from companies that, with the benefit of hindsight, I probably shouldn't have. There's a lesson in that reality, itself, that's humbling and teaches that good intentions alone won't accomplish anything. Doing one's homework, following through, acknowledging when help is needed and getting some, learning to ask the right questions, taking measurements along the way and learning from them, having the right people on your side, and lots of other factors are immensely more important than good intentions. Luck can play a role, too, if, of course, it's good luck.

You just read about three companies that went out of business and a fourth that will inevitably follow suit, though without the gore of the others. I elected to tell these companies' stories because their pathologies were not only so different from one another, but that all of them provide students of business a range of instructive lessons about what keeps companies moving forward, what can get in their way to frustrate long-term viability, and how some things were either beyond the owners' control or beyond any realistic means of repair and correction. I could fill a book with lots of other stories about businesses, including some of my own clients, that failed in our industry and why they failed, what could have turned them around, but that became hopeless inevitabilities. Or in the case of Crimson Creations, a self-fulfilling prophecy.

What the tale of **Superior Shirts** teaches is that partnerships can present challenges of their own despite successfully growing a good business. That Pat and Stan were brothers, deep-seated sibling rivalry eventually provided the seeds of the company's demise. I can tell you lots of stories about father-and-son, mother-and-daughter, and husband-and-wife operations that have happy endings and more often so than not. Businesses built on partnerships between old friends or co-workers can start well and end up with a variety of outcomes.

But anyone entering into a business partnership needs to realize the arrangement is a form of marriage. Given the nation's divorce rate, it's no wonder that partnerships can and often do take on a life of their own. If you're starting a business with a partner or are currently involved in one, formal arrangements about the company's management and the paperwork regarding down-the-road what-ifs are best effected at the enterprise's onset or, failing that, as soon as humanly possible once the company has commenced operations.

What Pat and Stan needed most, though, was counseling, a matter over my pay grade to be sure. But even with the intervention of a professional skilled at dealing with the dynamics of relationships, the chances of resolution are at best 50/50, in my opinion.

Take the story of Superior Shirts to heart if you'll be sharing ownership of a business with a partner, even if its your BFF, mother, or son.

The **Desert Fox Designs** narrative is one that occurs routinely throughout the world of small business. Someone buys a business without doing enough homework. Driven more by optimism and enthusiasm than knowledge and a sound game plan, most entrepreneurs who buy businesses in the decorated apparel industry fail. You read that right. *Most* will fail. My observation is that about half will go under within two years, though there's no statistical documentation about the failure rate in this industry regarding those who enter via the acquisition path. Most exit by unloading their mistake or getting the note-holding previous owner to take back the business, though some simply walk away and/or have to file for bankruptcy.

By the way, the failure rate for start-ups in our industry, especially for those who buy new equipment and focus on learning how to use it instead of focusing on building an account base, is, I believe, even higher. Many start-ups are owned by people who aren't experienced or skilled in running a business nor adept at selling. Oftentimes unwilling to "do sales," themselves, they look for seemingly easy solutions. "Well, I'll just have to hire me some salesmen," the logic goes. While the company has little work, is often priced too low or too high, and its ability to operate is compounded by being undercapitalized to begin with, more than half of the industry's start-ups expire within 12 to 18 months; about a third of them are gone within six months. Those that make it through the umbilical phase have a good chance to survive if they learn how to price, to sell, and to market. It is those entrepreneurs for whom this book will save a fortune in painful lessons ("tuition") and shorten the learning curve if they apply what they've read and get serious about developing a workable game plan.

Desert Fox owner Bob Zimmer is one of the fortunate ones who, while he didn't make it in this trade, was smart enough to get out while the gettin' was good. I spoke with him a few years later and learned he went on to become a successful flower broker, of all things, importing thousands of dozens of flowers every week from South America. As Bob told me, "Yeah, I'm now a *blooming* idiot – and lovin' it!"

The death of **Blue Ribbon Graphics** was the result of marital infidelity run amok, a serial philanderer's epic-proportioned mid-life crisis, and the complicity of a family member who engineered the embezzlement of key accounts while on Blue Ribbon's payroll. The creeps got away with commercial murder. Would that Jay Romanoff had been a man and settled for half of the company by buying out his wife's shares, the company would be doing $30 million today. But Jay wanted it all, not just what was his. Instead he lost everything, including a relationship with his only child, whose tragic death only compounded his loss. But I doubt highly he shed any tears for anyone, including himself.

The bankruptcy trustee did what many in his craft do when appointed to oversee the disposition of assets. He took the fastest, easiest way out to justify his assigned fee: He got an auctioneer to liquidate the company, in this case within weeks of its cessation of operations. No attempt was made to sell the business as a "gong concern," which it wasn't much of, or its accounts, art files, or assets beyond the equipment and inventory – at 10¢ on the dollar, or less. This story is what it is and one major "teaching moment" is that key employees in a position to damage a company as thoroughly as Justin's nephew Skip could and did, along with his inside accomplices, should be obliged to sign a professionally drafted non-compete agreement, which provides some basic protections for a business. But Blue Ribbon would have crashed and burned anyhow. Legal niceties and honor are not impediments to stupidity and vengeance.

I doubt Jane Romanoff would have ever gotten deeply involved or become knowledgeable of the company's culture and operations. But in most companies employing salespeople, it's smart for owners to become personally acquainted with their customers. It's among the easiest mechanisms for having any effective opportunity to keep the accounts a deceitful salesperson is planning to steal when he leaves for the seemingly greener pastures of a competitor. Or becomes one.

Crimson Creatives is perhaps the saddest case, because it adamantly refuses to change its modus operandi. If and when it ever might, my strong belief is that it will be too little too late. Meanwhile, at least it will keep its owner comfortable in his personal philosophy that "If it ain't broke, don't fix it." This common belief is anathema to astute marketers. Most people don't wait for a car to completely fall apart and stop running altogether before they buy a new one. Neither should folks in this industry. Though the industry evolves and at a pace where it's often hard to monitor from year to year, its dynamics are inexorable in their continuance. That word, "continuance," includes the word "nuance." But it's those nuances of change that constantly are occurring in decorated apparel, if one only looks for them.

Twice in my career, upon arrival for an assignment, I thought of turning around, refunding my fee, getting back on a plane, and going home.

The first time was in Winnipeg, early on in my consulting career in the mid-80s. A half hour after clearing customs, as the elevator door opened at the seventh floor of an old industrial building, I got one glance at the world headquarters of aptly-named Manitoba Mayhem, a cut-and-sew and apparel decorating business, and looked at my watch. The time read: "Mark, you can make it back to the airport for the return flight to Minneapolis and connect in time for the flight back to Philly."

I was staring at the biggest single mess I'd ever seen in this industry before or since. It was my professional inclination to recommend hiring an arsonist to fix things. I'm in over my head, I thought.

My ego prompted a quick excuse to stay the course, wondering to myself if I could in fact handle the toughest challenge of my young career and turn chaos into order and gloom into sunshine. I concluded it was in both my own interest and, of course, the client's for me to attempt to change the course of history.

In the longest three days of my life, I got owner Frank Richardson to swallow a pharmacy-full of bitter pills, who resolutely proceeded during the next 90 days to resurrect his failing enterprise. Whatever my own instrumentality in this miracle, I'll award most of the credit for the turnaround to Divine Intervention. Frank went on to sell his company and his Manitoba Mayhem trademark a year or so later, getting a real good price for his years of sweat equity, and moved on to his next career, as a very successful manufacturer's rep.

My second I-think-I'm-in-over-my-head challenge is painfully recounted in the next chapter.

CHAPTER

HOW TO RUIN YOUR BUSINESS –
AND SAVE IT FROM OBLIVION

Fajita's – Las Cruces, New Mexico

Jim and Belle Meadows were high school sweethearts in Las Cruces, New Mexico, graduated college together at New Mexico State University there, and got married. On their honeymoon in St. Lucia, they decided to live there! A few weeks later, with some help from family, Jim opened a shoe store. Ten years later they had built a chain of high-end shoe stores throughout the Caribbean, catering to American and European tourists vacationing in St. Lucia, Barbados, Ocho Rios, Grenada, Curaçao, St. Maarten, Cancun, Cozumel, and St. Thomas. Despite a wonderful life in St. Lucia, the couple decided it was time to sell their business and move the family back to Las Cruces. Their oldest son Rick was about to enter ninth grade and Jim and Belle wanted Rick and his two sisters to finish growing up in a place more in keeping with "the real world," not Fantasy Island. Planning their relocation back to their family's home town, Jim contacted a business broker in Las Cruces, who located a custom decorated apparel company. Jim flew up for a look-see and liked what he saw. As do many other would-be apparel graphics entrepreneurs, he contacted me for some insight on the industry's stability, operating ratios, typical return-on-investment (there is no such thing), and current industry trends. I didn't hear back from Jim.

It turned out that that deal fell through, but Jim asked the broker to keep looking, especially if he could find another apparel graphics company. A few months later, after soliciting some local firms, the broker brought a deal to Jim for a business that would finish the year at $1.6 million in sales.

Fajita's, a screen printing and embroidery company with 16 years of serving the area, soon had its third owner, Jim Meadows.

Sales dropped during Jim's first year to just under $1.4 million. Another year passed with the company dropping to $1.3 million and not producing sufficient profits for Jim to stay in business much longer.

After two years, I finally heard back from Jim, who told me a tale of great disappointment and growing concern. Juggling my schedule, I went to Las Cruces three weeks later to help Jim climb out of his hole. I usually get the client's financial data well before I land on site, but Jim never got the numbers to me – until he handed me a folder with the company's hot-off-the-press accounting reports after I got into his car at the airport. All buckled up, I looked at the materials on our way to the hotel. About a minute later, I knew why the company was sick and, without mincing words, apprised Jim that the situation was far worse than he had led me to believe. He showed no emotion as he listened to me prepare his soul to receive Last Rites as an apparel decorator.

A few figures jumped out at me, particularly the operating ratios for production labor, utilities, and advertising. At 34% of gross revenue, the production labor figure was "two times bad." The utilities, at 3.4%, were three times the industry's average for similarly-sized custom apparel decorators. Advertising, at .3%, was one tenth of what I recommend for maintaining accounts, replacing losses to attrition, and generating sufficient inflow of new leads. Other numbers weren't so good either, further revealing just how bleak the company's outlook was for survival. The patient's pulse was weak, its heartbeat dangerously slow, and the body exhibiting extreme diaphoresis (sweating). The patient was gasping for air.

The next morning, at Jim's business, we did a quick walk-through, during which time I asked a few questions of some of the employees. Their answers fully explained the reasons for the horrible numbers. What I learned in my first few minutes on the clock made my diagnosis of the illness that was killing Fajita's fast and easy. Reviewing the financial reports on the company's performance of two years earlier, when he bought it, I concluded he paid more than twice what it was worth and that the debt service on his mortgage alone would be all but impossible to meet at the current level of sales.

In the ground floor pressroom, I saw four manual screen printing presses, each with a small electric dryer next to it. And there were four screen printers on staff. Each dryer was up to temperature and running, but no jobs were being run. Huh?! Enlightened by the de facto department head, though no one had the formal title or responsibility of "Production Manager," I was told, "The first guy in, in the morning, turns on the lights and the dryers in the pressroom."

"Uh huh," I acknowledged.

"That way," the employee continued, "when the screens are done, we're ready to set up the presses and roll and don't have to wait for the dryers to heat up." In other words: Even though the jobs probably won't be ready to print for an hour or two or longer, the dryers are on, so the printers won't have to wait the usual 10 minutes for the infrared elements to reach the proper temperature. Given that electric dryers are usually the single, greatest juice-sucker in a screen printing shop, the company's electric meter was racing at blur-speed. Four dryers running at full tilt for four to eight hours of heavy energy use every morning before a single shirt was ready to be printed made the ridiculously high utility ratio simple to understand.

On the first floor there, one level up, was another pressroom with a mint-condition automatic press sitting idle, covered with dust, ready for someone to whip out a finger and write, "Wash Me!"

"When was it run last?," I asked another printer who was pulling some boxes from shelves.

"Uh, it's been a coupla' months."

"How come you don't use it?"

"Well, business has been real slow lately and if we were running jobs on it, there wouldn't be enough work for everyone [the four screen printers]."

"I see, " I replied, ending the conversation. I should have said "I see, I see, I see, "I see" – one for each of the four printers whose labor was sucking the company dry. But you can't blame the employees. Since Jim gave them carte blanche in production and really took no interest in how it was being done – only that it was in fact being done – the employees' sole interest in Fajita's was to feed their families.

In other words: The employees running the asylum determined it was preferable – in their view -- for the company to pay four screen printers to run jobs on four manual presses with four dryers running, letting the garments fall off the end of the dryer belt into a carton, and then for the printer to dump the shirts on a table to stack or fold them. Instead of: a.) running the jobs on the auto press, b.) running one dryer, and c.) cutting production labor costs to the bone -- enough to at least enable the company to get some oxygen into its lungs.

Later in the morning, Jim explained that incoming orders were way off from the previous year's figures, which were down from the previous year, too. In reviewing a census of the staff and their pay rates, I saw the highest wages for printers in New Mexico -- and maybe for all the land west of the Mississippi. Average hourly wage for production employees: $12 to $13 per hour, gross, costing the company $14 to $16/hr. per pressman – in 2002! After lunch I innocently (yeah, sure) asked the de facto printing manager, "When was the last time you guys got a raise?"

"Right before Jim bought the company from Choppy."

Investigating payroll records, I found that the previous owner awarded $2-per-hour raises to every single employee in the company two weeks before the sale to Jim. I presume it was a parting gift from him to the staff. Yessiree . . . Choppy gave the gift and got the thank-you's, Jim pays the bill and gets hosed. Veterans, you read it right: two bucks an hour. For everyone. With a staff of 11, not counting Jim, that was $22 per hour per employee extra, times 40 (hours per week), times 52 (weeks). Or, a whopping $45,760 in added payroll per year, not counting employer-paid taxes, workman's comp, unemployment, and benefits (one-half medical premiums). Cost over the two years Jim had owned the business, including payroll costs and fringes: $110,0000 extra before deducting what would have been at most about $10,000 in normally scheduled wage increases. So, there was another $100,000 worth of 'splainin' about Fajita's "two times bad" production labor ratio.

Advertising totaled $3,600 a year for a shrinking company, but one still doing $1.2 million. And that was all in Yellow Pages advertising and donations to a few high school yearbooks and church bulletins. "Why so little in advertising, Jim?," I asked.

"Well, basically, Choppy said it wasn't really necessary, since everyone in town knows us and we're right across from the high school."

Good ol' Choppy. He also told Jim the company didn't need a salesperson, nor that Jim would have to do any real selling, himself, proudly noting, "I rarely have to leave the shop." To Choppy's way of thinking, the company was well established, ergo it needn't need much in the way of marketing or advertising and it could run forever just the way it was. Perhaps once upon a time it was so.

With the patient in critical condition, going into a coma, and now on life support, late that first day, I outlined for Jim exactly what Fajita's would have to do to survive.

1. New Rules for Screen Printing

a. Two of the four screen printing production folks would have to be laid off the following day, indefinitely. One would have to be reduced to 20 hours a week, and would get additional hours of work as needed. The company would, however, continue paying half his medical insurance premiums.

b. All screen printing orders over two dozen pieces would be run on the automatic press. All orders of any quantity for multicolor work would exclusively run on the automatic.

c. Screens for the following day's production all would be completed, taped and retouched by the end of the day, and the first job for the following morning's production would be set up and registered by day's end as well.

d. A new minimum-wage employee would be hired to handle screen reclaiming, folding, and other lower-skilled tasks as assigned. (Note that none of the laid off printers was willing to work at a reduced rate).

Fortunately, the embroidery department was functioning well with one full-timer and one part-timer, who also could help out in other departments when necessary.

2. Name Change

As agreed to by Jim as a condition of my accepting him as a client, the company's name would have to be changed. "Fajita's" was a major impediment to repositioning the company. Jim, who never really liked the name, was justifiably concerned that after 16 years of business, the name was known in the community – or so he thought. As name changes are part of my stock in trade, I explained that his existing accounts knew it and that customers who left knew it. But new customers didn't care and the name was confusing. And lame. Invariably, people would walk into the showroom from time to time inquiring as to whether the company catered Mexican food.

"Fajita" was the nickname of the first owner, who named the company "Fajita's" after himself. It worked for that guy, who, after two years, sold the business to a friend who had built the business over the next 12 years and retained the name. How, after 16 years, it had outlived its usefulness over time. After an evening of brainstorming, the new name would be: Roadrunner Graphic Apparel & Promotions. The roadrunner is New Mexico's official state bird. It's comical and loveable in its behaviors and prefers running to flying. And it was a dream name -- it has an "ear" (it sounds good), it's easy to say, and everyone in New Mexico knows it's the state bird and is proud of it. The name could work as a company name, a brand, a store name, a line of apparel, and it could be extended to other marketing uses. It works well illustrated -- as a silhouetted logo, as a cartoon-y mascot, as a sleeve icon. And who doesn't know a roadrunner goes "Meep Meep!" when he's running – or at least that's what he does in Warner Brothers cartoons. The trademark for apparel was available. And the only thing I borrowed from Hollywood (OK, I stole it!) was adding the meep-meep sound in radio commercials.

3. New Rules in Marketing

a. The company would now actually do some marketing!

b. A massive advertising campaign would begin within 10 days. Radio would be critical to getting the name out quickly, get attention, and make the phone ring, as there was still ample time left in peak season to vacuum up leads and orders.

c. An express catalog and price list would need to be press-ready within a week, because it would have to be printed and mailed the following week to customers, chamber of commerce members, and certain key targeted local accounts. The mailing was designed to announce the new name, make it easy for customers to see what they want to buy, make it easy to order, and generate some badly needed order volume.

d. "Good phone" procedures would be implemented immediately

A new sign with the new name and tagline and descriptors would be installed within two weeks.

f. All customers who had bought from the company in the previous two years (a few hundred) would be contacted by Jim personally or by his customer service rep by phone within three weeks.

4. Create a Culture of Creativity in the Art Department

The artists were quite good, but their work-product was ordinary, traditional, typical. And boring. A morning meeting conducted by me teaching them a range of graphic techniques, new approaches to placement and color, and specialty inks was well received. Their assignment was to come up with speculative designs to show key customers and prospects what the firm could do for them in the way of fresh, creative graphics. And to get started immediately on executing the new catalog.

5. A New Job for Jim

With two years of ownership under his belt, Jim had certainly learned enough about the industry, its products, decorating technologies, and culture to understand what his company was selling. And as he had just completed his one-day crash course on why his company was so very ill, he knew the medicine was essential for keeping the ship afloat. The immediate goals were to stop the bleeding, reel in some business, reposition his enterprise for recovery now and, once the company was breathing better and eating regularly, move it to the next level and beyond.

As I learned much later, his marriage at the time was on the line, he feared losing his house along with his entire investment, and his personal guarantees on the note to the previous owner would essentially wipe him out financially and for years to come. Jim's choices were a.) lose everything or b.) do everything necessary in his power to attempt a comeback from the precipice. He picked the latter option.

I outlined his new job and its highest priorities.

a. Start calling customers, an effort he never once undertook since he assumed control of the company. He'd be calling to *sell* decorated apparel, not just to get acquainted and make nice -- and to "ask for the order" on every call.

b. Attend every function of the chamber of commerce to network with the area's business leaders, get in their faces, find out their needs, visit them if necessary, and ask for their orders, too.

c. Contact the NMSU alumni office to see if there was any work available and ascertain what was coming up on the group's calendar. As Jim was well wired to the university and well networked among the alumni, there was a good likelihood of getting a license to do NMSU work to sell to retailers, alumni, and create for special events.

d. Create a price list over the weekend, ready for the art department on Monday to format professionally.

After four days of providing triage and treatment of the patient, I left Las Cruces for the airport in El Paso on Friday morning.

So, what happened after my departure from Las Cruces?

Jim got right down to business. Staff was cut dramatically on Friday, resulting in a 40% drop in payroll the following week. That same day the company started running orders on the automatic press, resulting in an almost 60% reduction in Roadrunner's electric bill the following month.

Jim and his assistant, Kathy, got on the horn and spoke with nearly 200 customers that week. Jim opened a huge door with a local trucking company, Kathy hauled in a 2,300-piece order for a local 10K charity run, and together they booked more than 30 new orders, and nearly twice that the following week.

The art department cranked out some great new spec designs and the production guys even figured out how to print high-density and suede inks. Jim took some designs over to the alumni office to test the reaction, walked away with a provisional license to do NMSU designs for homecoming week (occurring three months away), and got to bid on a big order being placed by the HR department for NMSU's maintenance and security personnel.

By the end of the following week, the company had its new logo, a tagline, and descriptors in place. The express catalog was completed and along with the price list, everything was sent out for printing on Thursday evening and delivered after the weekend, on Monday. Mailing labels were ready to go and the day after all the printing was in hand, the labels were affixed to the envelopes and nearly 400 packets were taken to the post office that same day.

Roadrunner Graphic Apparel & Promotions

SCREEN PRINTING ▪ EMBROIDERY ▪ GRAPHIC DESIGN ▪ PROMOWARES
We Sell Attention! . . . Meep Meep!

On Friday, the new signage was up on the building. A press release with a photo showing the new sign with the new logo and a freshly painted exterior was sent to the local newspaper.

Yours truly produced radio commercials in Maryland the week after I left and the following Monday they started airing on three stations. Air time was done on a trade for printed tees and embroidered golf shirts and caps, but at very favorable rates and times.

A month after being on life support, Roadrunner was rockin'. Having gotten the catalogs and price lists distributed, seeing the Roadrunner photo and story on the front page of the newspaper, getting a good response from the radio campaign, (he and Kathy) having hooked up with almost the entire account base by phone, doing some solid networking, being out of his office hustling business and closing sales, watching orders being produced faster and more efficiently, and actually taking some money out of the business, Jim was feeling good about owning the company and was well on his way to getting it back on the road to black ink.

And for the first time since he bought the company, Jim was having fun and looked forward to going to work.

His marriage blossomed again. The constant unpleasant discussions with his wife about how bad things were going at Fajita's had been transformed to brainstorming sessions about designs, opportunities, and further strengthening the company's internal operations.

The following month, Jim personally closed two $100,000-plus deals that would happen over the next few months, including a monster order for a chain of supermarkets and a big hit for NMSU's homecoming week (garments that sold well throughout the whole year at retail locations and online). Sales were strong. Employees were being called back to work. The showroom got a long-overdue makeover.

By the end of the year, sales were up more than 20% to $1.5 million. Not as good as when he bought the company, but certainly a shot in the arm in terms of confidence-building and a huge cause for optimism for the following year's performance. Most importantly, the company had caught up on its bills, Belle was shopping at department stores again, and Jim had renewed his passion for golf. And when it got too cold to play in New Mexico, Jim took Belle for a long-delayed vacation to St. Lucia to see old friends there, hit the links, and rent a sailboat to wander the Caribbean for two weeks while they renewed their marriage and recharged their batteries.

Jim and Belle, devout in their faith, also made a very generous donation to Holy Cross Catholic Church to acknowledge Who was really to thank for their blessings.

Eight years since all this happened at Roadrunner, the company in the intervening years eclipsed the $3 million mark, established a children's clothing line that's sold in upscale stores throughout the Southwest, built a sales force, and moved into its own custom-built 19,000-square-foot facility just off I-10. With a staff of 30, considered among the most technically sophisticated apparel graphics firms in its region, and a dominant player in the state, Roadrunner has become a strong, progressive company with exceptionally high productivity in its decorating operations and maintaining extraordinary profitability for Jim and Belle Meadows.

And now you know...*the r-r-r-e-s-t of the story.*

As I stated at the beginning of the previous chapter, "Each one of the stories in this chapter and the following chapter is true." And I can assure you each one is. But as it would be painfully embarrassing for some to read about themselves and admit their places in them, unprofessional to disclose the real names and locations, and as I wouldn't want to receive a letter from their attorneys telling me I'm being sued, I can now tell you the names of the individuals, the companies, and the locations are all fictitious. Admittedly I had to create some references about the locations to make them appear factually coherent. And I trust you can appreciate why I waited until now to let you in on the white lies aspect of these two chapters.

But each story IS true. The events actually transpired. And the outcomes are accurate as I've written them. More importantly, the lessons they teach should alert readers to recognize when they are in (or are about to be in) similar straights, and, left unaddressed, what their futures may hold.

So, for the record . . .

All characters and all companies appearing in Chapters 38 and 39 of this book are fictitious. Any resemblance to real persons, living or dead, or real businesses, currently in operation or no longer operating, is purely coincidental and unintentional.

Oh, yeah, I can assure you unequivocally that no animals were harmed in the writing of this book. If anything, two animals had an absolute ball during the process, walking on my keyboard, sleeping on my elbow, sticking their noses in my coffee, and relocating papers, the TV remote, the phone, and other stuff on my desk to the floor.

CHAPTER

40

THE FUTURE OF THE APPAREL DECORATING INDUSTRY – IT'S YOUR MOVE!

The apparel graphics industry is healthy. The industry has been blessed with increases in units and dollars every year for nearly 40 consecutive years. The growth of our industry has been marked by the uninterrupted advance of ever-improving quality, higher value garments, and an ever-increasing demand for more sophisticated levels of screen printing, embroidery mastery, and other technological wizardry.

Resilient even through the recessions that have come and gone, the sales volume of custom decorated apparel, today at $20-some billion in sales, has proven strong and consistent. Propelling the sales of custom decorated apparel is the universal acceptance of our products across broad demographic categories of age, lifestyle, and socioeconomic class. Our products are by any measure, a staple of mainstream American and Canadian culture. Can you name a single person who doesn't own a single decorated T-shirt, golf shirt, sweatshirt, cap, or jacket? And who doesn't add a few during the year?

The underlying appeal and strength of custom decorated apparel can be seen today in its regular and ubiquitous applications in literally millions of businesses and organizations and tens of thousands of schools.

I tell you all this to put to rest any concerns whatsoever about the popular demand for custom decorated apparel and the vitality of the industry in the years ahead. For those readers contemplating entering into the ranks of the industry, I can assure you there's ample room for you and everyone else who takes the plunge.

The rate of growth we experienced through the 70's, 80's, and 90's has leveled off as the industry's penetration has attained "saturation" status. The good news here is that our product category has matured to the point where we no longer have to explain the benefits and applications of our products to buyers or to convince them about the quality and durability of our decorating processes. We might need to remind people about all this, but we don't need to explain it.

Those 1970s pioneers and the entrepreneurs who followed them in the 80's had a relatively easy time of it, as the mushrooming marketplace for our products was able to feed the burgeoning production capacity developed by so many new entrants in screen printing and embroidery. You didn't have to be particularly good at decorating garments, you just had to keep your shingle out and your doors open. The challenges of doing these things today, though, are vastly greater and the number of apparel decorators include some 50,000 year round, full-time enterprises in the US and Canada. Sellers of decorated apparel, including decorators, themselves, and encompassing promotional products distributor representatives, sporting goods retailers, and personalized products merchandisers number nearly 200,000 companies, individuals, and outlets. To all these sellers, add today's online companies and big-box office supply retailers.

In this staggeringly competitive 21st century environment, what will determine the success or failure of a decorated apparel business comes down two major factors: management skill in overseeing the enterprise and the company's effectiveness in creating a system for generating qualified leads, profitable orders, and loyal accounts.

That first factor means the owner or chief operating officer has to make certain that orders are processed in an efficient manner, production is well-orchestrated and well-executed, customers receive their orders when promised and pay their bills when due, and that employees, vendors, and tax collectors are all paid promptly and in full. All these things oblige entrepreneurs and their management to understand how the various component pieces of the puzzle -- administration, technology, finance, and more -- all fit into the picture.

The second factor comes down to the organization's basic ability to market itself and its products. Success here means management hasn't just the vision to read its audiences and accommodate their needs, but to do so on a continuing and consistent basis, ever aware of their customers' evolving needs, and ever able to address them and satisfy them. Anything less opens the door to a host of competitors trying to do these same these things better and faster.

If doing all this isn't enough of a challenge, add to these responsibilities having to keep up with advances in both business technologies
and decorating technologies, about emerging trends in garment styles
and color palettes, new governmental legislation and decrees, changing lifestyles, and other social and economic forces that impact what
we do and how we do it.

Major factors impacting our industry today, for better or worse, and
the future of your own business are catalogued below across nine issues.

1. The Impact of Online Sellers: When customink.com came on the
scene at the onset of the 21st Century, there was unprecedented concern
that online sellers would supplant the role of local apparel decorators
and eventually put them all out of business. Well, that hasn't happened
and it won't. That's because the big powers in online custom apparel
decorating – customink.com, zazzle.com, cafepress.com et al – all
sell at prices much higher, 20% or more, than local companies do. If
and when one or more of these online players decides to leverage their
economies of scale to offer lower-tier pricing, that's when you should
start to worry. My judgment is that you're safe for an eon or two from
this occurring.

As these companies all are dependent on scores of contract printers, direct-to-garment printers, and embroiderers who are required to
decorate quickly (1 to 3 day turnaround) and with a high level of satisfaction (which the vendors track rigorously with regard to customer
complaints and returns), any substantive decrease in their selling prices
would have to be done in conjunction with lowering the fees they pay to
their contractors. Right now those contractors are relatively happy with
what they're getting paid, but few, if any, would work for much less.

The development by customink.com of user-friendly online design
software, complete with a huge selection of layout formats and graphic
icon templates and tools for customers to select fonts, imprint colors,
modify the appearance of text, upload art (and sketches) along with
other options for the buyers, including seeing how the graphics appear
on different shirt colors, spawned competitors who developed the same
type software that's now available to just about everyone that's willing to pay for it. It also made the design efforts of apparel decorators
easier, as thousands of firms can now tell their customers to go online
to the various vendors, design their shirts, print out the design, and

bring it back in for the decorator to clone. Forget that it might not be legal, but it's done every day thousands of times by customers doing it at the suggestion of apparel decorators and sales agencies. The online companies cannot possibly or effectively police the activity nor would it be worth their time and expense to do so.

After several years in operation, the big online vendors haven't put anyone out of business, have helped to stimulate online decorating and design software competitors as well as assisted industry decorators to save lots of time and money from doing customers' graphics. And many decorators, themselves, go online to shorten their time to do speculative art and proofs of the designs they'll execute upon approval.

My read on the impact of the advent of online vendors promulgating design software for end-users on the apparel graphics industry? No big deal. They have their customers and you have yours. Everyone has learned to live with them and many benefit from them. My larger view is that they've also contributed to increasing awareness and demand, albeit marginally, for our products in the marketplace. Don't fear them...thank them!

2. The Impact of Mandated Increases in Wages and Healthcare Benefits: Philosophically I'm no fan of government telling us what we should pay our employees, especially with regard to minimum wage legislation. That said, whatever your politics or mine, we've all learned to live with minimum wage mandates, even though most apparel decorating companies pay more than the minimum anyhow to most of their workers.

Federally-mandated healthcare benefits, however, may in our industry have predictable unintended consequences and potential benefits for employers and equipment manufacturers. It's one thing to deal with rising minimum wage floors over time, it's quite another thing to absorb an extra $100 per week or more per employee in healthcare premiums. But because only 1 or 2% of apparel decorating companies -- at most -- have 50-or-more employees, almost no companies in our industry actually will be covering more employees as a result of the legislation. Scheduled for full implementation in 2014, the legislation might be targeted for modification (I'm predicting it here, folks) to encompass companies with fewer than 50 employees, so it's not a done done-deal. And at some future time, it may well impact *every* company. If so, I can safely predict it will precipitate demand for greater automation of the apparel decorating process before those larger firms accept absorbing labor increases of $2.50/hr. or more per worker without trying to get around the law. Automation is one answer.

I look for larger screen printing companies to buy more machinery featuring advanced pre-press and production equipment such as CTS (computer-to-screen) imaging systems (e.g., see Kiwo™), larger capacity printing presses, automatic take-off machines (robotic devices for removing shirts from the press and placing them on the dryer belt), automatic folding machines, more automated warehousing equipment, more advanced business software, and other labor-saving devices. I anticipate that embroiderers will be buying devices for faster hooping (sales of the Hoopmaster™'s magnetic hooping system should skyrocket!) and more multihead equipment. More teamwear providers will be buying cutting machines for better and faster production of player names and numbers.

As a result of discussions with some larger clients, I also expect that once lawyers and tax accountants figure how to circumvent the new laws, companies will spin off certain operations (art, screen making, sales departments) to newly established sister companies where they might keep their employment under the 50-threshhold. Well, until Congress figures out in return how to counter such actions. It's safe to say some of our larger enterprises, particularly those of 50 to 75 employees, will simply start contracting out a certain amount of work to trim their workforces below the 50-mark, if possible.

3. Technological Development: Direct-to-garment printing has earned a place in the industry. But at current levels of machine output per hour, its competitiveness with screen printing or heat printing for orders of several dozen garments and more just isn't there. Yet. I expect two major developments in this area of endeavor: a.) in time, speed will increase, though it's anyone's guess when or if it will become sufficiently competitive with screen printing and heat printing; and b.) the price of the equipment will eventually drop, probably sooner than later.

CAD-CUT® will see increasing penetration into the apparel decorating process, especially in areas involving the decoration of high tech and super-stretch fabrics. More and more screen printers, heat printers, and embroiderers are availing themselves of the technology's versatility in decorating garments as well as expanding into producing signs and vehicle graphics, and cutting appliqués, among other products.

Heat printing will see the development of more sophisticated capabilities as heat transfers, themselves, are further developed to better handle more types of specialty inks, rhinestoning, and other emerging heat print materials. I also foresee larger presses becoming more widely used, mainly for accommodating expanded decorating areas.

Digital printing, especially in large-format banners, will be a growth area for apparel decorators in the next decade, I'm confident, to expand into banners, pressure-sensitives, and other products.

Due to the advent of digital technology, the trend for more full-color graphics and more highly detailed graphics will accelerate.

It's easy to predict more and smaller companies will buy more sophisticated graphic software and online art design software for end-users purchasing online. This resource will become increasingly more common among both apparel decorating companies and sales agencies. The trend is already underway, albeit slow. But more and more software designers and vendors for this product are emerging, which means prices will come down. For firms catering to the youth and collegiate markets that the big online services currently target, owning this type of design software will become imperative. Removing the current technological advantage of companies in the customink.com mold will enable smaller, more localized apparel decorators to win back some customers.

4. Garments: Expect to see more styles and different types of garments for decorating continuing to find audiences hungrier for the latest fashions. This phenomenon isn't at all a new development, as it has been a core dynamic of the industry ever since it began.

From the industry's starting gate in the early 1970s when only black, white, heather grey, and the athletic palette (red, maroon, gold, yellow, royal, navy, kelly, black, orange and Texas orange) were available, by the end of that decade we saw the introduction of pastels. (Hey, it was a really big deal!) In the early 1980s, our manufacturers brought out hot fashion flavors, followed by neon colors a few years after that.

In the 1990s, ladies cuts in T-shirts and more figure-flattering tops were the first new garments to take the stage in what became a major expansion of the whole category of women's styles, which has continued to grow. At the start of the century's first decade, we saw the emergence of moisture-wicking or performance fabrics become available as garment staples and expand into more garment categories by the end of the decade.

What we'll see in the years ahead will be essentially what we've always been known to provide, but you can always expect to see a few tweaks and occasionally a new product or a new product category.

5. Graphics: As with evolving nuances in garments, what we'll put on them will constantly shift from smaller to bigger to biggest and back again, kind of like the width of ties and the length of skirts. The locations we decorate today finally include just about anywhere you can put ink on a garment (techniques I've been teaching and advocating since the 80's). New specialty effects – from specialty inks and burnouts to more multimedia and heat printing innovations – can safely be expected to emerge and recede and morph and then happen in ways we never imagined – or in ways that we return to after they've being off the radar for a decade or two -- and resurface to be dubbed "retro!"

6. Changes in the Supply Chain: Most of what we sell will continue to be manufactured in Latin America. The bulk of what we sell comes from Honduras, Guatemala, the Dominican Republic, Mexico, and elsewhere in Central America. But in addition to sources in these nations, we'll see the arrival of more goods from Columbia, Peru, and Brazil.

Goods sourced in our hemisphere put limits on what we'll import from Asia, which includes in our industry mainly caps, bags, and jackets, where I think we can all agree we're getting excellent quality and good pricing in these categories.

In distribution, where a decade ago we saw some major wholesalers acquired by a multinational conglomerate, we've seen privately owned family businesses – Bodek & Rhodes, San Mar, S & S, and most of our wholesalers – continue to compete effectively in our marketplace. They also continue to provide excellent service, so much so, they've actually increased their respective market share positions against a billion-dollar competitor. More good news: Knowing many of the principals at our leading wholesalers, I'm confident they'll remain independent for the foreseeable future, and perhaps much longer. Though they've gotten tighter on credit, these companies still view their relationships with their customers as partnerships, as most industry buyers have come to know. They're a major stabilizing force in the trade, because they're still run and owned by men and woman who intimately understand the culture of apparel decorating companies.

As for our major manufacturing sources of basics, Fruit of the Loom, Hanes, Gildan, and Jerzees will remain in their positions of dominance. I foresee no developments on any horizon indicating another firm of their scale will be moving into our industry anytime soon. If anything, I wouldn't rule out a merger of two of these companies in the next decade.

Through any lens they're seen through, our supply chains will remain largely as they are. And healthy.

7. Legal Issues: On this front, things are happening that affect you and your business. I'm not referring to legislation or court decisions here, I'm talking about the recent move to license shirts for schools – *public* schools! – to control where and how they're sold. High school-logoed merchandise has been sold at mass merchandisers and department stores for years. But while over 500 universities and colleges of every stripe have licensing agreements with decorators and vendors, such deals were unheard of with regard to high schools. Enter Licensing Resource Group. Based in Holland, Michigan, LRG has now emerged as the king of high school licensing programs, engineering itself into the lead position in controlling who sells high school logo-ed apparel, where it can be sold, and who gets paid what in the deal. Securing agreements with statewide organizations (e.g., state athletic associations, departments of education), LRG has carved out a piece of the pie for itself and pays royalties to schools to cede control of their goods at retail to LRG and approved outlets (e.g., Wal-Mart, Kmart, Kohl's and Walgreen's). The impact on price is to add a dollar or more per garment to the consumer, who bears the brunt of paying the piper here despite already paying property taxes to support local schools.

Right now high school licensing is where collegiate licensing was in the 1970s. With nearly 20,000 high school in the U.S., though, the process of selling to schools will inevitably become more complicated in the future for apparel decorators. Today you can still sell directly to schools, teams, and other groups within a school or a school district. All that will gradually change, I'd venture by 2020, to mirror the rules and systems by which collegiate licensing is done. I foresee a similar path down the road that will impact how we do business with elementary and middle schools, and private and parochial schools, though to a lesser extent and not quite as invasive as what is occurring with high schools. In the late 1990s many big corporations – IBM, Microsoft, Cisco Systems, American Express to name a few – began to place limits on who could apply their trademarks on apparel, paper, and just about everything else. The issue here isn't royalties, but rather better control and policing of the integrity of their marks. Expect to see more big companies limit access to using their marks and selling directly to them and their re-sellers. That means smaller companies will in a practical sense essentially be cut off from doing business with them or confronted with new hoops they never had to jump through before. From what I've seen, most small companies will have great difficulty complying with these emerging barriers.

More workplace regulations are likely as well, as states and provinces find ways to improve workplace safety, control of chemicals and environmentally responsible disposition of them, and more scrutiny of employees regarding their immigration status. And, who knows what new taxes and fees municipalities and other governmental entities will impose to create more ways to take money from businesses. Of course, these new revenue measures won't apply solely to apparel decorators, but to all businesses.

8. The Intersection of Decorated Apparel and Promotional Products: Since the inception of the industry there's been speculation that the promotional products and apparel graphics industries, given the overlap of some key product categories and our customer bases, will eventually converge professionally and/or politically (in trade associations and trade shows). I, too, made the same prediction about such an inevitability in a interview I gave in *Impressions* in 1982. I was wrong then and I'd be wrong today to make the same observation, though, many promotional products firms have since joined forces with apparel decorating companies either by merger or more commonly through acquisition of one by the other. Recent years have seen an increase in this activity, though nothing earth-shattering. It's a fact that virtually all promotional products distributors sell custom decorated apparel, usually by sourcing from our same wholesalers and engaging contractors for the decoration. And it's a fact that most apparel decorating companies sell promotional products. That cross-selling will continue as is.

There has indeed been a convergence of our industries. Promoware

companies and decorated apparel companies source from the same garment wholesalers. Note that the wholesalers' floor presence at promotional products trade shows is much larger than it is at apparel decorating shows, which should tell you where the wholesalers see their own
growth opportunities. So important is decorated apparel to promotional
products companies that decorated apparel is the No. 1 category of
product sales in that industry.

Look a little closer at the numbers. The Promotional Products Association International (PPAI), the trade association for the promotional
products industry measures 21 different product categories. According
to PPAI, of that industry's $18.3 billion in sales for 2008, wearables
accounted for 30.68% of the total revenue. (All figures discussed here
are for 2008). The next four categories combined totaled 29.95% (Writing Instruments - 9.04%; Calendars - 7.89%; bags - 6.92%; drinkware
- 6.09%; followed by desk/office/business accessories – 5.54%). With
bags at 6.92% and textiles (banners, flags, et al -- the No. 17 category
in sales) combined totaling 8.91% added to 30.68% for wearables,
items decorated for the most part by screen printing and embroidery,
all decorated textile products combined are just a hair under 40% of
the sales volume of the entire promotional products industry, while the
next four non-textile categories total only 28.56%.

In other words, the promotional products industry derives $2 of every
$5 dollars it sells from what apparel decorators decorate. But for more
than 95% of the apparel decorating firms that sell promotional products, the promotional products category represents on average only 3%
to 5% of their total revenue – at best, no more than only one in $20 in
revenue. The apparel graphics industry's trade publications and trade
shows have for three decades advanced the case – and still do – that
apparel decorators need to sell promotional products as an essential
component of their success. With 30 years of data to reinforce my own
counsel, I tell apparel decorators they need to do nothing of the sort.

As a practical matter, apparel decorators don't and won't make the
necessary commitments of time and money and in educating themselves
about the basics of selling promotional products to do themselves and
their customers justice. The small percentage that does make such commitments can and do enhance their sales and profitability. But the true
story is that selling promotional products makes little impact on the

bottom lines of most apparel graphics firms. Nonetheless, where I do recommend and endorse apparel graphics companies selling promotional products is mainly as a defensive effort to retain certain customers from moving their apparel business to promoware competitors. Note that the single most relevant product category that apparel decorators succeed in selling competitively (after apparel, of course) is "drinkware" (primarily mugs, travel mugs, and glassware). With a small investment in a mug press, most of this product category can be done in-house using sublimation transfers for running small to medium quantities, and for larger quantities, outsourcing the entire job.

I view the juxtaposition of the two industries as having evolved steadily toward a convergence, but stopping at that point and continuing on parallel courses to one another. The two sides won't get married anytime soon, and if they ever were to get hitched, it would be at best a marriage of convenience.

The two industries intersect mainly when competing for accounts. Their respective cultures are inherently different. One has the advantage of being focused primarily on sales, while the other has the advantage of controlling the means of production. Yes, some apparel graphics companies have thrown in the towel on trying to compete with the promotional products distributors, opting to become full-time contract decorators servicing an account base that's overwhelmingly promotional products companies. Some apparel decorators that focus on full-value selling accept contract work on occasion from PPDs, though most apparel decorators rightly eschew such business altogether except where it's with PPDs located outside the apparel decorators' geographical backyard.

On the front lines of selling, apparel decorators and PPDs are competitors, rivals often courting the same customers. Why have apparel decorators remained viable against competitors with the powerful advantage of being able to focus on sales? One reason is the differences in cultures. Another is that promoware salespeople sell decorated apparel primarily to the business market and, relative to apparel decorators, very little to schools, teams, events, and organizations. Ergo, smart custom apparel decorators realize they have an inside track in selling to non-business markets. But smart apparel decorators brook no competitors or barriers to sell business prospects. For most of the most successful custom apparel decorators in North America, business-to-business selling is their top targeted market and their most lucrative account sector.

9. Going Green, Selling Green: Instituting green practices and using green products in your business is wonderful. And it costs very little extra, if at all, to do so. In some cases, you might actually save some money. I advocate going green simply not for gaining some potential marketing "points" with green-oriented buyers, I advocate it for the basic reason that, in most cases, it's the right thing to do.

Regrettably, it's also my observation that the vast majority of companies in our industry are anything but green. Few recycle anything -- including cans and bottles, plastic, and cardboard or paper. That few of your competitors don't show evidence that they care about such things should not be an excuse for responsible businesspeople to emulate their competitors' insensitivity and ignorance.

"Selling green" is an altogether different issue for our industry and for most sellers – and most buyers – of decorated apparel. Garments made from recycled plastic spun into "yarn" (the term in textile manufacturing that describes what the rest of the population calls "thread") were introduced into our industry around 1980. And in all the intervening years the products have been available, they amount for only a small fraction of 1% of the fabric used in the entire apparel industry. Why? The cost. It's simply more expensive to make environmentally correct yarn and practical demand – in terms of what customers will pay – for garments made from the fabric is minuscule. Hence, the price-and-demand curve means it remains more costly for consumers at all levels.

Garments made from organically grown cotton also have been available for decades and have yet to make much of a splash in the marketplace for custom decorated apparel. As a matter of fact, I can discern hardly a droplet of it in industry sales, despite the fact that our trade publications heavily promote green garments.

I am NOT saying you shouldn't look at green garments and ignore it.

But as an essential to your success, I can tell you it doesn't make it onto the radar. At the courses I teach at the Imprinted Sportswear Shows, Imprint Canada Shows, and corporate events in Europe, I meet people (mostly newcomers and young entrepreneurs) who are committed to building their businesses frontlining green garments, green inks, and green thread. When I meet them a year or more later, about 99% of them report they've abandoned that focus when they found it sold like a lead balloon – even to environmental advocacy groups. I can also tell you from first-hand experience that even the most prominent environmental interest and advocacy groups in the Western hemisphere buy standard garments, decorated with standard materials, at standard prices and at typical price margins. I know this, because I've been (and still am) a consultant to the companies that sell them their shirts. Unless and until greenwear prices come down, it's not an issue for all but a tiny handful of professional apparel decorators.

It's nice to know it's out there, but, meanwhile, back in the real world ...

10. Global Economic Trends: Fluctuations in currency, trade surpluses and deficits, global markets, the emergence of China and India as major players on the world stage, Wall Street, the world of international economics, America's mounting national debt, yadda, yadda, yadda. It's all important, it all matters. But in terms of looking at the health of the apparel decorating industry, in terms of what our buyers want from us and how we run our companies, the very heavy subjects listed above have little special relevance for our industry. How they impact this industry will be little different from their general impact on the economies, polities, and societies of North America.

Why I even mention these subjects is to put the decorated apparel industry in context and in perspective for everyone who earns his or her livelihood in the industry, who contributes to the design and creation and sale of its products, and who studies it for possible entry into its ranks or looks at it from outside the field. The last group includes would-be entrants as owners or employees, Wall Street financial analysts (you'd be amazed at who monitors this industry), and college students working toward degrees in textile sciences, business, graphic arts, fashion merchandising, and other disciplines.

Among the audiences also addressed by this book are owners of businesses that easily could expand into decorated apparel from their current businesses in the signmaking, printing, sporting goods, graphic design, and recognition industries. For them, most of what has been written here about positioning, marketing, advertising, lead generation, customer service, and other subjects apply as well to businesses in those related fields. If what you read here entices you to expand into custom decorated apparel, come on in! And if by reading this you became convinced to stay out of it, I suppose I've done you a favor.

To everyone reading this book for whatever reason, I can state with absolute confidence that the state of the industry is not only strong and healthy, I can foresee virtually nothing that will change that fact for decades to come, if ever. Short of being outlawed by Congress, our society doing away with clothing, or the freedom of expression curtailed by an unthinkable event, all the fundamentals that make for a continued bright future are well in place. These include popular demand for custom decorated apparel, a highly competitive corps of producers and sellers, stable garment prices and interest rates, strong availability of garments with an ever-widening array of styles and colors, and an inexhaustible influx of eager, willing entrepreneurs. The forecast for custom decorated apparel: sunny skies and warm temperatures.

For those who own or manage apparel decorating businesses -- or who will in the future -- you've got your work cut out for you to keep your business strong and profitable. All the challenges ahead of you notwithstanding, remember that ours is a wonderful business where we get use our imagination and our creativity and to play with ideas and color and texture to make our customers love what we sell them.

In case you hadn't heard from anyone yet about the greatest benefit of being in this industry, you're allowed to have fun doing what you do, while hopefully also laughing all the way to the bank.

Two final thoughts: If you remember any lessons from me about the ultimate secrets of success in the decorated apparel industry, remember these:

1. Those who market, win. Those who don't, lo...uh... they find something else to do.

2. The most important ingredient in the success of any business is sales. Without sales, nothing else happens.

So, raise your right hand and repeat out loud: "I am allowed to make money!"

Now, go out and sell!

A SPECIAL MESSAGE TO NEW AND PROSPECTIVE APPAREL DECORATORS

Now that you've read the book, allow me to offer some additional food for thought and some recommendations . . .

1. Marketing Matters More Than Technology.

If you elect to become an apparel decorator, mastering your chosen technologies is essential to "earning your stripes." But practicing forever whatever technologies you've chosen as your core offerings before you begin your marketing and selling activities is no way to build a business. Aspiring to achieve perfection and sophistication is a wonderful ambition, but sufficiency is the goal you want to achieve first. To build your business means winning orders and establishing an account base. You can accomplish both well before you gain full command of your technologies. Waiting until you think you've learned all there is to know about technical matters is folly.

What most industry newcomers do is strive to get their equipment to do what it's supposed to do – and then wonder how they're going to get orders. If you're serious about making money in this business, the time to start getting orders is today, not tomorrow. Acquiring a solid command of technology comes from experience – by executing real orders -- and from what your customers demand from you.

I could tell you stories about highly talented, highly sophisticated apparel decorators whose businesses failed due to a lack of orders and the lack of a winning game plan for getting orders. But I can tell you lots more stories about apparel decorators who do satisfactory-level workmanship and make respectable money and have bright futures because they're marketers first.

2. Buying Your Start-Up Equipment Entails Much More Than Price.

You've probably heard the assertion "I sell price, quality, and service -- pick two!" Do shop around, but far more important than simply finding the lowest price is ascertaining which vendors have start-up specialists on staff, competent professionals who focus on start-up businesses and the evolving needs of the entrepreneurs who own them and who'll be there for you well after the sale to answer the questions you'll invariably have while learning to operate your equipment and while you're learning which products and consumables are the "best fits" for that equipment.

Ask about who's there to help you, how they'll help you, and how you reach them. Do establish which vendors respond by telephone and help you right "there and then" and which ones require you to first send a detailed e-mail with your questions and challenges.

If you buy on price alone, you'll likely have to "buy it again" sooner or later. You're certain to get better value when you make the buy with an eye to service after the sale. You can follow my advice here -- or wish you had followed it once you learn (the hard way) what I was preaching.

Do get references from prospective vendors to recent start-up customers of theirs and be sure to ask about written guarantees and warranties, refund policies, and what additional training is available.

3. Learn about the industry's information sources.

Smart businesspeople know that owning a business means staying current with technological developments, market trends, industry resources, and "buzz." All are easily accessed online and without charge. "Buzz" can be found on industry blogs, among many other places. For starters, go to www.t-shirtforums.com to read what's being discussed and participate by asking questions to fellow entrepreneurs.

I strongly recommend attending at least one major decorated apparel trade show every year and attending workshops and seminars relevant to your needs. Among your best choices are *The Imprinted Sportswear Shows* (Long Beach, Orlando, Atlantic City, Columbus, Atlanta, Ft. Worth > www.issshows.com), *The NBM Show* (Austin, Long Beach, Indianapolis, Baltimore > www.nbmshow.com), *Imprint Canada Shows* (www.imprintcanada.com > Toronto, Calgary) and the *Embroidery Mart* (Nashville > www.nnep.net). (My courses are offered exclusively at The Imprinted Sportswear Shows and the Imprint Canada Shows).

Sign up for every online industry newsletter you can find and subscribe to the industry's leading trade publications, most of which are free.

4. Call me. (410.641.7300 - Eastern Time)

If you find yourself floundering for answers or understanding, I'll be happy to help you (without charge) make decisions, learn more options, and, when necessary, refer you to technical experts and consultants who'll be happy to counsel you over the phone or via email.

AFTERWORD

Thank you to everyone who bought this book and perhaps for making it a gift to an employee, a partner, or the boss. Thank you as well to the management of GroupeSTAHL and its Chairman, a client for 29 years and my friend, Ted Stahl. Ted and his senior staff all understood the need for this book, underwrote my effort to write it, and took leadership in getting it published.

As the individual I regard as the industry's Chief Executive Visionary, Chairman Ted has had no equal in advancing the cause of expanding business education in the industries his company serves. This book is a direct result of Ted's commitment to help participants in those industries and especially for customers of Stahls' ID Direct, Transfer Express, and Imprintables Warehouse to have a roadmap for reaching their own goals for success. Ted's vision encompasses his strong belief that better prepared and better equipped businesspeople build more successful, more profitable enterprises. And that more profitable enterprises help build better, more sustainable communities. Yeah, it's corny. But it works, and everybody wins.

This book is a legacy contribution to the industry that has been very good to me personally. My only regret about it is that I didn't write it a decade or so sooner. But with the encouragement of CEO Jan Starr and Karin Bellinghausen at GroupeSTAHL and a big nudge from Ted, personally, I was able to take a sabbatical to devote several months to writing this book. If this effort helps you succeed in the decorated apparel business or any other business, I'll enjoy knowing I gave something back. Maybe it'll help you make so much money that you'll give plenty back, yourself.

Now, go make some money. And have some fun along the way!

-- Mark L. Venit